Power and Ideology in Brazil

*This book was written under the auspices of
the Institute for Social Research,
the University of Michigan
and
the Instituto Universitário de Pesquisas
do Rio de Janeiro,
Conjunto Universitário Cândido Mendes*

POWER AND IDEOLOGY
IN BRAZIL

PETER McDONOUGH

PRINCETON UNIVERSITY PRESS

Publication of this book has been aided by the
Whitney Darrow Publication Reserve Fund of
Princeton University Press

This book has been composed in Linotron Times Roman

Clothbound editions of Princeton University Press books
are printed on acid-free paper, and binding materials are
chosen for strength and durability

Printed in the United States of America by Princeton
University Press, Princeton, New Jersey

Library of Congress Cataloging in Publication Data

McDonough, Peter, 1939-
  Power and ideology in Brazil.

  Bibliography: p.
  Includes index.
  1. Elite (Social sciences)—Brazil—Attitudes.
2. Power (Social sciences)   3. Ideology.   I. Title.
HN290.Z9E45   305.5′2   81-47147
ISBN 0-691-07628-6   AACR2
ISBN 0-691-02203-8 (pbk.)

For Grace, Josefina, Graça, and Júlia,
and in memory of Joseph

Contents

List of Tables   xi
List of Figures   xiii
Acknowledgments   xv
Preface   xvii

INTRODUCTION   3
  Ambiguities of Authoritarianism   5
  Power   17
  Ideology   25
  Organization of the Study   48

PART ONE • *Structures of Power*
ONE. *Mobility and Recruitment*   55
  Origins   58
  Education   63
  Education and Class   70
  Marriage and Mobility   75
TWO. *Networks*   85
  The Form of the Power Structure   87
  The Separation of Kinship and Friendship Ties   92
  Class, Kinship, and Friendship   94
  Working Contacts   98

PART TWO • *Ideologies*
THREE. *Orientations toward the Distribution of Power*   109
  Perceptions of Power and Support   111
  Conciliatory and Conflictive Perspectives   118
  Preferences about the Redistribution of Power   121
FOUR. *Developmental Priorities*   130
  Variation in Developmental Agendas   138
  Elite Interpretations of Developmental Priorities   143
  Developmental Values, Policy Performance, and Government
    Support   153
FIVE. *Ideologies and the Limits of Legitimacy*   169
  Ideologies   175
  Bureaucratic-Authoritarianism versus Interest-Representation   189
  The Limits of Authoritarian Legitimacy   195
  Between *Arbítrio* and *Autonomia*   199

SIX. *Mutual Perceptions*   204
     The Lay of the Data   206
     A Model of Interelite (Mis)Perception   211
     Misperception as a Function of Stereotyping and Projection   213
CONCLUSION   228

Appendix. The Nature of the Evidence   247
     The Elite Samples   247
     The Interview Schedule   260
     Categorization of Elite Groups   262
     The Substance of Elite Ideology   264
     Elite Rationales   275
Bibliography   295
Index   323

List of Tables

TABLE 1.1   Father's Occupation by Elite Sector   61

TABLE 1.2   Elite Sector by Education   62

TABLE 1.3   University Specialization by Region of Origin   66

TABLE 1.4   University Specialization by Elite Sector   71

TABLE 1.5   Father's Class Position by Elite Faculty   72

TABLE 1.6   Father-in-Law's Occupation by Father's Occupation: Seven-Category Scales   77

TABLE 2.1   Promax Oblique Rotation of Factors from Kinship and Friendship Ties   93

TABLE 2.2   Factor Analysis (Varimax Rotation) of Working Contacts with Eight Major Groups: Normalized Factor Loadings   101

TABLE 2.3   Mean Standardized Factor Scores on Three Dimensions of Working Contacts, by Elite Sector   102

TABLE 3.1   Mean Perceptions of Government Support/Opposition among Thirteen Groups, by Elite Sector   115

TABLE 3.2   Correlations between Elite Perceptions of Attention Paid by Government to Thirteen Groups   120

TABLE 3.3   Mean Differences between Preferences about Attention Owed and Perceptions of Attention Paid to Thirteen Groups, by Elite Sector   123

TABLE 4.1   Relationship between Original and Revised Developmental Priorities   139

TABLE 4.2   Development Priorities across Elite Sectors   141

TABLE 4.3   Elite Evaluations of Governmental Performance in Ten Policy Areas   157

TABLE 4.4   Normalized Loadings, Oblique Factor Rotation, on Ten Performance Indicators   158

TABLE 5.1   Average Preferences on Twenty-Three Issues, by Elite Sector   177

TABLE 5.2   Correlations of Twenty-Three Policy Preferences with Left-Right Index, by Elite Sector   184

TABLE 5.3   Normalized Loadings, Oblique Factor Rotation, on Sixteen Issues   188

TABLE 5.4   Multiple Classification Analysis of Preferences on Three Issues, by Developmental Agendas and Elite Sector   198

TABLE 6.1   Mean Avowed (A) and Perceived (P) Opinions of Elite Sectors, by Issue   210

TABLE 6.2   Mean Differences between Avowed and Attributed Opinions on Foreign Investment, by Elite Sector   216

TABLE 6.3   Mean Differences between Avowed and Attributed
             Opinions on Government-Opposition Relations, by Elite
             Sector   216
TABLE 6.4   Mean Individual-Level Correlations between Perceptions
             and Actual Opinion of Seven Elite Groups, by Elite Sector   219
TABLE 6.5   Correlations between Elite Preferences and Interviewer-
             Assessed "Hesitation," by Issue and Sector   221
TABLE A.1   The Elite Sample in Detail, in Descending Order of
             Response Rate   253
TABLE A.2   Major Groups in the Elite Sample, As Aggregated for
             Data-Analysis   254
TABLE A.3   Average Importance Attributed to Fifteen Issues, by Elite
             Sector   267
TABLE A.4   Correlations between Importance Ratings, Fifteen Issues   270
TABLE A.5   Correlations between Importance Ratings (Ipsatized),
             Fifteen Issues   271
TABLE A.6   Correlations between Importance Ratings and Preference
             Scores on Thirteen Issues, by Elite Sector   273
TABLE A.7   Average Preference, Foreign Investment, by Rationale of
             Preference   279
TABLE A.8   Average Importance, Foreign Investment, by Rationale of
             Preference   280
TABLE A.9   Average Preference, Income Redistribution, by Rationale
             of Preference   284
TABLE A.10   Average Importance, Income Redistribution, by Rationale
             of Preference   284
TABLE A.11   Average Preference, Government-Labor Relations, by
             Rationale of Preference   288
TABLE A.12   Average Importance, Government-Labor Relations, by
             Rationale of Preference   289
TABLE A.13   Mean Preference, Government-Opposition Relations, by
             Rationale of Preference   293
TABLE A.14   Mean Importance, Government-Opposition Relations, by
             Rationale of Preference   293

List of Figures

FIGURE P.1   Number of Deaths under Torture and Political
              "Disappearances," 1966-1975   xviii
FIGURE 1.1   Distribution of Father's Occupation   60
FIGURE 1.2   Education by Region of Origin   65
FIGURE 1.3   Higher Education in Law, Engineering, and Economics/
              Administration, by Age Cohort   69
FIGURE 1.4   Elites with University Education, Whose Fathers Did Not
              Obtain a University Degree, by Elite Sector   74
FIGURE 1.5   Correlations between Father's Occupation and Father-in-
              Law's Occupation, by Father's Education   78
FIGURE 1.6   Correlations between Father's Occupation and Father-in-
              Law's Occupation, by Elite Sector   80
FIGURE 2.1   Two-Dimensional Smallest-Space Diagram of Pooled
              Kinship and Friendship Relations for Pre-Adult, University,
              and Present Time   89
FIGURE 2.2   Correlations between Kinship/Friendship Ratio and Total
              Number of Ties, by Elite Sector   95
FIGURE 2.3   Selected Upward-Mobile Linkages Over Time: Mean
              Densities by Elite Sector   97
FIGURE 3.1   Relationship between Mean Perceived Attention Paid by
              Government and Mean Perceived Support/Opposition among
              Twelve Groups   114
FIGURE 3.2   Two-Dimensional Smallest-Space Diagram of Differences
              between Preferences for Attention Owed and Perceptions of
              Attention Paid to Thirteen Groups   126
FIGURE 4.1   Average Government Support by Developmental Priorities   154
FIGURE 4.2   Standardized Factor Scores on Social and Economic
              Performance of Government, by Elite Sector   160
FIGURE 4.3   Relationship between Government Support and Performance
              Evaluations, Controlling for Developmental Priorities   164
FIGURE 5.1   Difference between Emphasis Given to Strengthening
              Representation and Strengthening Executive, by Elite Sector   192
FIGURE 5.2   Difference between Emphasis Given to Strengthening
              Representation and Strengthening Executive, by Elite
              Priorities   194
FIGURE 6.1   Mean Preferences and Perceptions of Seven Elite Groups   207
FIGURE 6.2   Mean Preferences and Perceptions for Five Key Issues   209
FIGURE 6.3   Two-Dimensional Smallest-Space Diagrams for Perceptions
              of Elite Sectors on Five Issues   227

Acknowledgments

Rumor has it that those with a flair for language enter the humanities, that those with a head for numbers go into the natural sciences, and that those with neither become social scientists. This is true, of course: I've had a lot of help along the way.

My first debt is to the anonymous respondents who endured the interviews. Their cooperation made the rest possible.

Fieldwork was undertaken with the Instituto Universitário de Pesquisas do Rio de Janeiro under a Ford Foundation grant to the Center for Political Studies, Institute for Social Research, University of Michigan. The idea for the study came from the late Kalman Silvert. The writing was facilitated by grants from the National Institutes of Health, the National Science Foundation, and the Tinker Foundation.

I am especially grateful to Cândido Mendes, Almir de Castro, Luis Alberto Bahia, and the perseverant generation of social scientists at IUPERJ for seeing the study through difficult times. I owe a debt past counting to Warren Miller, director of the Center for Political Studies, for seeing it through more lean years than I care to remember. Raburn Howland of CPS taught me the parts of project management that aren't written down.

Philip Converse, Amaury de Souza, and Youssef Cohen have been my collaborators in this study. Phil invested much more in it than he took out. Amaury forced me to discard the autocracy-in-Brazil/democracy-in-America mindset and still claims that I dance like a missionary. Youssef took charge of the fieldwork and led me to see things I would have otherwise ignored. Another colleague, Kenneth Organski, gave consistent support, all the while holding his nose in the presence of survey research.

Peter Evans read two earlier versions of the book, and Barry Ames got through one. Peter's suggestions made the final draft intelligible and possibly even readable. Barry's encouragement kept me going. Together, they pushed me to write the book I wanted to write.

Joyce Kaufman, Thomas Rochon, and Barbara Smela grew old processing the data. Joyce Meyer kept track of the drafts and put the pieces together, and Deborah Eddy filled in when Joyce could stand no more.

Tom McDonough set an example. The analysis of the economists, the social reformers, and the politicians in these pages is a distillation of our talks about the BMT, the IRT, and the IND people in the celestial railroad of the New York subway system.

The publishing history of this book has had nearly as many ups-and-downs as the research itself. Sandy Thatcher smoothed the path and Cathy Thatcher's copy-editing brought me to the verge of literacy.

Parts of this book have appeared in other forms as "Developmental Priorities Among Brazilian Elites," in *Economic Development and Cultural Change* 29 (1981), and as "Mapping an Authoritarian Power Structure," in *Latin American Research Review* 16 (1981). Permission to use these materials was granted by the University of Chicago Press and the *Latin American Research Review*.

Reading it over, I have the impression that the tone of the book alternates between Gibbon on the Roman Empire and a ringside announcer at a bantamweight fight, with a few moments of the good and the gray in between. It probably suits the subject. It also reflects, I would like to think, my frustration at not being able to write the original in Brazilian Portuguese, surely the most Elizabethan of modern languages.

Agradeço sobretudo Josefina: mulher, mãe, e feminista.

Preface

The graph on the following page shows the number of deaths under torture in Brazil from 1966 through 1975 and the number of unresolved disappearances during the same period. The figures may seem self-explanatory. They reflect the hardening of authoritarianism after the 1964 coup and then its decomposition during the seventies. Much the same rise and decline pattern would appear were we to plot the incidence of censorship or the frequency of military trials for political transgressions.[1]

But neither the meaning of this trend nor its causes are transparent. In the first place, it coincides only roughly with changes in the Brazilian economy. Repression of a kind peaked around 1971, before the drop in economic performance struck in 1973 and 1974. Even if a tighter association between economic and political cycles could be found, it is not clear what form the connection might take. Should repression be expected to increase in bad times? The graph suggests the opposite.

Second, the downward trend in political deaths and disappearances can be misleading if taken to signify a weakening of the Brazilian state. The movement away from despotism in Brazil has been substantial. At the same time, the size and administrative capacity of the government—for example, its ability to tax the citizenry—have grown, unabated, since 1964.[2]

[1] Although not quite: censorship of the press did not really begin to taper off until early 1975. See "A Fera Ganhou os 100%," *Veja*, June 18, 1980: 80-87. Furthermore, by the very nature of the case, reliable documentation of human rights violations is difficult to obtain, and data such as those presented in Figure P.1 must be treated with caution. See José Meirelles Passos, "A Tortura Ainda é uma Rotina nas Delegacias," *Isto É*, November 5, 1980: 26-27.

[2] For the period 1969 to 1971, Brazil's tax ratio—taxes divided by gross national product—placed it fourth highest among sixty-three developing countries; it fell to twentieth place in the same sample for the period 1972 to 1976. However, Brazil consistently ranks first or second in "tax effort" (real taxation divided by predicted tax level). The predicted tax is derived by, in effect, controlling for the structure of the economy—for example, large primary sector equals low tax capacity, high exports equals high tax capacity, and so on. See Raja J. Chelliah, Hessel J. Baas, and Margaret R. Kelley, "Tax Ratios and Tax Effort in Developing Countries, 1969-71," *International Monetary Fund Staff Papers* 12 (1975): 187-205, and Alan A. Tait, Wilfred L. M. Gratz, and Barry J. Eichengreen, "International Comparisons of Taxation for Selected Developing Countries, 1972-76," *International Monetary Fund Staff Papers* 16 (1979): 123-153. Brazil has traditionally relied on extremely high sales taxes as part of its fiscal effort. However, since the early 1970s, the number of Brazilians paying income tax has risen sharply.

The decline in torture does not mean that the Brazilian state has been made accountable.

Third, the idea that recourse to the harshest repressive measures follows a cost-effective logic, so that no more is applied than is thought to be needed, does not hold up. The fall-off in torture might be taken as evidence that such devices had achieved their goal—''social peace''—and that the application of the same or even greater amounts would represent a path-ological condition rather than calculated control. Yet, as the cruder forms of repression faded in Brazil, acts of rebellion mounted.

This is not to suggest that changes in Brazilian politics have nothing to

FIGURE P.1
Number of Deaths under Torture and Political ''Disappearances,'' 1966-1975

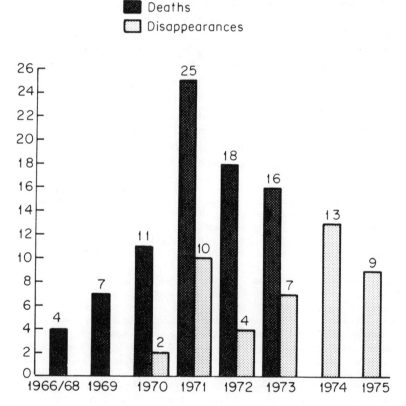

SOURCE: Reported in *Isto É*, October 4, 1978: 39. The original source is Amnesty International.

do with the factors just mentioned. But the causal linkages remain obscure. Very generally, it is plausible to attribute the erosion of authoritarianism in Brazil to two shocks that, from the viewpoint of the elites, were exogenous and unexpected: the sudden deterioration in the international economic system signalled by the oil crisis of 1973 and the outbreaks of popular discontent—work stoppages and strikes more often than guerrilla activity—that ensued on the regime's difficulties in furnishing a modicum of material benefits from the miracle years of 1968 to 1973.[3]

But these lines of explanation, however attractive, are incomplete. For the most part, they ignore crises internal to the government and to elites on the fringes of the state. Göran Therborn has argued that "the prevalence of dictatorships and large-scale violent repression is, first of all, a manifestation of the failure of the Latin American bourgeoisie to establish democracy for itself, and not primarily of its failure to contain the popular classes by other means than open state terror."[4]

A focus on elite politics may furnish insight not only into the onset of authoritarian rule but also into its decay. This book is about the tensions within the Brazilian establishment that have contributed to the undoing of authoritarianism. The objective is to clarify the understudied and, I believe, misunderstood complexity of interelite rivalries and their effect on the unravelling of dictatorial government.

My primary concern is with the ideological strains that have undermined the authoritarian coalition in Brazil. Although fully a third of the study is devoted to the structure and organization of Brazilian elites—to their recruitment, their familial and friendship ties, their functional networks, and

---

[3] Even if its causal meaning is opaque, the tightest structural-political correlation in recent Brazilian history seems to be between the rate of inflation and the degree of authoritarianism; the association is inverse. A primary rationale of the regime installed in 1964 was to control inflation, something it succeeded in doing through about mid-1973. Since then, the inflation rate has climbed back up to 1964 levels. It may be that the loosening of authoritarian restrictions implies an admission on the part of the government and its allies that a large part of the economic environment is simply outside their control. See José Paulo Kupfer, "Nas Asas da Inflação," *Isto É*, June 4, 1980: 66-71; "Alívio com a Dívida," *Veja*, July 9, 1980: 90-91; and Antonio C. Lemgruber, "Inflation in Brazil," in *Worldwide Inflation: Theory and Recent Experience*, ed. Lawrence B. Krause and Walter S. Salant (New York: Academic Press, 1977). Compare John Sheahan, "Market-oriented Economic Policies and Political Repression in Latin America," *Economic Development and Cultural Change* 28 (1980): 267-291, and Edmar L. Bacha, *Os Mitos de uma Década: Ensaios de Economia Brasiliera* (Rio de Janeiro: Editora Paz e Terra, 1976).

[4] Göran Therborn, "The Travail of Latin American Democracy," *New Left Review* 113-114 (1979): 74. A similar view is expressed by Juan J. Linz, *The Breakdown of Democratic Regimes: Crisis, Breakdown, and Reequilibration* (Baltimore: The Johns Hopkins University Press, 1978).

so on—the thrust of the analysis has to do with what the elites think about political issues and what they think about one another.

Given the state of the art of studies about Brazil and about authoritarianism generally, this may not seem a promising approach. Academic perspectives on the authoritarian condition can be divided, somewhat artificially but not entirely inaccurately, into two schools. One is the structuralist, the other is the culturalist.[5] The gist of the structuralist position is that the rise of authoritarianism in Brazil, and to varying degrees elsewhere in Latin America (if not in South Korea, or the Philippines, or Indonesia, et cetera[6]) can be traced to a developmental false start: the post-depression and, in some cases, postwar period of light industrialization and democratic experimentation generated expectations that could not be met. Large-scale, rapid industrialization, requiring huge investment in capital goods, meant the forceful postponement of consumer gratification and populist politics.

The culturalist perspective stresses the ideological roots of the authoritarian renaissance. The wave of repression that engulfed Latin America beginning in the 1960s was not exceptional or new. It derived from a tradition of hierarchy and subservience—from a view of an organic society in which elites felt entitled to rule over a compliant but irresponsible mass. The resurgence of authoritarianism was seen not simply as reactionary capitalism but as the reflection, as well, of a precapitalist, largely Catholic vision of social order.

As academic fashions go, the exegesis of authoritarianism in Latin America by way of cultural inertia has been a minority position.[7] Further inroads have been made against it by acceptance of the idea that authoritarian regimes are not ideological at all. In this view, the style and behavior of these regimes are pragmatic and technocratic and their use of ideological-sounding rhetoric is just that: rhetoric. Words are a screen for what they do.

However, whatever the utility of the structuralist perspective in accounting for the origins of developmental authoritarianism, it may be less helpful in understanding the failure of regimes like the Brazilian to attain

---

[5] References to the extensive literature from both schools can be found in the Introduction.

[6] See for example Robert B. Stauffer, "The Political Economy of a Coup: Transnational Linkages and Philippine Political Response," *Journal of Peace Research* 11 (1974): 161-177, which follows a fairly standard dependency approach to authoritarianism. For a more complex analysis, with careful attention to political variations in India, South Korea, and the Philippines, see Jyotirinda Das Gupta, "A Season of Caesars: Emergency Regimes and Development Politics in Asia," *Asian Survey* 28 (1978): 315-349.

[7] See Eldon Kenworthy, "Nonparticipation in Latin America: How We Explain the End of Democracy There," paper presented at the meetings of the American Political Science Association, Chicago, Illinois, September 2-5, 1976.

institutionalization. No sooner had scholars come to a loose agreement about the causes of the authoritarian revival in Brazil than the dictatorship started to grind down. This turn of events has posed questions about the instability of Brazilian authoritarianism that are difficult to answer by invoking structural and economic explanations.

It would be incorrect to assert that Brazilian elites are scrupulous ideologues, if what is meant by ideology is a unidimensional polarization of true believers on the left and right, with an inflexible and fanatic edge. It would be equally wrong to treat whatever ideological yearnings Brazilian elites harbor as the chief determinants of their conduct, above and beyond structural and organizational constraints, or to suppose that the elites are fully aware of the implication of either the range of alternatives open to them or of the institutional limits on their decisions. Once these caricatures are set aside, however, it is possible to probe what it is that might be truly ideological about the thinking and behavior of the elites and to see how these factors may circumscribe the stability of authoritarian rule.[8]

A key hypothesis of this study is that Brazilian elites are neither unideological nor unidimensional ideologues. Their belief systems can best be understood as complex but patterned—that is, as multidimensional. More precisely, many Brazilian elites think in terms of three axes of political choice. Furthermore, these cleavages can be viewed as the reflection of specific institutional conflicts rather than merely as a matter of personal psychology.

The most obvious although not necessarily the most explosive cleavage among Brazilian elites is of a class nature. It derives from the gulf between the leaders of urban labor and the rest of the elites. Ideologically, it divides the economic conservatives from the social progressives, the proponents of forced-march accumulation from the advocates of a less Draconian, more meliorative distribution.

This is not an inexorably zero-sum cleavage, pitting elite groups against one another in terminal combat. While many of those favoring greater attention to social equity are found among the labor leaders, more than

[8] The caricatures noted here, especially the second one, still appear to be taken seriously by scholars inveighing against "idealism," "psychologism," "humanism," "the subjectivist problematique," and worse. See Göran Therborn, *What Does the Ruling Class Do When It Rules?* (London: New Left Books, 1978); Terry Eagleton, *Criticism and Ideology* (London: New Left Books, 1976); and Barbara Laslett, "The Place of Theory in Quantitative Historical Research," *American Sociological Review* 45 (1980): 214-228. Contrast James H. Billington, *The Icon and the Axe: An Interpretative History of Russian Culture* (New York: Alfred A. Knopf, Inc., 1966); Vera S. Dunham, *In Stalin's Time: Middleclass Values in Soviet Fiction* (London: Cambridge University Press, 1976); and Michael Zuckerman, "Dreams that Men Dare to Dream: The Role of Ideas in Western Modernization," *Social Science History* 2 (1978): 332-345.

might be expected are scattered throughout the establishment—among the bishops, the politicians, the civil servants, and indeed the businessmen. There is no mechanistic correspondence between group affiliation (and presumed interest) and ideological propensities.

A second cleavage is perhaps equally glaring, and yet it is neither conceptually nor empirically identical to the first. This dimension of conflict separates the supporters of authoritarian order, of the top-down, centralized state, from those who place greater value on decentralized decision making and on the autonomy of organized interests.

Two properties of this split bear emphasis. First, it is not reducible to the accumulation-distribution dilemma. If it were, Brazilian authoritarianism would be an extremely polarized yet essentially simple phenomenon, with antagonists arrayed on opposite sides of a single macroissue.

To be sure, the accumulation-distribution and the order-autonomy axes are related. Many of the advocates of headlong development also condone outright authoritarianism as the mechanism to enforce their economic goals. But the convergence is far from perfect. Several of the elites who applauded the economic performance of the early post-1964 regime began to have second thoughts about the encroachment on what they considered their own spheres of action by the government. This is the sentiment behind the cries of "statism" heard from elites who would otherwise seem to have little to complain about under the authoritarian dispensation.

Conversely, not all of the elites distressed by the government's neglect of social needs can be described as upset by the absence of the rule of law and by the growth in the size of the government, anymore than those who became disillusioned with the monopolization of power by the military and their technocratic allies can be equated with the advocates of democracy in the sense of social justice. While the two cleavages resemble each other, they do not overlap completely. This partial separation makes for complicated coalitional possibilities among the elites.

Another feature of the order-autonomy split is that it is very sharp indeed. The trade-off between accumulation and distribution may be structurally more fundamental but it need not be politically more volatile than the rift between authoritarian order and civil liberties. Brazilian elites tend to perceive the conflict between the imperative of accumulation and the need for distribution relatively, in terms of more and less. By contrast, issues involving the autonomy of elite interests—for example, the right of political parties to organize on their own terms, as compared to the continuation of the military's hold on power—have an either-or quality. Conflicts over the distribution of aggregate growth are usually framed as a matter of degree. The explicitly political issues—those involving the control over and the autonomy of interests—are not so malleable. They put into question the foundations of the authoritarian hierarchy itself.

Neither of these lines of potential conflict—between accumulation and distribution and between control and autonomy—is new to observers of authoritarian politics. Very broadly, they correspond to the class and state-versus-society divisions common in discussions of authoritarianism. Yet systematic considerations of their interaction are hard to come by. Analysis of this interaction can reveal, among other things, how the elites behave ideologically—that is, how they cling to principle—on certain issues, while on others they are open to comparatively prosaic bargaining and negotiation.

The approach also casts the question of the ideological component of Brazilian elite behavior in a manageable framework. Instead of trying to decide whether or not Brazilian elites are ideological—an exercise virtually doomed to produce lexical contortions without much empirical substance[9]—the problem becomes one of estimating which issues are likely to generate seemingly irreconcilable differences and therefore heated, ideological conflict, and which are less touchy and open to compromise.

There is a third cleavage in Brazilian politics that is less familiar and much less frequently analyzed because it is usually thought to have almost no political significance whatsoever. Regional, linguistic, ethnic, and associated differences have not been at the center of elite conflict in Brazil. Although regional disparities are great, they have failed to ignite severe hostility, most probably because they are not intertwined with sharp linguistic or ethnic differences.

Of these primordial yet relatively weak nodes of conflict the one singled out for attention in this study is religion. The brunt of the argument presented so far is that Brazilian elites are not so unideological as they may appear. Yet neither are they given to disquisitions of the dogmatic sort. The strain of patrimonial softness, of conservative preemption, has been noted by several observers of the political culture of Brazilian elites.[10] The problem is how to explain it.

The hypothesis advanced here is that the reluctance of Brazilian elites to go at each other to the death, to cultivate extremist ideologies, and

---

[9] However, for an exceptionally useful schematization of the literature on ideology, see Giovanni Sartori, "Politics, Ideology, and Belief Systems," *American Political Science Review* 53 (1969): 398-411. Compare Douglas C. Bennett, "Defining Ideology: The Danger of Methodological Distortion," in *Terms of Conflict: Ideology in Latin American Politics*, ed. Morris J. Blachman and Ronald G. Hellman (Philadelphia: Institute for the Study of Human Affairs, 1977).

[10] For example, Paulo Mercadante, *A Consciência Conservadora no Brasil* (Rio de Janeiro: Editôra Saga, 1965).

indeed to impose a thoroughgoing authoritarianism can be traced in part to the virtual separation of religious controversies and of absolutist modes of thinking from most other political issues. The idea is not obvious, and it requires a brief explanation.[11]

The penetration of Brazilian society by the church has never been extensive, although the country remains nominally Catholic. The church has neither been unequivocally identified with the fate of the nation or with that of a particular government in Brazil, nor has it exercised significant influence on the educational system.[12] This last fact has particular importance for the socialization of the elites. By and large, they have not been acculturated to the cut-and-thrust of doctrinal debate; a lack of metaphysical certitude does not appear to bother them.

The dissociation between religious and secular-ideological modes of thought probably sets Brazil apart from other Latin cultures, from Spain, for example. A leading Spanish politician can declare "I am the conscience of Spain!" and not be thought an irredeemable crank. In Brazil, pronouncements in this vein would be met with ridicule and calls for psychiatric treatment.[13]

Religious and moral issues are not uncontroversial in Brazil. Some of them, such as the fight over the legalization of abortion, can become quite heated. At the same time, positions on these issues are compartmentalized from preferences regarding other controversies in which progressives and reactionaries are clearly visible. The religious cleavage, such as it is, stands apart from the divisions over accumulation and distribution and between order and autonomy. It is the isolation of moral issues in the cognitive frameworks of the elites that, I shall argue, deprives political combat in

[11] My thinking on the comparative salience of religion and its connection to secular cleavages has been greatly influenced by David Martin, *A General Theory of Secularization* (New York: Harper & Row, Publishers, 1978), and Bryan Wilson, "The Return of the Sacred," *Journal for the Scientific Study of Religion* 18 (1979): 268-280.

[12] See Ralph Della Cava, "Catholicism and Society in Twentieth Century Brazil," *Latin American Research Review* 11 (1976): 7-50.

[13] The message of the anecdote can be confirmed by more rigorous methods. Correlations between religious sentiment and left-right leanings in Spain have been consistently reported at very high levels, on the order of .4 to .5, at the top of corresponding associations in other nations for which comparable evidence is available. In Brazil, the correlation hovers around zero. Correlations between religiosity (frequency of church attendance) and left-right self-placement for ten Western European nations and the United States are reported by Ronald Inglehart and Hans D. Klingeman, "Party Identification, Ideological Preference and the Left-Right Dimension among Western Mass Publics," in *Party Identification and Beyond*, ed. Ian Budge, Ivor Crewe, and Dennis Farlie (New York: John Wiley, 1976), p. 268. Comparable figures for Spain are given by Juan J. Linz, "Europe's Southern Frontier: Evolving Trends toward What?" *Daedalus* 108 (1978): 175-209.

Brazil of the acerbity and intransigence which it might otherwise display.[14]

This tridimensional view of the ideology of Brazilian elites has several implications.[15] First, cultural factors such as religion are treated as variables rather than as conditions with either great explanatory power or else with none at all. The proposition that religious sentiment does not matter much among Brazilian elites and that it hardly constitutes a dimension of conflict in the normal sense of the term may be taken to mean that its weakness is unworthy of attention. Quite the opposite is intended. Brazil deviates

---

[14] There is another aspect to this argument that I do not develop in detail. Somewhat like that of the church, the political history of the Brazilian military has been ambiguous rather than strictly identified with the right, much less the left. The unity of the military with conservative forces, and especially the continuation of this role since 1964, represent a departure from its conventional role as the *poder moderador* (moderating power) of public life in Brazil as well as from its comparatively liberal function in the overthrow of the monarchy toward the end of the nineteenth century. See Edmundo Campos Coelho, *Em Busca da Identidade: O Exército e a Política na Sociedade* (Rio de Janeiro: Forense Universitária, 1976), and compare Don Whitmore, "Brazilian Positivism and the Military Republic," in *Religion in Latin American Life and Literature*, ed. Lyle C. Brown and William F. Cooper (Waco, Tex.: Baylor University Press, forthcoming). The point is that, traditionally, neither the Brazilian army nor the church has been equated with a single political current; this tradition engenders an ambivalence on both sides that takes some of the sting out of Brazilian politics.

Still another implication of the general argument about the weakness of establishment Catholicism in Brazil concerns the sensuality of Brazilian popular culture, a phenomenon about which both the regime and the church have been circumspect. It is difficult to discuss *tropicalismo* without lapsing into folklorisms about Zé Carioca, Carmen Miranda's fruit-salad headgear, steamy samba dancers, and the like. Nevertheless, at least in the zone running from Bahia in the North to Rio in the center-south, this strain in popular culture has almost certainly contributed to what might delicately be called a picaresque irreverence regarding exhortations to respectable behavior, political and otherwise. See Roger Bastide, *The African Religions of Brazil: Toward a Sociology of the Interpenetration of Civilizations* (Baltimore: The Johns Hopkins University Press, 1978).

[15] In part, this conceptualization resembles Daniel Bell's ideas about the "disjunction" among the "economic," "political," and "cultural axial principles and structures" in advanced industrial societies. See *The Cultural Contradictions of Capitalism* (New York: Basic Books, 1978) and *The Winding Passage: Essays and Sociological Journeys 1960-1980* (Cambridge, Mass.: ABT Books, 1980). However, Bell does not treat these phenomena as dimensions or cleavages in the sense used here. He argues that disorientation and conflict result from the incompatibility between, for example, the hierarchical principles of organization enshrined in the economic sphere and the participatory ethic of the political sphere. From this perspective, it is not clear how conflicts that emerge within these areas are to be interpreted. Furthermore, Bell argues that the various axes are disjoined without indicating the degree to which this is so and how one might go about estimating the extent of this differentiation. Compare Steve Barnett and Martin G. Silverman, *Ideology and Everyday Life: Anthropology, Neomarxist Thought, and the Problem of Ideology and the Social Whole* (Ann Arbor: University of Michigan Press, 1979).

from the stereotype of Latin political cultures in that the religious factor
is peripheral. While the comparative unimportance of the religious factor
qualifies a reading of the culturalist perspective that emphasizes the weight
of Catholic organicism, the marginality of an absolutist tradition may
contribute to the empirical and piecemeal style of thought favored by many
Brazilian elites. This interpretation differs from the claim that cultural
inheritance can be dispensed with altogether in the analysis of Brazilian
authoritarianism.

Second, the dimensions of conflict underpinning the ideologies of Brazilian elites are not free-floating attitudes. They reflect, albeit obliquely,
institutional cleavages within the power structure. For example, there is
an organizational as well as an ideological separation between the leaders
of Brazilian banking and industry, on the one hand, and the military and
the civilian technocrats in charge of the government, on the other. Despite
their near agreement on the broad lines of economic policy, they do not
see eye-to-eye on questions involving the autonomy of organizations outside the government.

On the whole, the institutional divisions of the power structure—the
splits between urban labor and most of the other elites, between private
economic interests and the military-technocratic stewards of the state, and
between the Brazilian church and the secular world of politics—form a
tripartite mapping of groups much like the tridimensional shape of elite
ideologies. This aggregate composition of political structure and culture
among Brazilian elites is not reducible to individual personality traits, nor
is there a simple link between social background and political opinion.

Third, this having been said, it is extremely important to remember that
the values and ideologies of the elites on any one of the three axes of
conflict cannot be matched impeccably with the groups to which individual
elites belong. Few of the elite estates can be thought of as formal organizations in the everyday sense of the term. To the degree that they have
explicitly stated codes of recruitment and rules of conduct, the military
and the church approach this standard. But the government and opposition
parties were homogeneous organizations mostly in name. In any event,
they no longer exist, having splintered into various smaller parties and
factions. ''The business community'' is a euphemism for multiple, specific
sectors; ''it'' does not speak with one voice. One of the ironies of Brazilian
politics is that there may be more de facto pluralism within any one of the
elite sectors, including the military, than there is in the relations among
the groups themselves—a tendency that helps explain the air of simultaneous disorganization and despotism.

The reason why this internal heterogeneity matters is that, although the
attitudes of individual elites are more than just psychological idiosyncracies

and regularities and although they can be traced to abiding institutional cleavages, they are only imperfectly organized in collective fashion. Many of the historically and culturally defined institutions of Brazilian politics do not take overtly organizational form.

This may be a weakness, particularly for the opposition, and one on which authoritarianism may thrive by default. In any case, it would be as simplistic to reify the ideologies of "the businessmen" versus the "politicians," for example, as if political combat were a morality play setting Vice against Virtue, as it would be to reduce their values to a kind of random individualism.[16]

Fourth, the fact that elite ideologies in Brazil cannot be reduced to a single master cleavage makes elite politics and the tensions underlying Brazilian authoritarianism complex and ambiguous. Societies in which the divide between religion and irreligion is very sharp and in which this division coincides with other cleavages (regional, ethnic, linguistic, and so on) are prone to protracted, bitter conflict. Such a convergence of tensions does not hold in Brazil.

And yet there may be cases where primordial attachments provide cultural moorings in the absence of consensus in other areas. Again, the experience of post-Franquist Spain comes to mind. There, popular religiosity and its identification with the monarchy have supplied the center-right with a psychological anchor during the transition toward a more democratic politics.[17]

In Brazil, no such centripetal force exists. The movement away from authoritarianism in Brazil is not liable to be especially violent—it has not been so far—but it is likely, because of the absence of a dominant political current, to be confusing and highly experimental. Thus, while Brazilian elites may not be given to extremes, their politics has no immediately recognizable center or dominant legitimizing strain. It is this vacuum among contending forces that the military has tried to fill.

A fifth implication of viewing the ideology of Brazilian elites as multidimensional touches precisely on the question of authoritarian legitimacy just noted. Most analysts have treated authoritarianism in Brazil as strongly conditioned by economic forces; the resurgence of antimass politics is seen as a response to the structural strains of catch-up development. I have suggested that since the onset and the undoing of authoritarianism are different things, pressures that may explain the former may not be of much help in coming to terms with the latter. A central thesis of this study is

[16] Compare Susan Kaufman Purcell and John F. H. Purcell, "State and Society in Mexico: Must a Stable Polity Be Institutionalized?" *World Politics* 32 (1980): 194-227.

[17] Peter McDonough, Antonio López Pina, and Samuel H. Barnes, "The Spanish Public in Political Transition," *British Journal of Political Science* 11 (1981): 49-79.

that ideology matters among Brazilian elites to the degree that it subverts the pretensions of the military-bureaucratic state to gain legitimacy.

But how, more precisely, does this process unfold? In one sense, the answer seems obvious, and it has little to do with ideology per se. Post-1964 governments have attempted to justify authoritarian measures on the grounds of efficiency. If the economy performs well, the rationalization would seem to be confirmed. If it does not, as has been the case since 1973, then the claim of efficiency becomes less compelling. The failure of the regime to manage economic policy at peak levels has contributed to its political troubles, even among many of its erstwhile supporters. According to this view, the fate of the regime is sealed by the practical, not the ideological, considerations on which it originally based its appeal.

But consider a different scenario, one in which the economy does well. (This is the environment of the early 1970s from which most of the data used here are drawn.) Even in this apparently favorable situation, the legitimacy of the regime is threatened, for two reasons.

First, increasing prosperity undercuts the supposed rationality of the belt-tightening, antipopulist measures enforced by the military. Although good times might redound to the credit of authoritarianism, they also call into question the continued necessity of repressive policies. Military rule was never justified in Brazil as a final solution. Instead, it was seen as a temporary, exceptional phenomenon to be abandoned to the degree that it succeeded. Ideologically, it was fugitive.

Second, whatever the causal connection between the two, economic growth in Brazil during the early seventies went hand-in-hand with the concentration of power. The regime was exclusionary; the mass of the population had no say in decision making. Somewhat less obvious is the fact that many formerly well-entrenched elite groups were also marginalized: politicians as a class, labor leaders, many intellectuals, some members of the business community and, gradually, the church. The concentration of power by the military and the civilian bureaucracy began to deprive these elites of their constituencies. They were made increasingly irrelevant.

The arbitrariness of Brazilian authoritarianism impinged on the limited pluralism to which rival elites had been accustomed. The problem was not that the economy was doing badly but that contending elites had to pay a very steep and, for some, unacceptable price for this success. Economic growth did not guarantee political good will among the elites. The regime did not fail, at least for some time. On the contrary, it did all too well, and its very triumphs incited resentment among elites with little to gain by unrestricted despotism.

This interpretation of Brazilian authoritarianism implies not only that the regime was insecure during the economic miracle years but also that specifically political issues, intrinsic to the balance of power among the elites, exerted a debilitating influence on whatever legitimacy the government enjoyed. A final twist remains to be added to this diagnosis, however. Among the elites, the proponents of authoritarian order and the advocates of political liberalization saw each other as outlaws. A profound enmity existed between the two camps: neither accepted the other as legitimate. But the law-and-order elites held the upper hand. They were joined by those who, ostensibly caring little about political or ideological refinements, opted for a crash program of economic development. The coalition between the ''authoritarians'' and the ''economists'' left the ''politicians'' virtually powerless.[18]

Virtually powerless but not entirely isolated. For there is another set of elites, scattered throughout the power structure but concentrated among the labor leaders, the bishops, and to some extent the politicians of both the government and opposition parties, that the alliance left out—those who gave primary emphasis to economic distribution and social reform. By the canons of liberal democratic theory, the ''social reformers'' are a puzzling lot. They want more—that is, palpable benefits for their clienteles. Yet while they are not so enamored of large-scale, long-term economic growth as some of the other elites, neither are they particularly sensitive to questions involving political liberties. Usually, they are the most accommodating and least ideological of the elites. As long as the authorities can deliver tangible benefits to their constituents, the social reformers are generally deaf to disputations over the form of government, its military make-up, its gargantuan size, and the like. The acceptance by the social reformers of the rules of the corporatist game and their extreme caution in openly challenging the state render them uncomfortable allies of the more stridently political elites.

Two factors move the social reformers closer to the politicians. The most obvious is the failure of the government to furnish the educational and welfare goods on which the coalition of convenience and subordination is based. A slowdown in economic growth, such as occurred in Brazil in 1973, can put this bargain into jeopardy, although the process cannot be thought of as automatic. In any event, to the degree that the social reformers are pragmatically rather than ideologically committed to the regime, they may begin to shop around for allies who they feel might be better able to come across for their constituents.

The other factor contributing to the disaffection of the social reformers

---

[18] These terms represent a linguistic convenience and are not meant to imply professional or occupational categories. Rather, they are intended to demarcate particular sets of attitudes— that is, developmental priorities—that are not necessarily identified with specific elite groups.

is the opposite of the first, and it is the one that I shall stress. It involves a reaction against the usurpation by the state of the little influence left to contending elites with the expansion of authoritarianism. Economically, this can occur in good times as well as bad. Although the social reformers are loath to stand up to the centralizing state, and although they cannot be called ardent defenders of a more open, parliamentary style of conflict-resolution, they can be driven into the arms of the politicians when their control over the distribution of material rewards is diminished to the point where their status as elites, with some power over the allocation of needed benefits in the eyes of their clienteles, becomes small to the point of vanishing.

Thus, it is when the social reformers uncharacteristically chafe at the coercive rather than the cooptative pretensions of the state—at the regime's increasing arbitrariness—that whatever legitimacy or acceptance the authoritarian coalition enjoyed begins seriously to unravel. The law-and-order types become more isolated, even from some of the elites who remain dedicated to rapid economic growth but who also retain vestiges of the liberal democratic faith.

This reconstruction of the conflicts leading to the delegitimization of authoritarian rule in Brazil does not, by itself, establish that the elites behave ideologically. Rather, it suggests that explanations of the decline of authoritarianism in Brazil in terms of broad economic factors do not take us very far. Consideration of crises of power internal to the establishment, in which normally compliant elites begin to raise what look like questions of principle as well as matters of specific group interests, permits an approximate understanding of the curious downturn in repression at the height of economic success depicted earlier. The elites act ideologically some of the time, and this unaccustomed polarization erodes the viability of authoritarian government.

The rest of this book is devoted to putting flesh on these abstract bones. Along the way, it is important to keep three ideas plainly in view. First, the lines of conflict between accumulation and distribution, between authoritarian order and political liberty, as well as the virtual noncleavage involving religion are partially distinct. To the extent that this is so, even such rudimentary beginnings can yield a complexity of political alliances. By contrast, the premise that Brazilian politics is totally polarized, such that all the advocates of rapid growth favor outright authoritarianism, and all the proponents of social reform are also committed to a liberal polity, and the conservatives and progressives on these cleavages are neatly as-

---

The relationship between elite sectors and developmental priorities is examined in Chapter Four.

sociated with deeply religious and fiercely secular positions, like monarchists and republicans, would be, I think, disastrously simplistic.[19]

Second, the cleavages should not be thought of as forming a static matrix. Legitimacy, authoritarian or otherwise, is a dynamic phenomenon; alliances shift. Potential partners in a coalition have multiple goals, some of them compatible, others contradictory. Much of the polemic surrounding Brazilian politics comes from an attempt to foist either-or diagnoses on what is, in fact, a confusing reality to the elites themselves.

Taken alone, however, the caveat is banal; bromides about the complexity and subtlety of authoritarian politics no longer pass as profound. In relation to the dynamics of cleavages in Brazil and the uncertain nature of the coalitions based on them, I have in mind two apparently unrelated things: the role of the church and the issue of foreign investment.

I have mentioned that the church is weaker at the mass level in Brazil than is sometimes thought, despite the publicity given to the grass-roots communities associated with it, and also that the elites prefer not to link moral controversies with debate on "modern" issues. This in turn keeps chronic ferocity out of elite conflict. But the situation is in flux. Powerful elements within the church have begun to side with the neglected and the oppressed.

At the same time, the church as an institution is changing. Vocations are down, and more priests are wearing civilian clothes. The one institutional symbol of traditional community, apart from the military, is itself straining for identity.[20]

The religious dimension in Brazil is not so much a cleavage as it is a remnant of a cultural community that cannot be retrieved, if it ever existed, even were the tensions between accumulation and distribution, order and autonomy, to be resolved.[21] The church is undergoing a transformation that does not lead it or its sympathizers to a new secular order, although the creative contribution of this change is likely to be at least as great as anything produced by the uncertain pragmatism of the normal run of Brazilian politics. It is in this sense that the church is ambivalent and that its actions provide a kind of Rorschach test for diviners of the future of the country.[22]

[19] Contrast Apásia Alcântara de Camargo, "Authoritarianism and Populism: Bipolarity in the Brazilian Political System," in *The Structure of Brazilian Development*, ed. Neuma Aguiar (New Brunswick, N.J.: Transaction Books, 1979).

[20] See Michael Dodson, "Prophetic Politics and Political Theory in Latin America," *Polity* 12 (1980): 388-408.

[21] Compare Marshall Berman, *The Politics of Authenticity: Radical Individualism and the Emergence of Modern Society* (New York: Atheneum, 1970).

[22] Conceivably, the Brazilian church as a body may become increasingly radicalized and

The foreign investment issue shares this ambiguity. Like the question of population planning, decisions taken on the issue have potentially serious repercussions. But, again like the moral issues, it is not supremely controversial among Brazilian elites. It does not divide them as some other expressly political issues do.

On the one hand, many of the elites try to deal with the multiple challenges of foreign investment through a mixture of brinkmanship and hard bargaining. The indebtedness of the country is enormous, but Brazil is not Zambia; much of its industrial infrastructure has already been put in place. On the other hand, the challenges are not simply economic. They also pose questions of cultural identity. As the economy of Brazil merges with the world market, the myth of *antropofagismo*—the capacity of the Brazilian vastness to cannibalize, to swallow up and to profit from, outsiders—has given way to fears about denationalization.[23]

The elites' position vis-à-vis foreign capital is therefore schizophrenic. While some of this conflict is expressed across the elite sectors, so that those on the left are generally less enthusiastic about foreign capital than their peers on the right, individual elites seem even more divided within themselves on the issue. For these reasons, although the internationalization of the Brazilian economy has fundamental importance for the future of the country, the process need not open deep fissures among the elites. On the contrary, it may cause the political culture to swing from a solidarity of euphoria to a consensus of despair, around a base line of grueling pragmatism.

What the bishops and foreign capital have in common, then, is that they are the trickiest things to analyze in Brazil by way of conventional parameters. In their own ways, both embody tensions evoking the frailty of Brazilian identity and community, and these tensions are registered less perfectly by other groups and other issues.

---

identified with what it believes to be the cause of peasants and workers. In order for this to happen, leftism with regard to domestic issues would probably have to become more closely aligned with a virulently nationalist position that conservatives would not be able to countenance, and this realignment would have to involve not only the bishops (who are for the most part anticapitalist, if not antiforeign, to begin with) but also many of the developmental elites. None of this is impossible, but I know of only one instance in which such a sea change has been cogently documented. See Emmet Larkin, "Church, State, and Nation in Modern Ireland," *American Historical Review* 80 (1975): 1244-1276. It is worth noting that the Brazilian church has never claimed for itself the role of establishing a "new order"; its contribution lies in working with other voluntary associations to amplify the scope of day-to-day democracy.

[23] See Nora Hamilton, "Possibilities and Limits of State Autonomy in Latin American Countries," paper presented at the meetings of the Latin American Studies Association, Pittsburgh, Pennsylvania, April 5-7, 1979.

The third idea to keep in mind is that while ideology constrains the consolidation of authoritarianism, "economics"—or rather, the set of organizations developed to manage social as well as economic change during the authoritarian period—restrains the movement toward political liberalization in Brazil.[24] These top-down planning and welfare instruments, now of mammoth size, do not self-destruct. One reason why not only the social reformers but also Brazilian elites with other priorities are usually so cautious in contemplating a root-and-branch renovation of the corporatist structure is that the anticipatory maneuvers of the state in the areas of welfare and service-delivery has been to some extent real as well as symbolic. The problem is not so much fear of mass politics as it is the opposite one of genuine doubt regarding popular receptivity toward radical change.[25]

On the whole, the Brazilian experience has been the reverse of the sequence, familiar in Anglo-Saxon democracies, according to which the achievement of political rights by autonomous parties and militant working-class organizations preceded the concession of social benefits.[26] Instead of "meeting demands," the Brazilian state tends to create and nurture clienteles, often taking mass support out from under dissident elites. This stratagem blunts ideological confrontation.[27]

Finally, just as the determinants of despotism and democracy in Brazil are multiple and probably have differential impacts, depending on which stage of the phenomena is analyzed, it helps to keep open the possibility that the two systems are not negations of each other. In Brazil, the absence

[24] See Julia Juruna, "Les Limites de la Libéralisation au Brésil," *Le Monde Diplomatique* (July 1980): 19-20.

[25] Compare Rose J. Spalding, "Welfare Policymaking: Theoretical Implications of a Mexican Case Study," *Comparative Politics* 12 (1980): 419-438.

[26] See Gaston V. Rimlinger, *Welfare Policy and Industrialization in Europe, America, and Russia* (New York: John Wiley & Sons, 1971), and T. H. Marshall, *Class, Citizenship, and Social Development* (New York: Doubleday & Company, Inc., 1964).

[27] While the foregoing paragraphs are pretty much a précis of the corporatist interpretation of Brazilian politics, no full-scale empirical study of authoritarian corporatism in Brazil has been conducted. There exists, however, an abundant comparative literature. See for example Lawrence Goodwyn, *The Populist Moment: A Short History of the Agrarian Revolt in America* (London: Oxford University Press, 1978); Alfred D. Chandler, Jr., *The Visible Hand: The Managerial Revolution in American Business* (Cambridge, Mass.: The Belknap Press of Harvard University Press, 1977); Charles S. Maier, *Recasting Bourgeois Europe: Stabilization in France, Germany, and Italy in the Decade after World War I* (Princeton: Princeton University Press, 1975); and David F. Noble, *America by Design: Science, Technology, and the Rise of Corporate Capitalism* (New York: Alfred A. Knopf, Inc., 1977). Goodwyn's study is particularly sobering as a demonstration of the obstacles against the creation of a sustained counterculture in the midst of capitalist modernization; it is germane to prognostications about the future of the grass-roots communities organized by the Brazilian church.

of one does not require the presence of the other. Neither political option is hegemonic; neither has been fully institutionalized. They represent zones along a continuum—or, more accurately, the partial resolutions of tensions formed by the incompatibility among several dimensions of conflict—rather than wholly alternate states.[28]

[28] Readers familiar with the literature on authoritarianism may want to skim through the Introduction. In addition to a critique of this literature, it contains a specification of the hypotheses to be tested and presents the plan of analysis.

Power and Ideology in Brazil

INTRODUCTION

[National development is] an integrated process of political, economic, and social development. The development of democracy is the first requisite in the political realm. We must develop and perfect our democracy. But this goal can be achieved only if we also further social development, if we improve our social life, if we raise the standards of living of the Brazilian people. And standards of living can only be raised through economic development. Thus it is clear that these are interconnected objectives: we cannot dream of a perfect democracy in a poor country or in a country where there are lacunas, defects, and inadequacies in the social realm.

—GEN. ERNESTO GEISEL, *President of Brazil, 1974-1979*[1]

Democracy is not dessert.

—*Opposition politician*

In 1964, the military seized control of the government in Brazil in order to avert what they and their upper- and middle-class allies saw as the menace of radical, mass-based rule. Popular organizations such as the peasant leagues were disbanded or their leadership replaced, as happened with the labor syndicates, or, as occurred with the political parties, they were reorganized in such a way as to diminish the threat of mass participation. The insulation of elites was preserved against the pressures attendant upon structural transformations in the larger society.

The novelty of this situation was not that the military intervened to restore order. They had done so on several occasions prior to 1964. Rather, it consists in their overt continuation in power. The extended tenure of the military is without precedent in Brazilian history. They chose to remain at the head of the government in order to ensure, so they claim, the conditions for economic growth that will make Brazil a world power by the end of the century.

During the late sixties and early seventies, when annual rates of economic growth stood at around 10 percent, the dictatorship came to be vaunted as an exemplar of capitalist modernization in the Third World. By 1974, with the growth rate reduced, inflation resurgent, and a mounting foreign debt, the Brazilian miracle showed signs of weakening. The government party suffered an electoral defeat, and there was talk of "decompression." Yet the military, who took over the government with dubious legitimacy,

[1] Quoted in *Jornal do Brasil*, June 30, 1977: 3.

had difficulty in finding a formula for giving it up. The "state of exception" continued on its way toward what was becoming a generation of authoritarianism.[2]

As the seventies wore on, Brazil alternately veered toward democracy and backtracked into factionalism. Strikes among manual and white-collar workers proliferated. The government made some wage concessions while removing the more obstreperous opposition leaders. By 1980, the rate of inflation had surpassed the level—over 100 percent—of that which had preceded and was thought to have precipitated the coup of 1964. Still, the government hung on. Criticism of virtually every aspect of government policy was permitted in the newspapers, but radio and television continued to be censored. Torture declined, yet the security apparatus stayed in place.[3]

The political system failed to resolve two fundamental questions: the relationship of elites to the public at large and the relationship of elites to one another. While authoritarian demobilization protects elites from the pressures of mass society, at least for a time, it is unable to establish the ground rules by which elites are protected from one another.

The present study concerns the interelite side of this drama. Although most of the elites would accord the armed forces the right to guard the nation, and themselves, from demagogy and communism, their willingness to accede to the military as the dominant actor in elite polities is questionable. The study concentrates on the early seventies, when the economic

[2] There are numerous studies of political and economic changes in Brazil since 1964. For an overview of Brazilian politics since the birth of the First Republic in 1889 to the military dictatorship (through 1977), see Peter Flynn, *Brazil: A Political Analysis* (Boulder, Colo.: Westview Press, 1978). Aspects of the post-1964 period are covered by Edmar L. Bacha, "Issues and Evidence on Recent Brazilian Economic Growth," *World Development* 5 (1977): 47-67; Bacha, *Os Mitos de uma Década: Ensaios de Economia Brasileira* (Rio de Janeiro: Editora Paz e Terra, 1976); Werner Baer, "The Impact of Industrialization on Brazil's External Development," paper presented at the meeting of the Midwest Political Science Association, Chicago, Illinois, April 20-22, 1978; Luís Carlos Bresser Pereira, *O Colapso de uma Aliança de Classes* (São Paulo: Editora Brasiliense, 1978); Georges-André Fiechter, *Brazil Since 1964: Modernization Under a Military Regime* (New York: John Wiley, 1975); Albert Fishlow, "Brazilian Development in Long-Term Perspective," *American Economic Review* 70 (1980): 102-108; Norman Gall, "The Rise of Brazil," *Commentary* 63 (1977): 45-55; Celso Lafer, *O Sistema Político Brasileiro* (São Paulo: Perspectiva, 1975); Pedro S. Malan and Regis Bonelli, "The Brazilian Economy in the Seventies: Old and New Developments," *World Development* 5 (1977): 19-45; Riordan Roett, ed., *Brazil in the Seventies* (Washington, D.C.: American Enterprise Institute, 1976); Roett, *Brazil: Politics in a Patrimonial Society*, rev. ed. (New York: Praeger, 1978); H. Jon Rosenbaum and William G. Tyler, eds., *Contemporary Brazil: Issues in Economic and Political Development* (New York: Praeger, 1973); and Ronald M. Schneider, *The Political System of Brazil: Emergence of a "Modernizing" Authoritarian Regime* (New York: Columbia University Press, 1971).

[3] Harry Mauer, "Is Brazil on the Brink of Democracy?" *New York Review of Books* 25, September 28, 1978: 43-48.

boom was at its height and political repression in full force.[4] Most of the data is drawn from personal interviews with over 250 members of the Brazilian elite: top civil servants, the heads of leading industrial companies and banks, senators and deputies of both the government and the opposition parties, bishops, and labor leaders.[5]

I focus on two aspects of the elite system: the structure of power and the nature of elite ideology. My interest is in understanding the tensions within and between these phenomena that gave rise to a situation in which for a time debate turned on not whether the military would or should go but on the phasing and terms of their departure and the make-up and policies of their replacements.[6] In order to set these questions in context, it is necessary to consider some of the clues and puzzles encountered by analysts of authoritarianism in Brazil and Latin America generally.

Ambiguities of Authoritarianism

A major contribution of the scholarly effort devoted to Brazil over the past years has been to clarify the structural bases of authoritarianism. The rise of authoritarian, as opposed to liberal-democratic and totalitarian, regimes during the course of industrialization is now less of an enigma than it once was.

Several interpretations of authoritarian capitalism draw on midlife crisis models of political development.[7] Although they exhibit enough variation from country to country to warrant skepticism about the prevalence of a uniform genotype, developmental dictatorships appear to be especially common at around the midpoint of the transition from a rural to an urban society. In outline, such systems are thought to be constituted out of a love-hate coalition between ascendant industrial interests and a declining agrarian elite who join forces, at least temporarily, against a growing urban proletariat and a presumably restive peasantry. From the stalemate between landed and urban interests, the authoritarian regime gathers strength to enforce the alliance against the lower classes, often at the expense of

---

[4] This period is also analyzed in Alfred Stepan, ed., *Authoritarian Brazil: Origins, Policies, and Future* (New Haven: Yale University Press, 1973).

[5] Sampling procedures are described in the Appendix.

[6] For a concise chronicle of events during the recent period, through early 1980, see Thomas G. Sanders, *Human Rights and Political Process in Brazil*, American Universities Field Staff Reports, No. 11 (Washington, D.C.: 1980).

[7] See Gino Germani, *Authoritarianism, Fascism, and National Populism* (New Brunswick, N.J.: Transaction Books, 1978); Barrington Moore, Jr., *Social Origins of Dictatorship and Democracy* (Boston: Beacon Press, 1966); A.F.K. Organski, *Stages of Political Development* (New York: Alfred A. Knopf, Inc., 1965); and Otávio Guilherme Velho, *Capitalismo Autoritário e Campesinato* (São Paulo: Difel, 1976).

particular capitalist interests, and to cope with the absorption of the nation into the world market.[8]

More recent interpretations give less weight to the decline of the aristocracy/rise of the bourgeoisie syndrome.[9] They devote greater attention to the economic crises of delayed dependent development—particularly, the bottlenecks associated with the changeover from light to heavy industrialization—and to the incompatibility of the accumulation imperative with populist politics and the expectations of consumer demand. Authoritarianism emerges as a reaction to the structural challenges and perceived threats of catch-up, take-off growth.[10]

A detailed exposition of the numerous revisions and criticisms of these formulations need not detain us here.[11] While it would be thoroughly misguided to claim that an academic consensus has crystallized around the domestic and international political economy of Brazil, the structural constraints on developmental options and their political repercussions are better understood now than they were a few years ago.

This makes my own task easier. In large measure, studies of the political economy of Brazil have rendered feasible the present analysis of the political demography and the political psychology of Brazilian elites. More than this, they have made such an analysis necessary. As many of the proponents of the concepts of bureaucratic authoritarianism, corporatism, and allied variants of Bonapartism recognize, the import-substitution phase

---

[8] For comparative critiques, see Philippe C. Schmitter, "Paths to Political Development in Latin America," in *Changing Latin America*, ed. Douglas A. Chalmers, Proceedings of the Academy of Political Science, Columbia University (1972), 3: 83-105; Peter Gourevitch, "The International System and Regime Formation," *Comparative Politics* 10 (1978): 419-438; Eldon Kenworthy, "The Function of the Little-Known Case in Theory-Building, or What Peronism Wasn't," *Comparative Politics* 6 (1973): 17-45; Juan J. Linz, "Totalitarian and Authoritarian Regimes," in *Handbook of Political Science*, ed. Fred I. Greenstein and Nelson W. Polsby (Reading, Mass.: Addison-Wesley, 1975), 3: 175-411; and Immanuel Wallerstein, "From Feudalism to Capitalism: Transition or Transitions?" *Social Forces* 55 (1976): 273-283.

[9] The most devastating attack on this line of reasoning has been mounted with specific reference to the English experience. See. J. H. Hechter, *Reappraisals in History*, 2d ed. (Chicago: University of Chicago Press, 1979), pp. 117-162.

[10] Guillermo A. O'Donnell, *Modernization and Bureaucratic-Authoritarianism* (Berkeley: Institute of International Studies, 1973). For an update, see the essays in David Collier, ed., *The New Authoritarianism in Latin America* (Princeton: Princeton University Press, 1979).

[11] See Fernando Henrique Cardoso, *O Modelo Político Brasileiro* (São Paulo: Difusão Européia do Livro, 1974); Richard Stuart Olson, "Expropriation and Economic Coercion in World Politics: A Retrospective Look at Brazil in the 1960s," *Journal of the Developing Areas* 13 (1979): 247-262; and Michael Wallerstein, "The Collapse of Democracy in Brazil," *Latin American Research Review* 15 (1980): 3-40.

of theory building directed against the errors of modernization and party-line Marxist theory has passed.[12]

For my purposes, the most pertinent feature of the literature on authoritarianism has to do with the questions it leaves unanswered. Indeed, they are not so much questions as ambiguities. This uncertainty is no doubt characteristic of the authoritarian condition itself. Early attempts to come to grips with developmental authoritarianism had as their primary aim not the explanation of such regimes in causal terms but rather their identification as a type of political system distinguishable from cold war polarities. The taxonomical goal was to isolate authoritarian regimes as distinct not only from democratic and totalitarian systems but also from traditional, plainly antidevelopmental polities.[13]

Analyses of the etiology of authoritarianism also reflect its elusive nature. The much-noted affinity between economic challenges and authoritarian solutions has been quite deliberately called "elective" to relieve the mechanistic air liable to surround such linkages.[14] The problems of social unrest facing Brazil and Venezuela in the fifties and sixties, to take only two instances, were broadly similar. Yet the political responses of the two countries have varied markedly. It seems too pat to invoke Venezuelan oil and the lack of an equivalent resource in Brazil as a sufficient explanation for the differences in political outcomes.[15]

[12] For example, Guillermo A. O'Donnell, "Reflections on the Patterns of Change in the Bureaucratic-Authoritarian State," *Latin American Research Review* 8 (1978): 3-38.

[13] The *locus classicus* is Juan J. Linz, "An Authoritarian Regime: Spain," in *Cleavages, Ideologies, and Party Systems*, ed. Erik Allardt and Yrjo Littunen (Helsinki: Academic Bookstore, 1964), pp. 291-341.

[14] Schmitter, "Paths to Political Development in Latin America," p. 94.

[15] One approach to unravelling the connections between economic pressures and political changes focuses on the relative autonomy of the state from society. In technical terms, the strong state/weak state heritage is treated as an intervening variable. But, while a centrist tradition is certainly stronger in some societies than others, it is extremely difficult to isolate the relative effects of differing cultural heritages. For useful attempts along these lines, see Magali Sarfatti, *Spanish Bureaucratic-Patrimonialism in America* (Berkeley: Institute of International Studies, 1966); Alfred Stepan, *The State and Society: Peru in Comparative Perspective* (Princeton: Princeton University Press, 1978); and Claudio Veliz, *The Centralist Tradition in Latin America* (Princeton: Princeton University Press, 1979). The classic interpretation of the drag of the statist tradition in Brazil is by Raymundo Faoro, *Os Donos do Poder: A Formação do Patronato Político Brasileiro* (Porto Alegre: Editora Globo, 1968). Critiques of this interpretation can be found in Simon Schwartzman, "Representatção e Cooptação Política no Brasil," *Dados* 7 (1970): 9-41, and Fernando Uricoechea, *The Patrimonial Foundations of the Brazilian Bureaucratic State* (Berkeley: University of California Press, 1980).

Part of the problem in assessing the effects of the centralist legacy in Brazil lies in the fact that, despite the presumed historical power of the state bureaucracy, the share of the public

However worthy the enterprise, the unresolved questions in the literature on authoritarianism are to some extent the result of trying to account for too much in too many places. In addition, theories elaborated to explain the onset of authoritarian rule are probably not suited for understanding its persistence, much less its downfall.

Even at a less panoramic level, puzzles linger, and it is here that I concentrate my efforts. Seen from a distance, the Brazilian political situation, at least during the high tide of authoritarianism, does not appear mysterious at all. It is an exclusionary, modernizing dictatorship run by the military and the *técnicos* to the benefit of capitalist interests, foreign and domestic.

But closer inspection reveals a melange of interests engaged in something more than palace politics and in something less than seismic revolution. Peter Evans has documented the jockeying among public companies, multinational corporations, and private domestic manufacturers in Brazil.[16] The constellation of forces depicted in the *tripé* model is a far cry from zero-sum renditions of imperialism. Yet even this sophisticated account omits the manueverings of the national and international banking sectors.[17]

Other approaches to political bargaining under authoritarianism also suffer from loose ends. It is not always clear what references to class fractions—for example, to the "agrarian bourgeoisie," the "state bourgeoisie," and the like—add, except detail, to our understanding of the dynamics of authoritarianism, or how they improve on analysis by way of more tangible collectivities and associations.[18] The trouble is not merely

---

sector as a proportion of the GNP has been rather modest, until fairly recently—that is, from 1930 (or 1964) onwards. See Nathaniel H. Leff, *Economic Retardation and Development in Brazil, 1822-1947* (forthcoming). Historically, the Brazilian state never seems to have attained the awesome sway of, for example, the Czarist bureaucracy. Compare Richard Pipes, *Russia Under the Old Regime* (New York: Charles Scribner's Sons, 1974). Consideration of this literature suggests that there are at least two dimensions to the tradition of the "heavy" state: one, its fiscal and confiscatory capacity and, two, its cultural penetration—a phenomenon that, in precapitalist societies, is closely associated with the dominance of a state religion and an accompanying religious bureaucracy.

[16] Peter B. Evans, *Dependent Development: The Alliance of Multinational, State, and Local Capital in Brazil* (Princeton: Princeton University Press, 1979).

[17] Compare Werner Baer and Annibal V. Villela, "The Changing Nature of Development Banking in Brazil," paper presented at the meetings of the Latin American Studies Association, Pittsburgh, Pennsylvania, April 5-7, 1979, and Jeff Friedan, "Third World Debt Industrialization: International Finance and State Capitalism in Mexico, Brazil, Algeria and South Korea," paper presented at the annual meetings of the American Political Science Association, Washington, D.C., August 28-31, 1980.

[18] See Guillermo O'Donnell, "State and Alliances in Argentina, 1956-1976," *Journal of Development Studies* 15 (1978): 3-33. This fine-grained study exemplifies the best in this tradition of analysis, and my reservations are as much aesthetic as substantive; the jargon—

that these studies are both complicated and incomplete. So is this one. Nonetheless, the addition of more and more actors and contingencies may serve just as well to confuse as to enhance comprehension of a complex reality.[19]

The serious problem, however, is twofold. In the first place, the vocabulary of class fractions implies that the crucial battles among competing

---

for example, "efficientist orientation," et cetera—occasionally obscures interpretation. The reasons for using such an approach for the study of Latin American politics are laudable. In many countries, formal organizations outside (and often inside) the state apparatus are weak or virtually nonexistent, and yet social interests, *camarillas*, and other associations in various forms of latency abound. It therefore becomes crucial to understand how these social forces are translated into political phenomena, as well as to keep separate the constellation of class forces and the types of political regimes based on them. Peter Gourevitch, among others, has elaborated on these points. See "The Second Image Reversed: The International Sources of Domestic Politics," *International Organization* 32 (1978): 881-911. Terminological and theoretical confusion is compounded by an absence of facts about the extent and modes of political participation in Latin America. The two volumes edited by John Booth and Mitchell A. Seligson, *Political Participation in Latin America* (New York: Holmes & Meier, 1978), help fill this gap. See also Booth, "Political Participation in Latin America: Levels, Structure, Context, Concentration and Rationality," *Latin American Research Review* 14 (1979): 29-60. The problem of the underorganization of interests is not, of course, unique to Latin America. For an analysis of an equivalent phenomenon elsewhere, see Clement Henry Moore, *Images of Development: Egyptian Engineers in Search of Industry* (Cambridge, Mass.: M.I.T. Press, 1980).

[19] Once we get beyond two or three elite groups, elite theory offers virtually nothing in the way of ideas about how they interact. For the most part, elites studies are taken up with the analysis of discrete elite and semi-elite groups; they are a mine of information about this or that set of powerful actors. See, for example, Joel B. Berner, "Educational Backgrounds of Latin American Legislators," *Comparative Politics* 6 (1976): 617-634; Mattei Dogan, ed., *The Mandarins of Western Europe* (Beverly Hills: Sage Publications, 1975); Heinz Eulau and Moshe M. Czudnowski, eds., *Elite Recruitment in Democratic Polities: Comparative Studies Across Nations* (New York: John Wiley and Sons, 1976); and the critique of the latter by Samuel J. Eldersveld, *American Political Science Review* 72 (1978): 727-728.

Certain pieces escape the narrow focus typical of many elite studies. See for example the monumental study by John A. Armstrong, *The European Administrative Elite* (Princeton: Princeton University Press, 1973); David S. Broder, *Changing of the Guard: Power and Leadership in America* (New York: Simon & Schuster, 1980); Hugh Heclo, *A Government of Strangers: Executive Politics in Washington* (Washington, D.C.: Brookings Institution, 1977); Gwen Moore, "The Structure of a National Elite Network," *American Sociological Review* 44 (1979): 673-692; Harold Perkin, "The Recruitment of Elites in British Society since 1800," *Journal of Social History* 12 (1978): 222-234; and W. D. Rubenstein, "Wealth, Elites, and the Class Structure of Modern Britain," *Past and Present* 26 (1977): 99-126.

However, while it is possible to collate these studies and, casting a benign eye on incompatibilities in sampling and other technical problems, to compare empirical regularities, it is extremely difficult to reconstruct a theory, or even a series of hypotheses, about the relations among elite groups. This is my principal topic, and I am therefore silent on the subject of elite theory as generally understood. For helpful explorations of this area, see Robert D. Putnam, *The Comparative Study of Political Elites* (Englewood Cliffs, N.J.: Prentice-Hall,

groups are essentially economic in origin.[20] I shall have more to say about this one-dimensional perspective later.

In the second place, discussions of Brazilian politics often focus on the clear winners and the obvious losers, the ruling elites and the underdogs, without much regard for those sectors whose institutional and ideological positions in the authoritarian landscape are ambivalent.[21] Omission of these groups—the lack of attention both to their complicity with authoritarianism and their "petty bourgeois" criticism of it—makes it difficult to understand either the durability of authoritarian governments or the interelite conflicts that contribute to their demise.

I am thinking particularly of the bishops, the labor leaders, and the politicians. The movement of 1964 was not only a class counterrevolution but also an attack by one segment of the Brazilian elite against another, a serious reordering of the membership and operative rules of interelite relations.[22] The Brazilian establishment is like an exclusive club with strict entrance requirements, whose members have yet to come to terms on the by-laws, that is, about how they should treat one another.

Thus, it is not self-evident that powerful or potentially powerful interests in Brazil can be treated as primarily economic actors. Nor can it be assumed that these groups behave as unitary blocs. Consideration of groups whose interests are presumably noneconomic increases the array of contending forces, and the situation is complicated further if we admit the possibility that elements within economic groups may act out of character, so that their driving motives escape explanation by way of transparent material interests. Brazilian authoritarianism contains a multiplicity of elite organ-

---

1976); Frank Bonilla and José A. Silva Michelena, *The Politics of Change in Venezuela*, vol. 1, *A Strategy for Research on Social Policy* (Cambridge, Mass.: M.I.T. Press, 1967); and Alan Zuckerman, "The Concept of 'Political Elite': Lessons from Mosca and Pareto," *Journal of Politics* 39 (1977): 324-344.

[20] This is not intended to mean that such analyses are deterministic or reductionist in a simplistic way but only that, almost always, the connections between economic conflicts and those that are expressed in cultural and political forms are opaque. For a helpful discussion, see Michael Buroway, "Contemporary Currents in Marxist Theory," *American Sociologist* 13 (1978), especially pp. 55-56; compare Howard J. Wiarda, ed., *Politics and Social Change in Latin America: The Distinct Tradition* (Amherst, Mass.: University of Massachusetts Press, 1974), and James A. Caporaso, "Dependency Theory: Continuities and Discontinuities in Development Studies," *International Organization* 34 (1980): 605-628.

[21] See, for example, André Gunder Frank, *Capitalism and Underdevelopment in Latin America* (New York: Monthly Review Press, 1967); contrast Robert W. Cox, "Ideologies and the New International Economic Order: Reflections on Some Recent Literature," *International Organization* 33 (1979): 257-302.

[22] For an account of the purges conducted by the military against their elite and semi-elite rivals, see Marcus Faria Figueiredo, "Política de Coerção no Sistema Político Brasileiro," Master's thesis, Instituto Universitário de Pesquisas do Rio de Janeiro, 1977.

izations that may, moreover, be divided internally as well as against one another.

One way to bring order to this scattering of interests and protogroups is to examine their ideological as well as their structural and organizational positions. The strategy may not seem parsimonious at all. The key idea, however, is not to extend the range of elites covered, although I shall discuss a greater number than that included in, for example, the triple alliance model of authoritarian domination. Instead, the idea is to introduce another variable, or set of variables—that is, ideology—across a slightly expanded set of groups. The approach does not guarantee simplicity, much less revelation. It does, however, introduce a variable with possible explanatory power rather than simply another subgroup, class fraction, or post hoc qualification.

A second problem remains. Even if examination of the ideological homogeneity and heterogeneity of various elite interests yields something more than smithereens of data, it is not clear that the strategy goes beyond the detection of comparisons and contrasts, of group-by-group patterns. However useful, this tells us nothing directly about the interactions among elite interests, the dynamics of which should be of primary concern once the number of groups becomes fairly large.

In brief, two problems have to be faced. One stems from the probability that there exists a multitude of rival interests within the Brazilian establishment, that these interests are divided within as well as among themselves, and that these divisions may be traced to ideological as well as more mundane factors. Second, making sense of the similarities and differences among elite factions requires an understanding of the relationships among the factions, of the ways in which they get along or fail to get along. Let us examine the latter question first.

Limited Pluralism

The question of interelite relations—of the balance of power between incumbents and potential dissidents with the capacity to make themselves heard—has been at the center of efforts to understand authoritarian politics as a distinctive type. In a seminal article, Juan Linz coined the phrase "limited pluralism" to characterize the bounded room for maneuver that exists among rival elites.[23]

The phenomenon of limited pluralism is significant because it draws attention to the importance of interelite relations in regimes that usually lack monocratic parties and explicit, dominant ideologies. In the absence

[23] Linz, "An Authoritarian Regime: Spain."

of such mechanisms for regulating political action, elites—certainly those in a society as complex and rapidly changing as the Brazilian—seek protocols of interaction.

But it is not at all certain that Brazilian elites have developed such a code or, if they have, that they adhere to it.[24] Limited pluralism can be understood in two different ways: as a description of the interelite squabbling that goes on in all but the simplest of polities and as a set of guidelines for how elites should behave toward one another. The former pretends to be a statement of fact.[25] The latter is supposed to be a code of conduct, a kind of ideology that distinguishes what is legitimate behavior from what is not.

As far as I can tell, this distinction between the behavioral and the normative facets of limited pluralism has never been drawn. Perhaps the reason is that no difference is thought to exist, at least in authoritarian regimes that function smoothly. The disjuncture evaporates if what is and what ought to be are congruent in the minds of the elites or if one supposes that elites under authoritarianism are thoroughgoing cynics.

On reflection, however, this eventuality seems improbable, first, because it presupposes a uniformity of socialization and a consensus on fundamental beliefs that, in a society undergoing massive transformation, strains credulity and, second, because it assumes a shared understanding of canons of behavior that are in fact vague and uncertain. The elite compact designated as limited pluralism may be stretched or restricted according to rules that are not obvious to the disinterested observer and are probably obscure to many of the elites themselves.

Limited pluralism does not constitute a positive ideology. At most, it is a procedural rather than a substantive truce that is subject to recurrent trespass and misunderstanding.[26] Perhaps symptomatically, there is no direct translation for "fair play" in either Portuguese or Spanish. Reservations

[24] Compare Arthur L. Stinchcombe, "Social Structure and Organizations," in *Handbook of Organizations*, ed. James G. March (Chicago: Rand McNally, 1965), pp. 171 ff, and Stinchcombe, "Political Socialization in the Latin American Middle Class," *Harvard Educational Review* 38 (1968): 506-527.

[25] A fact, it should be noted, that is not peculiarly authoritarian, since elite infighting is endemic to totalitarian systems as well. See William Pang-Yu Ting, "Coalitional Behavior among the Chinese Military Elite," *American Political Science Review* 73 (1979): 478-493. The hidden pluralism of totalitarian systems is an especially lively topic among students of the Soviet Union. Compare, for example, Alexander J. Groth, "USSR: Pluralist Monolith," *British Journal of Political Science* 9 (1979): 445-464, and Jerry F. Hough, *The Soviet Union and Social Science Theory* (Cambridge, Mass.: Harvard University Press, 1977).

[26] Compare David G. Lawrence, "Procedural Norms and Tolerance: A Reassessment," *American Political Science Review* 70 (1976): 80-100.

such as these have prompted some commentators to note that a concern with legitimacy in Latin American politics may be a waste of time.[27]

It seems preferable to view limited pluralism as a shifting, constantly renegotiated set of prescriptions defining acceptable gains and tolerable losses for multiple elite interests whose goals are unlikely to stay fixed.[28] The limits of pluralism in Brazil have never been codified. Or if they have, as, for example, through military decree, the characteristic response of the elites has been to read between the lines and probe for the true delimiters in their struggle for advantage. Limited pluralism is a kind of demi-ideology the scope and substance of which are subject to chronic redefinition.

Limited pluralism might just as well, although less felicitously, be called "moderated totalitarianism." The turn-around is not a lexical diversion. Just as the ruling elites in Brazil restrain freewheeling pluralism, contending elites have an interest in loosening the brakes. A major task of this study is to specify more precisely where elites draw the line—that is, how they handle the trade-off between their insulation from mass politics, which is the bedrock of limited pluralism, and the sacrifice of their own prerogatives associated with such insulation. It is with regard to this latter condition that the boundaries of limited pluralism are insecure and unexplored.

Mentalities and Ideologies

The notion of limited pluralism is as eminently ambiguous as the situation it seeks to describe. The role of ideology in authoritarian regimes is more slippery still. The convention has been to dismiss authoritarian elites as unideological carriers of pragmatic "mentalities."[29] They are supposedly unconcerned with the finer points of political dogma. At most, they vibrate to a sort of ersatz nationalism and a technocratic boosterism.

In some respects, this characterization rings true. Brazilian authoritarianism is first and foremost demobilizing. While not all regimes that favor or actively promote mass participation have ideological programs, by most

---

[27] See for example Irving Louis Horowitz, "The Norm of Illegitimacy: Toward a General Theory of Latin American Political Development," in *Latin America: The Dynamics of Social Change*, ed. Stefan A. Halper and John R. Sterling (New York: St. Martin's Press, 1972), pp. 67-93.

[28] Compare Juan J. Linz, "Opposition in and Under an Authoritarian Regime: The Case of Spain," in *Regimes and Oppositions*, ed. Robert A. Dahl (New Haven: Yale University Press, 1973), pp. 171-259, and Susan Kaufman Purcell and John F. H. Purcell, "State and Society in Mexico: Must a Stable Polity Be Institutionalized?" *World Politics* 32 (1980): 194-227.

[29] David Collier, "Industrialization and Authoritarianism in Latin America," *Items of the Social Science Research Council* 31/32 (1978): 5-13.

definitions it is impossible to find any political system that is at once ideological and demobilizing.

In addition, Brazilian elites themselves often take pride in their pragmatism, their adaptability, and their apparent lack of principle. As Skidmore observes, the attribution of Machiavellianism in Brazil is not necessarily pejorative; it may be a recognition of finesse in public affairs.[30] By such criteria, ideology is naive when it is not dangerous.

Furthermore, Brazilian elites have changed their minds on a variety of issues, and contradiction and inconsistency may appear to be the norm rather than the exception. "Responsible pragmatism" is the keynote. To take only two not very puzzling examples: anticommunist Brazil has enjoyed cordial trade relations with Communist China, and a previously pronatalist Brazil has moved gradually but steadily toward an antinatalist commitment because "circumstances have changed."

But this hardly closes the case. The distinction between mentalities and ideologies may be unduly restrictive.[31] The objection can be considered a definitional quibble, especially if what the elites believe and feel is thought to be irrelevant to how they behave. Before I tackle this conundrum, let me spell out some of the reasons for my discomfort with the notion of distinctively authoritarian mentalities, or rather with the use to which the original insight has been put.

First, whatever the theoretical status of the construct of unideological mentalities, no systematic empirical evidence has been presented on the concept. The supposition that elites in authoritarian regimes are unideological dispenses us from the chore of treating the matter as susceptible to investigation or from considering what the elites think or say they think as diagnostic of their behavior.

This will not do. If there is anything distinctive about the ideologies of Brazilian elites, it is that they are multidimensional rather than reducible to a single, progressive-conservative continuum. But this is something entirely different from the claim that the elites are unideological.

It is understandable that the multidimensional nature of their belief systems may make Brazilian elites seem unideological. They are not ideological in the mad-dog, foaming-at-the-mouth sense. Nor do they generally pursue Cartesian deductions. Yet something coherent, and not just vacillating, may exist between these extremes.[32]

---

[30] Thomas E. Skidmore, *Politics in Brazil, 1930-1964: An Experiment in Democracy* (New York: Oxford University Press, 1967).

[31] See the contrast between restrictive and inclusive definitions of ideology in Martin Seliger, *Ideology and Politics* (New York: The Free Press, 1976).

[32] Compare Clifford Geertz, "Common Sense as a Cultural System," *Antioch Review* 33 (1975): 5-26. Once the possibility that authoritarian elites might have ideologies of their own is admitted, even if we do not recognize immediately what these ideologies are, a humane

Second, authoritarian regimes are not so much unideological as they are characterized by two layers of ideology, the one public and the other private. The public ideology tends to be an alternatively assertive and apologetic mishmash. The real interest of the regime is in controlling collective as well as verbal behavior, in the sense of what may be expressed in public. The regime is less concerned, or only indirectly so, with the private thoughts of individuals. Censorship—controlling what people think about—rather than brainwashing—controlling what people think—is the prevailing norm. Mental reservation is permissible.[33]

Third, it is essential to distinguish between ideology as a property of individual elites and ideology as a more systemic phenomenon.[34] Some analysts, dissatisfied with what they consider a one-sided emphasis on the structural determinants of authoritarianism, have searched for the intellectual roots of the authoritarian revival in the Catholic, Luso-Hispanic tradition. The approach is historical rather than psychological. The search is for a latent hegemonic strain in Latin and Latin American intellectual history favoring a disposition toward hierarchical ideologies of statecraft.[35]

Treating this line of analysis as a separate school, utterly opposed to structuralist explanations, is unhelpful. The debate over the impact of

complexity replaces Procrustean typology. The emphasis turns from the presence/absence of ideology to ideologies in the plural. Compare J.G.A. Pocock's criticism of Louis Hartz's notion of a singular Lockean heritage in the "fragment" culture of the United States (one that is interpreted as virtually unideological and pragmatic) in *The Machiavellian Moment: Florentine Political Thought and the Atlantic Republican Tradition* (Princeton: Princeton University Press, 1975); see also the essays in John Higham and Paul K. Conkin, eds., *New Directions in American Intellectual History* (Baltimore: The Johns Hopkins University Press, 1979). For a review of the reasons for dismissing authoritarian regimes as unideological, see Gilbert Allardyce, "What Fascism is Not: Thoughts on the Deflation of a Concept," *American Historical Review* 85 (1980): 367-388.

[33] Since 1974, however, censorship in Brazil has been relaxed. Verbal attacks on the government are common. What the government is still reluctant to admit is organized confrontation.

[34] See David J. Elkins and Richard E. B. Simeon, "A Cause in Search of Its Effect, or What Does Political Culture Explain?" *Comparative Politics* 11 (1979): 127-145; Clifford Geertz, *The Interpretation of Cultures* (New York: Basic Books, 1973), pp. 194-233; and Bert A. Rockman, "Studying Elite Political Culture: Problems in Design and Interpretation," *Papers of University Center for International Studies,* University of Pittsburgh, 1976.

[35] Besides Stepan, *The State and Society,* see Louisa S. Hoberman, "Hispanic American Political Theory as a Distinct Tradition," *Journal of the History of Ideas* 41 (1980): 199-218; Frederick B. Pike and Thomas Stritch, eds., *The New Corporatism* (South Bend: University of Notre Dame Press, 1974); James M. Malloy, ed., *Authoritarianism and Corporatism in Latin America* (Pittsburgh: University of Pittsburgh Press, 1977); Howard J. Wiarda, "Corporatism Rediscovered: Right, Center, and Left Variants in the New Literature," *Polity* 10 (1978): 416-428; and Wiarda, "Corporatism in Iberian and Latin American Political Analysis: Criticisms, Qualifications, and the Context and 'Whys'," *Comparative Politics* 10 (1978): 307-312.

ideological as compared to structural-institutional factors in inducing authoritarian episodes in Brazil seems inconclusive. In the midst of this polemic, what has been overlooked is the possibility that a critical obstacle to the consolidation of authoritarianism or any other type of political system in Brazil is not so much the absence of ideology among the elites as it is the abundance of disparate ideologies, no one of which is able to dominate the other and all of which are reluctant to grant the others legitimacy.[36]

This perspective does not require the supposition either that the elites are purely and simply unideological or, on the other hand, that their ideology is all of a piece, a unique cultural trademark. It does imply that the ideologies of Brazilian elites are multifaceted and difficult to reconcile. By itself, this position reveals nothing about the content of Brazilian elite ideologies. It does, however, clear the way for discovering what this substance might be.

Fourth, if the construct of mentalities, as opposed to ideologies, is discarded, the task remains of specifying an alternative conceptualization of the schemes of the elites and of their compatibility with one another. This I do in the following pages. For now, it is worth noting that I do not rely on any single definition of what constitutes ideological thought. The widely accepted reading of ideology as a cognitively consistent belief system is more useful for identifying the levels of political sophistication that vary between elites and the mass public than for understanding the varieties of ideological thinking among elites themselves.[37]

By this standard, almost all Brazilian elites are ideological, or very close to being so. Their educational equipment and involvement in public affairs are such that they have little difficulty organizing political issues in a coherent, though not necessarily "correct," framework, if they choose to. My primary job is not to demonstrate that the elites are ideologues but to understand what kind of ideologies they have and then to determine what difference these ideologies make.[38]

Limited pluralism, as opposed to the ideal types of totalitarianism and democracy, and mentalities, as contrasted to full-blown ideologies, furnish the starting coordinates for the analysis that follows. One refers to the

[36] Not entirely overlooked, however: the point is expressed nicely by James R. Kurth, "Leading Sectors, Timing of Industrialization, and Political Change: A European Perspective," in Collier, ed., *The New Authoritarianism in Latin America*, pp. 319-362.

[37] The original formulation is by Philip E. Converse, "The Nature of Belief Systems in Mass Publics," in *Ideology and Discontent*, ed. David E. Apter (New York: The Free Press, 1964).

[38] The assertion of the unideological nature of authoritarianism and authoritarian elites does not enjoy universal assent. An argument for the opposite view, based largely on the Italian experience, is by A. James Gregor, *The Ideology of Fascism* (New York: The Free Press, 1969), and Gregor, *Italian Fascism and Developmental Dictatorship* (Princeton: Princeton University Press, 1979). Perhaps coincidentally, the notion that authoritarian elites are un-

institutional, the other to the cultural order of authoritarianism. When considered jointly, they point to a quandary that is central to this study: the ambivalent and circumscribed quality of political legitimacy in authoritarian regimes.

So far I have stressed the ambiguities in existing theories of authoritarianism. Now it is time to elaborate a more exact model of a notoriously imprecise condition.

Power

Assessing the utility of limited pluralism and concepts such as state corporatism, which share the idea that not only mass politics but also areas of elite behavior are repressed by a dominant elite sector, presupposes an understanding of the actual disposition of power among consequential actors. Quite apart from whatever ideological justification or resistance authoritarian regimes might elicit, the initial task is to estimate the functionalism and potential contradictions within the material structure of power.

My analysis of the Brazilian structure has less ambitious goals than these general observations might suggest. For the most part, I focus on the diversity of linkages among various elite groups, on what Martin has called "the configuration of power among participants in politics whose stakes and resources derive from positions in differentiated structures" rather than on "the systemic features of these structures that give rise to the configuration of power."[39] The object is not to discover the power structure, as if there were serious doubt about its existence or even much mystery about its composition, but rather to map the complexity and estimate the permeability of the power structure in Brazil.

The first and simplest step takes up the question of recruitment in the conventional sense, of variation in the background of the elites. The idea

ideological was advanced when the end-of-ideology thesis was still in vogue. This perspective continues to have some currency; see, for example, Lewis S. Feuer, *Ideology and the Ideologists* (New York: Harper & Row, Publishers, 1975). Occasionally, a disclaimer about the "mentalities" approach surfaces in the Latin American literature; see, for example, Robert R. Kaufman, "Industrial Change and Authoritarian Rule in Latin America," in Collier, ed., *The New Authoritarianism in Latin America,* and Carlos Steven Bakota, "Getúlio Vargas and the Estado Novo: An Inquiry into Ideology and Opportunism," *Latin American Research Review* 14 (1979): 205-210. The reason I do not spend much time establishing whether or not Brazilian elites are ideological is that, by the criterion of cognitive consistency, most elites routinely turn out to be ideologues or near-ideologues. See Herbert M. Kritzer, "Ideology and American Political Elites," *Public Opinion Quarterly* 42 (1978): 484-502. Compare Frederick D. Herzon, "Ideology, Constraint, and Public Opinion: The Case of Lawyers," *American Journal of Political Science* 24 (1980): 233-258.

[39] Andrew Martin, "Political Constraints on Economic Strategies in Advanced Industrial Societies," *Comparative Political Studies* 10 (1977): 342.

is to capture one feature of the much-noted separation of the state from society in Brazil—namely, the reliance that certain elites, especially the civil servants, place on formal education, as compared to purely class advantages, in the process of mobility.[40] This part of the analysis also has a broader but still fairly straightforward purpose: to illustrate the selective absorptive capacity of the power structure.

On the whole, Brazilian industrialists and financiers are not self-made men; many of them are the sons of prominent figures in industry and banking. At the other extreme are the labor leaders, who are almost exclusively of working-class provenance. In one respect, however, the businessmen and the labor leaders resemble each other. For both groups, class tends to be a more important determinant of their careers than education. It is primarily among the civil servants and, to a lesser extent, the politicians that formal education assumes a crucial role in mobility.

Thus, although different by most measures of status, the businessman and the labor leaders share a significant trait: they are the least mobile of the elites. Their class positions are not much different from those of their fathers. In between come the state managers. Most of them are from middle sector families, and they depend on higher education to surpass their class origins. This pattern should not surprise those familiar with contemporary Brazil; indeed, it is not peculiarly Brazilian.[41] Nevertheless, it suggests a certain flexibility in recruitment channels into the Brazilian elite under authoritarianism.

[40] A forceful statement about the links between changes in the social bases of elite recruitment and political outcomes is by Ellen Kay Trimberger, *Revolution from Above: Military Bureaucrats and Development in Japan, Turkey, Egypt, and Peru* (New Brunswick, N.J.: Transaction Books, 1978). The general notion, derived from Barrington Moore, of revolution-from-above seems applicable to post-1964 Brazil. For a review of the utility (or lack of it) of examining elite origins, see William A. Welsh, "Methodological Problems in the Study of Political Leadership in Latin America," *Latin American Research Review* 5 (1970): 3-34.

[41] The tendency for technocratic elites to rise from the middle sectors by way of formal education seems to be associated with a heavy industrialization/rapid urbanization course of development followed in certain socialist countries (for example, the Soviet Union) as well as by late capitalist modernizers. This is the basis of Nathan Keyfitz's otherwise puzzling reference to the "Brazilian-Russian pattern of development" (as contrasted to the Chinese under Mao). See Keyfitz, "World Resources and the World Middle Class," *Scientific American* 235 (1976): 28. Compare Kendall E. Bailes, *Technology and Society Under Lenin and Stalin: Origins of the Soviet Technical Intelligentsia, 1917-1941* (Princeton: Princeton University Press, 1978); Sheila Fitzpatrick, *Education and Social Mobility in the Soviet Union, 1921-1934* (London: Cambridge University Press, 1979); Stephen Sternheimer, "Administration for Development: The Emerging Bureaucratic Elite," in *Russian Officialdom: The Bureaucratization of Russian Society from the Seventeenth to the Twentieth Century*, ed. Walter McKenzie Pinter and Don Karl Rowney (Chapel Hill: University of North Carolina Press, 1980), pp. 316-354; and Robert C. Tucker, "Stalinism as Revolution from Above," in *Stalinism: Essays in Historical Interpretation*, ed. Robert C. Tucker (New York: W.W. Norton & Company, Inc., 1977), pp. 77-108.

But the standard socioeconomic indicators tell us little about the subtler modes of mobility and of the consolidation of power.[42] For this reason, I take up the question of the formation of class alliances among the elites by way of marriage. Endogamy—interclass marriage—is more common among Brazilian economic elites than among the state managers and the politicians. Control over large amounts of wealth is liable to be at stake in marriages in which business families enter. While this is not a timeless law, it seems to be sufficiently prevalent among Brazilian industrialists and bankers to set them apart from the noneconomic elites. For this latter group, the marriage contract may also represent a social risk or opportunity. Yet political power is a more nebulous and less transferable quantity than property, so that it enters less certainly into the calculus of marriage.[43]

Up to this point, interpretation of the Brazilian power structure is comparatively simple, entailing two complementary ideas: that the establishment exhibits some flexibility in admitting new members, and that at the same time it uses marital arrangements to preserve the inner core of the capitalist class. Two less obvious ideas must be added: one involves the form of the power structure and the other the multiplex nature of linkages between elites.

Three Dimensions of the Power Structure

Many observers would agree that, in broad terms, the Brazilian power structure is founded on two dimensions. A primary cleavage is one of class, separating the establishment proper from urban labor. Another cleavage operates within the establishment itself, dividing the state—the military and their technocratic allies in the civil service—from elites "on the outside"—principally, industrialists and financiers.

As rudimentary as this characterization is, it is nevertheless more realistic than a one-dimensional rendition in which political and economic power

[42] One factor influencing political outcomes may not be the socioeconomic backgrounds of the state managers, for example, but rather the momentous growth in the size of the state itself. See Werner Baer, Isaac Kerstenetsky, and Annibal V. Villela, "The Changing Role of the State in the Brazilian Economy," *World Development* 1 (1973): 23-34, and José Roberto Mendonça de Barros and Douglas H. Graham, "The Brazilian Economic Miracle Revisited: Private and Public Sector Initiative in a Market Economy," *Latin American Research Review* 13 (1978): 5-38.

[43] Compare the studies conducted by Maurice Zeitlin and his colleagues in the United States and Chile of family ties among economic elites: for example, Zeitlin and Richard Earl Ratcliff, "Research Methods for the Analysis of the Internal Class Structure of Dominant Classes: The Case of Landlords and Capitalists in Chile," *Latin American Research Review* 10 (1975): 5-61, and Zeitlin, "Corporate Ownership and Control: The Large Corporation and the Capitalist Class in Chile," *American Journal of Sociology* 79 (1974): 1073-1119. See also Sara Heller Mendelson and Miriam Slater, "The Weightiest Business: Marriage in an Upper-Gentry Family in Seventeenth-Century England," *Past and Present* 85 (1979): 126-140.

coincide. Agrarian bureaucracies governed by a comparatively homogeneous elite may approximate this ideal-type. The Brazilian dictatorship does not.[44]

Yet there are sound reasons for skepticism about the two-dimensional, upper-class-versus-lower-class/state-versus-society portrait. Not only may some detail be lost, as is indisputably the case, but certain key parameters may also be missing. A central contention of this study is that the church-state nexus or, more generically, the nature of relations between religious and secular authorities, constitutes one of these parameters.[45]

The proposition is twofold. One the one hand, the power of the Catholic church in Brazil is limited. While the bishops may speak out, their institutional presence within the establishment has traditionally been confined to moral issues, such as family planning, and their penetration of the larger society is uneven and shallow. The church has little influence over the educational system, for example, and the state has not become entangled in a concordat with the church.

In recent years, parts of the church have pulled away from their initial sympathy with the anticommunism of the military, and some bishops have been at the forefront of the social justice and civil rights movements in Brazil. As the military donned mufti in their capacity as executives and administrators of the authoritarian bureaucracy, the clergy have also exchanged their cassocks for civilian clothes and have provided leadership as well as shelter for the dissident and the oppressed. But the Brazilian church as a whole remains very ambivalent about the military government and, indeed, about what might come after.[46]

On the other hand, the marginality of the church is an important fact in itself. The bishops stand apart from or are divided about many political controversies in Brazil, and the relation between church and state forms more of a separation, strictly speaking, than a cleavage. "Tradition" and

[44] The comparison with agrarian bureaucracies is merely illustrative; their elite structures may be simpler than those of developmental dictatorships, but they are prone to elite factionalism all the same. Small-scale communal societies may exemplify the ideal-type more closely. See John M. Maguire, *Marx's Theory of Politics* (London: Cambridge University Press, 1978), and Theda Skocpol, *States and Social Revolutions* (London: Cambridge University Press, 1979).

[45] Compare Thomas C. Bruneau, *The Political Transformation of the Brazilian Catholic Church* (London: Cambridge University Press, 1974).

[46] Some observers would credit the church in Brazil with a firmer commitment to social and political action than I do here. See for example Penny Lernoux, "The Latin American Church," *Latin American Research Review* 15 (1980): 201-211, and Lernoux, *Cry of the People* (New York: Doubleday & Company, Inc., 1980). In my view, a subtler account, sensitive to the factionalism within the Brazilian church and to its transitory role as a political actor, is Ralph Della Cava, "Church Leads the Cause of Human Rights in Brazil," *International Development Review* 22 (1980): 40-43; see also Sérgio Buarque de Gusmão, "Um João Paulo II para Cada Gosto," *Isto É*, July 9, 1980: 30-35.

"modernity" are not reified; they lack conspicuous institutional referents, unlike some other Latin societies.

The institutional and cultural peripherality of the Brazilian church, its comparative dissociation from blatantly conservative currents as well as its relative weakness at the mass level, add to the complexity and flexibility of the structure of power. The multiplicity of organizational cleavages within Brazilian elite politics does not make for a convergence of disparate interests. But neither does it galvanize and polarize latent conflicts. Many controversies that would seem to be so fundamental as to precipitate intolerable contradictions and head-on combat are viewed by the elites themselves as ambiguous and are dealt with in piecemeal fashion.[47]

The Multiplex Nature of Interelite Linkages

If one reason why the relations between religious and secular authorities are ignored in the study of Brazilian authoritarianism is that they are not easily reducible to economic or class-fraction models, it can also be argued that a similarly narrow view overlooks the importance of the fact that all but the simplest of elite networks are multistranded. Not only should the proximity and distance among several actors, including the church, be examined but the probability that the ties between them may be of several kinds and therefore capable of generating alternative networks should also be analyzed.[48]

[47] To make the same point, it might appear that I could just as well have focused on the weakness of regional or linguistic cleavages as on the peripherality of the church in Brazil. But special attention is given to the institutional frailty of the church in Brazil to counter the possible misconception that the "church in Latin America" is a uniformly powerful presence. At least three problems, for which data are either scarce or tendentious, must be considered in assessing the influence and political direction of the church. First, comparative studies are needed of the linkage between the power and political leanings of the church and the social structure—particularly the proportion of the population that is labelled "peasant" or in some sense "pre-capitalist"—of various countries in Latin American and Latin Europe. Second, systematic studies of the *communidades de base*—Christian grass-roots communities—are needed to assess the hold of the church over them as well as the political commitments of their members. See Alba Zaluar Guimarães, "On the Logic of Popular Catholicism," in *Brazilian Social Studies Annual*, ed. Simon Schwartzman (New Brunswick, N.J.: Transaction Books, 1980), and contrast Michael T. Taussig, *The Devil and Commodity Fetishism in South America* (Chapel Hill: University of North Carolina Press, 1980). Third, the demographics of the ecclesiastical heirarchy must be sorted out. Even though the older bishops and priests are not necessarily more conservative than the younger cohorts, it is sometimes assumed that natural mortality will move the church in a more progressive direction. A further hitch in this argument is that religious vocations have been falling off rapidly in Brazil. See Thomas C. Bruneau, "The Catholic Church and Development in Latin America: The Role of Basic Christian Communities," *World Development* 8 (1980): 535-544.

[48] Several scholars of Latin America have noted that elite as well as nonelite networks may be composed of several kinds of linkages. But it is rare to encounter a formalization of the idea that different ties may produce different networks. A seminal work for the

The first qualification to a two-dimensional mapping of the Brazilian power structure boils down to the statement that it fails to include potentially crucial, if not all-powerful, interests. The second objection is directed not at the number of actors, and hence at the possible number of meaningful axes around which the power structure is built, but at the possible variety of linkages among a given set of actors.

Less abstractly, the configuration of power produced by mapping a single strand—say, kinship ties—need not be the same as that yielded by plotting friendship linkages, for example, or indeed by charting attitudinal clusters across elite groups. Multiple ties of different kinds—of kinship, friendship, organizational dependence, and the like—bind the Brazilian elites together. These networks overlap, but only loosely. It is the partial differentiation among various linkages that permits the power structure to absorb ambitious candidates by offering alternative channels of mobility, and it is this flexibility that in turn prevents the system from becoming easily vulnerable to attack from below. It allows mobility at one level and promotes stability at another.

Thus, marital linkages are specific instances of a wider set of mechanisms by which the Brazilian establishment renews itself. A series of complementary mechanisms preserves the position of the inner core of the capitalist class while facilitating the mobility of "deserving elements" from below. Not only is endogamy typical of the marital patterns of Brazilian industrialists and financiers; these men are also amply endowed with the most intimate sort of interelite linkages—that is, kinship ties. On the other hand, although the state managers do not start out with comparable class advantages, or marry into the inner sanctum of business families with great frequency, or enjoy so many blood ties with the economically powerful, they cultivate bonds of friendship and close working contacts with powerful individuals and groups at the various peaks of the Brazilian hierarchy.

In summary, I am concerned with both the shape and the substance of the Brazilian power structure. The shape of the power structure is its outward form, the visible configuration of dominance. It is composed of three main polarities. A fundamental cleavage, which insulates the elites as a whole from urban labor and its leadership, is one of class.

Another major division is the one between those who manage the state, the military and the civilian bureaucrats, and those in whose presumed interest it is run: the industrialists, bankers, and landowners. While the military and the government apparatus may not be autonomous in any

understanding of social networks in Brazil is Anthony Leeds, "Brazilian Careers and Social Structures," *American Anthropologist* 66 (1964): 1321-1347. For comparative analyses, see Steffen W. Schmidt et al., eds., *Friends, Followers, and Factions: A Reader in Political Clientelism* (Berkeley: University of California Press, 1977).

definitive, long-term sense, the state managers are neither recruited from the dominant strata nor are they accountable to them in any institutional fashion.

A third line of demarcation within the Brazilian elite is constituted by the peninsulalike position of the church, with the bishops and the clergy practically off in a corner of their own away from the other elites.

A clue to the substance of the power structure, how it holds together without ossification, is the division of labor between kinship and friendship ties. The importance of kinship ties relative to friendship linkages is greater for the businessmen and for the upper class elites generally than for the middle sector state managers; the density of kinship is thicker among the former and thinner among the latter. Conversely, while the elite estates maintain a certain distance among themselves through class-selective marriage and related means, the proliferation of friendship linkages is a critical element in the mobility and the power of the state managers.

If this was all there was to the Brazilian power structure, its gears might seem to mesh very smoothly. But at least three considerations argue against this conclusion. The first is that the distribution of power within the Brazilian establishment is steeply hierarchical, and there is no reason to believe that the imbalance of power between, for example, the technocrats and the politicians is self-correcting.

Second, while the evidence supports the hypothesis of a certain separation between state and society—less grandly, of a division in the sources and mechanisms of recruitment of businessmen and civil servants—the question remains of whether this development is peculiar to authoritarian, as compared to previously democratic, Brazil. Is it a new trend that distinguishes the Brazil of the post-1964 period from earlier times?

I suspect that the movement, although genuine, is not especially novel and that the renovation of the elite—in particular, the ascendance of the *técnicos* and the demise of the politicians—can be understood in part as a response to cyclical blockages among cohorts of elite incumbents and elite candidates. Besides protecting established capitalist interests and institutions, the regime opened up opportunities for the middle sectors. In the process, it removed many representatives of the older upper strata, most notably the politicians, who had been associated with Brazil's earlier bourgeois revolution headed by Getúlio Vargas in the 1930s.[49]

While considerable research into the social composition of Brazilian political and economic elites from 1930 onward would be required to verify the existence of "disordered cohort flows," the notion of generational

---

[49] See Glaucio Ary Dillon Soares, *Sociedade e Política no Brasil: Desenvolvimento, Classe e Política durante a Segunda República* (São Paulo: Difusão Europeía do Livro, 1973), pp. 36 ff, and Boris Fausto, *A Revolução de 1930* (São Paulo: Editora Brasiliense, 1970).

renewal within the bourgeoisie as contributing to the dynamic, rather than purely reactionary, character of Brazilian authoritarianism is entirely plausible. The passage of time wears down the welcome of any elite group or age cohort that tries to monopolize power. This is one of the reasons why the longer the military stays in power in Brazil, the less legitimate its hold on power becomes. For all the selective permeability of the Brazilian power structure, flexibility in recruitment depends on constant adjustment and expansion of the channels of mobility. This is not an automatic process.[50]

Finally, whatever the forces of equilibrium and contradiction within the power structure itself, the configuration of power may be at odds with the ideologies of the elites or of the pretenders to power. There is a trivial sense in which this must be so. Unless Brazil is a totalitarian monolith, which the notion of limited pluralism and common sense suggest it is not,

[50] Studies of cyclical blockages in mobility have grown in recent years and some are plainly relevant to the succession problem among elites. See Joan M. Waring, "Social Replenishment and Social Change: The Problem of Disordered Cohort Flow," *American Behavorial Scientist* 19 (1975): 237-256; I. William Zartman, "The Study of Elite Circulation," *Comparative Politics* 6 (1974): 465-488; Valerie Bunce, "Leadership Succession and Policy Innovation in the Soviet Republics," *Comparative Politics* 11 (1979): 379-401; Jerry F. Hough, *Soviet Leadership in Transition* (Washington, D.C.: Brookings Institution, 1980); John D. Nagle, *System and Succession: The Social Bases of Political Elite Recruitment* (Austin: University of Texas Press, 1977); John H. Kautsky, "Patterns of Elite Succession in the Process of Development," *Journal of Politics* 31 (1969): 359-396; Michael Yahuda, "Political Generations in China," *China Quarterly* 80 (1979): 793-805; Michael Oksenberg, "The Exit Pattern from Chinese Politics and Its Implications," *China Quarterly* (1976): 501-518; Oksenberg, "Getting Ahead and Getting Along in Communist China: The Ladder of Success on the Eve of the Cultural Revolution," in *Party Leadership and Revolutionary Power in China*, ed. J. W. Lewis (London: Cambridge University Press, 1970), pp. 304-347; Theodore L. Reed, "Organizational Change in the American Foreign Service, 1925-1965: The Utility of Cohort Analysis," *American Sociological Review* 43 (1978): 404-421; and Ivan Volgyes, "Modernization, Stratification, and Elite Development in Hungary," *Social Forces* 57 (1978): 500-521.

In Brazil, enormous pressures were brought to bear on the government for high-level patronage during the early sixties, a generation after the emergence of the middle sectors and just before the military coup. This occurred simultaneously with the packing of the labor ministry and the social security institutes with lower-class personnel and with the rise in the number of congressional seats captured by the Brazilian Worker's Party. It is also likely that the decline in economic growth at this time brought pressures on the elite as well as the mass job market. See Lawrence S. Graham, *Civil Service Reform in Brazil* (Austin: University of Texas Press, 1968), especially pp. 103-158, and Maria do Carmo C. Campbello de Souza, *Estado e Partidos Políticos no Brasil (1930 a 1964)* (São Paulo: Editora Alfa-Omega, 1976). Others have noted the role of cyclical blockages among elite cohorts as a precipitate of revolution. See, for example, Immanuel Wallerstein, "Class Conflict in the Capitalist World-Economy," Working Paper Series, Fernand Braudel Center for the Study of New Economies, Historical Systems, and Civilizations, State University of New York, Binghamton, November 3, 1976, pp. 6-7; D. A. Brading, ed., *Caudillo and Peasant in the Mexican Revolution* (London: Cambridge University Press, 1980); and Eric R. Wolf, *Peasant Wars of the Twentieth Century* (New York: Harper & Row, Publishers, 1969), p. 24.

even the incumbent elites are bound to be disgruntled about something or other.

Glimmers of this sort of disquiet do not warrant the inference that the republic is in imminent danger of collapse. We need only try to imagine what a polity in which the reality and the ideology of power were at one would look like to gain an appreciation for the elasticity and variety in the standards used to judge the acceptability of governments. Incongruity cannot be equated with illegitimacy or presumed illegitimacy with the willingness and the ability to engage in action designed to overthrow the regime.[51]

Another route is more promising. A reading of the kaleidoscope that is Brazilian intellectual history indicates that, aside from the problem of a possible mismatch between the reality of Brazilian politics and what elites feel ought to be, a determining factor in conflicts among elites has been the multiplicity of criteria used to evaluate the roles of the state and the citizenry.[52] Ideologies of political good and evil abound. On the face of it, this heritage does not seem incompatible with a healthy pluralism. But while rival elites may come to an accord on certain fairly important controversies, they have extreme difficulty in reaching agreement on other, even more fundamental issues. Typically, such issues bear on the rules by which decisions are reached in the first place—that is, on the norms that determine who has the right to govern, the right to compete for power, and the right to be consulted. The notion of a gradient of increasingly polarized issues is at the heart of my concept of the nature of elite ideology in Brazil and it is central to the notion of legitimacy as the acceptance by elites of the guidelines for political participation.

Ideology

My analysis of the ideology of Brazilian elites is directed at three closely related problems: the form and substance of their political beliefs, the degree of consensus among the elites on specific policy issues, and the priorities of the elites insofar as they reflect differing visions of the development strategy that Brazil should follow and differing commitments

---

[51] See Bert and Michael Useem, "Government Legitimacy and Political Stability," *Social Forces* 57 (1979): 840-852.

[52] See Carlos Guilherme Mota, *Ideologia da Cultura Brasileira, 1933-1974* (São Paulo: Editora Atica, 1974); José Honório Rodrigues, *Conciliação e Reforma no Brasil* (Rio de Janeiro: Editora Civilização Brasileira, 1965); Wanderley Guilherme dos Santos, "Liberalism in Brazil: Ideology and Praxis," in *Terms of Conflict*, ed. Morris J. Blachman and Ronald G. Hellman (Philadelphia: Institute for the Study of Human Issues, 1977); and Thomas Skidmore, "The Historiography of Brazil, 1889-1964: Part I," *Hispanic-American Historical Review* 55 (1975): 716-748.

to a common political arrangement. I am concerned with the *opinions* of the elites, with their *perceptions* of one another, and with their *values*.

Opinions

A natural, if preliminary, question in studying the ideologies of the elites has to do simply with what they believe, with the variation in their political preferences across a range of issues. The initial problem is to get them to state their opinions. For all its curiosity value, this is essentially a technical challenge involving access to genuine elites under authoritarian conditions; the methods used to overcome such obstacles are described in the Appendix.

With the information in hand, and once the distribution of opinion among the various elite groups has been plotted, a first approximation of the nature of elite thinking can be obtained by determining how opinions on a variety of issues hang together.[53] A classic left-right continuum turns out to be the principal cleavage of elite politics in Brazil. There are clearcut reactionaries and there are straightforward progressives, and they are distributed across the elite sectors in expected ways. The businessmen, for example, are plainly more conservative than the opposition politicians.

However, the left-right dimension is not the only line of conflict among Brazilian elites, even though it is a major one. The preferences of the elites can also be aligned along a subset of issues independent from their positions on the controversies of left versus right. Typically, these are moral issues having to do with birth control, the legalization of divorce, the legalization of abortion, and the like.

In the Brazilian context, the distinctiveness of this cleavage from the left-right dimension is not at all puzzling. Both Marxists and Catholics, who tend to diverge on the conventional left-versus-right issues, are often in agreement about the nefariousness of population planning and related measures.[54]

This is a rough sketch. While it serves to call into question the view of authoritarian elites as peculiarly unideological, it is more of a statistical description than a theoretical explanation. Two further limitations should also be noted.

[53] In technical terms, the procedure is to derive a correlation matrix from the indicators of opinion on a set of issues. For a valuable critique of the application of correlational methods to the analysis of ideology, see Michael R. Coveyou and James Pierson, "Ideological Perceptions and Political Judgment: Some Problems of Concept and Measurement," *Political Methodology* 4 (1977): 77-102. The rationale behind the method is simple. If the preferences of the elites on several issues did not correlate with one another, or if the correlations were weak, it would be difficult to make a case for the coherence of elite ideology. The presence of strong correlations does not mean, however, that the elites are necessarily unidimensional thinkers.

[54] See J. Mayone Stycos, *Ideology, Faith, and Family Planning in Latin America* (New York: McGraw-Hill, 1971).

First, what has been labelled "the left-right dimension" is in fact a composite of at least two partially separate cleavages, one involving social, distributional issues, and the other controversies that bear directly on the political tension between authoritarian control and interelite competition. On both cleavages, conservatives and progressives are clearly recognizable; yet elites with progressive preferences on one axis may hold conservative or centrist views on the other, and vice versa.

Second, while gauging the extent to which the opinions of the elites on diverse issues fall into a coherent, albeit multidimensional, framework is a necessary first step, it is one that is designed primarily to estimate the facility of individuals in sorting out and linking political issues. But my interest is less in classifying individual elites than in ranking the issues themselves along a gradient of conflict-potential.[55] Certain controversies are likely to be touchier than others in Brazil, and these are the ones that might galvanize the elites over the question of the legitimacy of the regime. Let us start with the type of controversy that does not strike this nerve, then work our way up.

The moral issues are the ones that are most remote from the deepest cleavages in Brazil. Debate on these issues may at times appear inflammatory. Yet the polemics do not get at the vital interests of the elites, with the possible exception of the bishops, and even they are concerned with a host of other issues. It is interesting to observe that the government joined with the opposition party to push through the legalization of divorce in 1975, against the vociferous protests of the church. Even more interesting, the reform was pulled off without disturbing the disposition of power and opinion on other issues. This is compelling evidence for the separateness of the moral axis from the more pressing concerns of Brazilian political life.[56]

Once past this set of controversies, we are in the realm of issues on which the elites take fairly predictable progressive or conservative stands. Still, the left-right dimension is not seamless. It is a composite of finely graded controversies, escalating toward the most explosive.

At the bottom is the broad and complex bundle of issues falling under

[55] The approach is similar to the classification of public policies pioneered by Theodore Lowi, "American Business, Public Policy, Case-Studies and Political Theory," *World Politics* 16 (1964): 677-715. One difference is that I am concerned with the sensitivity of the elites themselves to the supposed distinctions in degree and kind among issues. For an assessment of Lowi's work that criticizes it for the failure to provide empirical verification, see George D. Greenberg et al., "Developing Public Policy Theory: Perspectives from Empirical Research," *American Political Science Review* 71 (1977): 1532-1543.

[56] The moral issues are special in other respects as well, and a separate volume has been devoted to mass as well as elite attitudes on this set of topics. Peter McDonough and Amaury de Souza, *The Politics of Population in Brazil: Elite Ambivalence and Public Demand* (Austin: University of Texas Press, 1981).

the rubric of "foreign investment." Opinions on this controversy can be sorted out in left-right terms, the pro-position being conservative in Brazilian political culture and the anti-position progressive.

But such a rendering is a bit strained, and it misses most of the subtlety in elite thinking. Some of the otherwise conservative elites are strident nationalists, and many of the progressives are committed to a full-speed-ahead developmentalism that reserves a place for foreign capital and has little sympathy for what they consider an anticosmopolitan romanticism.[57] In short, opinions on the issue are subject to strong cross-currents. The elites cling to the left-right terminology, but just barely, and they do not favor the extremes.

The idea that the bundle of issues surrounding foreign investment is not perceived by the elites as so controversial as some of the literature on dependency suggests does not mean, of course, that the area is free of structural conflicts. Such an interpretation would be bizarre for a country with a debt burden of over fifty billion dollars.[58]

But some issues, despite or because of the presumption that they are fundamental and extremely difficult to solve, may not be extremely divisive. In the early seventies, when the foreign debt was about six times smaller than it became in the eighties, the attitude prevalent among elites was that foreign capital was by and large manageable and beneficial. Subsequent assessments of the issue were less cavalier, to such an extent that a consensus of desperation seems to have taken hold of elites on the left and the right.[59] In either case, the magnitude of the problem does not

[57] The argument developed here is generally in line with that presented by Evans, *Dependent Development*. See also Fernando Henrique Cardoso and Enzo Faletto, *Dependência e Desenvolvimento na América Latina: Ensaio de Interpretação Sociológica* (Rio de Janeiro: Zahar Editores, 1973); Florestan Fernandes, *Sociedade de Classes e Subdesenvolvimento* (Rio de Janeiro: Zahar Editores, 1972); Irving Louis Horowitz and Ellen Kay Trimberger, "State Power and Military Nationalism in Latin America," *Comparative Politics* 8 (1976): 223-244; and Jay R. Mandle, "Marxist Analyses and Capitalist Development in the Third World," *Theory and Society* 9 (1980): 865-876. Contrast the more pessimistic essays, including one by Evans, in Richard R. Fagan, ed., *Capitalism and the State in U.S.-Latin American Relations* (Stanford, Calif.: Stanford University Press, 1979).

[58] In 1972 and 1973, at the time the elite interviews were conducted, the foreign debt of Brazil was approximately eight billion dollars.

[59] See Richard Ensor, "The Great Brazilian Tightrope," *Euromoney*, January 1980: 50-68; Paulo Fona and Rolf Kuntz, "A Cruz e a Caldeirinha," *Isto É*, April 30, 1980: 84-86; Penny Lernoux, "Brazil Spends its Way to the Guardhouse," *The Nation*, June 28, 1980: 780-782; and Everett G. Martin, "Big Borrower: Brazil Counts on Banks to Lend More Billions as Tough Year Looms," *Wall Street Journal*, February 4, 1980: 1, 17. The tenor of these diagnoses is gloomy regarding Brazil's capacity to refinance its debt, much of which comes due in the mid-eighties. But, except for noting that debt-servicing demands cut into the ability of the government to deliver the welfare goods expected from the political opening, they have little to say about the effects of these difficulties on elite politics. One factor that

automatically generate rancorous antagonism among the elites themselves. If the elites define such issues as virtually intractable, the issues might not be so polarizing as expressly political but apparently more trivial controversies, since their resolution tends to be viewed as outside the control of most individuals and groups.[60]

Issues such as income redistribution and agrarian reform illustrate a third, more polarized level of controversy. Forming the basis of the great economic and social struggles in Brazil, they are undeniably important, and the elites recognize them as such. In general, there is no mistaking what constitutes progressive and conservative opinion on these issues. They fall squarely on the left-right cleavage.

At the same time, for a variety of reasons, they are seen as negotiable issues. Income, like capital, is thought to be divisible. The elites tend to view an issue like income redistribution as a question of more or less, not either-or, just as they approach the foreign investment controversy as one involving the amount, the kind, and the terms of such capital, not its presence or absence. They can conceive of a number of compromise policies on such issues, with the result that bargaining, sometimes of a highly technical sort, becomes possible.[61]

---

might mitigate the nightmare scenario of default is that the debt, although huge in absolute terms, is fragmented across several lenders. See Carl Gerwitz, "Varied Terms Sought for Brazil," *International Herald Tribune*, July 21, 1980: 9. Furthermore, while an extremely high 60 percent of Brazil's export earnings go to service its foreign debt, this burden must be set in perspective. The comparable figure for Poland is 92 percent. See Clyde H. Farnsworth, "Strikes in Poland: The Risk for Western Banks," *New York Times*, August 31, 1980: F1, F4, and Howard M. Wachtel, "A Decade of International Debt," *Theory and Society* 9 (1980): 504-518.

[60] There was a time in Brazil, during the late fifties and early sixties, when the ideologies of "nationalism" and "cosmopolitanism" were thought to represent polar opposites. See Helio Jaguaribe, *O Nacionalismo na Atualidade Brasileira* (Rio de Janeiro: Instituto Superior de Estudos Brasileiros, 1958), and Jaguaribe, *Economic and Political Development: A Theoretical Approach and a Brazilian Case Study* (Cambridge, Mass.: Harvard University Press, 1968). Redistributive issues and polemics over political equity and governmental form were not generally central to the nationalism-cosmopolitanism debate. Although this axis of controversy is still quite lively, it no longer monopolizes political discourse. As will be shown, Brazilian elites distinguish rather sharply between the actions of specific foreign corporations, toward which they can adopt a very combative stance, and foreign investment policies in general. For a similar distinction, see H. Jeffrey Leonard, "Multinational Corporations and Politics in Developing Countries," *World Politics* 32 (1980): 454-483.

[61] The literature on income distribution in post-1964 Brazil is extensive. See for example Roberto B. M. Macedo, "A Critical Review of the Relation between the Post-1964 Wage Policy and the Worsening of Brazil's Size Income Distribution in the Sixties," *Explorations in Economic Research* 4 (1977): 117-140, and Lance Taylor and Edmar L. Bacha, "The Unequalizing Spiral: A First Growth Model for Belinda," *Quarterly Journal of Economics* 90 (1976): 197-218. For especially vivid descriptions of social disparities, see "A Face Cruel do Brasil," *Veja*, July 16, 1980: 84-92, and São Paulo Justice and Peace Commission, *São*

There is still another reason for the workability of issues like income redistribution that can best be understood by comparing them to controversies a rung higher on the escalation ladder. Brazilian history is replete with instances of paternalistic social reform. "Let us make the revolution before the people do" goes the proverbial wisdom of a regional politician of the 1930s. Getúlio Vargas, the most famous of Brazilian politicians, was better known for his cooptative beneficence to the urban poor than for his sensitivity to civil liberties. The selective distribution of social opportunities (for example, education) and benefits (pensions, medical care, et cetera) is a familiar prop in the repertoire of political control in Brazil.[62]

What all this maneuvering suggests is that, short of economic catastrophe, at least some of the social issues are manageable—perhaps not well, or even rationally; but the elites cope. While these issues may pose severe threats to the evolutionary development of the country that so many of the elites desire, they do not strike unequivocally at the position and the prerogatives of the elites themselves. In retrospect, it is not difficult to see why it may be in the interest of the elites to bargain their way around social demands rather than retreat into their bunker.[63]

Paulo: Growth and Poverty (London: Bowerdean, 1978). On the agrarian question, see Shepard Forman, *The Brazilian Peasantry* (New York: Columbia University Press, 1975), and the critical review by William H. Nicholls, "Professor Forman on the Brazilian Peasantry," *Economic Development and Cultural Change* 26 (1978): 359-383.

[62] See Kenneth P. Erickson, *The Corporative State and Working-Class Politics in Brazil* (Berkeley: University of California Press, 1977), and Kenneth S. Mericle, "Corporatist Controls of the Working-Class: The Cast of Post-1964 Brazil," in Malloy, ed. *Authoritarianism and Corporatism.* Compare Janice Perlman, *The Myth of Marginality: Urban Poverty and Politics in Rio de Janeiro* (Berkeley: University of California Press, 1976).

[63] This commonsensical observation makes no sense at all if it is supposed that the elites suddenly decide to come to terms with a seething mass. As noted earlier, there is a longstanding tradition in Brazil of patrimonial cooptation that is not merely symbolic. Part of this stems from the softness of the Brazilian variant of Catholicism. Another strand is more tangible. It derives from the corporatist style of preemptive, defensive social expenditures. Even during the Médici period, the harshest of the governments since 1964, spending on compensatory programs—health care, unemployment insurance, and so on—rose relative to what had gone before, even while real wages fell and infant mortality in some areas actually increased. Investment in such programs grew even further during the Geisel and Figueiredo presidencies. Whatever its contradictions, the pattern is "normal" in Brazil. See Wanderley Guilherme dos Santos, *Cidadania e Justiça: A Política Social na Ordem Brasileira* (Rio de Janeiro: Editora Campus, 1979), and compare the discussion of "popular-concern rhetoric" in Alejandro Portes, "Housing Policy, Urban Poverty, and the State: The *Favelas* of Rio de Janeiro, 1972-1976," *Latin America Research Review* 14 (1979): 3-24. A similar dialectic of exploitation and compensation has been characteristic of Spanish economic and social programs as developed during the later Franco period. See Thomas D. Lancaster, "Toward an Assessment of the Spanish Social Security System," in *Economic Development and Cultural Change* (forthcoming).

However, there is at least one important difference between Franquist policies with regard to labor and those adopted in Brazil. Provisions with respect to job security in Spain made

The same potential for compromise, however, does not hold when it comes to issues like the autonomy of the labor organizations or the freedom of political parties. Here the stakes are more truly zero-sum, since controversies over, for example, the right to organize autonomously and compete freely have an either-or quality lacking in most of the quarrels over the distribution of material rewards. These issues are just below the most explosive level of conflict. They evoke the passions of the elites whose very right to exist as elites—that is, to compete for, if not to assume, power—is in question.

Thus, for example, in classic carrot-and-stick fashion, the government will often reward the acquiescent elements of the labor leadership by buying them and their membership off, at the same time that it eliminates those who do not go along. The success of this ploy depends on dispensing more than just symbolic benefits—that is, on having enough material resources to go around to increasing numbers of demand makers.[64]

But even successful measures in this vein are double-edged. To the extent that they work in mollifying the clienteles of potentially dissident elites, they may drive the elites themselves further into opposition. In trying to coopt their constituents, the government preempts the leadership of the labor organizations, the political parties, and other interest groups. The dissident and fence-straddling leadership is thereby threatened with the loss of its role as an intermediary between the state and the clientele citizenry. This function is its reason-for-being. In trying to isolate ambivalent, dissaffected elites from their clienteles, the ruling elites take a great risk. Everything hangs on being able to deliver more than the semblance of material benefits to a vulnerable but not infinitely patient following.[65]

---

it virtually impossible to fire workers, and this corporatist legislation has become the object of attack by employers during the post-Franco period. In Brazil on the other hand, at least from the early through the late seventies, the job security of urban labor seems actually to have worsened, because labor legislation provided incentives for companies to dismiss workers before they could accumulate enough seniority to guarantee benefits. See José Márcio Camargo, "A Nova Política Salarial, Distribuição de Renda, e Inflação," mimeograph (Rio de Janeiro: Pontifícia Universidade Católica, 1980).

[64] Much the same point is made by William Gamson, *The Strategy of Social Protest* (Homewood, Ill.: Dorsey, 1975).

[65] If the government succeeds in driving a wedge between, for example, labor leaders and the rank-and-file through its control of the welfare system, then the protestations of the syndical elite may appear to be mere "politics" in the eyes of their constituents. An exception to this scenario was the prolonged strike of the metalworkers in São Paulo, culminating in 1980 with the arrest of over a dozen labor leaders. A distinctive feature of this episode was that the leadership and portions of the rank-and-file were unwilling to settle for wage hikes; they demanded among other things bargaining autonomy, which the government refused to grant. See Warren Hoge, "Brazil's Army Regime Under Attack from All Sides," *New York Times*, April 30, 1980: A3. The larger syndicates were subsequently dismantled into smaller units. For a careful analysis of the continued frustrations of organized labor during the

There is a fine line between meliorative issues, like income redistribution, and issues involving the autonomy of organized interests, such as the labor syndicates. Yet the difference is a vital one, for elites would not be elites if they were not jealous of their prerogatives. In Brazil, the either-or issues cut at the nub of the corporatist ethos. At a minimum, the appearance of mutual consultation must be maintained, and the "representative" elites must be given some credit for what is bestowed from on high. When this does not happen, and when the regime cannot deliver over the heads of the elites it is trying to ignore, it is in deep trouble.

One key factor prevents this fourth level of controversy from becoming more serious. Issues in which the autonomy of various groups is at stake often tend to set these groups against one another and not necessarily just against the regime. For example, the question of the freedom of political opposition vitally concerned the MDB, the opposition party in the years our study was conducted. But a majority of the members of the government party, the ARENA, were not equally upset by the infringements of their colleagues' freedom, and some of them were certain to become nervous at any sign of a loosening of these curbs. In this way, for some time, the regime was able to divide and conquer.

The principal difference between controversies involving the autonomy of specific interests and those that may be even more volatile is that the touchiest issues have the potential for uniting acquiescent as well as dissident elites against the regime. Such issues entail a generalization of the disparate interests of particular groups in gaining room for maneuver.

The question of the party system—of the number of parties legally entitled to compete for power—is a prime example of this kind of issue. The question of the participation of the military in politics provides an even more striking case in point. The strong and persistent differences between the ARENA and the MDB politicians on a variety of battlefronts should not obscure their joint dissatisfaction, as politicians, with the abolition by the military of the multipartism prevailing before the revolution and, indeed, with the military's (and the technocracy's) usurpation of the powers of decision making and of the sources of patronage.[66]

movement away from brute authoritarianism, see John Humphrey, *As Raízes e os Desafios do 'Novo' Sindicalismo da Indústria Automobilística* (São Paulo: Estudos CEBRAP, 1980); compare Regis de Castro Andrade, "Política Salarial e Normalização Institucional no Brasil," mimeograph (São Paulo: CEDEC, 1980). Again, it is extremely important to recognize that the key issue in such disputes, at least among the contending elites, is not wage policy per se but rather the right of labor organizations to act as autonomous units. In fact, the government has rather consistently gone around the labor leadership in decreeing compensatory wage-hikes and other benefits for the poor, regardless of their affiliation or nonaffiliation with the *sindicatos*. See Ann Crittenden, "Brazil Sets Historic Plan to Redistribute Income," *New York Times*, September 4, 1979: D1, D4.

[66] The statement that Brazilian elites view bipartism as artificial may seem peculiar in light

As these examples suggest, it would be mistaken to argue that the counterelites are motivated solely by selfless interests and noble ideals in resisting the incursions of the state. They have a good deal to gain from pushing back the boundaries on their own freedom of action. For all this, the issues that strike most closely at the heart of the authoritarian ethic are those on which the usually pliable, cooptable elites share a common interest with the customary dissidents in getting rid of the restrictions imposed by the ruling elites.[67]

Three further points are worthy of note. Elites in an authoritarian situation continuously reassess what they have to win and lose from the perceived threat from below, that is, from fuller mass participation, and from the menace from above, represented by the sultanic proclivities of the authoritarian state. There is no magic number that tells them, or us, where the optimal trade-off lies. The five-tier gradient of controversiality just outlined suggests, however, that the "mass" issues, those involving the distribution of social benefits and even political rights to the citizenry, may not always be freighted with such terror for the elites as is generally supposed.[68] Nor may this threat, however terrifying the perception of it,

---

of the protests, especially on the part of the opposition MDB, against the decree of 1979 abolishing the two-party system and "permitting" a return to multipartism. This turnabout was correctly understood as a ploy to fragment the opposition after the strong showing of the MDB in the 1974 and 1977 elections. The stratagem, as well as others in the same vein, are discussed by Bolivar Lamounier in "Notes on the Study of Re-Democratization," Working Paper No. 58, The Wilson Center, Smithsonian Institution, Washington, D.C., 1980. The evidence to be presented in Chapter Five indicates that, at least during 1972 and 1973, the bipartism/multipartism controversy was a borderline issue, approaching those that directly impinge on the legitimacy of the regime but also dividing rival elite groups.

It should be noted that the ARENA and the MDB, established by the military in 1966, were formally abolished in 1979 as the system returned to multipartism. The successor of the MDB is the PMDB (the Brazilian Democratic Party); another opposition organization, the PT (Labor Party), has emerged from the labor strike in São Paulo. ARENA has split into the PD (Democratic Party) and the PP (Popular Party). There are, in addition, a host of smaller parties. All of these parties are readying themselves for the national assembly elections scheduled for 1982.

[67] Compare the discussion of "reserved" or "untouchable" versus more-or-less open policy areas in Richard Gunther, *Public Policy in a No-Party State: Spanish Planning and Budgeting in the Twilight of the Franquist Era* (Berkeley: University of California Press, 1980).

[68] Even during periods of poor economic performance, demands for social redistribution and justice may be less threatening than more narrowly political issues to the degree that the organizations for expressing these demands are, or traditionally have been, deprived of their freedom of action by the government. The lack of such autonomous organizations does not prevent mass violence, as is indicated by such occurrences as the periodic outbursts prompted by food shortages, hikes in public transportation rates, and so on. However, these flash movements have petered out. The government has learned either to stand aside and let them run their course, or, failing that, to apply repression swiftly and in an almost surgical manner; it has also played skillfully on the craving for order shown by many lower- as well as upper-

be sufficient to enforce a unity among elites for a long period of time. The elites may be at least as concerned with protecting themselves from the arbitrariness of those who insist on remaining in power after the panic times of mass politics have passed.

Second, the tendency for counterelites to resist the hegemonic ambitions of ruling elites who try to impose a set of rules impinging on their prerogatives does not mean that they rally around a positive alternative program. Theirs is a unity of opposition. While it may be more than just this, there plainly exist gradations from a commonality based on mutual disaffection from the prevailing system to the consolidation of a different political order.[69]

Third, a correspondence can be discerned between the multidimensional structure of power linking the various elite groups and the hierarchy of conflict-potential in the issues confronting the elites. In its simplest form, the power structure is a two-dimensional array dividing the labor leaders from the rest of the elites and, within the establishment, the military and the civilian bureaucrats from the private sector. Complicating this picture are the bishops, whose locus of power and contacts cannot be plotted along either of these coordinates.

Similarly, the distribution of opinion among the elites, and especially the intensity of and the antagonism involved in this opinion, changes with particular issues. Preferences on the moral issues—birth control, divorce, and so on—are pretty much disengaged from opinions on other issues. Among the left-right issues, some tend to be more sharply polarized than others. The distributive conflicts—income redistribution, for example—are class issues in a limited sense; typically, they involve trade unionist rather than incendiary demands. Issues involving the autonomy of interest

---

class persons in times of economic hardship. See "Golbery na ESG: Abertura pelo Centro," *Isto É*, July 9, 1980: 36. For a graphic analysis of the same tactics in another authoritarian regime, see William Chapman, "New Leaders in Seoul Exploit General Yearning for Stability," *Washington Post*, September 4, 1980: A33.

[69] In the transition away from authoritarianism in Brazil, dissident elites are vulnerable to the charge that they cannot agree on a positive political arrangement that is something more than a negation of the authoritarian tradition. The most difficult questions seem to center around the problem of establishing innovative elite-mass linkages—that is, representative and responsive mechanisms that depart from the paternalistic, corporatist heritage. See Bolivar Lamounier, "O Discurso e o Processo: Da Distensão às Opções do Regime Brasileiro," in *Brasil 1990*, ed. Henrique Rattner (São Paulo: Editora Brasiliense, 1979). The opposition-in-disarray theme applies not only to the political parties but to the labor syndicates as well. In fact, the government encourages and enforces "multipartism for the working class" through typically corporatist restrictions against the formation of large, centralized unions. However, the theme can also be overworked. It is not clear that a close relationship between urban labor and a single political party in Brazil would work to the benefit—that is, restore the autonomy—of either one.

groups and the equity of the rules of the game split those who actively support the authoritarian state from those who oppose or are ambivalent about it.

The conflict hierarchy implicit in the issues facing the elites has been presented as a statement of fact but, at this point, it is nothing more than a plausible taxonomy. In the following discussion of the perceptions and the values of the elites, I develop a set of hypotheses for testing these ideas.

Perceptions

From the outside, most elites in authoritarian systems would seem to know where one another stand. This does not imply that they agree on everything, a requirement that would violate the code of limited pluralism. But it does mean that the elites understand one another.

The problem involves not so much consensus defined as the coincidence of individual opinions as it does a reciprocal awareness of the positions of major actors. But as observers look more closely at the actual workings of authoritarian rule, the more interelite behavior takes on the appearance of a buzzing confusion.[70] It becomes crucial to understand the degree to which the elites themselves know what is going on.

Thus, in examining the perceptions of the elites, I am interested in the common recognition among several elite groups of the extent of their agreement or disagreement on several issues. The inquiry differs fundamentally from the analysis of the coincidence or divergence of opinion.[71] The trouble with this latter sort of investigation as a device for the study

[70] See Linn A. Hammergren, "Corporatism in Latin American Politics: A Reexamination of the 'Unique' Tradition," *Comparative Politics* 9 (1977): 443-461.

[71] Although I do not stress the point here, the perceptual approach to ideology has a long, essentially Durkheimian, tradition in the social sciences and has, after a period of neglect, received much attention. See Murray Edelman, *Political Language: Words That Succeed and Policies That Fail* (New York: Academic Press, 1977); Paul Harris and Paul Heelas, "Cognitive Processes and Collective Representations," *Archives Européennes de Sociologie* 20 (1979): 211-241; Thomas Luckmann, ed., *Phenomenology and Sociology: Selected Readings* (London: Penguin Books, 1978); Paul Rabinow and William M. Sullivan, eds., *Interpretative Social Science* (Berkeley: University of California Press, 1979); and Richard J. Bernstein, *The Restructuring of Social and Political Theory* (New York: Harcourt, Brace, Jovanovich/ University of Pennsylvania Press, 1978). Unfortunately, in his critique of mainstream and, in particular, functional social science, Bernstein ignores the attention that figures like Merton, who are otherwise removed from the Marxist perspective, pay to perceptual distortions such as the self-fulfilling prophecy. The phenomenon has been discovered independently by several scholars working out of different orientations. Perhaps the most familiar source is W. I. Thomas, who stated that "if men define situations as real, they are real in their consequences." This theme is taken up recurrently by Daniel Chirot, *Social Change in the Twentieth Century* (New York: Harcourt, Brace, Jovanovich, 1977), pp. 52-54, 201.

of consensus is that it implies perfect or near-perfect information. This assumption is convenient but not especially realistic. Brazil has a complex, authoritarian system. Complexity makes for an abundance of information that is difficult to process. Secrecy, official and otherwise, makes information a scarce commodity.

In either case, pluralistic ignorance may breed as much conflict as do genuine differences in opinions and interests. Or it may be that the segmentation of the elites leads them to engage in a kind of parallel play, with each of the sectors enveloped in their own concerns at the expense of any but the most rudimentary comprehension of what their allies and rivals in other areas are up to.

Three outcomes of an analysis based on the mutual perceptions of the elites are possible.[72] One is that they understand one another more or less completely. This is unlikely, except under conspiratorial conditions in a simple, small-scale political system.

Another outcome is chaos: that is, the elites engage in wild guessing, and their perceptions of one another have only a random connection with their actual preferences. This, too, is unlikely. The elites make it their business to know, approximately, what is going on.

A third outcome deserves to be taken more seriously. This happens when the elites misunderstand one another systematically. A regular but presumably mistaken process of stereotyping and projection occurs. The elites use preconceptions about their peers to stylize reality. The result is a simplification of collective perception, much as ideology serves to coordinate political facts and impressions for individuals.

This emphasis on mutual perceptions among the elites has several implications. First, in the context of a study including various elite groups and multiple political issues, it poses an obvious question: Do the elites recognize the scope of their (dis)agreement on policy controversies? The question is obvious but the answer is not. This part of the analysis permits us to analyze conflict and consensus realistically, or surrealistically, through the eyes of the elites themselves.

Second, the perceptions of the elites furnish criteria against which to compare their own preferences. Elite opinions in Brazil have a suspiciously progressive cast, and the question arises whether they can be taken at face-value as indicators of the elites' intentions and actual behavior. The opinions that the elites attribute to one another serve as a partial corrective to

---

[72] In reality, there are many more outcomes from the interplay between preferences and perceptions. The number is a multiple of issues times groups. Some groups may understand certain others on particular issues, misunderstand others on other issues, and so on. Thus, while the three outcomes posited here do not exhaust the logical possibilities, they capture the major variations.

the assertions of enlightenment and liberal sympathies that the elites claim as their own.

Third, there is an important sense in which elite definitions of reality become reality because they are the views of powerful individuals. Even authoritarian elites are not free to misconstrue the facts of political life at will. But, as elites, they are compelled to impose meaning, an ideological structure, on events and persons. Through this dynamic, the environment becomes partly of their own manufacture. Perceptions, like organizations, take on a life of their own.[73]

But how, specifically, might the attributions that the elites make of one another's opinions be patterned? Two hunches mentioned in the discussion of elite opinions are relevant. The first is that, at least in authoritarian regimes, public and private ideologies differ, the former being more conservative than the latter. So long as personal views do not become a matter of disruptive public debate, the elites are free to indulge in verbal liberalism. Indeed, it is difficult for them not to do so, since outright fascism is no longer a defensible political platform. In general, then, it is not surprising that some gap should emerge between the opinions that elites divulge in confidential interviews and those that they attribute to one another as public figures.

At the same time, there is no reason to expect this gap to remain constant across all issues, and this is where the notion of a hierarchy of polarization among issues becomes useful. If it is true that an issue like the limits on political opposition is touchier than one involving population policy, for example, one sign of this differential polarization should be an increase in the discrepancy between public image and private opinion as the issues become more controversial. Elites who off the record claim to hold enlightened views on such issues are prone to label others, and to be labelled in turn, as comparatively reactionary. Conflict-laden issues are those on which, by definition, compromise is difficult and the pathology of self-fulfilling prophecy sets in. The elites develop an interest in stereotyping one another as virtual extremists, disinclined to bargain, while viewing themselves as more conciliatory.

The same incentive-structure of perception does not take hold on the less conflictful issues because the vital interests of the elites are not at stake and the gap between public and private opinions is therefore diminished. Even if the positions of the elites on these issues are relatively ill-defined and even if, because of their low salience, information about the opinions of others on such issues is thin, the elites can exhibit an inadvertent accuracy

---

[73] See Peter L. Berger and Thomas Luckmann, *The Social Construction of Reality* (New York: Doubleday & Company, Inc., 1966).

about the preferences of their colleagues (as opposed to their presumed rivals). The operative premise is of agreement rather than antagonism.[74]

Aside from the fact that it is readily testable, this set of hypotheses provides a way of furthering the understanding of two ideas prominent in theorizing about authoritarian regimes: the postulate of the unideological nature of authoritarian elites and the concept of limited pluralism. Although the psychological roots of perceptual distortion are of interest in their own right, I am primarily concerned with the regularity with which this distortion occurs, issue-by-issue, and with the ability of the elites to structure reality—that is, to construct a series of expectations about the intentions of their peers—in a situation that is in many ways unstructured and susceptible to praetorian unpredictability.

The images that the elites hold of one another are not, of course, "reality." But without these schema, it is difficult to see how the elites could navigate their way at all through the complexities of Brazilian politics. The more uncertain and disorganized their institutional setting is, the more ideological, in the reality-constructing sense, the elites are compelled to be.

Moreover, my focus on the growing distance between what the elites claim to believe in private and how they are seen in public, by their peers, as the conflict-potential of issues increases, forces a reconsideration of the limits of limited pluralism. It leads to an examination of the frailty of shared understanding and, by extension, mutual acceptance among competing elites. This endeavor leads in turn to a consideration of the meaning of authoritarian legitimacy by way of a study of the multiple values of the elites.

Values

Whatever they are, "values" are often thought to be as useless for the understanding of elite, authoritarian politics as they seem to be nebulous in fact. Yet it is hard to discuss the tensions underlying the authoritarian condition without taking them into account. Hirschman, for example, in speculating on the swings in Latin America back and forth from closed to open politics, distinguishes between the "entrepreneurial" and "reformist" impulses and hints of a cyclical balance between them, one gaining on the other as the hegemony of each is exhausted and replenished

[74] Compare the analysis of the relationship between "intensity of crisis" and "perceptual distortion" by Ole R. Holsti, "The 1914 Case," *American Political Science Review* 59 (1965): 365-378. See also Anthony Oberschall, "Protracted Conflict," in *The Dynamics of Social Movements*, ed. Mayer N. Zald and John D. McCarthy (Cambridge, Mass.: Winthrop Publishers, 1979), and D. A. Strickland and R. E. Johnston, "Issue Elasticity in Political Systems," *Journal of Political Economy* 78 (1970): 1069-1092.

over time.[75] These tides in the priorities of regimes appear to be ideologically as well as structurally conditioned, even though we know little about how this actually happens.

By "values" I do not mean the characterological traits of the elites.[76] I take the values of the elites to signify abiding commitments to distinctive models of economic, social, and political change. The argument runs like this:

Brazilian elites are divided between those fixated by the imperative of aggregate growth and those who take a more distributive view of the developmental process. They are also split between the advocates of greater autonomy vis-à-vis the bureaucratic state and those who accept the authoritarian machine. This cleavage divides the elites who comply with and to some extent approve of the authoritarian state and those who, even if they may not be partisans of mass democracy, recoil from the threat that the military-technocratic complex poses to their own prerogatives. The coordinates of conflict may be visualized thus:[77]

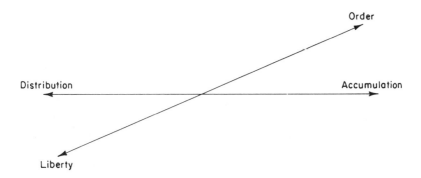

[75] Albert O. Hirschman, "The Turn to Authoritarianism in Latin America and the Search for its Economic Determinants," in Collier, ed., *The New Authoritarianism in Latin America*, pp. 61-98.

[76] This statement does not mean that I consider the psychohistory of elites irrelevant for the study of politics; I simply do not have the data to follow up on this sort of analysis. For suggestive works in this direction, see Lloyd Etheredge, "Hardball Politics: A Model," *Political Psychology* 1 (1979): 3-26; Mostafa Rejai with Kay Philips, *Leaders of Revolution* (Beverly Hills: Sage Publications, 1979); David Shapiro, *Neurotic Styles* (New York: Basic Books, 1965); and George E. Vaillant, *Adaptation to Life: How the Best and the Brightest Came of Age* (Boston: Little, Brown and Company, 1977).

[77] The graph is a simplification. Since the trade-off between accumulation and distribution is not necessarily zero-sum, this single axis may more properly be thought of as the abscissa and ordinate along which the priorities attached to accumulation and distribution are placed. A similar qualification holds for the order-liberty trade-off. It should also be noted that the words "liberty" and "autonomy" are used interchangeably to refer to what are generally understood as political freedom and civil rights, including the right to the organization of dissident interests. Although a distinction is often made in theory between individual liberty

The two axes are not utterly different, but neither do they overlap completely. If they did, constant polarization of conflict would be unavoidable, and the authoritarian system would probably not be tenable at all. For example, not all the elites who place supreme value on aggregate economic growth are ardent believers in the beneficence of authoritarian rule, especially as it implies the indefinite postponement of minimal political guarantees. Similarly, not all the advocates of a more socially equitable mode of growth care much for what are generally understood as civil liberties.[78]

In one respect, this is simply another way of saying that choices among the various goals are not, in principle, zero-sum. But in practice, most Brazilian elites admit that all the goals cannot be maximized simultaneously. They must set a developmental agenda. Because such choices constitute strategic decisions about the future of the nation and about the fate

and collective autonomy, the Brazilian elites do not dwell on this point, and neither do I. See Giovanni Sartori, "Liberty and Law," in *The Politicization of Society*, ed. Kenneth S. Templeton, Jr. (Indianapolis, Ind.: Liberty Press, 1979), pp. 249-311.

[78] For a presentation of a similar two-dimensional model in a very different context, see William Schneider, "Democrats and Republicans, Liberals and Conservatives," in *Emerging Coalitions in American Politics*, ed. Seymour Martin Lipset (San Francisco: Institute for Contemporary Studies, 1978), pp. 183-267. Compare the more one-dimensional but still useful theory presented by Robert Kelly, "Ideology and Political Culture from Jefferson to Nixon," *American Historical Review* 82 (1977): 531-562. The fourfold classification of developmental goals presented here is used to characterize elites. But, for those with an interest in taxonomies, it can also be adapted as a classificatory device for different regimes. Most polities seem to emphasize pairs of priorities, such as order-and-accumulation, order-and-distribution, and so forth. It is instructive to match these combinations with the four ideal-types of polities set forth by Philippe C. Schmitter: authoritarian-state corporatist (order/accumulation); pluralist-societal corporatist (liberty/accumulation); monocratic-Maoist (order/distribution); and, perhaps the most hypothetical of all, anarcho-syndicalist (liberty/distribution). See "Still the Century of Corporatism?" *Review of Politics* 36 (1974): 85-131.

The value of such an exercise is limited, however, by restricting it to combinations of two goals. Even starting with only four priorities, it is logically possible to imagine twenty-four different rank orderings, and the variety of these orderings adds some realism to the artificiality of ideal-types. There are almost no empirical studies of the trade-offs between "hard" and "soft" goals in less developed countries, although many analysts recognize the importance of the multiple goals dilemma. See Mark S. Granovetter, "The Idea of 'Advancement' in Theories of Social Evolution and Development," *American Journal of Sociology* 85 (1979): 489-515, and Michael S. Lewis-Beck, "Some Economic Effects of Revolution: Models, Measurement, and the Cuban Evidence," *American Journal of Sociology* 84 (1979): 1127-1149. Compare Valerie Bunce and Alexander Hicks, "Capitalism, Socialisms, and Democracy: Beyond Present Political Economic Tradeoffs," paper presented at the annual meetings of the American Political Science Association, Washington, D.C., August 28-30, 1980, and John M. Echols III, "Does Socialism Mean Greater Equality? A Comparison of East and West Along Several Major Dimensions," *American Journal of Political Science* 25 (1981): 1-31.

of particular groups, interests, and classes, and because they seem to be fairly deep-rooted, I call them *values*.

The important thing to understand, first of all, is that the elites are confronted with several difficult-to-reconcile goods. It is not as if the choice were only between "entrepreneurship" and "reform" or some combination of the two. To treat the strategic dilemma this way is to elide the fact that in Brazil (and elsewhere, to greater and lesser degrees) social reform has sometimes gone hand-in-hand with authoritarian politics, as during much of the Vargas period, and that rampant capitalist accumulation has at certain times—for example, the postwar period through the presidency of Juscelino Kubitschek—been accompanied by a respect for political liberties, civil rights, and other "bourgeois" decencies.

Second, the two strategic axes that summarize the developmental values of the elites resemble the coordinates that underly their opinions on a variety of issues. For some purposes, both may be situated in left-right terms. This interpretation would not be wrong in the Brazilian context, but it would be superficial. The trade-offs between accumulation and distribution and between order and liberty are distinct, just as the preferences of the elites with respect to income redistribution are of a different order from their views on the political role of the military and the autonomy of interest groups.

Hence, it would be simplistic to identify the emergence of authoritarianism in Brazil with the imperative of accumulation, just as it would be wrong to equate progressive social policies with guarantees of civil liberties.[79] To be sure, analysts since Marx have recognized that "the bourgeoisie" (not to mention vast portions of the working class) can be compensated for their loss of the right to rule by preservation of their right to make money, and the squeamishness of sectors of the Brazilian elite about the incursions of the authoritarian state may be discounted at least in part.[80] Nevertheless, the two axes of choice—those involving the relative weight attributed to accumulation and equity, on the one hand, and to order and liberty, on the other—are different.

Third, even though the elites are asked to choose among four partially separate goals, for most purposes, only three types of elites—those who give priority, respectively, to economic development, social reform, and

[79] Compare José Serra, "Three Mistaken Theses Regarding the Connection between Industrialization and Authoritarian Regimes," in Collier, ed., *The New Authoritarianism in Latin America*, pp. 99-163.

[80] See Eli Diniz Cerqueira, "Os Limites Políticos do Empresariado," *Isto É*, June 7, 1978: 70-71, and Diniz Cerqueira, "Industrial and Agro-Export Sectors in Brazil: Interest Differentiation and Institutional Changes (1930-1945)," paper presented at the annual meeting of the Latin American Studies Association, Pittsburgh, Pennsylvania, April 5-7, 1979.

political liberalization—need to be distinguished. Those who give top ranking to "order," or who refuse to set priorities and claim that all developmental goals can be maximized at once, are so few in number, or subsumed by one or another of the principal types, that they do not generally require a category of their own. For the sake of simplicity, I call the three major variants "economists," "social reformers," and "politicians."[81]

With these types of elites in place, several hypotheses can be generated. Whether the developmental priorities of the elites are called priorities or values matters less than the idea that their agendas constitute basic, long-term commitments. I shall argue that their economists, the supposed technocrats, are at least as tenacious as the presumably more ideological politicians.[82] Furthermore, if there are any elites in Brazil who can be called unideological, it is the social reformers, who tend to be less interested in questions of economic grandeur and political niceties than in providing their clienteles with a modicum of material well-being.

But who are these elites? As might be expected, there is an appreciable correlation between the group affiliation of the elites and their developmental values. There are more economists, for example, among the state managers and the businessmen than among the opposition politicians, and the labor leaders as well as the bishops harbor a disproportionate number of social reformers.

Yet the correlation is quite imperfect; the elite groups cannot be treated as undifferentiated blocs. For some purposes, not much information is lost by considering the elite sectors to be unitary actors. But when the issue comes down to the legitimacy of the regime, the loyalties of the elites cannot be predicted by the overall fit between their routine group interests and their developmental values.

In order to understand how the basic priorities of the elites might have an effect on their allegiance to the regime above and beyond their specific and presumably short-term group interests, it is necessary to recognize that the normal, noncrisis position of the men whom I have called the social

---

[81] The label "social reformers" is, perhaps appropriately, something of a compromise; it is difficult to find an exact and at the same time concise phrase for the idea in the Brazilian context. The essential notion is that these elites do not care much about who rules so long as they are in a position to keep some control over the distribution of benefits to their followers. Although they cannot be called radicals, and although most of them are quite paternalistic, they are more populistic than the austere economists. Many of them are the Brazilian version of ward heelers. But some are more than just low-profile bargainers. There is a subset of social reformers who resemble the others in their disregard for "politics" as usually understood but who are seething with resentment at social injustice in Brazil.

[82] Compare Merilee Grindle, "Power, Expertise and the 'Tecnico': Suggestions from a Mexican Case Study," *Journal of Politics* 39 (1977): 399-426, and Bolivar Lamounier, "O Mito da Tecnocracia," *Isto É*, May 25, 1977: 72-73.

reformers is one of tentative acquiescence. Of all the elites, they tend to be the most ambivalent and vacillating. By contrast, the positions of the economists and the politicians are easier to predict. They are usually at loggerheads because of the direct threat posed to the autonomy and indeed to the very existence of certain elites by the perpetuation of authoritarian rule.

The social reformers lie somewhere in between. During the heyday of the Brazilian boom, they were probably closer to the economists than to the politicians. Although the social reformers are scarcely committed to aggregate growth for its own sake, they cannot be termed staunch allies of the politicians who fell into disgrace during the populist uproar preceding the 1964 revolution. And whatever the social reformers might feel about the politicians in general, on practical grounds they did not view the politicians as being in a position to help them when authoritarian economics was riding high. Thus, the authoritarian coalition was held together not only by force but also by the partial cooptation of elites who desired some distribution of social benefits yet whose memories of the populist era were so negative that they were unwilling to align themselves with the more political types.

But the commitment of the social reformers to the authoritarian regime, and probably to any regime, is rarely wholehearted. They shift around, trying (unlike many of the economists and the politicians) to minimize their losses rather than maximize their gains. In this sense, even though they are not the most powerful or the most combative of the elites, they hold a swing vote. Legitimacy may therefore be a partial rather than a perfect harmony, a working majority rather than a complete accord. In effect, it may be more realistic to speak of the tenability rather than the legitimacy of regimes, authoritarian and otherwise.

But this is to get ahead of the story. Here it is useful to consider the factors that might lead the usually malleable social reformers into disaffection from the economists and their allies in the military. One such factor has been pinpointed by Linz. Whatever support the authoritarian regime enjoys comes from its pragmatic, utilitarian accomplishments. As soon as its performance falters, the regime is in trouble—a diagnosis quite in line with the dissatisfaction ensuant on the oil crisis and the downturn in economic growth in the post-1973 period.[83]

But the difficulties of the regime also thicken with success. Not only the dissident but also the usually compliant elites become uneasy as the regime bears down on them and outbids them for the allegiance of their

---

[83] Juan J. Linz, "The Future of an Authoritarian Situation or the Institutionalization of an Authoritarian Regime: The Case of Brazil," in Stepan, ed., *Authoritarian Brazil*, pp. 233-254.

traditional clienteles. The social reformers are driven from their almost exclusive focus on the distribution of material benefits and patronage, away from their cynicism about the utility of openly competitive politics, toward a concern with "democratization"—that is, with a loosening of the bonds on their organizational autonomy.

Put more generally: Brazilian elites are prone to ideological anxiety, and this tension undermines the legitimacy of the regime. To the extent that the authoritarian solution is successful—to the degree that economic growth is sustained—authoritarian ideology is subject to obsolescence. Exclusionary and repressive policies justified in the name of national recuperation are supposed to lose their rationale as growth proceeds. In the eyes of the elites, the dynamics of development should lead to the dissolution of authoritarian politics.

If, on the other hand, authoritarian measures prove unsuccessful beyond the short term, the pragmatic pretensions of the regime are undercut. "The only excuse for this situation," declared one of our respondents, "is that it promotes economic growth. If it can't do that, what is the point?" This is the double bind of Brazilian authoritarianism. It renders the system ideologically vulnerable, even during its periods of apparent triumph.[84]

This line of argument is, I believe, straightforward. The challenge is to see how it holds up under the evidence. I reconstruct the hypothesis empirically, first by drawing on the dual premise that issues involving elite competition and the autonomy of interest organizations are among the most tension-ridden in authoritarian politics and that the social reformers, of all the elites, are usually the least sensitive to such issues. They try to follow their own group interests without provoking the economists and without wasting time with the politicians. To the degree that this is true, and to the degree that the developmental values of the elites are also more or less in accord with their group interests, we can arrive at reasonable explanations of the preferences of the elites simply by looking at how they vary across their sector affiliations. In graphic terms:

Elite Sector ─────────────────────────────▶ Policy Preferences

There is nothing mysterious about this model. While there may be substantial policy differences among the elite groups, for example, among the identifiable conservatives and progressives, their sectoral interests gen-

---

[84] Again, the fact that the ideologies of the elites may be out of joint with the structure of power does not imply that the regime is doomed to an abrupt collapse. Almost certainly, however, this disjuncture winnows away support from the regime and contributes to the immobilism of the government in its relation with opposition forces. See Fernando Henrique Cardoso, "A Coragem de um Gesto," *Veja*, August 27, 1980: 130.

erally provide a satisfactory explanation for these divergences. This is politics-as-usual among rival elites. Their ideologies, in the low-grade sense, mirror their group interests.[85]

My central hypothesis, however, is that preferences on certain issues, those that bear on interelite comportment, can be better understood as the outcome of the developmental values of the elites than as the product of their divergent group interests, thus:

In such cases, differences in the orientations of the elites cannot be satisfactorily accounted for by their sectoral affiliations or their immediate group interests. More precisely, although the economists and the politicians stay just about where expected—at opposite poles of the conservative-progressive continiuum—the social reformers pivot leftward, closer to the politicians. The economists become isolated, and the cooptative underpinnings of the regime crumble.

This break is possible only if the developmental priorities of the elites are not wholly consonant with their group interests in the first place. That is, the elite groups are not uniform entities. On occasion, the social reformers cease to behave like *pelegos* (roughly, puppets of the incumbents) and begin to resist the depredations of the authoritarian state. This happens, I hypothesize, when the issue comes down to the persistent lack of equity— that is, of even limited pluralism—in the interelite game.

By and large, because of the threat of a breakdown in control over mass participation, the elites are reluctant to give up on one another. The social reformers are extremely cautious about contemplating an overhaul of the prevailing order, even when they fail to get their way on certain policy questions. Only when their primary values are persistently threatened are they likely to abandon their fondness for *convivência* (accommodation) and engage in *contestação* (confrontation). This happens when they see that on the "rules-of-the-game" issues, such as the participation of the

[85] In one respect, the model is not simple at all. It implies that the social origins of the elites have no independent effect on their attitudes that cannot be accounted for by their group affiliations. This is in fact the case; I found practically none. While such an outcome corroborates the reasonable expectation that most measures of socioeconomic origin for elites are not powerful determinants of their beliefs or their behavior, it is not entirely satisfactory. I suspect that the nonfinding is partially a function of the inadequacy of the data on elite socialization.

military, they have little to gain either for themselves or their constituents, despite the formidable costs of resistance.

This, then, is my model of the determinants of and the factors undermining authoritarian legitimacy. I assume that the legitimacy of the regime is deeply flawed. The problem is to identify the criteria by which the elites judge it to be so, just as the question at an earlier stage of the investigation is to determine what kinds of ideologies the elites entertain and not to decide whether they are ideologues to begin with.

The model draws on several approaches to the study of political legitimacy. If there is any assumption that I reject in this literature, it is that political legitimacy reflects a positive consensus about what the good polity should be. A substantive covenant of this sort, adhered to by rival interests, seems most improbable in Brazil.[86]

The key question is not whether any one of the major ideological currents among the elites can dominate the others—whether, for example, the economists can gain sustained hegemony. Instead, it concerns the degree to which elites with profoundly discrepant priorities about the challenges facing Brazil, and themselves, manage to put up with one another. Such a compact is not identical to a consensus on specific issues, for the very concept of legitimacy involves the manner in which elites live with one another in the chronic absence of agreement about important policy questions. Neither, by postulate, is it reducible to the particular interests of disparate groups. It refers to a procedural *entente* rather than to a consensus on specific issues.[87]

Conceptualizations of political legitimacy in terms of such rules are not without precedent in the study of authoritarian systems. Anderson has argued that the politics of Latin American countries, including Brazil, is characterized not so much by an absence of prescriptions for interelite behavior as by "the normal rule . . . that new power contenders may be added to the system, but old ones may not be eliminated." He proposes further that elites usually try "to restrain destructive conflict between

[86] On the other hand, the notion of legitimacy as reflecting the capacity of elites to accept one another's differences—a definition toward which I lean—tends to dodge the problem, most evident in times of economic setbacks and scarcer-than-usual resources, of getting the elites to agree on a minimally common program. Compare Douglas A. Chalmers and Craig H. Robinson, "Why Power Contenders Choose Liberalization: Perspectives from Latin America," paper presented at the annual meetings of the American Political Science Association, Washington, D.C., August 28-31, 1980.

[87] See Richard Hyman, "Pluralism, Procedural Consensus, and Collective Bargaining," *British Journal of Industrial Relations* 16 (1978): 16-40.

[themselves] and to protect their established place in the political order.''[88] The problem in militarized Brazil is that many of the elites have been "disestablished"; they are threatened with becoming nonentities.

Approaches to political legitimacy that have been developed without specific reference to the Latin American context are also utilized. Two of these merit special attention. James Scott and others have elaborated a "phenomenological" theory of peasant movements in Southeast Asia in an attempt to identify the norms—the cultural definitions of justice—that motivate subsistence farmers to strike out against tyrannical and improvident governments.[89] The interesting feature of this work is that it can be read, not as a conceptualization of legitimacy, but as a theory of illegitimacy—that is, as a set of values that prescribe how far the state may intrude on the "established places" of its citizens before provoking serious disaffection from a regime that most people are otherwise able to endure. Like mine, Scott's model does not require dissidents to adopt a full-blown alternative to the existing order in order to call its legitimacy into question.[90]

At least in spirit, the theory used here bears a strong resemblance as well to models of consociational politics.[91] The ideas connected with this approach have been elaborated with reference to societies split by linguistic, ethnic, regional, and religious cleavages. They have been directed at the ability of the elites representing black-and-white interests to keep the polity running short of civil war.

In Brazil, cleavages of this sort have not been salient. Yet the elites are riven with analogous disputes—those involving the autonomous representation of interests, for example, versus the impositions of the bureaucratic-authoritarian state. These conflicts may be less visible and clearcut than the problems typical of consociational democracies, but they are harsh nonetheless. The major difference between the consociational model and

[88] Charles W. Anderson, *Politics and Economic Change in Latin America* (Princeton: D. Van Nostrand, 1967), pp. 102-104. See also Peter H. Smith, *Labyrinths of Power: Political Recruitment in Twentieth-Century Mexico* (Princeton: Princeton University Press, 1979), p. 5: ''. . . if authoritarianism consists of limited pluralism, it becomes necessary to determine who falls on which side of the limits—who does (and does not) have the functional right to organize and compete for power. There is an equally urgent need to gain some understanding of the behavior of authoritarian elites and the 'rules' of their political game.''

[89] James C. Scott, *The Moral Economy of the Peasant* (New Haven: Yale University Press, 1976). See also Edward Friedman, *Backward Toward Revolution* (Berkeley: University of California Press, 1974).

[90] For an excellent critique of the "alienation" literature, much of which seems to hold to this assumption, see James D. Wright, *Dissent of the Governed* (New York: Academic Press, 1976). For a spirited defense, see David Easton, "A Re-Assessment of the Concept of Political Support," *British Journal of Political Science* 5 (1975): 435-457.

[91] Arend Lijphart, *Democracy in Plural Societies* (New Haven: Yale University Press, 1978).

mine lies in the hypothesis that the normally conciliatory elites, and not the representatives of diametrically opposed interests, hold the key to the legitimacy of the regime.[92]

However, perhaps the broadest implication of my argument is one whose geneology cannot be traced so simply. It is possible that for the foreseeable future no single ideological current will enjoy hegemonic status in Brazil. While it is clear that the days of virtually exclusive dominance by authoritarian technocrats are over, coalitions based primarily on opposition are notoriously liable to disintegrate. Situations of this sort, in which no single class or set of interests is able to gain majority power, are precisely those in which authoritarian interventions are thought to thrive.

Put slightly differently, the multiplicity of contending values among Brazilian elites makes it difficult to create an abiding consensus, and it leaves open the temptation of imposing one.[93] The weakness of political institutionalization in Brazil suggests an anomic quality to interelite relationships. Scholars have come to recognize that this "post-hegemonic" condition is hardly peculiar to Brazil, even though it may be more pronounced there than in more fully industrialized settings.[94] But these speculations are better left to the end of the analysis, after we have seen how the ideas developed here bear up under empirical scrutiny.

Organization of the Study

The presentation is divided in two unequal parts. The first section is devoted to the structure of power in Brazil. Chapter One lays out the variable

[92] Compare Ian Lustick, "Stability in Deeply Divided Societies: Consociationalism versus Control," *World Politics* 31 (1979): 325-344. The reason why I believe it is the generally conciliatory rather than the usually combative elites who determine the legitimacy of Brazilian regimes has much to do with the nature of the religious factor in Brazil, the "third dimension" about which little has been said in the last few pages in discussing the accumulation-equity and order-liberty cleavages. The Catholic church is not only comparatively weak in Brazil, as are absolutist modes of thought; denominational differences, while prolific, have not been associated with political movements or parties. See Fausto Cupertino, *As Muitas Religiões do Brasileiro* (Rio de Janeiro: Editora Civilização Brasileira, 1976). Popular cults in Brazil are, among other things, expressive support networks that provide a variety of social services; they have not been noted for their doctrinal or political disputes.

[93] The priorities of the elites are not only "contending" but also incommensurable. How is "liberty," for example, to be weighed against "equity"? The problem of noncomparability almost certainly adds to the difficulty that the Brazilian elites experience in reconciling disparate priorities, and it is one that is discussed at length as a universal dilemma in politics by Isaiah Berlin in *Against the Current: Essays in the History of Ideas* (New York: Viking Press, 1980). Compare Eugene Goodheart, *The Failure of Criticism* (Cambridge, Mass.: Harvard University Press, 1978).

[94] See Alan Wolfe, "Has Social Democracy a Future?" *Comparative Politics* 11 (1978): 100-125, and Nicos Poulantzas, "La Crise des Partis," *Le Monde Diplomatique* (1979): 28.

emphasis given by different elite groups to alternative mechanisms of mobility, including their efforts in linking themselves to the inner sanctum of the establishment by way of marriage. I am particularly interested in tracing the rise of technocratic cadres from the middle sectors, and in seeing how their partial separation from already entrenched elites may contribute to the consolidation of the authoritarian system.

Chapter Two extends this analysis, first, by mapping the multidimensional structure of networks among Brazilian elites and, second, by examining the complementary and reinforcing functions of various types of linkages, principally of kinship and friendship. The chief purpose of this chapter is to gain a sense of the balance between the functional and the disruptive components of the power structure.

Taken together, these chapters provide a view of the institutional context of and the intergroup strains within the Brazilian establishment. They establish the backdrop for the more extensive analysis of the ideologies of the elites.

The second part of the study begins in Chapter Three with an examination of the orientations of the elites toward the distribution of power. The main question here entails the degree to which the elites see beyond their immediate quarrels and envision something approaching a redesign of the structure of power itself.

The elites, of course, understand what the power structure is, even if they suffer from a myopia brought on by their own positions in it. The intriguing piece of evidence presented in Chapter Three suggests the existence of a negative consensus among progressives and conservatives alike with respect to a common enemy—that is, elite groups who, they all feel, have too much power and therefore deprive them of what they consider their just share of position and privilege.

The suggestion of a profound fissure within the establishment, of a latent unity of opposition, leads me to explore further, in Chapter Four, the deep-seated tensions among the elites. It is here that I examine the validity of classifying the elites in three basic types: the "economists," the "social reformers," and the "politicians."

This is done in two ways. The first step involves an inspection of the discursive responses the elites gave when asked to elaborate on their developmental priorities. The results belie the image of the economists as cool professionals. "Development," as the then finance minister was fond of claiming, "is the moral equivalent of war."[95] The necessity of distinguishing between the empirical manner of the economists and the determination with which they pursue their goals soon becomes evident. In the

[95] Delfim Netto, address to the Conference on Indicators of Nation-Building, Rio de Janeiro, April 1972.

degree of their commitment, the economists are much like the politicians, even though the substance of their values differs.[96] This characterization of the economists and the politicians, together with the depiction of the social reformers as chameleonlike middlemen, will become the centerpiece in the subsequent analysis of the determinants of legitimacy.[97]

The second way in which the measures of developmental values are validated is by correlating the priorities of the elites with their evaluations of the performance of the government and with their support for it. While neither of these indicators taps what I understand as legitimacy, they help estimate the sensitivity of elites with discrepant agendas to fluctuations in specific governmental outputs. They also reveal how ready or reluctant the elites are to translate their judgments of governmental performance into political support and opposition.

Chapter Five is devoted to an analysis of the factors undermining the legitimacy of the regime. The investigation proceeds in two phases. The first step is to obtain a picture of the ideologies of the elites as a multi-dimensional configuration—that is, to reduce the connections between the preferences of the elites on a variety of issues to their underlying coordinates. Here the independent locus of opinions on the moral issues begins to emerge, as does the conflict-ridden nature of issues concerning the autonomy/subjugation of interest organizations and the even greater polarization of controversies touching on the rules of the interelite game itself.

The final step is to specify the determinants of elite positions on the hierarchy of issues. The basic idea is that variation in preferences on most of the issues facing the elites—indeed, on all of them save those that touch directly on the legitimacy of the regime—can be understood as a reflection of the divergent interests of the elite groups.

On the legitimizing issues—for example, those concerning the role of the military and the role of interest representation generally vis-à-vis the dominion of the centralizing state—the basic values of the elites are engaged. In particular, the social reformers, who more often than not shade their positions toward the economists in order to salvage what they can,

[96] Although it was not at all common during the miracle years of the early seventies, the notion that certain Brazilian businessmen and technocrats were reckless proponents of *capitalismo selvagem* (savage or jungle capitalism) had become widespread by the end of the decade. An equivalent interpretation has been made of late nineteenth- early twentieth-century capitalism in the United States. See John P. Diggins, *The Bard of Savagery: Thorstein Veblen and Modern Social Theory* (New York: Seabury Press, 1978).

[97] This tripartite categorization of the elites does not imply a levels-of-conceptualization hierarchy of the sort usually associated with the study of ideologues, near-ideologues, and nonideologues. For a similar argument, see Andre Modigliani and William A. Gamson, "Thinking about Politics," *Political Behavior* 1 (1979): 5-30.

display an unaccustomed solidarity with the politicians. They withdraw their allegiance from a regime that deprives both supporters and opponents of their organizational autonomy. The transgression of the code of limited pluralism provokes an ideological reaction among the least ideological of the elites and forces them into the camp of the erstwhile opponents of the regime.

The analysis concludes with an examination of the mutual perceptions of the elites. The objective is to gather independent verification of the consequences of issue-polarization. As the stakes increase, as we move from the moral issues to the distributive controversies and onto questions about the legitimacy of the political order, the gap between the avowed opinions of the elites and the positions that they attribute to one another widens. An "everybody-is-a-fascist-except-me" pathology takes hold. Under these conditions, both the legitimacy of authoritarianism and the probability of reconciliation are diminished.[98]

[98] Chapter Six has another objective as well. It is to suggest that the gulf between "objective" and "interpretative" (read perceptual, hermeneutic, et cetera) modes of analysis may be more accidental, and less wide, than has been argued by practitioners in both camps. See J. Donald Moon, "The Logic of Political Inquiry: A Synthesis of Opposed Perspectives," in *Political Science: Scope and Theory*, ed. Greenstein and Polsby, vol. 1 of *Handbook of Political Science* (Reading, Mass.: Addison-Wesley, 1975).

PART ONE

Structures of Power

ONE

Mobility and Recruitment

Almost all Brazilian elites are mobile; they do not form a strictly hereditary caste. The important questions have to do with the variable range of mobility of elites from diverse social origins and with the differential effects of class and education, among other factors, on their career trajectories.

Whatever the mix of devices they use to reach their positions, the upward mobility of Brazilian elites is a significant fact in itself. Revolutions open channels of mobility. The Brazilian system may be more restrictive in this regard than leftist movements, at least in their early days. Nevertheless, in the aftermath of the 1964 coup, the structure of opportunity improved for the bourgeoisie. Emphasis was placed not just on education but on technical credentials and at times competence as criteria for advancement.

The rise of the state managers reflects this shift. Recruitment to the command posts of Brazilian society differs from the pattern in some dictatorial systems where partisan allegiance and occasionally anti-intellectualism have been standards of promotion. In Brazil, as the series of *cassações* (proscriptions and early retirements) demonstrates, political disloyalty has been a criterion of exclusion. Yet ideological fealty alone does not guarantee inclusion in the elite ranks.[1]

The elites who have travelled fastest have done so through education. This does not mean that education is a weightier determinant of mobility and power than class. Below a certain threshold—in effect, the middle class—education does not help much, because access to the universities is cut off. And those who have moved with the greatest speed have not necessarily caught up with elites like the businessmen whose family back-

---

[1] Compare Robert E. Blackwell, Jr., "Elite Recruitment and Functional Change: An Analysis of the Soviet Obkom Elite, 1950-1968," *Journal of Politics* 34 (1972): 124-152; Monte Ray Bullard, "People's Republic of China Elite Studies: A Review of the Literature," *Asian Survey* 19 (1979): 789-800; William Jannen, Jr., "National Socialists and Social Mobility," *Journal of Social History* 9 (1976): 339-366; and Jack Grey, "The Two Roads: Alternative Strategies of Social Change and Economic Growth in China," in *Authority, Participation, and Cultural Change in China*, ed. Stuart R. Schram (London: Cambridge University Press, 1973).

grounds give them a class advantage. In addition, the truly upper-class elites can scarcely be described as undereducated. Finally, class endowment and educational attainment among the elites are positively correlated, so that it is difficult to separate their contributions to mobility. For all this, the contrast in the ways the different elite sectors use education as a mechanism of class mobility and class consolidation is striking, and it is a major theme of the present chapter.

Several other factors besides class endowment and educational attainment matter in the selection of Brazilian elites. One of these is regional. The elites can be sorted into those who come from the geographic periphery—most of the politicians as well as the bishops—and those who come from the center—the majority of the businessmen, bureaucrats, and labor leaders. There is also a division within the center between the industrial heartland of São Paulo and the government-oriented city of Rio de Janeiro. Regional insularity may contribute as much to the isolation of the elites from one another as differences in class and educational background.

At the same time, the effects of regional differences on elite politics have not been nearly so great in Brazil as, for example, in Spain. Region does not now form a primary cleavage in Brazilian politics; it has never been intertwined with linguistic or ethnic differences.[2] And yet it counts in a negative way. Although the rise of the state managers is not an entirely novel phenomenon in Brazil, the ascendancy of these men, most of whom have been recruited from the center, goes together with the decline of the politicians under authoritarianism, and the politicians, by law, come from all over Brazil.[3]

Thus, in somewhat roundabout fashion, the centralizing policies of the regime have contributed not only to the marginalization of the politicians as a corporate body but also to the peripheralization of regions outside the center. This imbalance is exacerbated by the maldistribution of resources for higher education across the country.

Another factor that plays a significant role in elite recruitment is age, or rather the historical and generational differences that age represents. Despite the cross-sectional nature of the data, some variations in the com-

---

[2] Inter-regional economic differences, however, are great in Brazil. See D. E. Goodman, "The Brazilian Economic 'Miracle' and Regional Policy: Some Evidence from the Urban Northeast," *Journal of Latin American Studies* 8 (1976): 1-27, and the literature cited therein.

[3] Compare Alvin W. Gouldner, *The Dialectic of Ideology and Technology* (New York: Seabury Press, 1976); Gouldner, "Prologue to a Theory of Revolutionary Intellectuals," *Telos* 26 (1975-1976): 3-36; and Robert D. Putnam, "Elite Transformation in Advanced Industrial Societies: An Empirical Assessment of the Theory of Technocracy," *Comparative Political Studies* 10 (1977): 383-412.

position of the elites, such as the decline in lawyers and the increase in economists and trained administrators among the younger cadres, can best be accounted for by historical and generational transformations.

By the early sixties, the Brazilian middle sectors were hemmed in not only from the bottom, by mass mobilization, but also from the top by a lack of vacancies in elite positions filled by the upper and middle sectors who had begun their rise to power a generation before. Overlaying the conflict between a growing working class and a capitalist class nearing the end of the growth period based on import-substitution was a conflict between cohorts of the bourgeoisie.

The authoritarian response to the dual problem of class and cohort conflict is in one respect obvious: the demobilization of the working class. But the elites also renovated their own ranks. The ascendancy of the *técnicos* and the demise of the politicians correspond to this strategy. Age-specific differences in the social origins and mobility mechanisms of the elite cohorts are fairly strong, and the notion of generational renewal within the bourgeoisie as a partial explanation of the dynamic, rather than purely reactionary, character of Brazilian authoritarianism is altogether plausible.

Finally, because the standard socioeconomic indicators are pale and incomplete measures of the recruitment process, I consider the question of elite marriage patterns. There are two complementary rationales for this undertaking. One stems from the supposition that marital arrangements entered into by the elites are designed largely for the purpose of consolidating the power and social position of different social strata. Of special interest in Latin America is the extent of intermarriage between landed and industrial-commercial families. While this tendency does not prove that the two segments form a unified class, it raises doubts as to the degree of conflict between them, undermining the notion of an ineluctable split between "the rural oligarchy" and "the modernizers" during the shift toward an urban society.[4]

A second way of analyzing elite marriages is as a mechanism of vertical mobility from the viewpoint of those on the way up. This perspective is not the opposite of the first. Rather, the focus shifts to the ways in which sponsored mobility through marriage reinforces the structure of power by bringing into it promising, instead of incompetent or merely adventurist, elements from below.

Upward mobility by way of marriage may not always or even usually require fulfilment of the melodramatic convention that the son-in-law follow the same line of work or enter the same organization as his father-in-

[4] Compare Ronald H. McDonald, "Patterns of Patrimonial Leadership in Latin America," paper presented at the annual meeting of the American Political Science Association, Washington, D.C., August 31-September 3, 1979.

law. It suffices that the marriage increase the number of contacts and mutual obligations, facilitating the access of the husband to strata in which he would otherwise be less likely to move and providing the family of the bride with links to the innovative sectors of a changing society. The assumption is that the absorptive capacity of elite families enhances rather than dilutes their power.

In this chapter, I examine elite marriages from both perspectives. The procedure involves correlating the social origins of the elites with the occupational ranking of their fathers-in-law. In particular, I try to determine how marriage patterns vary from one elite grouping to another. Since considerations of wealth are supremely important in the business sector, the industrialists and the financiers are likely to be among the most endogamous of the elites. Lastly, I attempt to pick out glints of change in marriage patterns across age cohorts. If the Brazilian middle sectors have been on the rise since 1964, and indeed during most of the post-war period, this movement may be reflected in an opening-up of the marriage system over time.

Origins

On the average, Brazilian elites come from the middle class. More than a third of them claim that their fathers were of the middle sectors: shopkeepers, highschool teachers, middle-level government functionaries—in short, the petty bourgeoisie. If we add to these the professionals (doctors, lawyers, engineers, accountants, university professors, et cetera) and routine nonmanuals (low-level public functionaries, elementary school teachers, enlisted men, salesmen, et cetera), nearly two-thirds of the elites can be categorized as middle class in origin.[5] The pattern would not be so

---

[5] The seven-category classification is a simplified version of an original twenty-category code. Briefly: "manual" includes urban and rural labor, both skilled and unskilled; "routine nonmanual," "middle class," and "professional" are as described in the text; and the top three categories are largely self-explanatory. "Top military/political," for example, takes in nationally known politicians, ministers, generals, and admirals. On occasion, I collapse the three highest categories into one to form a five-point scale, since it is impossible to rank-order the top categories. The name given this grouping is "upper class." A full discussion of the extensive controversy surrounding class as opposed to stratification approaches to background analysis is unnecessary here. Much of the argument is not pertinent to the present study, insofar as it has taken place with reference to advanced industrial societies and, in any event, has little to do with the social origins of elites. See, however, F. Lancaster Jones and Patrick McDonnell, "Measurement of Occupational Status in Comparative Analysis," *Sociological Methods and Research* 5 (1977): 437-459; Sugiyama Iutaka and E. Wilbur Bock, "Determinants of Occupational Status in Brazil," in *Social Stratification and Career Mobility*, ed. Walter Muller and Karl Mayer (The Hague: Mouton, 1973); Archibald O. Haller, Donald B. Holsinger, and Hélcio U. Saraiva, "Variations in Occupational Prestige Hierarchies:

impressive were it drawn from an advanced industrial society. As it is, the distribution expresses the unrepresentativeness, in descriptive terms, of the Brazilian establishment.[6]

Of course, the class backgrounds of the elite groups are not uniform. Table 1.1 confirms the fact that the labor leadership is a caste apart. Three-quarters of them are from manual or routine nonmanual backgrounds; none of them comes from the upper class proper.[7]

The businessmen are more likely than the other elites to come from families already prominent in industry and banking. There is a father-to-son quality to the transmission of class in the business sector, just as there is among the labor leaders. Class and kinship differences reinforce rather than contradict one another. In addition, powerful military and political antecedents figure conspicuously in the business families, even more so than among the politicians themselves.[8] The businessmen are extremely well-connected.

Brazilian Data,'' *American Journal of Sociology* 77 (1972): 941-945; March D. Szuchman and Eugene F. Sofrer, ''The State of Occupational Stratification Research in Argentina,'' *Latin American Research Review* 11 (1976): 159-171; and Theodore D. Kemper, ''Marxist and Functionalist Theories in the Study of Stratification: Common Elements that Lead to a Test,'' *Social Forces* 54 (1976): 559-578.

[6] In Figure 1.1, and in analysis throughout the study, occasional missing data are eliminated. The base of calculation is always less than the full sample of 251. In addition, in most of the present chapter, the bishops are omitted. The main reason is that there are too few of them for the type of analysis conducted here. Also, the social background of the bishops is not viewed as theoretically crucial compared to that of the other elites. When such information may be of interest, documentation on the origins of the bishops is given in the footnotes.

It is worth mentioning, finally, that the labor leaders are included in Figure 1.1, as they are in subsequent tabulations (except where otherwise noted). The inclusion of the labor leaders, whose origins are predominantly lower class, makes the background of the elites as a whole appear more modest than it actually is. This is noted when relevant. For example, the distribution of parental occupation, without the labor leaders, is 2 percent manual, 5 percent routine nonmanual, 41 percent middle sector, 23 percent professional, and 29—as compared to 22—percent upper class.

[7] Note that the divide is not precisely between ''blue collar'' and ''white collar''; the routine nonmanual category also supplies many labor leaders. Compare Reeve Vanneman, ''The Occupational Composition of American Classes,'' *American Journal of Sociology* 82 (1977): 783-807, and Arno J. Mayer, ''The Lower Middle Class as Historical Problem,'' *Journal of Modern History* 47 (1975): 409-436.

[8] Although the ARENA and MDB politicians are far apart on most matters of public policy, there are essentially no differences in their social origins, so that they remain undifferentiated in this part of the analysis. For an extensive study of the occupational composition of Brazilian politicians (rather than of their fathers and fathers-in-law), see David V. Fleischer, ''Thirty Years of Legislative Recruitment in Brazil: An Analysis of the Social Backgrounds and Career Advancement Patterns of 1548 Federal Deputies, 1945-1975,'' paper presented at the Tenth World Congress of the International Political Science Association, Edinburgh, Scotland, August 16-20, 1976.

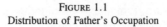

FIGURE 1.1
Distribution of Father's Occupation

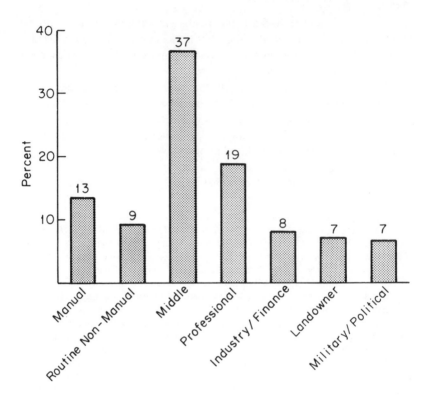

By contrast, the civil servants have shallower roots in the top political and military echelons and, indeed, with the capitalist class as a whole—that is, with the large businessmen and landowners. The tendency is highlighted by separating the directors of the public companies, the technocrats *par excellence*, from the ministerial bureaucrats. On the average, the directors of the state-owned corporations are the quintessential sons of the middle sectors. In this respect, they are very close to the military.[9]

Two facts emerge from these tabulations. The most obvious is the huge distance between the labor leadership and the rest of the elites, particularly the businessmen; the class division is unmistakable. There are also less pronounced divisions among the state managers, the politicians, and the businessmen. The ministerial and public company bureaucrats are distinctly

[9] The predominantly middle sector origins of the Brazilian officer corps are documented by Alfred Stepan, *The Military in Politics* (Princeton: Princeton University Press, 1971).

TABLE 1.1
Father's Occupation by Elite Sector

Father's Occupation	Elite Sector					
	Labor	Public Companies	Ministerial Bureaucrats	Politicians	Business	Totals
Manual	52%	8%	3%	2%	1%	13% (29)
Routine Nonmanual	23	17	8	—	5	9 (20)
Middle Class	21	42	41	44	40	37 (83)
Professional	4	17	28	28	18	19 (42)
Large Industry & Finance	—	10	10	2	16	8 (19)
Landowner	—	6	5	15	8	7 (16)
Top Military & Political	—	—	5	9	12	7 (16)
Totals	100 (48)	100 (12)	100 (39)	100 (43)	100 (83)	100 (225)

NOTE: Row and column totals are in parentheses, as they are in subsequent tabulations.

middle class in origin, whereas the businessmen are more truly of the upper class.

A qualitative difference also exists between the businessmen and the politicians. A high proportion of the latter come from the landed elite, as might be expected from the dispersion of their geographical base. While a few of the businessmen are drawn from the agrarian sector, they are more typically second-generation industrialists and bankers or the sons of military and political leaders.[10]

The pattern is repeated with the educational background of the elites. Again, the gulf between the labor leaders and the true elites is enormous. While there is some dispersion of men of poorly educated fathers into the key sectors—for example, a quarter of the elites whose fathers have only primary schooling or less become politicians, and almost half of those

[10] As shown in Table 1.1, differences in parental occupation within the elite establishment proper are statistically very modest, and conclusions about dissimilarities between the businessmen and the civil servants, for example, cannot be firmly drawn from this evidence alone. Nevertheless, the differences are replicated and reinforced by other measures presented in this and the following chapter; the cumulative signs of the heterogeneity of the elites are substantial.

whose fathers failed to get beyond high school become industrialists and bankers—most of the elites themselves are university graduates. The lack of a university education inclines potential elites to the labor leadership, and the exceptions are symptomatic. For example, a substantial number, nearly a third, of the elites with only secondary education enter the business community, where formal schooling counts for less than it does among the politicians and the civil servants.

These results contain in embryo much of what is elaborated in the remainder of the chapter: the ostracism of the labor leaders, the class division between them and the businessmen, and the variable functions of class endowment and educational attainment for the businessmen and the elites associated with the state itself.[11]

TABLE 1.2
Elite Sector by Education

Elite Sector	Father's Education			
	Primary	*Secondary*	*University*	*Totals*
Labor	40%	25%	2%	22% (53)
Civil Service	15	28	28	23 (54)
Politicians	25	6	24	20 (47)
Business	20	41	46	35 (83)
Totals	100 (87)	100 (63)	100 (87)	100 (237)

Elite Sector	Elite Education			
	Primary	*Secondary*	*University*	*Totals*
Labor	93%	59%	6%	22% (53)
Civil Service	—	4	30	23 (54)
Politicians	—	6	25	20 (43)
Business	7	31	39	35 (84)
Totals	100 (15)	100 (49)	100 (174)	100 (238)

NOTE: "Primary" includes a few fathers with no formal schooling.

[11] The bishops depart somewhat from these patterns. Their class origins appear to be

Education

Regional Variations

Brazil is remarkable among developing countries for having maintained its geographical boundaries over a period of centuries. Yet the national territory is so large that regional variations are considerable, even with most of the population concentrated near the litoral and toward the center-south.[12]

The impact of regional inequalities on educational attainment is easier to predict for the general population than for the elites. The rural areas are backward, and the opportunities of those born there are diminished by this fact. The disadvantages of being born in the interior are all the more pronounced if access to higher education is considered. The metropolitan areas provide the widest variety of educational opportunities, and migration becomes practically a prerequisite for entrance into the prestigious universities.[13]

---

extremely mixed. About one-fourth of the sample of bishops for whom information is complete ($n = 11$) come from the working class; another one-fourth are from truly upper-class families (the top three categories of the seven-point occupation scale). The educational status of the fathers of the bishops is a bit lower on the average than that of the fathers of the other elites. In sum, the bishops tend to be socially heterogeneous and more upwardly mobile than the rest of the elites. Although it is impossible to prove the hypothesis with the available evidence, this configuration fits well with the special nature of the bishops' political views, analyzed in subsequent chapters.

[12] Because it is not essential to understanding the power structure, I omit a full discussion of the regional origins of the elites and their migration patterns. It should be noted, however, that at the elite level São Paulo is the most insular of the regions. Although few of the elites who are born there leave São Paulo, only a negligible fraction of outsiders take up residence in the state. Rio is just as possessive of her native sons as São Paulo, but she admits a greater number of out-of-staters to elite status. The temptation to view São Paulo as cosmopolitan stems from the state's variety of European and Asian ethnic groups. But first-generation immigrants do not gain public office, and they seldom become captains of industry. Most of the Paulista elites are businessmen rather than politicians or civil servants. They control vast amounts of wealth, and they make up the largest pool of entrepreneurial talent in Brazil. They are also extremely private, a collectivity with tribal qualities. See Simon Schwartzman, *São Paulo e o Estado Nacional* (São Paulo: Difusão Européia do Livro, 1975); Schwartzman, "Twenty Years of Representative Democracy in Brazil," in *Mathematical Approaches to Politics*, ed. Hayward Alker, Jr., Karl Deutsch and Antoine H. Stoetzel (San Francisco: Jossey-Bass, 1973); Richard M. Morse, *Formação Histórica de São Paulo* (São Paulo: Difusão Européia do Livro, 1970); and Paulo Nogueira Filho, *Idéais e Lutas de um Burguês Progressista*, 3 vols. (Rio de Janeiro: José Olympio, 1965-1967). It should also be noted that many top positions in the armed forces have been filled by men from outside Rio and São Paulo, most notably, from Rio Grande do Sul. There seems to be a tacit recognition among the military that their own top people, and indeed the president of the republic, should not be drawn from the most powerful "civilian" states.

[13] See Michael P. Todaro, "Rural-Urban Migration, Unemployment, and Job Probabilities:

As for the elites, it is unlikely that regional parochialism alone keeps them from the universities. On the whole, they are well-educated. Nevertheless, the kind of education they receive may be affected by their regional origins. The variety of professional specialization in the periphery is restricted. The elites may overcome this obstacle by migrating to the central cities. Even so, the experience of growing up in the interior may limit their educational horizons, with the result that their choice of university specialization turns out to be traditional in comparison with the paths followed by their peers from Rio and São Paulo.

Figure 1.2 addresses the simpler question of regional variation in the amount of formal education. Elites raised in the interior began with a handicap and those who grew up in Rio, the cultural capital, were advantaged. Fewer fathers of the regionally peripheral elites attended the university than those from the center. The low incidence of university education among the fathers of the Paulista elites reflects the business ambience of the state. Although the Paulista elites tend to have more education than their fathers, there are still fewer university graduates among them than among their colleagues from other states. A university diploma is not so indispensable a credential in the marketplace as in the public sector.[14]

We are now in a position to examine the kind as well as the quantity of elite education. Elites raised in the interior, it has been proposed, should filter into the more traditional faculties either because the range of offerings at the universities in the interior is limited or because, even if they pass through universities at the center, a certain parochialism has limited their vocational horizons.

Table 1.3 shows that some regional maldistribution between traditional and modern preparation exists. The most venerable professions are law and medicine, with engineering of more recent but still respectable vintage. The newest professions are economics and business administration, so new that they hardly enjoyed professional status until after 1964.

Law is by far the most common specialization among Brazilian elites, and those raised in the interior take up the law with greater frequency than

---

Recent Theoretical and Empirical Research,'' in *Economic Factors in Population Growth*, ed. Ansley J. Coale (New York: Halsted, 1976); Lorene Y. L. Yap, ''Internal Migration and Economic Development in Brazil,'' *Quarterly Journal of Economics* 90 (1976): 119-137; and Yap, ''Rural-Urban Migration and Urban Underdevelopment in Brazil,'' *Journal of Development Economics* 3 (1976): 227-243.

[14] The bivariate association shown in Figure 1.2 is not spurious; it is not a result of the small importance that businessmen attach to formal schooling. Paulista businessmen differ not only from the elites generally but from other businessmen as well. When the relationship between regional origins and education is broken down for each of the three major groups—politicians, state managers, and businessmen—the contingent from São Paulo has the least formal education among industrialists and bankers.

FIGURE 1.2
Education by Region of Origin

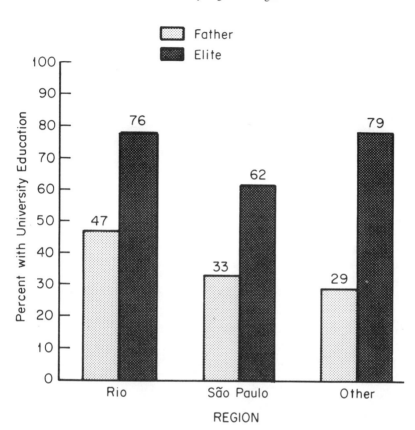

those born in the center. Conversely, members of the more technocratic professions, such as engineering and economics, come disproportionately from the Rio and São Paulo regions.[15]

Thus, if only the amount of education is considered, elites from the interior would seem to have caught up with their peers from the center. The peripheral elites have taken the first step in catching up by overcoming

[15] The predominance of lawyers among the geographically peripheral elites is not due to the prevalence of politicians from the interior. When the politicians are set aside, the total number of lawyers is naturally reduced, since most of the politicians are graduates of law faculties. But the tendency for nonpoliticians from the interior to be trained in the law remains just as strong. Thus, whatever the sectoral affiliation of the elites—politics, business, or the civil service—the incidence of lawyers among the elites from the interior is higher than among elites from the center.

TABLE 1.3
University Specialization by Region of Origin

	Region of Origin			
Faculty	*Rio*	*São Paulo*	*Other*	*Totals*
Law	41%	44%	54%	47% (81)
Engineering	25	22	12	19 (33)
Economics[a]	16	20	7	13 (23)
Medicine	5	2	12	8 (12)
Other[b]	13	12	15	13 (23)
Totals	100 (63)	100 (41)	100 (68)	100 (172)

[a] Includes public and business administration.
[b] Includes a mixture of mostly traditional specializations: the military, philosophy and letters, fine arts, and the like.

the educational deficit of their fathers. Yet they have not taken the second step, in appreciable numbers, of specializing in the modern professions. The obverse of this pattern is the upsurge of technocratic training among elites from the center.

The lag of the periphery behind the center does not constitute an iron law. Individual departures from the pattern can be cited, perhaps the most notable being Reis Veloso, an economist and long-time minister of planning from one of the most peripheral of Brazilian states, Piauí. Furthermore, it is conceivable that the continued spread of higher education in Brazil will correct this disequilibrium.

But there is no evidence of a countertrend among the present generation of elites. The regionally marginal elites might have been expected to take up "deviant" specializations precisely because they are peripheral. Born of fathers whose education does not meet traditional elite standards, they may have less of the burden of tradition to bear. Yet little leapfrogging seems to have occurred. On the whole, the peripheral elites have passed through a more traditional educational experience, on their way beyond a poorer educational inheritance, than the elites at the modern core of Brazil.[16]

[16] This two-stage sequence is analogous to a pattern found in various countries, including

One other question remains to be answered about the relationship be-tween regional and educational differences. It concerns where, specifically, the elites receive their higher education. Are there in Brazil one or more universities recognized for socializing elites-to-be in the habits of com-mand, as in England (Oxbridge), Japan (Tokyo University), and the United States (the Ivy League)? For the Brazilian military, the Superior War College carries out this function. But the pattern among civilian elites is varied.

No single university dominates elite higher education, even though two of them come close to a monopoly in their regions. One is the federal university in Rio (UFRJ), the other is the state university of São Paulo (USP). Nearly half (43 percent) of the elites have graduated from these two universities, and no other faculty accounts for more than 3 percent of the elites. The politicians, being the most regionally diverse of the elites, are the likeliest to have attended universities in the interior. But these are separate universities, located in the capitals of the various states.

While such dispersion suggests the variety of educational experiences that the elites have undergone, it is not by itself a mark of heterogeneous socialization. However, the common experience implicit in attending the same university is probably less standardizing for the civilian elites than for the military. The Superior War College is a unified faculty located in one place, like a seminary. By contrast, the UFRJ is composed of several faculties without a central campus and without common living quarters for students. The Superior War College has developed a homogeneous program of professional and political training. But, the bishops aside, no such course of study prevails in the scholastic history of the civilian elites.

In summary, with the exception of the military, no one university ex-ercises a predominant role in the socialization of Brazilian elites.[17] What-ever public identity the elites acquire at the universities seems instead to be a matter of professional specialization. Moreover, the variety of spe-cialization is concentrated rather than spread evenly across the regions. Elites born and raised in the center are more likely than those from the interior to have received technical training. By comparison, the peripheral elites tend to be unmodern. To a degree, therefore, regional and profes-

---

the most developed. In South Asia, Srinivas has dubbed the phenomenon "Sanskritization." As peripheral groups modernize, moving away from "the little tradition," they adopt the "great tradition" of the elites. At the same time, the modernizing elites begin to abandon the great tradition for more secular, developmental values. The result is a phasing of the differences between the cultures of the center and the periphery, with those on the outside wearing the hand-me-downs of the vanguard elites. See M. N. Srinivas, *Social Change in Modern India* (Berkeley: University of California Press, 1967).

[17] This pattern stands in striking contrast to the Oxbridge phenomenon in England and to the traditions of the *grand corps* in France, examined by Ezra N. Suleiman, *Elites in French Society: The Politics of Survival* (Princeton: Princeton University Press, 1978).

sional solidarities overlap. But they do so only indirectly, for few of the elites have actually attended the same faculties. On balance, the university experiences of Brazilian elites are diverse. There is no civilian counterpart to the designed camaraderie of the military.[18]

Cohort Differences in Education

All of the evidence adduced so far about regional variations in elite education suggests that the pattern of higher education among elites has been changing. Rio and São Paulo are vanguard regions. If elites from these areas are more likely than their colleagues from the interior to enter faculties like economics and business administration, it may also be that the younger elites are more likely to do so than the older cohorts. Figure 1.3 confirms this expectation.

Enrollments in law have declined; enrollments in economics and administration have gone up; the numbers of elites with degrees in other fields (not shown) fluctuate irregularly over time.

There is little doubt that the decline in law graduates and the increase in specialization in engineering and economics reflect historical change. Economists could be early starters, entering the elite at a young age and leaving for one reason or another sooner than the lawyers, who might start late but last longer. Such differential career cycles might have produced the configuration interpreted here as a historical trend. But the possibility seems farfetched. Brazil produced almost no professional economists until after 1945. Until then, there were virtually no economics faculties and little programmatic planning. There are more economists as well as engineers in Brazil now, and it is natural that movements in university specialization mirror this change.[19]

A more serious possibility of misinterpretation lies in another direction. Despite the upsurge of the *técnicos*, the lawyers have not disappeared from the corridors of power. Even when the politicians are discounted, many lawyers remain within the banks and the large industrial companies and in the governmental bureaucracy. The lawyers are no longer the lords of creation in Brazil, but they retain considerable power in an expanding and complex polity, even in an authoritarian one that craves legitimacy.

To recapitulate: temporal as well as regional differences are manifest

[18] Stepan observes that between 1950 and 1967, 50 percent of the graduates of the Superior War College were in fact civilians, a policy that was encouraged by the military command. See Stepan, *The Military in Politics*. It is extremely doubtful, however, that a similar proportion of the active military has attended civilian universities.

[19] Compare Peter M. Blau, "Inferring Mobility Trends from a Single Study," *Population Studies* 16 (1962): 79-85.

FIGURE 1.3

Higher Education in Law, Engineering, and Economics/Administration, by Age Cohort

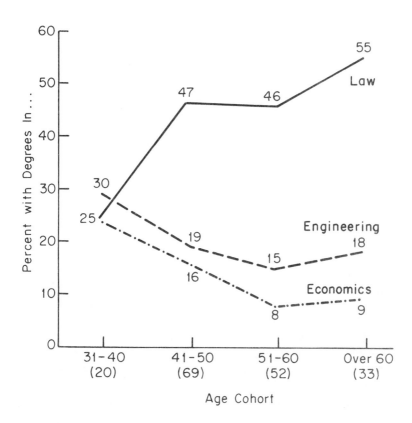

among Brazilian elites. Cohort attachments may be no firmer than those based on regional parochialism. It is difficult to identify civilian elite cliques in Brazil whose membership is based on old school ties. There are many more new and separate schools than old and select schools through which the elites have filtered.

Yet it is also evident that the educational experiences of the central and peripheral, and the younger and older, elites differ in ways that accord with an aggregate transformation of the elite structure, in particular with a renovation in the make-up of the state bureaucracy. During the late sixties and early seventies, the time of the great spurt in Brazilian development, the cutting edge of elite recruitment was concentrated on the central regions and on the younger middle sectors.

Education and Class

The task is no longer to verify the basic association between class and education, since this was made plain enough at the beginning of the chapter. Instead, the objective is to clarify the interaction between the two factors: to trace the variable use of both mechanisms in the recruitment of elites into different sectors.

The fundamental hypothesis is straightforward. Formal education tends to compensate for class deficiencies. Its efficacy, however, is contingent on a middle-class background or better. Even then, a university education is generally more useful as an entree to the public sector; it means less in the world of Brazilian business. The confluence of this pair of factors produces a stratum of highly educated state managers from modest families.

The simplest way to proceed is to start with the outcome of the mobility process—for example, with the educational composition of the elite sectors—and to estimate the differential importance of class and education as sorting devices. Table 1.4 provides this base line. It shows the distribution of professional specialization for the elite groups. Most of the politicians are lawyers, as are nearly half of the businessmen. Law is also the most common area of preparation for the civil servants, but it does not weigh so heavily in this sector as it does among the politicians, the industrialists, and the bankers.

The interesting fact is not the popularity of law among the politicians but rather the incidence of lawyers among the businessmen, joined with the technocratic cast of the civil servants. The pattern confounds black-and-white renditions of the chasm between state and society. The businessmen need legal skills to cope with the bureaucracy. The businessmen are also a comparatively traditional group; traditional professions such as the law are likely to be common among them.

It is primarily among the state managers, and to a lesser extent the businessmen, that the technical professions, engineering and economics, assume significance. In large measure, the technocratic qualifications of the state managers explain the skew in governmental recruitment toward the center, where increasing numbers of technical specialists are produced.

The argument can be taken a step further. Elites who rise from the middle sectors depend not only on access to higher education but also on training in technical skills for which the demand is great. It is the kind and not simply the amount of education that puts them on the elite track. Table 1.5 substantiates this hypothesis.

Among the lawyers, for example, a higher-than-average proportion is drawn from the leading military-political families, and the engineers come disproportionately from industrial-banking backgrounds. On the other

TABLE 1.4
University Specialization by Elite Sector

| Faculty | Elite Sector | | | Totals |
	Politicians	Civil Service	Business	
Law	63%	29%	49%	47%
				(82)
Engineering	9	27	23	21
				(34)
Economics	5	23	12	13
				(23)
Medicine	14	4	6	7
				(12)
Other	9	17	10	12
				(14)
Totals	100	100	100	100
	(44)	(52)	(69)	(175)

NOTE: Labor leaders are omitted. Only ten of them have attended universities. The bishops are also deleted. All of them have, by training, the equivalent of higher education (in theology); in addition, two of the eleven bishops interviewed have law degrees.

hand, the economics and business administration faculties are crowded with elites from the middle sectors.

The sons of good families enter, more often than not, the traditional faculties of law and engineering. Their problem is not upward mobility in the conventional sense. They may surpass their fathers by reaching the apex of Brazilian society, above mere respectability, but university specialization is not apt to be crucial to this climb. In the absence of definite signals from the educational system, save that a university degree is desirable, the sons of upper-class fathers can be expected to enter the traditional faculties.

But upward mobility is still a challenge to the sons of middle-sector families, and the university furnishes an important mechanism for overcoming the deficiencies of their class endowment. They can be expected to choose faculties that are less crowded and whose graduates are in demand. The more lawyers there are, the more competition there is likely to be among them for the few truly elite positions. And if a law degree itself does not distinguish among the applicants for these positions, then the criteria of discrimination and selection are likely to involve nonmeritocratic factors such as class style and family connections. In the struggle for preferment, the traditional professionals from upper-class families have

TABLE 1.5
Father's Class Position by Elite Faculty

Father's Occupation	Faculty					
	Law	Engi-neering	Economics	Medicine	Other	Totals
Manual	6%	—	—	—	—	3% (5)
Routine Nonmanual	3	3	19	—	9	5 (9)
Middle Class	35	33	62	58	35	40 (67)
Professional	25	33	5	33	17	24 (40)
Large Industry & Finance	8	18	5	8	9	10 (16)
Landowner	9	6	5	—	22	9 (15)
Top Military & Political	14	6	5	—	9	10 (16)
Totals	100 (79)	99 (33)	101 (21)	99 (12)	101 (23)	101 (168)

NOTES: Labor leaders are omitted.

Because of rounding error, marginal totals will occasionally stray from 100 percent in tabulations throughout the text.

other resources besides their diplomas; those from below do not. Certification in the traditional professions is thus less valuable a means of mobility for the middle sectors than training in technical areas.

Economics and administration are the faculties that the sons of middle-sector families probably perceived as being accessible in the first place. They promise middle-management security. We need not impute historical prescience to the middle sectors for their luck in choosing careers that were to yield them a bonanza. It would be fanciful to argue that the sons of the middle sectors devoted themselves to economics and administration for the purpose of becoming elites. If anything, the process works the other way around: they became elites by reason of their professional qualifications, and they were in the right place (the regional center) at the right time (after 1964). Yet they are all undeniably ambitious men, and university education is a key step toward upward mobility. Specialization in economics and administration imparts a competitive advantage, relative to their modest origins.

University education, then, may be characterized as a necessary but not sufficient condition for entrance into the Brazilian elite. For some groups, like the businessmen, it is less necessary than for others. For the civil servants, it is crucial. For the politicians, higher education seems to function more as a pathway beyond regional parochialism than as a device for mobility beyond their class inheritance.

The most striking feature of the workings of class and education is the interaction between them. Not only is access to education conditioned by class, as we would expect; it is also the case that the uses to which education is put, the significance of its role in elite mobility, depend on class origins. As a rule, the more modest the social background of the elites, the more crucial is the role of formal education. Educational qualifications affect, in turn, the sorting of the elites into the public and private sectors.

The telling point is thus the contribution that university education makes at the margin. The tendency is illustrated in Figure 1.4, which presents, for each of the major elite groups, the incidence of university education among those whose fathers did not obtain a university degree.

The characteristic immobility of the labor leaders is clear. They are below the middle-class threshold that makes higher education attainable to begin with.[20] More generally, across the elites as a whole, education is the key factor in the mobility of those from the middle sectors, the civil servants being the most thoroughly middle class of the elites. Virtually none of the elites has less education than that attained by the previous generation; but this fact is trivial, since by definition elites are not downwardly mobile. The decisive pattern is the extent of upward mobility that education provides for elites of modest origins. Thus, for example, while only 16 percent of middle-sector fathers attended a university, four out of five of their sons have a university degree.

The importance of education for the middle sectors can be specified more precisely by correlating the educational levels of the elites and their fathers within each parental occupational category. For all categories except the middle sectors, the correlation is about .30, signifying that the amount of education that the elites receive depends significantly on the education of their fathers.[21] This is as true for elites of working-class families (low

---

[20] It is questionable that higher education improves the mobility chances even of the few labor leaders with a university degree, a point suggested by the following detail. The average age at which the nonlabor elites receive their diplomas is twenty-two. Most of the labor leaders, however, are in their thirties by the time they graduate. There is a night-school quality to the formal studies of the labor leaders. The later they obtain their degrees, the less useful they are likely to be as a resource for moving up.

[21] The coefficient is Pearson's *r*, calculated using six-point scales ranging from no formal schooling to complete university education.

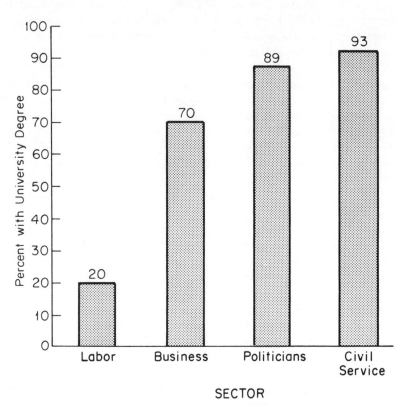

FIGURE 1.4
Elites with University Education, Whose Fathers Did Not Obtain a University Degree, by
Elite Sector

education) as for the sons of upper-class fathers (high education). But for
the elites of middle-sector background, the father-son correlation is a mere
.05. The elites from this stratum, more than any other, use formal education
to bypass the handicaps of their social origins.

There is a certain just proportion to the distribution of class and educational attributes among Brazilian elites. The labor leaders are at the lower
end, and the businessmen on top. The bureaucrats tend to be in the middle
not only because so many of them are from middle-class families but also
because they depend so much on education and are in a social position to
take advantage of it, as a way up from their origins. The politicians have
more distinguished origins. But their training appears outmoded, and historical circumstance rendered them, during the height of the authoritarian
period, obsolete.[22]

[22] In one respect, the foregoing analysis reveals more about where the elites come from

Marriage and Mobility

The smoothness of the findings presented so far is partly a reflection of the fact that analysis has been restricted to a few variables. The problem is not so much the occasional deviant case—the successful capitalist born to a working-class family or the state manager with an impeccably aristocratic heritage—as that the elites do not survive by class and education alone, at least as measured until now. Inspection of the marriage patterns of the elites helps clarify their mobility paths.

Elites, like ordinary people, tend to marry within their own class. To the extent that this is true, it is natural to expect the distributions of occupations among fathers and fathers-in-law to be similar. In principle, a significant amount of cross-class marriage may underlie this similarity, just as the relation between two variables is constrained but not determined by their marginal distributions. But a stronger case can be made for exogamy when the distributions of occupations are discrepant. If more fathers-in-law than fathers are drawn from among leading industrialists and bankers, while most of the fathers are of middle-sector origins or below,

---

than about how they arrived where they are. Class background and educational attainment, modulated by regional and cohort differences, provide the basic resources, but the influence of these factors may taper off with time. As the elites progress in their careers, various contingencies come into play, reducing the impact of earlier socialization on mobility. The most important of these contingencies is the set of organizational rules and professional roles that influence the direction and pace of advancement, beyond the initial positioning traceable to class, education, and the like. The elites were asked: "We would like to know in what positions and in which companies or organizations you have worked (since leaving the university)? Could you tell us what were your three most important jobs, the name of the company or government agency, and the dates associated with each one?"

The resulting information must be treated gingerly. The older elites regularly claim that their first important jobs were of high status, compared to the rather second-string ranking of jobs in which the younger elites report having started their careers. The elites upgrade their standard of "importance" as they grow older and accumulate job histories replete with prestigious positions, forgetting to mention their first and no doubt humbler classifications in the career track. Their junior colleagues do the opposite. Having skimpier *vitae*, they mention their first rather than their first important job.

This methodological detour aside, it is possible to trace the kinds of positions through which the elites pass: (1) "private," including the practice of law and medicine as well as "business" generally; (2) "public," that is, governmental and political activities; and (3) "other," usually either education (for example, university teaching) or some other form of parastatal activity such as work in the labor syndicates. The upshot of this analysis is that the politicians are the most laterally mobile of the elites, moving with the greatest frequency from one sector to another. Next in line are the civil servants, then the businessmen, and finally the labor leaders. In brief, class roots cling more tenaciously to the labor leaders and the businessmen than to the politicians and the state managers; formal education creates opportunities for lateral as well as vertical mobility. The ranking of the four elite groups in ascending order of lateral mobility corresponds closely to their ranking according to the amount of education.

the putative evidence for upward mobility is compelling, even before the relative frequency of shifts from one category to another is ascertained.

When the respective distributions are examined side-by-side, no significant differences emerge between the occupations of fathers and fathers-in-law in any of the elite groups. Even if the incidence of exogamy is considerable, it has not resulted in a set of fathers-in-law much different occupationally from the fathers of the elites. By and large, the elites do not seem markedly upward- or downwardly mobile through marriage.

With this overall pattern in view, Table 1.6 broaches the question of endogamy/exogamy directly, depicting the incidence of within- and between-strata marriage for the entire elite sample.[23] Endogamy is most common at the lowest, manual end of the occupational spectrum. More than three-quarters of the elites born to fathers designated as manual workers marry into working-class families, and none of them marries above the middle sectors. Endogamy is also very common at the other, upper-class end of the hierarchy, while a bit more movement becomes visible along the middle ranges. Tracing the probability of endogamy from the bottom of the stratification system to the top produces a U-shaped curve, high at the extremes and lower in the middle. Where class positions are well-defined, within-class marriage prevails.[24]

Yet there is also appreciable movement among segments of the upper class. For example, the relationship between the landed and the industrial-banking families is notably asymmetrical. Landed families are more likely to marry into industrial-banking families than vice versa, in part because backgrounds in large-scale business are more common than proprietorship over land among both the fathers and the fathers-in-law of the elites. This is less likely to have been the case a generation or two ago in Brazil.[25]

Furthermore, on the assumption that the landed gentry is not so powerful as it once was, elites from this stratum have an incentive to exogamy with members of a class on the rise, like the industrial-banking community. Elites from leading military and political families also show a disproportionate tendency to marry into industrial-financial families. Conversely, the scions of the business elite proper, those born into industrial and banking

[23] An index of endogamy has been devised that can be used with the type of data presented in Table 1.6; see David J. Strauss, "Measuring Endogamy," *Social Science Research* 6 (1977): 225-245. However, the percentage differences used here are adequate to the task of assessing the extent of endogamy/exogamy, and they focus attention on the shifts between specific occupational categories.

[24] Endogamy within the upper class may appear to be lower than it actually is because Table 1.6 retains the tripartite disaggregation of this stratum. When these categories are joined, it can be seen that endogamy at this level reaches 60 percent.

[25] See Warren Dean, *The Industrialization of São Paulo, 1880-1945* (Austin: University of Texas Press, 1969).

TABLE 1.6
Father-in-Law's Occupation by Father's Occupation:
Seven-Category Scales

Father's Occupation	Father-in-law's Occupation							
	Manual	Routine Non-manual	Middle Class	Profes-sional	Large Industry & Finance	Land-owner	Top Military & Political	Totals
Manual	76%	12%	12%	—	—	—	—	100% (26)
Routine Nonmanual	44	13	25	13	—	5	—	100 (16)
Middle Class	4	12	52	16	4	8	4	100 (77)
Professional	8	5	31	28	10	10	8	100 (39)
Large Industry & Finance	—	—	12	29	29	24	6	100 (17)
Landowner	—	—	—	29	50	14	7	100 (14)
Top Military & Political	—	6	13	31	25	13	13	101 (16)
Totals	17 (34)	8 (17)	31 (63)	19 (39)	11 (23)	9 (19)	5 (10)	100 (205)

families, are the least likely of all genuinely upper-class elements to marry outside their stratum, although they show some inclination for marriage into landed families. In brief, within the upper class, there is a tendency for the elites to marry into families who exercise control over investment and production.

However, while 60 percent of the upper-class elites marry within their class, close to a third of them report having married into families identified with the liberal professions. The offspring of professional fathers may enter upper-class families with greater ease than the children of the plain middle sectors. If a family has professional status, and especially if the status goes back as far as the father, the members of the family participate in a transitional stratum linking the middle sectors and the upper class.

The role of education in promoting limited exogamy deserves emphasis. Figure 1.5 presents the correlations between the occupations of fathers and fathers-in-law for the three main levels of parental education. The pattern is linear: exogamy is most common among the most highly educated families. To be sure, all of the correlations are positive; it would be unrealistic to suppose that education actually reverses the inertia toward endogamy. But it is equally clear that higher education erodes class-based barriers to exogamy.[26]

It should be remembered, however, that the businessmen are exceptional among the true elites in their comparatively low levels of formal education. Since education increases the chances of exogamy, the businessmen should be the most endogamous of the elites. The determining factor is not their

FIGURE 1.5
Correlations between Father's Occupation and Father-in-Law's Occupation,
by Father's Education

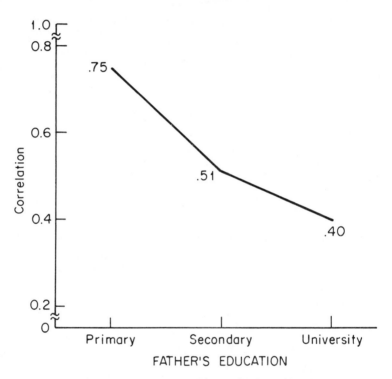

NOTE: Correlations are based on five-point occupational scales. Correlation for entire sample, regardless of father's education, is .69.

[26] Technically, it is possible for correlations between the occupational rankings of fathers and fathers-in-law to be quite high even though elites do not marry within the same class. There could be a constant difference between the rankings, such that the manual category marries regularly into the routine nonmanual, the routine nonmanual into the middle sectors, and so on. But inspection of the empirical distributions shows that this is not the case. Hence, the correlations shown here (and in Figure 1.6) are proper measures of endogamy, and they permit a more economical presentation than a series of cross-tabulations.

relative lack of education per se but the imperative of keeping control of property "within the family."[27]

Figure 1.6 documents the endogamous inclinations of the businessmen. The two elite groups most clearly defined in class terms, the businessmen and the labor leaders, are also the most endogamous. The politicians and the civil servants are also more endogamous than not, but the tendency is less pronounced in these sectors. The businessmen form the elite estate that is least permeable by way of marriage.[28]

The tendency of endogamy/exogamy to vary across the elite estates, peaking among the businessmen and declining among the politicians and civil servants, is plausible. The basis for demonstrating that marriage patterns may have changed over the years is much less secure, for longitudinal evidence is lacking. Yet the theoretical expectation is quite uncomplicated. It is reasonable to suppose that strict endogamy on the part of the elites should give way with changes in the social composition of elite recruits. University education has spread in Brazil, together with the entrance of the middle sectors into elite positions. As increasing numbers of candidates from the middle sectors appear on the boundaries of the establishment, more of them marry into segments of the upper class than was previously the case. Social mobilization, an aggregate phenomenon, implies individual social mobility, and the rise of the middle sectors may entail a certain democratization of marriage patterns among the elites.[29]

The problem of isolating such a trend across age cohorts is severe for most of the elites, but it is less acute within the business community. The careers of the politicians and the labor leaders, and probably of the civil servants, are more subject to unpredictable turns of political fortune than those of the businessmen, who are less exposed to public life. The indus-

[27] Distinctions between "class" power, "political" power, educational resources, and the like, and their differential effects on endogamy/exogamy have been around for some time. See, for example, William J. Goode, "Family Systems and Social Mobility," in *Families in East and West*, ed. Reuben Hill and Rene Konig (The Hague: Mouton, 1970), pp. 120-136.

[28] To say that businessmen are inclined to marry within their class does not mean that they all marry into business families. It does mean that they are less mobile by way of marriage than the other elites. In principle, this suggests that the occasional businessman who rises from working-class or routine nonmanual origins is more likely to have married into a family of similar background than into a "business family." In practice, there are very few businessmen from the lower classes. It is their "studied" lack of education that seems to be the key factor in the relative immobilism of the industrialists and bankers.

[29] See Donald J. Treiman, "Industrialization and Social Stratification," in *Social Stratification: Research and Theory for the 1970s*, ed. Edward O. Laumann (Indianapolis: Bobbs-Merrill, 1970), and Lawrence E. Hazelrigg and Maurice A. Garnier, "Occupational Mobility in Industrial Societies: A Comparative Analysis of Differential Access to Occupational Ranks in Seventeen Countries," *American Sociological Review* 41 (1976): 498-511.

FIGURE 1.6
Correlations between Father's Occupation and Father-in-Law's Occupation, by Elite Sector

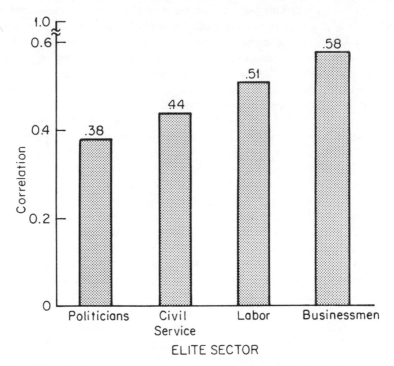

NOTE: All correlations were computed using the five-category occupational scales.

trialists and the bankers are not usually purged, exiled, or otherwise de-
toured by political forces. In their case, differences in the social origins
of younger and old cohorts may be taken as a reflection of demographic
changes in the social composition of candidates for leadership positions
in the business world. In the case of the politicians, by contrast, the
supposition that the older cohorts constitute a representative sample of a
prior historical generation is considerably more tenuous. Political events
have intervened at least as much as demographic transformations to alter
the social composition of political cohorts.

The methods for justifying this set of assumptions and for testing the
hypothesis of a decline in endogamy among the younger cohorts of businessmen are rather involved, but the outcome of the inquiry may be stated
simply.[30] The younger businessmen tend to be more exogamous than their

---

[30] The first step is to trace differences in the occupations of fathers and fathers-in-law

predecessors. Although the trend is not monotonic, it is clearly in the expected direction; the tradition of endogamy within the capitalist class has probably faded during the postwar period.[31]

Increasing exogamy among the industrialists and bankers is not simply the result of greater upward mobility through marriage on the part of the junior executives. When the data are examined case-by-case, both downward- as well as upwardly mobile marriages emerge with frequency among

---

across elite cohorts. It is only among the businessmen that the correlations between age and the occupational classifications of fathers and fathers-in-law are significantly positive (.26 and .22 respectively). The older the industrialist or banker, the higher the social ranking of his father and father-in-law. However, the cohort-related differences may reflect a career-cycle pattern rather than a historical trend. It may be that the younger businessmen are not true elites but rather junior executives, many of whom fail to make it to the top. Perhaps the younger cohorts during any historical period are drawn from a mixture of middle- as well as upper-class candidates. After an initial testing, the upper-class recruits may be more likely to succeed to the key positions, while a disproportionate attrition takes place among executives of humbler origins.

While there is no way to exclude this possibility altogether, one bit of side information renders it less damaging to a historical interpretation of the data than it may appear at first glance. It is conceivable that the younger businessmen are high executives in the companies ranked toward the bottom of the top five hundred manufacturing and the top two hundred financial enterprises and that they are under-represented in the board rooms of the largest companies. If the corporations that the younger executives manage were smaller and presumably less important than the ones headed by the older elites, the business community would be stratified such that the more youthful (and generally middle-sector) types controlled organizations peripheral to the inner circle of major enterprises, and there would be no reason to view this hierarchy-by-age as indicative of generational change. However, the correlation between the liquid assets of industrial corporations (deposits in the case of bank) and the age of the corporate executives is a wholly insignificant -.07. Nor is there any association between the class origins of the business elites and the size of the companies they direct. It is still possible that, within a given corporation, the older executives are more powerful than their junior partners. The normal operation of the rules of seniority would seem to guarantee this internal stratification by age. On the other hand, the practice of maintaining aged figureheads seems to be fairly common. It is difficult, inside the executive offices of Brazilian companies, to rank the directors along a hierarchy of power by their age and titles.

In summary, there is no evidence that the stratification of the business community by age and social origins can be reduced to a career-cycle pattern alone. Certainly, the distribution of younger and older, and middle-sector versus upper-class, businessmen among the larger and smaller companies is random. The imputation of historical change in the selection of industrialists and bankers from different social strata is therefore a reasonable inference.

[31] The relevant correlations drop from .62 within the oldest cohort of businessmen (those sixty-one years of age and older) to .44 within the youngest (the thirty-one to forty year-olds). This trend can be expected to continue. The post-1964 economic plan in Brazil has placed a very high premium on recruiting "professionals"—for example, business school graduates, many of them with foreign training—rather than on simply hiring "relatives and friends." The skyrocketing salaries of these essentially middle-class managers have made them economically acceptable candidates for marriage into the upper class. See Jonathan Kandell, "The Bonus Babies of Brazil," *New York Times*, July 11, 1976: F3.

the younger cohorts. While males from middle-sector or professional families marry into upper-class families, it is also true that the sons of the upper-class businessmen often take brides from families "beneath them." It is in this dual sense that cross-class marriage has increased among the businessmen: the system has opened up, and down.

Thus, two significant historical trends are apparent within the business community. One is the opening-up of the recruitment system itself. There seem to be more business executives drawn from the middle sectors during the postwar period than was typical of an earlier generation.[32] Second, the exclusiveness of marital arrangements among the business elites has suffered some erosion. Cross-class marriages tend to be more common in the present than in the past.

Although a middle-sector endowment prevails among Brazilian elites, the politicians and in particular the businessmen have an upper-class edge. The civil servants make up for their modest origins by relying more than their fellow elites on university education in technical fields like economics and administration.

Very generally, the finding that like tends to marry like—that elite marriages take place more often within than between classes—is hardly surprising. Yet it reminds us that the family is at least as important a unit of mobility and of the consolidation of power as the individual in the process of elite selection.

University education blurs the differences between the middle sectors and the upper class. The sons of upper-class fathers are more likely to marry into professional families than into families identified with the ordinary middle sectors. It is a fine point whether such movement represents downward mobility on the part of the upper class. Though increasingly more common, university diplomas are possessed by only a tiny fraction of the Brazilian populace, and they carry a prestige that augments the chances of marriage into the true upper class. The absorption of ambitious and competent elements from the middle sectors does not represent, on the face of it, a threat to or a dilution of the power of the ruling class. On the contrary, it may serve to defuse potential conflict and to renovate, and thus sustain, the hierarchy.

It is precisely among the sectors where formal education counts for relatively little, among the businessmen and the labor leaders, that within-class marriage is most prevalent. The barriers against marriage between individuals from clearly disparate classes are formidable. To some extent,

[32] See the similar finding reported by Hartmut Kaeble, "Long-Term Changes in the Recruitment of the Business Elite: Germany Compared to the U.S., Great Britain and France since the Industrial Revolution," *Journal of Social History* 13 (1980): 404-423.

the tradition of endogamy among the businessmen is breaking down. But on the whole, like the labor leaders, they are still a more clannish group than the politicians and the state managers. By most standards, the social background of the politicians is as respectable as that of the businessmen. Yet the industrialists and the bankers are generally wealthier and less educated than the politicians, and considerations of class are more evident in their marital decisions.[33]

The process of elite recruitment has been scrutinized from various angles in order to convey a sense not only of the paths of elite mobility but also of the composite rationale of the structure of selection. The system affords mobility to the "qualified" sons of the middle sectors, while keeping working-class elements in quarantine and preserving the transmission of advantage from one generation of the upper class to the next. Viewed in the aggregate—that is, not merely as a series of background factors with differential weights for the life-changes of individual elites but as a structure for renewing and maintaining class dominance—the processes of elite recruitment in Brazil are complementary. The social composition of the system has probably changed, especially among the ranks of the state managers, but the elite hierarchy stays in place.

However, it would be misleading to infer from these materials that the wheels of the Brazilian power structure grind smoothly. The apparent complementarity of the class and educational routes to elitehood is only part of the story. The educational experiences of the elites do not seem especially coherent or conducive to integration, and there are strong traces of regional disparities among the elites that the universities do little to erase.

No binding association between diverse social backgrounds and political orientations need be posited to see that such differences constitute a potential source of interelite feuding. It is not so much that interests enter into conflict directly as a result of disparities in social origins and socialization. Rather, the variety of skills needed to direct a society like Brazil, hurtling toward development, impels the system to recruit elites from

---

[33] A similar tendency has been verified by Peter H. Smith, *Labyrinths of Power: Political Recruitment in Twentieth-Century Mexico* (Princeton: Princeton University Press, 1979), especially pp. 205-216. While there appears to be little intermarriage between business and political families in Mexico, as in Brazil, one important difference should not be forgotten. None of the top officials in Brazil is elected by popular vote, and there are significant divergences in the social profiles of Brazilian politicians compared to state managers. The distinction between politicians and bureaucrats-technocrats is not so sharp in Mexico. Furthermore, some Brazilian businessmen have prominent forebears in military and political circles.

previously untapped areas. The system becomes highly diverse and, in the economic sense, mobilized; yet it remains extremely hierarchical. Under these conditions, complexity itself may generate conflict, suggesting a need for the elites to establish codes of interaction. This is the topic of the next chapter.

TWO

Networks

The safest and least interesting assumption about elite networks in Brazil and elsewhere is that their full complexity will always be shrouded from view. Not even the members of these networks, much less outside analysts, can be expected to be aware of all the ramifications of social ties, even when they agree on the basic contours of the power structure.[1]

This observation relieves us of the naive assumption that a conspiratorial consciousness guides whatever regularities are encountered in elite linkages. Instead, it turns analytical interest toward the structures of elite relationships that do not depend on purposeful manipulation and that abide after the intrigues of powerful individuals are long forgotten. Brazilian elites are situated in a structure of interaction that is flexible in its capacity to absorb new elements while at the same time sturdy in its resistance to modification at the hands of individual actors.

The allied assumption that elite networks are powerful to the degree that linkages among elites are close is also fallacious. Inferences of this kind imply a tenuous extrapolation from the individual, or dyadic, to the structural level.[2] An elite system in which practically all ties are strong might be imposing yet brittle, lacking the capacity to absorb vigorous candidates from the outside and inclined toward an isolation with few resources for adapting to a changing environment. This perspective furnishes the point

[1] The seminal work on social networks in Brazil is by Anthony Leeds, "Brazilian Careers and Social Structure," *American Anthropologist* 66 (1964): 1321-1347.

[2] See Mark S. Granovetter, "The Strength of Weak Ties," *American Journal of Sociology* 78 (1973): 1360-1380. Almost all of the recent literature on social networks aims at the development of general solutions, and the empirical evidence used to test the models is drawn from a variety of sources, many of which do not involve "important" (for example, elite) data. As a rule, nothing substantive is assumed about the evidence. For an exception, see Ronald S. Burt, "Corporate Society: A Time Series Analysis of Network Structure," *Social Science Research* 4 (1975): 271-328. See also Mark Granovetter's critique of Edward O. Laumann and Franz U. Pappi, *Networks of Collective Action* (New York: Academic Press, 1976), *American Journal of Sociology* 83 (1978): 1538-1542.

of departure for my approach to the complementary functions of kinship and friendship bonds in Brazil.[3]

Because the data are complex, it is helpful to keep the main lines of analysis plainly in sight. The basic idea is twofold. First, the Brazilian power structure is formed by three major cleavages: one between urban labor and the elite establishment proper; another between those who run the state and those, like the businessmen, in whose presumed interest the state is run; and, finally, another between the church and the rest of the elites. Second, there is a class-specific division of labor between kinship and friendship linkages such that the density of kinship ties among the truly upper-class elites, like the businessmen, is greater than among the elites of predominantly middle-sector origins, where friendship ties prevail.

Thus, I am concerned with two aspects, the shape and the substance, of the Brazilian power structure. One involves mapping the sociometry among the elites: that is, depicting the axes of power around which elites in different positions are tied to and kept distant from one another. The second entails an investigation of the specific ways in which elite groups are bound together: that is, through multiple ties, principally of kinship and friendship.[4]

These two concerns are interconnected. At one extreme, a crystalline power structure can be imagined—one that is organized along a single dimension (the economically powerful and not-so-powerful, for example) and bound together by a single type of linkage, say, kinship. Relations

[3] The emphasis on kinship and friendship ties should not be viewed as an attempt to suggest that informal linkages among the elites supersede class loyalties on the one hand and, on the other, organizational and institutional affiliations. Except in ideal-typical discussions of bureaucracy and modernization, this perspective has never gained much currency. Jettisoning the dichotomy between formal and informal, or instrumental and effective, ties simply clears the way for the task of showing how they complement and reinforce one another. Nevertheless, it should be emphasized that class is an indirect relation; there is no such word as "class-ship." Compare Peter Flynn, "Class, Clientelism, and Coercion: Some Mechanisms of Internal Dependency and Control," *Journal of Commonwealth and Comparative Politics* 12 (1974): 133-156; Robert R. Kaufman, "The Patron-Client Concept and Macro-Politics: Prospects and Problems," *Comparative Studies in Society and History* 16 (1974): 284-308; Keith R. Legg, *Patrons, Clients, and Politicians: New Perspectives on Political Clientelism* (Berkeley: Institute of International Studies, 1975); Legg, "Political Participation, Ideologies of Participation, and Regime Stability: A Comparison of Pluralist and Clientelist Systems," paper presented at the meetings of the Midwest Political Science Association, Chicago, Illinois, April 24-26, 1980; L. E. Shiner, "Tradition/Modernity: An Ideal Type Gone Astray," *Comparative Studies in Society and History* 17 (1975): 245-252; and Richard A. Thompson, "A Theory of Instrumental Social Networks," *Journal of Anthropological Research* 29 (1973): 244-265.

[4] Compare Lois M. Berbrugge, "Multiplexity in Adult Friendships," *Social Forces* 57 (1979): 1286-1308, and Douglas Heckathorn, "The Anatomy of Social Network Linkages," *Social Science Research* 8 (1979): 222-252.

among Brazilian elites are considerably more complex than this. They are multistranded as well as multidimensional, and these properties render the power structure both permeable and resilient.

Indicators of kinship and friendship were gathered for three time periods: childhood, the university, and the present. The elites were asked whether they had friends and/or relatives in each of thirteen groups, ranging from politicians ("governors, senators, and federal deputies") through "large industrialists" to "lower- or middle-level public functionaries." Information on kinship was obtained for t_1 (childhood) and t_3 (present); information on friendship is available for t_2 (university) and t_3.[5]

The items generate an enormous amount of data. For each of the first two time points, there are thirteen variables, corresponding to the number of groups. For the present time, there are twenty-six variables, split between kinship and friendship linkages. The number of possible correlations between these indicators is a multiplicative function of their number.[6]

Let us begin by depicting the overall shape of the power structure, and use this as a bench mark for subsequent examination of the internal workings of the system.

The Form of the Power Structure

For the sake of simplicity, we may start by pooling information from the three time periods, ignoring the distinction between kinship and friendship ties. While the results of the analysis represent a composite, the general structure remains the same no matter how it is calibrated.[7]

---

[5] The questions are as follows: (1) "When you were growing up, before you reached the age of 18, do you recall if any of your relatives or members of your family belonged to the following 13 groups?" (2) "Could you tell me if any of your colleagues from the university now occupy positions in the following 13 groups?" (3) "Could you tell me if any of your relatives or friends currently occupy any position in the following 13 groups?" When responses were positive to (2) or (3), the elites were asked whether they had contact with their friends and/or relatives in the groups. In addition, for (3), kin were divided into *familiares* (immediate family) and *sogro ou cunhado* (father-in-law or brother-in-law). These distinctions have been abandoned in the analysis because they are practically nonexistent empirically: that is, contact is almost always maintained, and degrees of *parentesco* (kinship) are almost never distinguished.

[6] In general, with *n* groups, there are $n(n - 1)/2$ dyadic relations.

[7] Some features of the Brazilian power structure are not treated, even though the data are available to do so, because they are peripheral to the main lines of analysis. One of these should be mentioned, however, for it has theoretical and substantive importance in its own right: the question of asymmetry in elite linkages—that is, the problem of uneven reciprocity between the ties reported, for example, by the politicians with the state managers, as contrasted to the incidence of ties reported by the state managers with the politicians. The problem is significant since asymmetry in self-reported ties is often a sign of differential ranking in the

Networks are constructed not from the mere number of elite relationships but from the relations between relations—that is, from the tendency for ties with one key group to lead to ties with other significant actors and from the propensity for these linkages to cluster apart from those joining the lesser figures. Figure 2.1 locates the groups according to their proximity to one another, the proximity between any two groups being defined as the probability of having a linkage with one, given a linkage with the other. Thus, smoothing over differences in the period of ties and in the type of linkages, the sociogram is a condensed rendition of the relative distances between the groups with whom the elites have contact.[8]

The sharpest division is between the labor leaders and the rest of the elites, a division that is plainly one of class. The members of the elite establishment cluster to the right, yet within this grouping they are differentiated in significant ways. The military are located at some remove from the civilians. The politicians and, to a lesser extent, the top civil servants are positioned midway between the military and the economic elites. There are also small but consistent distances between the higher and lower echelons within each of the functional groupings. The state managers

---

pecking order. It is known that very powerful individuals sometimes report fewer links than the number attributed to them by others, because they are too busy to notice all but their most intimate and salient contacts. See Ronald S. Burt, ''Positions in Networks,'' *Social Forces* 55 (1976): 93-122, and James Davis and Samuel Leinhardt, ''The Structure of Positive Interpersonal Relations in Small Groups,'' in *Sociological Theories in Progress*, ed. Joseph Berger (Boston: Houghton-Mifflin Company, 1972).

With the Brazilian data, there is some suggestion that the state managers may under-report the extent of their ties. However, on close inspection, the asymmetry in the interpersonal relations of the civil servants turns out largely to be confined to their pre-adult kinship ties. Many of the elites report having kin among the top civil service when they were growing up, with the exception of the civil servants (and the labor leaders) themselves. But the asymmetry disappears by the present time. The pattern seems to reflect accurately the middle-sector milieu of the civil servants-to-be. The bishops, on the other hand, present the most interesting case of ''over-reporting'' linkages, even at the present time: they are inclined to report many more ties with the other elites than the other elites report having with them. The lack of reciprocity reflects in part a real lack of power among the bishops, as well as the fact that they are few in number and dispersed away from the centers of power. In general, the fact that the number of elite respondents in each of the sectors does not correspond proportionately to their numbers in the elite population makes it difficult to arrive at precise interpretations of the phenomenon of asymmetry in linkages. For a discussion of this and related problems, see Ronald S. Burt, ''Positions in Multiple Network Systems, Parts One and Two,'' *Social Forces* 56 (1977): 106-131 and 551-575.

[8] The method used is smallest-space analysis. It generates results similar to those of factor analysis without some of the latter's restrictive assumptions (for example, interval-level measurement). See Joseph B. Kruskal and Myron Wish, *Multidimensional Scaling* (Beverly Hills: Sage Publication, 1977); David McFarland and Daniel Brown, ''Social Distance as a Metric: A Systematic Introduction to Smallest-Space Analysis,'' in *Bonds of Pluralism*, ed. Edward O. Laumann (New York: John Wiley, 1973); and Kenneth B. Bailey, ''Interpreting Smallest Space Analysis,'' *Sociological Methods and Research* 3 (1974): 3-29.

FIGURE 2.1

Two-Dimensional Smallest-Space Diagram of Pooled Kinship and Friendship Relations for Pre-Adult, University, and Present Time

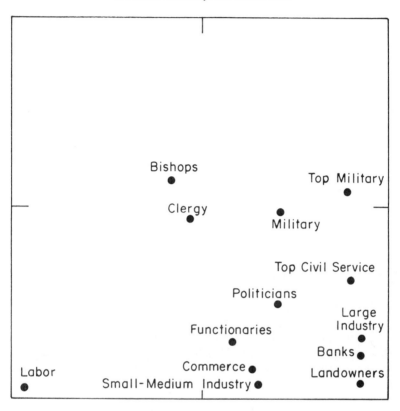

DIMENSIONALITY OF SOLUTION

	One	Two	Three
Kruskal's Stress Coefficient	.20	.11	.06
Guttman-Lingoes' Coefficient of Alienation	.24	.15	.09

NOTE: The diagram is equivalent to a sociogram in which the relative distances between groups represent the degree of contact between them; to eliminate clutter, lines are not drawn between pairs of groups.

are separated from the mere functionaries, the bankers from the merchants, and so on.

None of this contradicts informed observations about the configuration of power in post-1964 Brazil.[9] The state managers, especially the military,

[9] Fernando Henrique Cardoso, *O Modêlo Político Brasileiro* (São Paulo: Difusão Européia do Livro, 1974), and Helio Jaguaribe, *Brasil: Crise e Alternativas* (Rio de Janeiro: Zahar, 1974).

are indeed distinguishable from the industrialists, the financiers, and the landowners. The labor leaders are isolated. If the power structure has a center, it is represented by the politicians. On the average, among all the elite sectors, the latter maintain the shortest distance between themselves and the other groups.[10]

Three cautionary notes should be sounded. On the one hand, the real-world flavor of Figure 2.1 is encouraging as a sign of the validity of the data. On the other hand, the diagram elides some important details. For example, the top civil servants are not nearly so bloclike as they appear. Although the distance between the civilian and military cadres captures the differentiation between the security apparatus and the bureaucratic management, there are also factions and functional divisions within these groups. As we shall see, one that is particularly consequential is the divide between the noneconomic bureaucracy, the men responsible for the care-taking and cultural operations of the state, and the economic bureaucracy, those charged with the developmental push of the country.[11]

Second, the bishops and the ordinary clergy do not fit neatly along the labor-versus-elite or state-versus-society coordinates. While they are not so isolated as the labor leaders, they are not really integrated with the other elites. Were the spatial rendition of the power structure carried to three dimensions—an option not taken here because the graphic presentation becomes unduly busy—the church would in fact emerge on a dimension of its own.[12]

Several factors contribute to the odd-man-out position of the ecclesi-astical hierarchy. Although most of the bishops supported the anticom-munism of the 1964 revolution, they have become increasingly alienated

[10] This was determined by inspecting the matrix of "derived coefficients" output from the smallest-space analysis. These coefficients are comparable to measures of intergroup distance. A similar pattern was encountered among Venezuelan politicians by Allan Kessler, "The International Structure of Elites," in *A Strategy for Research on Social Policy*, vol. 1 of *The Politics of Change in Venezuela*, ed. Frank Bonilla and José A. Silva Michelena (Cambridge, Mass.: M.I.T. Press, 1967). The centrality of the politicians does not make them the most powerful of the elites; it only indicates that their contacts are extensive and rather evenly spread. The scope of their contacts exceeds their span of control.

[11] See Celso Lafer, *O Sistema Político Brasileiro* (São Paulo: Perspectiva, 1975).

[12] The coefficients at the bottom of the diagram indicate the success of the technique in reducing the thirteen ties to one, two, and three dimensions: the lower the coefficients, the better the fit. The one-dimensional solution is unsatisfactory. It would reduce the power structure to a split between the labor leadership and all other groups. The two-dimensional solution shown here is acceptable. The three-dimensional solution, which would place the church on a separate axis, is even better. The fact that the ecclesiastical hierarchy forms the basis of the third, but still significant, axis of the power structure conforms to theoretical expectations.

by the poor human rights and social welfare record of the regime. More generally, the Brazilian clergy forms a humanistic as well as spiritual estate that falls in the interstices of the secular and largely economic dimensions of the power structure. In one sense or another, all of the elites except the bishops and the priests are public men, and the divisions among them are broadly recognizable as matters of public policy. The church, however, has a moral and private mission that cannot be reduced to the usual political conflicts. The locus of the clergy in the Brazilian power structure is therefore ambiguous.[13]

Third, there is a double-edged quality to the representation of the power structure unveiled so far. The results do not seem peculiarly Brazilian. This is both a virtue and a defect. The distances between the groups are not strikingly different·from what might be expected to emerge in any capitalist society that has attained a moderate level of development. Since the Brazilian system is a variation on state-capitalist models that are widespread, its generic similarity to this design is to be expected. It can be argued, further, that this structural resemblance belies the democratic pretensions of advanced capitalist societies, at least insofar as the distribution of power rather than benefits is concerned.[14]

Still, despite the broad similarities, some distinctive traces of the authoritarian nature of the Brazilian system appear. The labor leaders would probably not be so remote from the center of action in advanced European democracies, and the proximity found in Brazil between the state managers and the large industrialists is an empirical question in other capitalist systems. Finally, there is no guarantee that the structure of power, defined as an arrangement of kinship and friendship relations, corresponds to the ideological bias of the system, in Brazil or anywhere else. In short, the within- as well as the between-system comparability of the patterns uncovered until now is limited.

[13] Compare Glen Caudill Dealy, *The Public Man: An Interpretation of Latin American and Other Catholic Countries* (Amherst, Mass.: University of Massachusetts Press, 1977).

[14] The sociometry presented in Figure 2.1 does not provide an optimal basis for cross-national comparisons. The smallest-space analysis uses correlation coefficients as measures of similarity—that is, proximity—in such a way that relative rather than absolute distances are portrayed. Comparing Figure 2.1 with an equivalent representation from, say, the United States has the same limitations as using correlations, rather than regression estimates, in cross-national research. In any event, elite network data that are truly comparable are quite rare. One analysis that closely resembles the one presented here, though some of the elite actors are different, is by John Higley, C. Lowell Field, and Knut Groholt, *Elite Structure and Ideology* (New York: Columbia University Press, 1976), especially p. 266. See also Robert J. Mokken and Frans N. Stokman, "Corporate-Governmental Networks in the Netherlands," *Social Networks* 1 (1978/1979): 333-358.

The Separation of Kinship and Friendship Ties

In view of the evidence presented so far, the Brazilian elite network seems remarkably coherent. In one respect, this coherence may not be remarkable at all, for in most ways, with the exception of the ambiguous locus of the church, it confirms standard accounts of the power structure. Yet this obviousness is also partly traceable to the fact that we have not plumbed very deeply. The contours of the power structure are its surface architecture, its form. With this outline in place, the interior and the foundations of the structure can be examined.

Until now kinship and friendship linkages have been treated as the same; they have been merged, as have the time periods of the linkages. Kinship and friendship ties among the elites are indeed similar in that the networks derivable from them look alike. The elites have few friends and fewer relatives among the labor leaders, and they tend to have more of both within the business community. In this sense, kinship and friendship linkages go together.

However, an elite system in which kinship and friendship with specific groups coincide is probably not very supple. Configurations of power in which all friends "are family" suggest an inbreeding and lack of resilience that do not make for adaptability. This is not to argue that a hypothetically optimal elite network would be one in which kinship and friendship ties were wholly separate, for such a situation would entail a rigid segregation of the modalities of interelite contact. The argument does imply a certain differentiation between kinship and friendship linkages. In operational terms, this means weak correlations between the two, even if separately they yield similar aggregate structures.

The fundamental claim, then, is that inside the Brazilian power structure there is at most a moderate overlap between kinship and friendship ties. The record of elite linkages at t_3, the present time, provides a good test of this proposition, since the data register kinship and friendship simultaneously. The twenty-six variables (thirteen kinship and thirteen friendship links) were first correlated and factor-analyzed, reducing them to nine dimensions. The factor scores on these dimensions were then factor-analyzed themselves for the purpose of determining whether substantively meaningful dimensions might be extracted. The results of this second-order analysis are presented in Table 2.1.[15]

[15] See Harry H. Harman, *Modern Factor Analysis*, 3d ed. (Chicago: University of Chicago Press, 1967), and R. J. Rummel, *Applied Factor Analysis* (Evanston: Northwestern University Press, 1970). The oblique (as opposed to orthogonal) rotation is used because the elite cleavages are not independent of one another. "Promax" rotation is simply a version of oblique rotation, performed after computing a varimax (orthogonal) rotation from the principal components results. See S. A. Mulaik, *The Foundations of Factor Analysis* (New York:

TABLE 2.1
Promax Oblique Rotation of Factors from Kinship and Friendship Ties
(present time)

| | | Factors | | Commu- |
		I	*II*	*III*	*nalities*
F:[a]	Landowners, Large				
	Businessmen	1.01	−.25	.09	1.09
F:	Military, Top Civil				
	Service, Politicians	1.01	.03	.16	1.04
F:	Church	.91	.26	−.19	.94
F:	Commerce, Functionaries,				
	Labor	−1.00	.00	.01	1.00
K:[b]	Labor	.11	1.04	−.32	1.20
K:	Landowners, Large				
	Businessmen	.15	−1.00	−.01	1.02
K:	Military, Top Civil				
	Service, Politicians	−.08	−.91	−.19	.87
K:	Commerce, Functionaries	−.07	.67	.55	.75
K:	Church	−.07	−.06	1.03	1.06
Sum of Squares		3.92	3.48	1.57	

Correlations between Factor Scores

	I		
I	—		
II	.09	—	
III	−.15	.34	—
	I	II	III

[a] "F" = friendship
[b] "K" = kinship

The key feature of the tabulation is the separation of kinship and friendship linkages. It is easier, perhaps, to interpret the configuration by rec-
ognizing what does not happen. For example, ties of kinship and friendship
with the landowners, the bankers, and the industrialists do not cluster
together. Instead, the first factor encompasses all friendship linkages, and
within this factor there are evident corporate and class gradations. Similarly, the remaining two factors take in all kinship ties, with the third
dimensions reserved for the special case of the celibate clergy.

Something else fails to happen: the factors are not negatively correlated.
That is, kinship and friendship are not the obverse of each other. But

McGraw-Hill, 1972), pp. 300 ff.; compare Duncan MacRae, Jr., "Direct Factor Analysis
of Sociometric Data," *Sociometry* 23 (1960): 360-371, and Phillip Bonacich, "Factoring and
Weighting Approaches to Status Scores and Clique Identification," *Journal of Mathematical
Sociology* 2 (1972): 113-117.

neither are they rigorously interdependent. The correlations between the kinship and friendship factors are insignificant.

Thus, the basic idea that kinship and friendship do not go in lockstep and that, by implication, the elite system exhibits a certain flexibility, is confirmed. But the point is rather abstract. The parallelism between kinship and friendship, as opposed to either an intimate interlocking or an even less plausible mutual exclusiveness between them, helps account for the fact that kinship and friendship generate more or less equivalent network structures, without forcing us to assume that they are the same for all sectors of the elites. But it raises a further question. It may be that kinship and friendship perform complementary functions and have differential importance for the various elite sectors. They may be connected in particular ways within certain sectors and in another but equally specific way among elite groups of a different kind. This would tend to cancel out the correlations between the types of ties, when calculated for the elites as a whole.

Hence, the parallelism between elite ties is a first approximation of the internal workings of the power structure. There may not be a typical elite or a seamless uniformity to the functioning of kinship and friendship.

Class, Kinship, and Friendship

All elites are privileged, but some are more privileged than others. Multiple indicators—class differences, recruitment patterns, marital mobility—place the elites on a reasonably clear-cut gradient, with the businessmen on top and the labor leaders at the bottom. The question now is the extent to which the various elites make different use of kinship and friendship links with different classes.

Two propositions can be extracted from the argument that kinship and friendship linkages fulfill complementary functions among Brazilian elites. One is that, at any point in time, kinship ties should be more abundant within sectors populated by elites from upper-class families than within groups where elites are recruited mainly from the middle sectors. The other is that, over time—that is, during the career cycles of the elites—upper-class sectors such as the businessmen should continue to rely on kinship linkages, and especially on kinship linkages with the upper class, whereas the middle sector, education-dependent civil servants should rely more on friendship ties as primary devices of mobility.

A central feature in both propositions is the "density" of kinship ties, computed simply as the ratio of kinship to friendship linkages. My interest is in the relative number of kinship bonds, not in their absolute quantity. Figure 2.2 gives the results of an exact test of the idea that kinship ties are comparatively numerous among the upper-class elites. What has been done is to correlate, within each of the principal groups, the kinship/ friendship ratio with the total number of ties reported by the elites. A strong positive correlation indicates that as the absolute number of linkages increases, so does the density of kinship ties.

As the lower-class and lower middle-class labor leaders gather more linkages, they collect a disproportionate number of friendship ties, relative to their small base of kinship connections. The businessmen, on the other hand, start with an ample supply of familial linkages, and those with the largest number of ties have very dense kinship networks. The politicians, many of whom are from landed families, approach this pattern. Finally, there is no association between the proliferation of ties among the civil servants and their kinship linkages. Although they are not destitute of such connections, neither are they especially well-supplied with them.

FIGURE 2.2
Correlations between Kinship/Friendship Ratio and Total Number of Ties, by Elite Sector

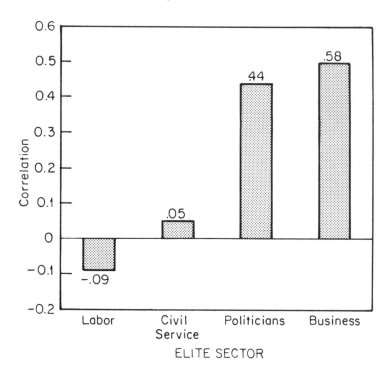

NOTE: Kinship/friendship ratio = number of kinship ties / number of friendship ties

Hence, as the number and extent of ties increases, as it does from the "poor" to the "rich" elites, so does the importance of kinship over friendship ties. If the labor leaders, the poorest of the elites, are to augment their connections, they must do so by cultivating friends, for they have little chance of marrying into middle- or upper-class families. By contrast, the most powerful of the businessmen have little incentive to expand their network of nonfamily connections. Their problem is not mobility but the protection of property. In summary, the data convey a sense of the inertia behind the genuinely upper-class elements of the elite, of the latent solidarity among them, and of the obstacles against breaking into the inner sanctum.[16]

The basic pattern can be refined. Implicit in my argument is the notion that upper-class elites enjoy a cumulative advantage. They build on their kinship networks over time. This is not to say that they neglect other types of connections but only that the largely middle-sector elites do not catch up with the comparatively well-born, like the businessmen, in the density and amplitude of their kinship networks, especially with the upper class itself.

One way to demonstrate the cumulative nature of kinship ties is to calculate a dynamic ratio—for example, of present-day kinship ties relative to childhood kinship ties. The higher the ratio, the greater the cumulative density of these linkages. Furthermore, kinship (as well as friendship) bonds can be subdivided into those with upper-class groups (large bankers, large industrialists, top civil servants, et cetera) and those with middle-class groups (*comerciantes*, medium-to-small industrialists, and so on). A ratio can then be formed, for example, between present-day kinship linkages with upper-class groups and childhood kinship linkages with middle-class groups. The higher the ratio, the greater the growth of kinship ties with key sectors of Brazilian society.

Figure 2.3 illustrates two patterns of upward-mobile linkages for five elite groups. The overall trend is evident. The businessmen are the most successful in building their networks with upper-class elements, and their networks tend to be of the best—that is, the presumably strongest—kind, favoring kinship over friendship. The accumulation of upper-class kinship linkages is considerably more modest among the other elites, especially among the civil servants, the bishops, and the labor leaders. The politicians are the only sector that can compete with the businessmen in cultivating

[16] See Nicholas Abercrombie and Stephen Hill, "Paternalism and Patronage," *British Journal of Sociology* 27 (1976): 413-429, and Maurice Zeitlin, Lynda Ewen, and Richard Ratcliff, "New Princes for Old? The Large Corporation and the Capitalist Class in Chile," *American Journal of Sociology* 80 (1974): 87-123.

FIGURE 2.3

Selected Upward-Mobile Linkages Over Time: Mean Densities by Elite Sector

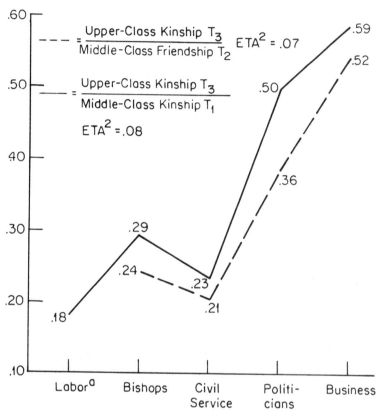

[a] Too few cases for analysis where base equals middle-class friendship t_2.

the most intimate ties with the upper class, and even they come out in second place.

The complement of these results—namely, the upper- and middle-class friendship densities for the various elite groups over time—can be summarized simply. Ties with middle-class groups grow proportionately faster, from the university to the present time, for example, among middle-sector categories like the state managers than among the businessmen, with the politicians falling in between.

In brief, while it would be erroneous to claim that middle-sector mobility into the Brazilian elite is purely nonparticularistic, following exclusively the meritocratic route of formal education, it is clear that a dominant mechanism of sponsored mobility works through the cultivation of friend-ships, sometimes with upper-class individuals but often, as well, with individuals of less than true upper-class standing. With the still rare but important exception of the sons of the "respectable" (professional) middle sectors who marry into landed, industrial, or banking families, few middle-sector elites establish the tightest kind of bonds with the core of the upper class.

Working Contacts

The day-to-day maneuverings of the elites may appear more haphazard and generate more intricate configurations than their kinship and friendship linkages. Nevertheless, it is improbable that they are wholly without pattern or that they violate the general thrust of networks based on kinship and friendship.[17] The advantage of registering the working contacts of the elites is the finer-grained resolution they afford of groups within groups—for example, within the top civil service, the military, and so on. In addition, these materials provide a feel for the similarities between the interorgan-izational and interpersonal relations among elites in a semi-institutionalized system.[18]

When the elites were asked to nominate the "five or six men with the greatest influence in matters of national importance," the qualification "within your own area of interest" was added to make the responses less obvious. Even so, the president himself and the finance minister, Delfim Netto, received many more citations than any other individuals. This re-flects the enormous concentration of power in Brazil during the Médici years.[19]

[17] Compare Michael Gurevitch and Alex Weingrod, "Who Knows Whom? Acquaint-anceship and Contacts in the Israeli National Elite," *Human Relations* 31 (1978): 195-214.

[18] Compare James R. Lincoln and Jon Miller, "Work and Friendship Ties in Organizations: A Comparative Analysis of Relational Networks," *Administrative Science Quarterly* 24 (1979): 181-199, and the literature cited therein. Although the analysis of interorganizational linkages would seem to be directly pertinent to the testing of corporatist models of Brazilian politics, the literature on Latin American authoritarianism is devoid of references to the wider tradition of interorganizational studies. I have discovered only one application of interor-ganizational theory to Latin American (in this case, Mexican) politics: Susan Eckstein, "Po-liticos and Priests, the Iron Law of Oligarchy and Interorganizational Relations," *Comparative Politics* 9 (1977): 463-481.

[19] President Médici was nominated as "most influential" by 41 percent of the elites and Delfim Netto by 17 percent. No other individual approaches these men in the hierarchy. Correcting the power rankings in the light of reported contact restores some balance to the hierarchy. The president is more powerful than the finance minister, but the elites have more contact with the latter. This does not work for any other individuals, because they are cited so rarely. Compare Maria Lúcia de Oliveira, "A Tendência à Centralização e o Fenômeno

All told, the elites nominated thirty individuals, including the president and the finance minister, as having great influence in their own fields of activity. Moreover, the elites reported the frequency of their contact with these individuals.[20] It is possible but inelegant to trace the prodigious number of direct and indirect linkages between the persons cited. This yields a highly and, for present purposes, too detailed picture of the power structure. It also produces a transitory snapshot, for most of the personages who figured among the mighty in 1972 and 1973 have since left the scene. However, they can be grouped in functional clusters. This aggregation captures the principal coalitions and subcoalitions without loss of verisimilitude.

The thirty individuals were sorted into eight categories. Since they were mentioned so often, the president and the finance minister each form a minority of one, and there is no need to align them beforehand with other individuals.

Aside from these two men, there are six significant groupings. The first can best be described as "the presidency," that is, the men directly attached to the executive office—principally, the chief of staff of the military, the head of the civil office, the director of the security apparatus, the generals of the standing armies, and the heads of the three armed services. This is the cockpit of the Brazilian state, occupied almost exclusively by repressive forces.[21]

Another set of actors comprises the economic bureaucracy: men such as the minister of planning and coordination, the minister of industry and commerce, the minister of transports, and the heads of the state-owned industries and banks. A third set of state managers makes up the non-economic bureaucracy: all of the civil servants whose main responsibilities have to do with education, foreign and labor relations, the judiciary, and the like.

The economic bureacrats form the entrepreneurial core of the state. Their role is to drive Brazil toward great power status. The functions of the noneconomic bureaucracy are not entirely routine, yet they spend a good

---

do Autoritarismo no Brasil," *Dados* 15 (1977): 83-99. Delfim Netto remains the first-among-equals of the civilian ministers, a role that he has cultivated through extensive contacts. His "at-homes" on Christmas Eve, where about a thousand elite guests are received, have become an institution. See "Dom Antônio Exercita seu Poder," *Isto É*, December 31, 1980: 68.

[20] Actually, the elites nominated more than thirty individuals as influential; the total figure is close to two hundred. However, if a person was not cited by at least 2 percent of the elites, he was grouped with other persons in his own field (for example, business, government) rather than treated individually. In short, only thirty individuals were nominated as influential by 2 percent or more of the respondents.

[21] For a description of the information-gathering side of the security apparatus, see Carlos Alberto Sardenberg, "O Mundo das Fichas," *Isto É* June 25, 1980: 12-17.

deal of time in what amounts to cleaning up after their developmental colleagues: assuaging, controlling, and servicing various clients who are victims or bystanders of the great leap forward.

The three remaining groups are businessmen, politicians, and "others," this last group a residual miscellany gathering in ecclesiastics, labor leaders, journalists, members of the liberal professions, and the like. All in all, the eight-part categorization brings a preliminary order to the dispersion of influence and contacts among individual elites. However, it is only a classification, and the question remains concerning the extent to which the various groups and persons interact with one another. To some degree, they deal with separate clienteles, and their patterns of working contacts should mirror this differentiation. The appropriate method for summarizing the networks of operational linkages is to reduce the twenty-eight pairwise connections between the eight actors to the coordinates underlying them. The factor analysis in Table 2.2 does this.[22]

The three dimensions that emerge from the analysis crystallize the main lines of the working relationships within and between the nexus of technocratic power represented by the finance minister and his minions in the economic agencies, and the political sector generally, including the titular supporters as well as opponents of the government. The economic planners move in a world largely separate from that of the elected representatives. On occasion, the politicians may be consulted, but this is the exception rather than the rule, certainly during the Médici regime. The politicians rarely participate in the making of key decisions.[23]

The president and his entourage also occupy a distinctive place in the power structure. There is some overlapping between this institutional clique and the economic bureaucracy, and it also maintains some contact with the politicians (of the government party, as will be shown). The presidency is most remote from "the others," the collection of mostly powerless figures in the church and the labor syndicates.

The third dimension of operational contact divides the businessmen and to a lesser extent the politicians from the noneconomic bureaucracy. The axis has a state-versus-society flavor. While the business leaders are fairly close to the economic bureaucrats, they have little use for the rest of the

---

[22] The variables entered into the analysis are the measures of contact scored from "1" (no contact) to "4" (frequent contact). Virtually identical results are obtained when the influence measure is used. In this case, "greatest influence" (that is, cited at the top of the list of the "five or six" most powerful figures) receives a score of "6," the second-to-the-top score of "5," and so on, with "0" representing "not mentioned as influential."

[23] Compare Luciano Martins, "A Expansão Recente do Estado no Brasil: Seus Problemas e Seus Atores," unpublished manuscript, São Paulo, March 1977, and Carlos Estevam Martins, *Capitalismo de Estado e Modelo Político no Brasil* (Rio de Janeiro: Editora Graal, 1977).

TABLE 2.2
Factor Analysis (Varimax Rotation) of Working Contacts with Eight Major Groups:
Normalized Factor Loadings

Contacted Groups	Factors			Commu- nalities
	I	*II*	*III*	
Economic Bureaucracy	.81	− .03	.07	.67
Finance Minister	.73	.39	.12	.69
President Médici	− .02	.77	− .20	.64
Presidency	− .01	.71	.15	.53
Business	.06	− .21	.73	.57
Other Bureaucracy	.06	− .19	− .69	.51
Politicians	− .55	.14	.30	.41
Other	− .30	− .37	− .04	.23
Sum of Squares	1.59	1.49	1.17	
Percent of Variance	19.9	17.7	14.6	

Factor I: Technocrats versus Politicians
Factor II: The Presidency-Security Axis
Factor III: Businessmen/Noneconomic Bureaucracy

state apparatus, especially as it interferes with their freedom of action and in general complicates their affairs.

However, it is not clear why the politicians are aligned with the industrialists and bankers in a protoclique apart from the noneconomic agencies, nor is it certain that both the ARENA and the MDB can be located at the same remove from the bureaucracy. These ambiguities are resolved in Table 2.3. Factor scores were computed for each dimension, and their mean values are presented for each of the elite groups. The scores indicate how the various sectors are linked to the diverse spheres of day-to-day influence.

The ordering of the elite estates along the first dimension specifies a primary cleavage within the Brazilian establishment: the technocratic-business alliance stands apart from the politicians, the bishops, and the labor leaders. The split is not only between the technocrats and the politicians; it also divides the business elite from labor. The supremacy of the technocrats is more than an interelite problem, for it entails the domination of one class over another as well as the internal stratification of the elites proper.

The second axis of working contacts reveals the coercive element behind the exclusion of lower-class groups. Political power emanates from the

TABLE 2.3
Mean Standardized Factor Scores on Three Dimensions of Working Contacts,
by Elite Sector

	Factor Scores		
Elite Sector	I	II	III
MDB	− .81	.06	.23
Church	− .69	− .78	− .12
Labor	− .41	− .41	− .57
ARENA	− .20	.90	.02
Business	.28	− .01	.43
Civil Service	.43	.01	− .15
ETA²	.17*	.17*	.14*

*p ≤ .01

presidency, and both the labor leaders and the church are isolated from this center.

The third orbit of contact revolves around the noneconomic bureaucracy. It is the only one in which the bishops and the labor leaders move with ease. When the data are examined in detail, it becomes apparent that the contacts of the syndical operatives are almost exclusively with the ministry of labor and the labor courts, and those of the bishops with the ministry of justice. The labor leaders depend on the syndical bureaucracy in numerous ways—for example, for the allocation of union funds controlled by the government. Much of the church's dealings with the state involves coping with human rights violations. The noneconomic bureaucratic network may thus be characterized as one of patronage and administrative control.[24] For this reason, the ARENA politicians are somewhat more closely enmeshed in it than the representatives of the MDB, while the businessmen try to avoid the underside of the state machine altogether.

The common denominator of all three networks is that they converge on the state. If the government can be termed autonomous in any meaningful sense, it is as a derivative of the multiplicity of functions it carries out and the corresponding proliferation of its clientele. No single organization or institution on the outside has the capacity to monitor or effectively counterbalance the activities of the Brazilian government. The one sector

[24] The fact that the labor leaders and the bishops are both enmeshed in the noneconomic bureaucracy does not mean that they form a common front, even though a tentative alliance has emerged between them (and the peasantry). See Warren Hoge, "Brazilians Battle Over Land, with Church Backing Poor," *New York Times*, March 4, 1980: A2, and Paul Sigmund, "Latin American Catholicism's Opening to the Left," *Review of Politics* 35 (1973): 61-76.

that may qualify as a quasi-equal partner is the business community. The alliance of the technocrats, the military, and the large businessmen against the politicians and the church as well as against urban labor has been the foundation of the authoritarian power structure in Brazil.

The gray eminence of the Brazilian establishment is neither this nor that individual nor the shape of the power structure itself. Rather, it is how the system holds together. This "how" is a composite of reinforcing mechanisms. The clearest feature of the system is the quarantine of the working class and its leadership through a variety of coercive and cooptative devices. Among the elites proper, power is unevenly distributed: the politicians and the bishops have little, the businessmen and the state managers a lot.

Yet the system renews rather than simply reproduces itself. Although many of them receive enormous advantages from their forebears, not even the businessmen inherit their positions automatically. Compared to their fathers, almost all Brazilian elites are upwardly mobile. The state managers exemplify this success story. Born in general to families of modest status, they have reached the command posts of Brazilian society through their educational attainment, their technical credentials and, we may suppose, their competence, however narrowly construed. In the process, they have not been averse to exploiting personal contacts. But they have had to work at these connections, since they are not typically brought up among, nor do they usually marry into, the *gente bem*, the best families.

There is a division of labor among the ties that bind Brazilian elites. Although the capitalist class is well-knit through endogamy and other kinship linkages, the power structure is not a seamless web. Less ascriptive channels of mobility are open to the well-educated sons of the middle sectors who find their way into the public bureaucracy.[25]

It is not surprising that the Brazilian power structure exhibits such differentiation, for Brazil can hardly be described as a traditional agrarian society. On the other hand, differences in the kinship and friendship networks of the upper-class and middle-sector elites do not prevent them from coalescing in the management of development. The compartmentalization of the elite estates is scarcely total. The predominantly upper-class businessmen have few qualms about developing close working contacts with the largely middle-sector bureaucrats in charge of capital accumulation, while they have little use for the noneconomic civil service or for the

---

[25] It seems probable that local politics in Brazil is even more strongly influenced by *parentesco* ties than I have plotted at the national level. See Linda Levin, "Some Historical Implications of Kinship Organization for Family-Based Politics in the Brazilian Northeast," *Comparative Studies in Society and History* 21 (1979): 262-292.

politicians, even though the family background and networks of the latter group are quite respectable.

The multiplex nature of linkages among the elites is complemented by the multidimensionality of the power structure itself. Although some convergence is evident between the line demarcating urban labor from the elites as a whole and the separation of the state managers from the industrialists and the bankers, the axes of latent conflict are themselves differentiated. The virtual independence of the cleavages underlying the power structure is clearest in the case of the bishops, who for the most part are structurally unaligned with the other elites.

There are two partial exceptions to these patterns, and both of them make sense in the authoritarian context. First, while the position of the bishops as determined by their kinship and friendship linkages is ambiguous, the effect of their particular configuration of working contacts is not only to separate but also to exclude them from the power structure and to place them alongside the labor leaders in tentative opposition. The bishops who supported the 1964 revolution were never really made a part of it, however willing some of them may have been to join in an anticommunist crusade. By the early seventies, and even more dramatically later on, the insensitivity of the regime to its potential allies as well as to its enemies had begun to drive the church leftward.

Second, the position of the politicians, like that of the bishops but for somewhat different reasons, is also ambiguous. They are not off to the side of the establishment, as are the bishops. Instead, the variety of their kinship and friendship linkages locates them at the center, if the structure of power can be said to have a center at all. They are at the crossroads of multiple cleavages, sometimes close to the civilian bureaucrats but most of the time far from the top of the establishment. To some extent, this ambiguity reflects the fact that the politicians are made up of both opposition and allegiant figures. However, the politicians as a class were marginalized under authoritarian rule, and it is this exclusion from power—and, indeed, their reduction to powerless actors—that led to a certain corporate solidarity between the ARENA and the MDB representatives vis-à-vis the military-bureaucratic state.[26]

Of course, the patterns mapped here are tendencies, not hard-and-fast

[26] The counterpart to the marginalization of the politicians and other formerly powerful elites in Brazil has been, as already noted, the expansion of the military and the technocrats into previously "private" areas. This simultaneous concentration and expansion of power has proceeded steadily since 1964, so that even with the movement toward liberalization that started in the mid-seventies, it is difficult to imagine a serious dismantling of the bureaucratic apparatus. See Cândido Mendes, "The Post-1964 Brazilian Regime: Outward Redemocratization and Inner Institutionalization," *Government and Opposition* 15 (1980): 48-74.

regularities. Variation in the density of kinship ties across elite groups is probabilistic rather than deterministic. The statistical and substantive connection between the various types of linkages may be termed expanding-sum: the better-endowed the elites are with one kind of tie, the better their position to cultivate others. Furthermore, the distinction between kinship and friendship is not merely biological. It is blurred by cultural definitions, as suggested by the common usage of "brother" and "son" in Brazil to signify long-standing friendships.

The impression of orderliness may derive from the fact that I have been at pains to systematize the complementarity of the devices used to facilitate mobility and consolidate power. Brazilians have an impressively variegated nomenclature for informal ties—*grupinhos, panelinhas, igrejinhas*, and so on. Yet the patterns implicit in such linkages can be quite systematic. Elite interactions may appear to be more disorganized than they are on account of severe obstacles to measurement. This is our problem, not a failing of the cliques.[27]

But there is a danger of confusing this orderliness with stability. Despite the fact that the elites supplied recall information about the development of their networks since childhood, the data are essentially cross-sectional, and dynamic inferences are therefore restricted. And apart from this limitation, the parameters of interelite relationships are not the only components of political stability in Brazil.

The Brazilian state is clearly not an agrarian bureaucracy. The power structure is differentiated, and there is a certain complementarity, not to say functionalism, to the ways in which its constituent parts interact. And yet it is difficult to come to firm judgments about the balance between functional and disruptive forces on the basis of information about the social backgrounds and networks of the elites alone. For example, the military are probably the most uniformly socialized of the elites, even more so than the bishops, who have been educated in various seminaries. By contrast, the education of the civilian elites has been heterogeneous. But what this tells us about the latent solidarities and intrinsic contradictions of the power structure is moot. The fraternalism of the military may heighten their

[27] It is true, however, that the account presented here does not transmit a sense of the warm Machiavellianism that is a trademark of interelite relations in Brazil: the hugging (rather than backslapping) with two arms (ceremonial) or one (casual); the *compromissos* (commitments) made enthusiastically, with uncertain deadlines; and the ironic humor that often sets the stage for serious discussion. A social anthropology of elite relations in Brazil is waiting to be written. For a fascinating analysis of the general area (although in a very different setting), see Abner Cohen, *The Politics of Elite Culture* (Berkeley: University of California Press, 1981).

isolation in the eyes of the civilian elites, even if the civilians have little in common besides their antimilitarism.

One way to reduce this ambiguity is to examine the ideological correlates of the power structure. I have ignored the issues around which elites form coalitions and enter into conflict. In this respect the power structure depicted so far lacks political content. The purpose of the ensuing analysis is to specify this content.

PART TWO

Ideologies

THREE

Orientations toward the Distribution of Power

Brazilian elites are well acquainted with the intricacies of their own niches within the structure of power. Even if corners of it go unnoticed, the overall configuration is easy to make out. However, the ability of the elites to comprehend the disposition of power, while less acute than might be expected of expert practitioners, is not a crucial issue here. The central question involves the degree to which the elites see beyond their immediate quarrels and envision something approaching a redesign of the power structure itself.

In effect, three issues are involved. First, the elites are split into various groups with diverse interests. Their views of exactly what constitutes the power structure are influenced by their positions inside the system. "Reality" is thus liable to be perceived in biased, though not entirely idiosyncratic, ways. The specialization of the elites fosters astigmatism: wishful thinking, projection, stereotyping, ideology as false consciousness—in short, a systematic distortion in the way they view themselves and their rivals.

Perceptual distortion among elites is not simply a curiosity, another demonstration of the psychological vagaries in which the powerful and willfully obtuse may indulge. The elites, however deluded they may be, are not whimsical. Their tendency to bend the prevailing order to their liking is diagnostic of the different stakes they have in maintaining and changing it.

Second, if there is disagreement among the elites about what would seem to be the elementary facts of Brazilian political life—that is, about the distribution of power—their differences may become all the more apparent when preferences about the redistribution of power are considered. A substantial amount of interelite conflict over who should get what is more plausible than serious misapprehension about who actually gets it.

Yet, third, the idea that elites will disagree in their preferences about the allocation of power can be just as erroneous as the supposition that the structure of power, being crashingly obvious, will be described in the same fashion by informed participants. The imputation of an atomistic disagreement among the elites must be qualified in several respects.

On the one hand, much interelite squabbling can be attributed squarely to the inclination of each of the major actors to place himself at the top, or very close to the top, of an idealized hierarchy. Again, this is not a psychological curiosity alone. It is brought on by the fact that Brazilian authoritarianism, despite its corporatist airs, is a disorganized, uninstitutionalized phenomenon. The rules of competition are uncertain. The inevitable result of the maximization of separate group interests under these conditions is that no consensus emerges about the substance of political change, even if most of the elites declare themselves in favor of change. Carried to the ultimate, unrestrained elite competition means king-of-the-hill politics.

On the other hand, even when the elites fail to come to terms about who should rule, their views about who should not rule may be considerably more consensual. It is quite possible for the elites to exhibit a negative unity of opposition. This is less than a positive alternative to the existing order, but it is something more than a total fragmentation of interests. There are latent coalitions among the diverse elite actors that tend to get lost in the midst of their evident difficulty in articulating hegemonic models.

Other factors work to restrain the elite impulse toward fratricidal and self-destructive infighting. One of these is a recognition of the hazards of nonelite participation in the struggle for power. Although the elites tend to close ranks against the arbitrariness of protracted military rule, most of them are not ardent defenders of mass democracy. They have a common, albeit vaguely shaped, interest in (a) protecting their own areas of influence from the military, and (b) controlling the entrance of new groups into the political arena. It is this tension that makes their perceptions of and preferences about the distribution of power ambiguous and complex.

However much they desire and thrive on power, many of the elites are not primarily concerned with seizing power from one another. Some of them seem more preoccupied with keeping what they have gained than with monopolizing authority, since the risks and costs of a defensive posture are almost certainly lower than the potential losses of a war of all-against-all. Among Brazilian elites, there are differential propensities to view power and conflict relations in variable-sum or zero-sum terms. Such orientations are generalizations of the tendency for the elites to see the power structure differently, depending on their own position in the hierarchy.

The characteristic style of Brazilian elites is to approach power relationships as variable-sum tensions rather than as winner-take-all struggles.[1] This inclination is common among the elites whose own positions are comfortable, and less common among the progressive elites. Nevertheless, even the dissidents are reluctant to challenge the power structure head-on. The initial impulse is to imagine that contenders can be brought into the system without seriously endangering those on the inside.

It can be argued that the views of the elites, for all their ambiguity and complexity, are superficial precisely because a fundamental rearrangement of the power structure, with full extra-elite participation, is not contemplated. The elites are not suicidal. At the same time, it is uncertain just how harmless their equivocations might be. There is a fault line in the authoritarian edifice rather than a gaping divide. But this narrow fissure may go very deep. The task is to probe beneath the surface to obtain a more exact sense of how profound the crack might be.[2]

What gives elite opinions about the distribution of power a cutting edge is an awareness that the interelite game is not, by definition, infinitely expandable. Even the conservatives realize that some of their colleagues may have to be sacrificed or pushed aside if the system of interelite accommodation is to be preserved.

In summary, then, I am interested in the perceptions of the elites regarding the distribution of power, in their preferences about the redistribution of power, and in their propensity to view conflicts inherent to the structure of power in a conciliatory rather than a combative light. The analysis proceeds in two stages. First, I consider elite perceptions of the distribution of power and of the allocation of benefits. Then I examine the degree to which and the ways in which the elites want to change the structure of power. Running through the analysis is the implication that, while a good deal of interelite conflict can be understood as skirmishing among gentlemen rather than as world-historical drama, the game may get out of hand, and that what is at stake, besides who wins and who loses, is a change in the rules of the game itself.

Perceptions of Power and Support

Subjective Linkages

The notion that support and opposition flow more or less directly from the distribution of benefits and sanctions by the government is crude and subject

---

[1] Compare Charles W. Anderson, *Politics and Economic Change in Latin America* (Princeton: D. Van Nostrand, 1967), pp. 87-114.

[2] Compare Allen H. Barton, "Fault Lines in American Elite Consensus," *Daedalus* 109 (1980): 1-24.

to all sorts of emendations.[3] Still, it provides a base line from which to proceed toward an understanding of the more involved concept of legitimacy. Even this apparently simple beginning is deceptive, for the problem is to discern the connections that the elites themselves, and not the hypothetical objective observer, make between political support and government action in Brazil. No matter how it is treated, the link between governmental outputs and elite support retains a strong subjective cast.

As a first approximation to estimating this connection, the elites were asked to state the degree of support/opposition that, in their view, several groups, ranging from the peasantry to the armed forces, display toward the regime.[4] There is room for variation in responding to such a question, especially on the part of elites who lack information or simply do not care about the political opinions of certain groups.

However, short of outright lying, it is difficult for the elites to misconstrue the contours of support and opposition among major interests. Exploited groups, such as rural and urban labor, may not be so alienated from authoritarian regimes as mechanistic interpretations of class consciousness suggest, and the multinationals have their misgivings about certain of the policies adopted in the name of high-speed development. Nevertheless, the gross outlines of support and opposition are clear. For example, it is quite unlikely that the businessmen as a group should be, or should be seen as, more critical of the government than the MDB politicians.

The concept of rewards and sanctions is less straightforward. On the one hand, it suggests the differential power of groups—how successful they are in pressing their demands on and in winning concessions from the government. On the other, it implies the more passive notion of relative autonomy from the government—that is, success in fending off the extractive and regulatory ambitions of the state. While the positive and negative versions of power are not mutually exclusive, the first is probably more familiar in the Brazilian context than the second. In any case, asking the elites for their perceptions of the distribution of "power" would produce virtually invariant answers, because the distribution of active influence is in fact highly skewed.

A middle course was steered by eliciting from the elites their perceptions of the "degree of attention which the government gives" to various groups

---

[3] See Deane E. Neubauer and Lawrence D. Kastner, "The Study of Compliance Maintenance as a Strategy for Comparative Research," *World Politics* 21 (1969): 629-640.

[4] The question reads: "In your opinion, what is the degree of support or opposition of the following groups with respect to the government?" The five-point scale goes from "strong opposition" to "strong support."

"in making decisions of national importance."[5] The purpose of this item is to capture the sense of the elites regarding the treatment of diverse interests, particularly their impressions about the inclusion of groups in the policy process.[6]

Figure 3.1 portrays, for the elites as a whole, the association between the perceptions of the attention paid to various groups and their support for the government, ignoring for the moment individual and sectorwise variation.[7] The aggregate correlation is nearly perfect ($r = .85$). The working assumption of the elites is that the delivery of benefits by the government induces support for the government and that the deprivation of benefits engenders opposition.

If the association between perceptions of governmental attentiveness and political support were such that groups were seen as backing the government exactly in response to the rewards they receive, all of the groups would lie along the line $y = x$. As it is, deviations from this standard are readily explicable. For example, the ARENA politicians tend to be viewed in a lackey role, giving more support than is warranted for the attention they receive. At the other extreme, the MDB politicians are seen as opposing the government out of proportion to their exclusion from the corridors of power.

Thus, the diagonal represents a purely instrumental relationship between payoffs and support, and departures from this line an "irrational"—that is, not strictly utilitarian—commitment or withdrawal of support: in rough terms, legitimacy or the lack of it. The elites view the MDB as "incor-

[5] The "attention" question, like the "support/opposition" item, is directed at the perceptions of the elites regarding thirteen groups. All of the groups but two match across the items. In the attention question, one of the groups is "the middle class"; in the support/opposition question, one of the groups is "state governors." Hence, Figure 3.1 incorporates only twelve groups. It should also be noted that responses to the attention item are scored on four-point scales, where 1 = no attention; 2 = little attention; 3 = some attention; and 4 = much attention.

[6] The selection of a middle course between "power" and "autonomy" by way of "attention" creates ambiguities that must be considered in the interpretation of results. It is not clear whether "attention" signifies the inclusion of groups in policy deliberations or simply the probability that they will benefit from policy decisions. The interests of powerful groups, whether or not they get their way on every decision, are probably taken into account in decisions that affect them. The interests of powerless groups are not, even if the outcome of decisions happens to work to their benefit. See William G. Roy, "Inter-Industry Membership in a National Polity Over Time," unpublished manuscript, Ann Arbor, University of Michigan, 1974. The distinction between incorporation and autonomous political activity, in the liberal-democratic sense, is a familiar one in studies of Latin America. See Lars Schoultz, "The Socio-Economic Determinants of Popular-Authoritarian Electoral Behavior: The Case of Peronism," *American Political Science Review* 71 (1977): 1423-1446.

[7] The points are the grand means of the two variables for each of the groups. Differences within and between elite sectors are omitted.

FIGURE 3.1
Relationship between Mean Perceived Attention Paid by Government and Mean Perceived
Support/Opposition among Twelve Groups

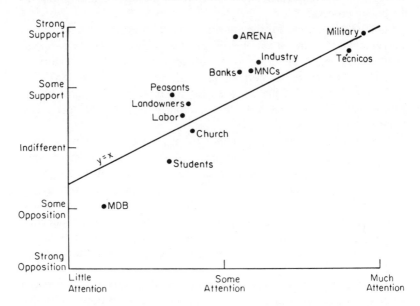

rigile,'' in the sense that the opposition party does not respond in equal
measure to the bits and pieces of beneficence dispensed by the government.
Conversely, the ARENA's appreciation of the government is seen as ful-
some, excessively loyalist in the face of the attention it actually receives.
This is not legitimacy/illegitimacy as I define it, but it is a fair approximation of partisan politics, as opposed to calculating objectivity.

Despite the departures from a one-to-one relationship between attention
and support, the basic association is unmistakable. At the top are the groups
composing the government itself, the military and the technocrats. In
between, but still toward the top, come the industrialists, the bankers, and
the multinationals, together with the government party. Below them are
the more doubtful collectivities: not only urban labor but also the rural and
traditional sectors (landowners, peasants, and the church) who are variously
exploited, downgraded, or ignored by the government. At the bottom lie
the university students and the MDB politicians, the unreconstructed losers.

Variations in Perception

Although the main link between the elites' perceptions of government
attentiveness and political support have been outlined, the results gloss
over systematic differences among the elite sectors. The perceptions are

those of actors with diverse stakes in the political process. It is natural to expect that, being perceptions, they are colored by the political preferences of the elites. Table 3.1 documents the bias in the views of the elites about the distribution of support for and opposition to the government.

The elite sectors inclined to perceive groups as being in opposition to the government are arrayed to the left, and the groups themselves are listed from top to bottom in descending order of perceived opposition, such that the MDB comes first and the military last. Thus, each row represents a separate analysis of variance, with the elite sectors (in the columns) giving their perceptions of the "MDB," the "students," and so on.[8]

The perceptions of the elites regarding the distribution of support and

TABLE 3.1

Mean Perceptions of Government Support/Opposition among Thirteen Groups, by Elite Sector

Perceived Group					Civil			
	MDB	Church	Business	Labor	Service	ARENA	Mean	ETA²
MDB	1.5	1.8	2.0	2.4	2.0	2.0	2.1	.05
Students	2.1	2.0	2.6	3.1	3.0	3.5	2.8	.10
Church	2.2	2.7	3.0	3.5	3.3	3.7	3.2	.09
Labor	2.4	2.7	3.6	4.1	3.7	3.7	3.6	.11
Landowners	3.3	4.4	3.7	3.7	3.9	4.0	3.8	.03
Middle Class	2.2	3.6	4.1	3.7	4.0	4.2	3.9	.18
Peasants	3.2	3.4	3.7	4.2	3.8	4.6	3.9	.13
Banks	4.3	4.4	4.5	4.2	4.6	4.4	4.4	.04
MNCs	4.6	4.9	4.6	4.0	4.6	4.3	4.5	.09
Industry	4.3	4.7	4.6	4.3	4.8	4.5	4.6	.07
Técnicos	4.7	4.9	4.8	4.8	4.8	4.9	4.8	.01
ARENA	4.6	5.0	4.9	4.7	4.9	4.9	4.8	.02
Military	4.9	5.0	4.9	4.9	5.0	5.0	4.9	.01
Mean	3.4	3.8	3.9	4.0	4.0	4.1	4.0	.12

Perceiving Elite Sector

NOTE: "In your opinion, what is the degree of support or opposition of the following groups with respect to the government?" 1 = strong opposition; 2 = some opposition; 3 = indifferent; 4 = some support; 5 = strong support. An ETA² of .07 or larger is significant at the .01 level. The larger the ETA², the greater are the discrepancies among the elites in the support/opposition imputed to a group. The coefficients reach a peak for vaguely defined and/or heterogenous collectivities (for example, "the middle class").

[8] The original Portuguese for the groups listed in Table 3.1, from top to bottom, is: (1) *MDB*, (2) *estudantes*, (3) *igreja*, (4) *sindicatos trabalhistas*, (5) *grandes fazendeiros*, (6) *classe média urbana*, (7) *trabalhadores rurais*, (8) *banqueiros*, (9) *investidores estrangeiros*, (10) *grandes industriais*, (11) *técnicos governmentais*, (12) *ARENA*, (13) *forças armadas*.

opposition are influenced by their own orientations with respect to the government. For example, the ARENA politicians view most groups as giving strong support to the government. The MDB politicians lean in the opposite direction, imputing below-average compliance to the groups. The average level of perceived support, given at the bottom of the array, summarizes this bias. It varies significantly across the elite sectors, with the progressives regularly imagining less and the conservatives more support for the government.

Thus, there are important differences between progressive and conservative sectors in their tendency to perceive groups generally as in support or opposition. The conservatives and those directly dependent on the government, like the labor leaders, have a rosier view of public opinion than the dissidents. But it is not only that actors such as the ARENA politicians characterize conservative groups, like the industrialists and indeed themselves, as supportive of the government. They also tend to perceive the usual suspects—the MDB, the church, and so on—as fairly appreciative of the ministrations of the government.

This is not an obvious result. We could just as easily have imagined the conservatives stereotyping the putative leftists as fiercely hostile to the government, counterposing their own protestations of loyalty against the "exaggerations" of the left. But if there are any elites disposed to view the political world in Manichean terms, labelling some groups as uncritically supportive and others as unswervingly in opposition, it is the progressives: the MDB politicians and the church.[9]

None of the elite groups is autistic; the average rank-order of groups generated by their perceptions of support and opposition is realistic. The MDB politicians are seen as the group most strongly opposed to the government, and in fact they are. The military are seen as the most supportive, and they are the government.

Yet it is as if the elites are looking through a partially reflective window. The disposition of groups is recognizable, but the self-images of the elites also move into focus, superimposed on their vision of the world outside. Perceptual bias is relative. None of the elite sectors, not even those most sympathetic to the regime, claims that the peasants receive more attention from the government, or give it more support in return, than the industrialists. Instead, the bias in perception deflates or inflates, systematically, estimates of the various elite sectors. This bias closely follows the position of the elite sectors themselves within the structure of power.

[9] Compare Lee D. Ross, Teresa M. Amabile, and Julia L. Steinmetz, "Social Roles, Social Control, and Biases in Social-Perception Process," *Journal of Personality and Social Psychology* 35 (1977): 485-494, and, more generally, Richard Nisbet and Lee D. Ross, *Human Inference: Strategies and Shortcomings of Social Judgment* (Englewood Cliffs, N.J.: Prentice-Hall, 1980).

Another factor working to produce discrepant observations is the variable specificity or lack of definition of the perceived groups. Everyone knows that the MDB opposes the government and that the ARENA supports it. At the same time, the perceptions of conservatives and progressives differ most sharply when the groups under consideration are ill-defined entities, like "the middle class" and "peasants." In such cases, the elites are freer to interpret the world as they please. The degree of support/opposition that the MDB politicians assign to "the peasants," for example, is widely discrepant from the imputations made by the ARENA politicians, and from those made by the conservative elites generally.

There is one instance of divergent perceptions that cannot be explained either in terms of the incumbent/outsider positions of the elites or with reference to the vagueness of the groups. Most of the elites believe that "urban labor" is at best mildly supportive of the government, and the MDB politicians and the church claim that the working class stands in patent opposition. The chief exception to the ascription of disaffection comes from the labor leaders themselves, who view the *sindicatos trabalhistas* as largely supportive of the government.

The reasons for this discrepancy are multiple, ranging from the *peleguista* (roughly, "government-oriented") tendencies of the labor leadership to the vulgar Marxist premise of the other elites that the exploitation of the Brazilian working class translates more or less automatically into political resentment.[10] A primary motive of the labor movement, such as it is under authoritarianism, is to become assimilated into, rather than to overthrow, the developmental program of the regime. As we shall see, the "social reformers" are not usually picky about who rules, so long as they get some share of the spoils. The perceptions of the elite establishment, by contrast, seem to be a mixture of guilt and fear.[11]

---

[10] For an analysis of the compromised position of the labor leaders, see Amaury de Souza, "The Nature of Corporatist Representation in Brazil," Ph.D. dissertation, Massachusetts Institute of Technology, 1978. For a study of short circuits in political consciousness in the Brazilian public, see Youssef Cohen, "Popular Support for Authoritarian Governments: Brazil under Medici," Ph.D. dissertation, University of Michigan, 1979. None of this implies that labor organizations in Brazil are uniformly incapable of serious mobilization against the government; it does suggest that the weight of the corporatist tradition, among the rank-and-file as well as the leadership, is very heavy indeed.

[11] Much the same pattern emerges when the bias in perceptions of the attention that the government pays to various groups is considered; for this reason, the data are not presented here. The MDB politicians and the bishops take a gloomier view of the responsiveness of the government than the other elites, just as they are inclined to see greater opposition against the government. The labor leaders surpass even the ARENA politicians, as well as the state managers, in their estimates of the attention that the government gives to different groups. This tendency may be attributed to a belief that certain groups are the object of governmental

In summary, the angle of vision of the elites changes according to their institutional positions in the power structure, and the distorting effects of this tendency are compounded when the objects of perception are themselves ambiguous. The composite result is rather like a cubist painting. The outside world impinges on but does not determine the perceptions of the elites.

Conciliatory and Conflictive Perspectives

In a power structure as steeply stratified as that of Brazil, we might expect that the attention given to some groups would be perceived as depriving others, insofar as governmental responsiveness is a scarce commodity. Yet most of the elites do not see things this way. When the correlations between the attention-paid indicators for the thirteen groups are computed, they all turn out to be positive.[12] This suggests that the elites perceive the government as dispensing or withholding attention generically, across all groups.

Some of the elites, usually the progressives, peg the responsiveness of the government as low while others—typically, the conservatives—give the government high marks. The progressives are a bit more inclined to perceive groups in polarized terms, with some receiving a lot of attention and others very little. But this tendency is secondary to the overall inclination to view the government as expansive or restrictive toward social actors in general, in part regardless of their identity.

On occasion, this way of looking at the power structure yields odd results. For example, the perception of the attention paid to the military correlates with the perception of the attention paid to the MDB on the order of .42. The corresponding correlation between *técnicos* and students is .36, between peasants and ARENA politicians .26, and so on.

Not all the statistics are so bizarre. Usually, when the groups are very disparate, the connection between the attention paid to one and the attention

---

care in the coping or repressive sense. But the possibility seems remote in light of the fact that the labor leaders view themselves as receiving below-average attention. A likelier interpretation is that, with the exception of the civil servants themselves, the labor leaders are the most statist of the elites. Since Brazilian labor organizations were created by and form part of the state, the labor leaders are accustomed to a state-centric world in which all groups, even the opposition, are supposed to orbit around the government. See Heloísa Helena T. S. Martin, *O Estado e a Burocratização do Sindicato no Brasil* (São Paulo: Editora Hucitec, 1979).

[12] Purists may object to the use of product-moment correlation coefficients with the kind of data analyzed here and in other parts of the study. Technically, measures of association designed for ordinal data might be more suitable. In the end, however, the results are the same, and the interval-level measures are probably more familiar. See Sanford Labovitz, "In Defense of Assigning Numbers to Ranks," *American Sociological Review* 36 (1971): 521-522.

paid to the other becomes attenuated. The correlations between urban labor and the multinationals is only .09, and that between landlords and peasants is zero.

Yet it is impossible to retrieve anything like a zero-sum vision of group conflict from these results, and we are left with the recourse of invoking the propensity of the elites to use the state, and no groups outside the state, as the arbiter of the fate of social interests. Apparently, the elites believe that all groups gain and lose at the sufferance of the government. Their gains and losses are unequal, but neither do they seem to be made directly at the expense of one another. The inference fits nicely with models of the Bonapartist state. All groups are more or less supine and dependent on the authoritarian executive.

Yet appearances are not quite what they seem. When presented with a list of groups that may receive varying degrees of attention from the government, the elites are not forced to make invidious comparisons. They go down the roster serially, imputing "more or less" attention to the groups. The contrast between groups is only implicit, since there is no need to rank interests precisely, one behind the other. In this way, the perceptions of the elites undergo inflation. The progressives constitute a minor exception to this rule; they deflate the responsiveness of the government. But not even the progressives rank groups exactly in order.[13]

This cordiality muffles the trade-offs that the elites may perceive but do not openly admit between contending groups. This bias can be corrected by calculating for each elite the attention that he believes each group receives from the government, above or below his average tendency to ascribe responsiveness to the government. The way to do this is to compute the mean "attentiveness" ascribed to the government, across the thirteen groups, by each of the elites, and to subtract the mean from his rating of each of the groups. The operation serves as a deflator, adjusting the perceptions of the elites in light of their base-line feelings about the government's responsiveness.[14] These scores, adjusted for inflation, can then be correlated.

Table 3.2 demonstrates that the correlations are much more in line with

[13] In other words, the consistently positive associations reflect the tendency of the elites to impute responsiveness to the government, whatever the specific target of this attention. The progressive elites are less prone to do this than the conservatives. But the progressives are a minority, and even they are not unfailingly contentious. The reaction of most of the elites is to slide over conflicts between groups and to suggest that some inequities may develop between social actors generally and the state itself. Compare Bolivar Lamounier, "Ideologia Conservadora e Mudanças Estruturais," *Dados* 5 (1968): 1-29.

[14] See William H. Cunningham, Isabella C. M. Cunningham, and Robert T. Green, "The Ipsative Process to Reduce Response Set Bias," *Public Opinion Quarterly* 41 (1977): 379-384.

TABLE 3.2

Correlations between Elite Perceptions of Attention Paid
by Government to Thirteen Groups
(calculated from ipsatized scores)

	(1)	(2)	(3)	(4)	(5)	(6)	(7)	(8)	(9)	(10)	(11)	(12)	(13)
(1) Military	—												
(2) Técnicos	.55	—											
(3) MNCs	.27	.09	—										
(4) Banks	−.03	−.05	.30	—									
(5) Industry	.23	.08	.50	.46	—								
(6) Landowners	−.04	−.21	.20	.26	.26	—							
(7) Church	−.12	−.15	−.15	−.16	−.20	−.03	—						
(8) ARENA	−.22	−.24	−.33	−.16	−.35	−.20	−.05	—					
(9) Governors	−.06	.11	−.27	−.12	−.24	−.21	−.13	.17	—				
(10) Peasants	−.40	−.27	−.39	−.41	−.36	−.22	−.05	.00	−.11	—			
(11) Students	−.34	−.28	−.44	−.29	−.43	−.29	−.03	.02	−.02	.46	—		
(12) Labor	−.33	−.30	−.42	−.40	−.44	−.28	.04	.09	−.05	.43	.38	—	
(13) MDB	−.40	−.21	−.40	−.28	−.41	−.19	.03	.17	.08	.16	.15	.15	—

NOTE: The raw scores on each of the thirteen variables are subtracted from their mean and computed for each respondent.

the intuitive notion of conflictful trade-offs between groups. The matrix abounds in negative coefficients, which capture the sense of the elites that some groups gain at the expense of others. What has been done is to remove the perceived ability of the government to expand and contract the field of competition and to allow the implicit, direct trade-offs between groups to emerge. Now the correlation between the attention attributed to the military and to the MDB is − .40, between the *técnicos* and the students − .28, between industry and labor − .44, between the multinationals and the peasants − .39, and so on.

Not all of the perceived relations between groups are conflictive. The military-*técnico* axis remains intact, as do the positive links between peasants and urban labor and between other collectivities with presumably common interests. Even the members of the rival political parties are perceived, to a slight but significant extent, jointly. Under authoritarianism, politicians have a common fate, and they share a latent solidarity because of their humiliation before the state machine.

In their own way, both versions of elite perceptions regarding the attentiveness of the government are true. Eliminating the softness produced by the propensity of the elites to assess the responsiveness of the government in across-the-board terms exposes the underlying conflicts among groups. Yet the response-set displayed by the elites has substantive meaning in its own right; it is not merely a methodological artifact but rather a mixture of courtesy and hypocrisy that men with pretensions to being reasonable and civil maintain in the face of dilemmas they prefer not to dwell on. In the Brazilian context, the idea that the state should assume a major role in smoothing over conflicting demands is a familiar one.[15]

We should be careful not to impute too much purposefulness to their manner, nor should we imagine that the elites have a paternalistic state explicitly in mind in giving responses that lead to the impression that the government has a vast capacity to reconcile social demands. The elites were not confronted with mutually exclusive alternatives. These are precisely the kinds of decisions they would probably rather avoid. The reality of politics in Brazil rarely presents elites with absolute choices. In fact, they spend some time trying to structure this reality so that it has more give to it than a perfectly inflexible, reciprocal system.

Preferences about the Redistribution of Power

Even if Brazilian elites are disinclined to envision the distribution of power in confrontational terms, beneath this affability there is more than a touch of awareness that interests are in fact competitive and that some win at the expense of others. In the absolute sense, putting numbers on these perceptions can be a misguided enterprise, for power is a relational property. Neither the generous nor the harsher perceptions of the elites are necessarily true; one without the other produces a one-sided illusion.

In a relative sense, however, the views of the elites are much less ambiguous. This becomes apparent when the normative opinions of the elites about the structure of power are examined. Now the question shifts to their preferences regarding how governmental attention, and by implication power, might be redistributed.

Initially, it appears that the tendency of the elites is to assert that most groups should be given more attention. The pattern is plausible but not very incisive. It corresponds to the variable-sum principle that actors be

---

[15] The sort of response-set discussed here is even more common in the data from the nonelite samples, expecially among the lower, less-educated classes. It is important to recognize that the methodological and substantive facets of the tendency are not mutually exclusive. The propensity for "yea-saying" parallels quite closely the more theoretical notion of mass acquiescence and dependence on a paternalistic state. Compare Henry A. Landsberger and Antonio Saavedra, "Response Set in Developing Countries," *Public Opinion Quarterly* 31 (1967): 214-229. This tendency needs to be sharply distinguished, however, from the more generic and much less firmly established phenomenon of mass authoritarianism. See Ken Rigby and Eric E. Rump, "The Generality of Attitudes to Authority," *Human Relations* 32 (1979): 469-487, and J. J. Ray, "Do Authoritarians Hold Authoritarian Attitudes?" *Human Relations* 29 (1976): 307-325.

admitted to the political arena without displacing those whose interests are already taken care of.

However, some of the elites would like to see not only a broadening but also a reallocation of power. The most telling datum is the difference between the attention that the elites feel should be given to various groups and the attention that they think the groups actually receive.[16] The departure from what has been considered so far is fundamental yet straightforward. I no longer compare the elites' perceptions of power held by diverse interests. I contrast these perceptions with what the elites think the distribution of power should be.

Table 3.3 arrays the elite sectors and the perceived groups to bring out the principal contrasts. Those who favor change are aligned to the left, and the groups are ranked from top to bottom in descending order of the relative attention that the elites feel they should receive. The views of the elites regarding the desirable amount of change in the structure of power are summarized in the column of averages toward the right, which gives the average difference between the attention owed and the attention paid for each of the groups.

The elites claim that three actors—the multinational corporations, the technocrats, and especially the military—should be given less attention. These are the groups who, the elites believe, have too much power. Conversely, the inclination to accord groups more attention increases for those, like the MDB, who are seen in opposition and for those, such as rural and urban labor, whose interests have been trampled on.

While all the elite sectors desire some reallocation of benefits, they do not push for the same amount of change. The MDB politicians are the strongest advocates of change, and the ARENA politicians are the most cautious. None of this is puzzling, given the divergent stakes of the elite sectors in the status quo.

But some aspects of elite preferences about the distribution of power are less obvious. A self-serving quality can be detected in the preferences of the elites about the groups to receive the greatest increment in attention from the government. The labor leaders put themselves in first place, as do the MDB and the ARENA politicians. There is a generalized tendency for the elites to maximize their own interests. While the businessmen do not assign themselves much more power under the new order, since they

---

[16] The elites were asked "What is the degree of attention which the government *should* give to the following groups in taking decisions of national importance?" Responses to the earlier question, "In your opinion, how much attention *does* the government give to the following groups in taking decisions of national importance?" were subtracted from responses to the *should* question. The resulting differences for all the groups are the scores shown in Table 3.3.

TABLE 3.3

Mean Differences between Preferences about Attention Owed and Perceptions of Attention
Paid to Thirteen Groups, by Elite Sector
(negative sign = less attention owed than paid)

Perceived Group	Perceiving Elite Sector							
	MDB	Bishops	Labor	Business	Civil Service	ARENA	Mean	ETA^2
MDB	1.79	1.44	.91	.63	.90	.43	.82	.12
Labor	1.77	1.70	.98	.55	.47	.16	.69	.19
Students	1.71	1.40	.91	.51	.49	.34	.68	.15
Peasants	1.54	1.80	.88	.56	.48	.16	.67	.18
Governors	.93	1.11	.26	.38	.27	.29	.38	.08
ARENA	1.43	.67	.09	.11	.22	.44	.27	.15
Church	1.38	1.40	.22	−.06	.02	.03	.17	.22
Landowners	.69	.11	−.18	.20	.16	.10	.12	.06
Industry	.46	−.11	−.08	.24	−.12	.03	.06	.06
Banks	.69	.11	−.25	.15	−.10	−.03	.01	.08
MNCs	.00	−.44	−.42	.03	−.04	−.03	−.11	.05
Técnicos	−.50	−.11	.02	−.20	−.02	−.26	−.14	.06
Military	−.71	−1.00	−.33	−.42	−.41	−.26	−.41	.05
Algebraic Mean	.83	.75	.23	.21	.18	.12	.25	.18
Absolute Mean	1.22	1.12	.63	.57	.45	.36	.59	.22

NOTES: An ETA^2 of .07 or larger is significant at the .01 level. The larger the coefficient, the greater the disagreement among the elite sectors about the attention owed to a group, relative to the attention it is perceived as getting from the government. In general, ETA^2 is low for the groups perceived as having a good deal of power and high for the less powerful. In other words, there is more agreement about the "common enemy" than about the distribution of benefits to contenders for power and less favored people.

In one respect, the *absolute value* is a more meaningful figure than the *algebraic difference*, since it is not affected by the tendency for positive and negative differences to cancel each other out, thus reducing the magnitude of the mean index. For the thirteen groups considered separately, however, the algebraic difference is more appropriate, for it shows the direction of desired change.

are well-off under present conditions, they still yearn for a bit more solicitude from the government, just as they feel that the power of the *técnicos* and the military should be curtailed. For their part, the state managers feel that they themselves have about the right amount of power (very great) and that the influence of the business community should be reduced.

In short, it is easier to identify the groups against which the elites are united—the multinationals, the technocrats, and the military—than to discern the make-up of an alternative coalition. Each of the elite sectors tends to put itself at the top, or very near the top, of the revised pyramid, so that no positive agreement appears about the composition of an antiforeign, antistatist, antimilitary alliance.[17]

The fact that even conservative elites such as the businessmen and the civilian *técnicos* feel that the military has gone too far for too long is, of course, significant in itself, especially since the data reflect the state of mind of the elites at the peak of the boom period in Brazil, when both self-congratulation and censorship were at their height. Nevertheless, while the elites are more or less united in opposition, the opposition can hardly be termed a coherent one, for there is little sign of a positive counter-coalition.[18]

But this outcome is in part built into the question posed to the elites. They were asked how much attention various actors should receive from the government; it is doubtful whether they feel that their favorite interests should actually take over the state. Not even the most progressive of the elites are likely to contemplate with equanimity, much less enthusiasm, a polity in which labor organizations are the most powerful groups.

The way to read these data is a reflection of a restitutive and, in certain quarters, redistributive impulse among the elites. The message seems to be that a balance of power should be introduced, or restored, within the establishment and that the most blatant inequities in elite-mass relationships should somehow be compensated for. Any reconstruction of a full-blown utopia from these data would be unwarranted.

Yet the preferences of the elites for change are not simply a function of their separate interests. This is most obvious in the case of the bishops, who place both urban and rural labor ahead of themselves. More generally, there appears to be a functional solidarity among certain elite sectors. For example, the ARENA politicians accord their colleagues in the MDB almost as much influence as themselves in their idealized version of the new order. Similarly, the MDB politicians feel that members of the ARENA should be given much more attention—more, for instance, than the bankers and the industrialists. Clearly, the MDB politicians are not self-effacing, nor are they arguing that their rivals in the ARENA should take power. But it is equally clear that both the MDB and the ARENA want greater influence for the political class as a whole.

[17] The best summary indicator of the consensual-versus-dispersed nature of elite preferences is the eta-squared statistic in the right-most column in Table 3.3. It tends toward insignificance for the groups about whom the elites agree—that is, for those whose power should be restricted. It becomes much larger for the groups who, on the average, the elites believe should be more fairly treated. While all the elite sectors feel that the MDB should be handled less roughly by the government, they do not agree about how much power such interests should enjoy.

[18] Compare H. R. Kedward, *Resistance in Vichy France: A Study of Ideas and Motivation in the Southern Zone 1940-1942* (London: Oxford University Press, 1978).

Thus, the elites tend not only to unite in their opposition to what they consider the excessive dominance of the military and the technocrats; they also form tentative coalitions among themselves. Although it is possible to gain an impression of comparative gains and losses by going through Table 3.3 cell-by-cell, both the oppositional and the protocoalitional structure of elite preferences can more easily be visualized by correlating the differences between attention owed and attention paid for the diverse groups and then reducing them to their underlying sociometry. The groups in Figure 3.2 are plotted according to their perceived proximity to and distance from one another: the greater the perceived distance, the more zero-sum is the elites' characterization of the relationship between groups.[19]

The most striking feature of the coalitional geometry is the segregation of the military. Their closest allies are the *técnicos* and the MNCs. All of the other groups are perceived at greater or lesser distances from this triumvirate. Among themselves, these groups are dispersed, and it would be forcing the case to impose a strong unity on such a constellation of interests. But, although unity-in-opposition may be fragile, the very legitimacy of the reigning coalition seems problematic. The consensus of the elites is that the technocrats, the multinationals, and their military protectors must be brought to account.[20]

The supremacy of the military and, to a lesser degree, the technocrats and the multinationals reinforces their isolation in the eyes of the elites who have been shorn of direct influence in the power structure. The military and their few allies, by gathering so much power in their hands and leaving so little for anyone else, cut themselves off not only from obviously downtrodden groups like peasants and workers but also from potential sources of support within the elite establishment. This centralization-without-integration promotes latent alliances between otherwise improbable partners.[21]

[19] The algorithm is the same version of smallest-space analysis used in Chapter Two. In correlating the attention-owed/attention-paid differences for the thirteen groups, the assumption is that a strong positive correlation indicates that two actors are perceived as sharing a common interest or fate; the relative gains or losses of one are thought to be in tandem with the ups-and-downs of the other. Compare Donald T. Campbell, "Common Fate, Similarity, and Other Indices of the Status of Aggregates of Persons as Social Entities," *Behavioral Science* 3 (1958): 14-25.

[20] It can be argued that the isolation of the military is an artifact resulting from the omission of military figures in the sample of elite respondents. Quite possibly, leaders of the Brazilian military do not see themselves as so cut off from the rest of the elites. But none of this changes the fact that the civilian elites, including the most conservative among them, perceive the military as having too much power and believe that this power should be curtailed.

[21] Compare Bernard Schaffer, "Organization is not Equity: Theories of Political Integration," *Development and Change* 8 (1977): 19-43.

FIGURE 3.2

Two-Dimensional Smallest-Space Diagram of Differences between Preferences for
Attention Owed and Perceptions of Attention Paid to Thirteen Groups

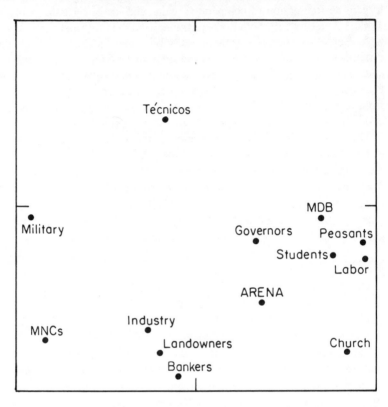

	DIMENSIONALITY OF SOLUTION		
	One	*Two*	*Three*
Kruskal's Stress Coefficient	.22	.07	.03
Guttman-Lingoes' Coefficient of Alienation	.26	.09	.05

It is not only the rural and urban workers, the standard objects of
progressive concern, who are seen as meriting greater attention. The politicians generally—the MDB, the ARENA, and the appointed governors—
also tend to be perceived as deprived. While the ARENA politicians and
the governors are looked upon with less sympathy than the urban and rural
working classes, as politicians they are included in the antimilitarist, antibureaucratic, antiforeign bloc.

In addition, the fate of the most repressed actors, like the peasantry, is
perceived as linked to changes in the predicament of intermediate collec-

tivities, such as the governors and the ARENA politicians. The configuration of direct and indirect connections among nominally disparate groups implies an inchoate alliance between leftists and moderates against the dominance of the military, the technocrats, and the multinationals. It is these latent, submerged protocoalitions that charge the question of political liberalization with more than the usual menace of palace intrigue.

A subsidiary axis is formed in Figure 3.2, running vertically between the technocrats on one side and the businessmen, including the landowners, on the other. The church and even the multinationals also stand at some distance from the bureaucratic state. The elites evidently distinguish between their military and foreign, as compared to their civilian, predators.

The perceived distinction between the *técnicos* and the business community gives the impression of a genuine split between the public and private sectors. This division is partially separate from the left-right cleavage polarizing the military and the civilians. Neither the technocrats nor the businessmen can be placed at one extreme or the other of the promilitary/antimilitary axis. The elites seem to consider them as key forces in the modernization of Brazil. As such, they are beyond the reach of superficial changes in the organization of power. All the same, there exists a perceived trade-off between the businessmen and the technocrats, one that can be traced to a traditional rivalry between private enterprise and state control.

The church remains distant from these clusters. Very broadly, the bishops are aligned with leftist and progressive groups: with urban and rural labor, with the students, with the MDB politicians. Yet they are also seen as distinct from these interests. Even though most of the elites believe that the bishops should be heard, the church can never be a full participant in the secular world of Brazilian politics. The most notable feature of the position accorded the bishops is that they are perceived as the farthest of all interests from the military. They form the only elite corporation in Brazil that can confront the military with some hope of not being crushed in return.[22]

The multidimensional reorganization envisaged by the elites makes it difficult to characterize their preferences in a summary statement. Yet if a diagonal line is drawn in Figure 3.2 from the lower left to the upper right, the essential features of elite reformism can be understood. The multinationals, the military, and the *técnicos* fall on one side of this divide and the rest of the elites on the other. All of the elite sectors desire some

---

[22] One group that, at least in recent times, approaches the bishops in this respect is the *Orden dos Advogados do Brasil*, the national bar association. The military recognize the role of the lawyers as important arbiters of constitutional legitimacy. See Maurício Dias, ''Os Anos Faoro, Tempo de Bom Combate,'' *Isto É*, April 4, 1979: 28-30.

redistribution of power. The opposition politicians and the bishops want the most extensive reallocation. But even the conservative elites agree that the power of the military and the *técnicos*, together with the prerogatives of the multinationals, should be curbed.

Again, this does not constitute an alternative model of the political order. But if the desired configuration of interests shown here is compared with the actual sociometry of the power structure depicted in the previous chapter, it can be seen that one is practically the reverse image of the other. This suggests, in turn, the inability of the authoritarian alliance to gain ideological hegemony.

Of the several regularities that have emerged in analyzing the elites' perceptions and preferences regarding the distribution of power, three deserve emphasis. The first involves the disposition of the elites to view conflicts and their solutions in variable-sum terms. The second involves their agreement that the power of three actors—the military, the *técnicos* and the multinationals—should be curtailed. Third, there does not appear to be any firm consensus as to the make-up of an alternative ruling coalition.

The reluctance of the elites to define political combat as a game of winner-take-all is probably not distinctively Brazilian. Power holders in most societies, even those who are more conspicuously ideological than the Brazilian elites, seem disinclined to force an either-or vision, at least on domestic politics, for this runs the risk of mobilizing enemies as well as allies.

Where signs of a zero-sum view do appear is among the dissident elites. The MDB politicians have less reason to be satisfied with the authoritarian condition than the incumbents. Not only are their objections harsher but they also tend to see the distribution of power in more polarized terms.

Yet once their tendency to inflate the possibility of redress is held constant, the views of all the elites of the inequities between groups take on greater contrast. Social interests are seen as gaining and losing at the expense of one another, when the system of competition and distribution cannot expand. Even when we allow for a certain expansiveness on the part of the elites in considering rearrangements of the power structure, most of them, including the conservatives, admit to the desirability of reducing the power of the military, the *técnicos*, and the multinationals. This is the second major finding.

The third discovery—that the elites are not consensual about the make-up of an alternative to the military-technocratic-multinational triumvirate— is in part a reflection of a failure to ask the question directly. If inferences are limited to estimates of how much and in which directions the elites want to change the distribution of power, considerably more agreement emerges regarding the identity of the losers than the winners. All these tendencies fall short of a thoroughgoing condemnation of the prevailing order. Since the respondents are elites, such an outcome would be far-fetched.

But the data also suggest that the reigning coalition is more than just unpopular; it is unanimously unpopular, even if the intensity of this judgment varies from one elite group to another. Progressive and conservative sectors alike resent sustained intrusions into their own spheres of privilege and influence. The consensual point is the desire for some modicum of autonomy from the depredations of the authoritarian state and some measure of control over the advantages enjoyed by the multinationals.[23]

What this convergence of tendencies suggests, in brief, is a sense of the elites that the military and their allies have overstepped the bounds of appropriate intervention and that their continued occupation of the command posts of Brazilian society is not only unpopular but also in violation of some fundamental rules of interelite behavior. In the eyes of the elites, the power structure lacks legitimacy; the ruling coalition is too narrow. In the next two chapters, the nature of these rules is ascertained more precisely.

[23] Compare Amaury de Souza and Bolivar Lamounier, "Escaping the Black Hole: Government-Labor Relations in Brazil in the 1980s," paper presented at the symposium on "Brazil 1980-2000," sponsored by the Research Institute on International Change, Columbia University, Rio de Janeiro, August 20-22, 1980. See also Dale Krane, "Opposition Strategy and Survival in Praetorian Brazil," paper presented at the annual meetings of the Southern Political Science Associations, Atlanta, Georgia, November 6-8, 1980.

FOUR

Developmental Priorities

Brazilian elites not only want changes in the structure of power, they are also unanimous about whose power should be reduced. The military, the multinationals, and the *técnicos* have transgressed the norm of limited pluralism. The gravity of the situation could be dismissed were it only a matter of grumbling from expected quarters—from the opposition politicians, for example, whose business it is to criticize the regime. But this is plainly not the case. Although the conservative and ambivalent elites, such as the labor leaders, are less enthusiastic about direct confrontation than the progressives, they all become contumacious when faced with the aggrandizing pretensions of the ruling triumvirate.

But there is much that is incomplete and unsatisfactory about this diagnosis. While we never expected to discover among the elites an elaborate alternative to the authoritarian condition, certainly not with the rather skimpy evidence examined so far, in retrospect—in light of the turmoil following the halcyon days of authoritarianism in Brazil—the existence of a negative consensus among the elites, the unity-in-opposition against the military, the multinationals, and the *técnicos*, hardly constitutes a revelation.

However, negative unity is not all there is to the political thinking of the elites. Even if we fail to uncover any single hegemonic current among the elites, and even with due regard to the fissiparous tendencies of elite interests, it may be that the elites judge the political system according to standards that are neither unanimous nor wholly fragmented.

What I am searching for are the simplifying guidelines of elite politics in Brazil,that, at the same time, do justice to the divergence of interests that lies barely below the surface of antimilitary, antiforeign, and antibureaucratic sentiment. These rules-of-thumb are the developmental priorities of the elites. Such partially conflicting values not only help explain the cross-purposes at which the elites often operate. The tentative coalitions formed among elites with different values also determine the contingent nature of authoritarian legitimacy.

In order to understand this, it is useful to begin by recalling the philosophy of growth summarized by Ernesto Geisel, quoted at the outset of the study. The model of development outlined by the fourth in a line of generals heading the government of Brazil since 1964 is fairly explicit. Strategic options are arranged in a schedule of orderly, if loosely timed, stages, beginning with capital accumulation and the expansion of the economic infrastructure, followed by a wider distribution of social benefits, and culminating in political liberalization. While the linear sequence of progress with order does not constitute a detailed policy package, it does express the grand design of the Brazilian "miracle."

The strategy corresponds to the "benign line" pattern of growth.[1] Although no Brazilian elites can be described as opposed to economic growth in principle, they are not of one mind about the primacy given to this goal at the expense of social and political change. Decisions on such matters are not taken on the basis of rational calculation alone.

I shall argue that the elites rank their developmental priorities along two partially separate and difficult-to-reconcile axes, one involving a trade-off between growth and equity and another between order and liberty. Consideration of these two dimensions provides a parsimonious way of comprehending the dilemmas of Brazilian development, as decision makers and contenders for power perceive them.

In addition, the developmental priorities of the elites reflect their fundamental values. They represent not only abstract causal models but also basic commitments to options implying gains and losses for specific interests as well as for the nation as a whole. Let us examine each of these aspects of elite agendas in turn.

The Perceived Multidimensionality of Development

The supposed conflict between growth and equity—in Williamson's phrase, "the classic correlation between accumulation and inequality"—is a staple of the literature on development.[2] Among Brazilian elites, the judgment that a trade-off must occur in favor of economic over social development derives not only from academic principle or from the casual observation that resources are limited and the time to catch up is short but also from their recollections of the populist era immediately preceding the 1964

[1] The phrase is from Samuel P. Huntington and Joan M. Nelson, *No Easy Choice: Political Participation in Developing Countries* (Cambridge, Mass.: Harvard University Press, 1976), pp. 17-41.

[2] Jeffrey G. Williamson, "Inequality, Accumulation and Technological Imbalance: A Growth-Equity Conflict in American History?" *Economic Development and Cultural Change* 27 (1979): 231. See also Douglas W. Rae, "The Egalitarian State: Notes on a System of Contradictory Ideals," *Daedalus* 408 (1979): 37-54.

coup.[3] However short-lived, the experience of double-digit inflation and of stagnation in real growth during the last year of democratic rule left many of the elites with a deep skepticism about the feasibility of equitable development.[4]

Hence, the priority given to aggregate growth over "premature" distribution derives from eminently political considerations. This is so not only because the exact terms of the trade-off between growth and equity are obscure but also because capital accumulation is not self-generating. The mechanism of enforcement in Brazil has been the authoritarian state.

Yet the "elective affinity" between economic growth and authoritarian rule in Brazil may be tenuous. There is little evidence that the relationship is either causal or permanent. Even if at a given time the imposition of wage restraints and the accompanying demobilization of mass politics are conducive to spurts in the gross national product, recourse to the sword has been viewed by Brazilian elites, even by conservatives, as an expedient rather than a stable solution.[5]

The official model, promulgated in the late sixties and early seventies,

[3] Compare Alejandro Portes and D. Frances Ferguson, "Comparative Ideologies of Poverty and Equity: Latin America and the United States," in *Equity, Income, and Policy: Comparative Studies in Three Worlds of Development*, ed. Irving Louis Horowitz (New York: Praeger, 1977); Irma Adelman and Cynthia Taft Morris, *Economic Growth and Social Equity in Developing Countries* (Stanford: Stanford University Press, 1974); Hollis Chenery et al., *Redistribution with Growth* (London: Oxford University Press, 1974); and Arthur M. Okun, *Equality and Efficiency: The Big Tradeoff* (Washington, D.C.: The Brookings Institution, 1975).

[4] It should be clear that I am concerned with the elites' perceptions of the relationship between economic performance and political institutions, not with the structural linkages between the two. Edmar Bacha, among others, has made the case that the Brazilian economy tends to move in cycles affected by world market fluctuations and that the causal impact of political decisions for which the technicians of the Médici era took credit has been overestimated. See Edmar L. Bacha, "Issues and Evidence on Recent Brazilian Economic Growth," *World Development* 5 (1977): 47-67. The perceptual distortions of the elites are not, of course, arbitrary, since the connections between public policy and policy performance are hardly transparent in Brazil, and there is leeway for honest disagreement. See Bacha and Lance Taylor, "Brazilian Income Distribution in the 1960s: 'Facts,' Model Results, and the Controversy," *Journal of Development Studies* 14 (1978): 271-297; Werner Baer, "The Brazilian Boom, 1968-1972: An Explanation and Interpretation," *World Development* 1 (1973): 1-15; and Gary S. Fields, "Who Benefits from Economic Development?—A Reexamination of Brazilian Growth in the 1960's," *American Economic Review* 67 (1977): 570-582.

[5] This has not always been the case. During the 1930s, a number of political theorists in Brazil argued that a corporatist authoritarianism was the manifest destiny of the country. They fought with both the "instrumental authoritarians" and the "doctrinaire liberals" of the time. See Wanderley Guilherme dos Santos, "Liberalism in Brazil: Ideology and Praxis," in *Terms of Conflict: Ideology in Latin American Politics*, ed. Morris J. Blachman and Ronald G. Hellman (Philadelphia: Institute for the Study of Human Issues, 1977).

is essentially a stage theory of development. As a causal chain, as a theory about the relation of means toward an end, it is rife with ambiguities. The role of coercion in maintaining the conditions for accelerated growth is never explicitly mentioned, perhaps because it is so painfully obvious. What makes many of the elites uncomfortable with the model may not be the "regrettable necessity" of force in the march toward economic growth but the growth in the monopolizer of the means of violence: the Brazilian state. The functions, prerogatives, and future of the state are left unspecified in the authoritarian model.

Similarly, the model says nothing about the composition of the ruling coalition. It is easy to deduce the identity of those who are excluded from participation and those who pay the costs of development. But these negative criteria do not constitute a positive political framework. This may seem a trivial intrusion of personalistic considerations into the debate over strategic alternatives. In the broadest of senses, the criticism is correct. No group or coalition or coalition of groups has the desire or the capacity to stop, much less to reverse, the course of Brazilian development from industrialization back to an agrarian past. By such a test, it does not matter who rules Brazil. All promoters and opponents of the regime are united in this macroconsensus that, because it is so broad, has no political significance. Membership in the ruling coalition and the composition of those left out are important to the extent that the elite actors disagree about the means toward and the pace of further development.

Put bluntly, under Brazilian authoritarianism, banishment from the ruling circles means not only a loss of power but all the loss of the right to protection from the excesses of power. This is so even when, as often happens, "exiled" elites such as the politicians and most of the business community, not to mention the labor leaders, benefit materially from authoritarian policies. The imposition of a developmental model in the absence of consensus—more precisely, in the absence of a hegemonic ideology—entails not only mass demobilization but also severe restraints on interelite competition. This leads to an atmosphere of suspicion and policing that is extremely costly to sustain.

Thus, the relative weight to be given to accumulation and equity is not the only command decision facing Brazilian elites. They must also decide about the costs involved in the balance between authoritarian order and political liberty.[6] At times, the two axes may overlap. The genius of

[6] The following statement by Fernando Henrique Cardoso, made during an interview when he was running for a senate seat from São Paulo in 1978, captures this distinction:

They [my supporters] are looking for something in the direction of socialism. Or better, something in the way of a more just society because, if you tried to express this socialist tendency, you wouldn't be able to pin it down. But a more just, more egalitarian society,

Brazilian authoritarianism, if it has one, is that more often than not the choices are partially separate and muddled. They are conceptually distinct and, in practice, confused.

Casting these differences in empirical form poses a challenge to measurement. The investigation hinges on a brief question, which reads:

> We would like to know your opinions about some fundamental issues for Brazil today. There is little doubt that economic development, social well-being and political development are three objectives of great importance for Brazil. In your opinion, which of the three objectives should receive, over the next five years, the greatest priority? And which should receive the least?[7]

Respondents to this question can be categorized into four types: those who give priority to economic development, to social equity, to political liberalization, and those who refuse to set priorities and argue that all the goals can be maximized at once.[8] This last alternative is intriguing. It

---

you can see right away that this is what people want. I think that here in São Paulo, today, you have three great demands: liberty, wages and autonomy. Everything turns around this: liberty, wages, autonomy. The wage question is not new. Everybody always wants more. Liberty is also an old demand. What strikes me as interesting is the demand for autonomy. People today really want to organize themselves to fight for their own ideas. They don't want you to come and formulate a doctrine or a galvanizing idea. It's not that.
Quoted in *Isto É*, September 13, 1978: 37.

[7] The Portuguese for the key words is *desenvolvimento econômico, bem-estar social*, and *desenvolvimento político*. In the text, I switch back and forth among "social development," "social reform," "social well-being," and the like to avoid repetition. The most ambiguous of the terms is "political development." Usually, the elites take it to signify liberalization. But sometimes, as we shall see, they understand it to mean the strengthening of the power of the state. Nor is "economic development" a completely unambiguous concept. Certainly, it cannot be equated with "accumulation" alone. Nevertheless, during the early seventies in Brazil, many of the elites did not bother to make any such distinction.

[8] Discounting ties and incomplete orderings, six different rankings of the three goals are possible. The analysis presented here focuses on the first priorities of the elites, ignoring for the most part their second and third choices. The reason for this condensation is that statistical consideration of the complete rank-orderings adds nothing of consequence even though, in principle, the differences between elites with priorities of the form "social-political-economic," for example, and "social-economic-political" may be great. In effect, these variations are taken into account in the section entitled "Elite Interpretations of Developmental Priorities," where the discursive responses of the elites to open-ended probes about their agenda are examined. Since the rank-orderings are not treated in exhaustive form, no transitivity is implied. As an example, elites who give top priority to economic development do not necessarily place social welfare second and political development last, in that order. The lack of transitivity renders the indicator of developmental priorities a nominal attribute, analogous for methodological purposes to indicators of religious denomination, ethnicity, and the like. See James Davis, "Contingency Table Analysis," *Quality and Quantity* 80 (1980): 117-154.

seems the opposite of the hard-nosed, growth-at-all-costs model; it suggests instead a holistic, humanistic ethic. Yet the "all-good-things-go-together" model lacks a cutting edge.[9] It suggests an evasion of the conflicts inherent in developmental decision making. As will be shown, the model is oriented toward the status quo.

Taken literally, these response patterns do not permit identification of the elites who give priority to "order." The omission of this alternative was motivated by the need to maintain rapport, since it is awkward even for the most reactionary of the elites to admit that they prize stability above all, virtually for its own sake. But the problem is not as difficult as it may first appear. Immediately after the elites ranked economic, social, and political goals, they were asked to explain their choices in a discursive manner. The open-ended responses enable us to detect those who intimately associate the need for capital accumulation with the need to impose this priority by force.[10]

Developmental Priorities as Values

There are at least two ways to interpret the development agendas of the elites. One is to consider the priorities as reflecting generic causal chains. This perspective is manifest in the officially approved model, with economic development coming first and political liberalization last. But other, equally "universal" prototheories of development are imaginable. For example, some of the elites contend not only that the fruits of economic development deserve to be more widely shared but also that serious redistribution is a necessary precursor to sustained and autonomous economic growth. Others argue that no such redistribution will occur as long as political power remains in the hands of incumbent elites and that a thorough liberalization of political life must precede advances in social well-being as well as a genuine economic take-off.

Yet the question was not directed at the priorities of the elites *sub specie aeternitatis* but rather at their agendas for the country "over the next five years," after the economic boom that began in 1968 had taken place and before the signs of the post-1973 downturn had become unmistakable. The distribution of elite priorities is therefore time-contingent.

Now, there is an important sense in which the apparently situational, tactical agendas of the elites may be more acute indicators of their basic

[9] See Robert A. Packenham, *Liberal America and the Third World: Political Development Ideas in Foreign Aid and Social Science* (Princeton: Princeton University Press, 1974).

[10] Despite some overlap, it is important to maintain a distinction between the "economists" and the pure "law-and-order" types, a distinction that the use of "technocrats" tends to elide. As the open-ended probes demonstrate, not all the economists are outright authoritarians. For a good analysis of this difference, see Howard P. Greenwald, "Scientists and Technocratic Ideology," *Social Forces* 58 (1979): 630-650.

values—that is, of their strategic commitments—than their supposedly timeless models of growth.[11] Elites who still gave primacy to economic development during the boom times of the Médici era can be considered true believers in the imperatives of accumulation and national grandeur. By the same token, elites who under the repressive atmosphere of the Médici regime insisted on political liberalization may be considered equally resolute. In this situation, considerable courage and conviction were required to uphold the urgency of a political opening.

The supporters of social reform fall between the "economists" and the "politicians." The government itself promulgated a number of welfare measures during the early seventies. These programs were well within the bounds of authoritarian paternalism and hardly represented concessions to dissident groups. A preference for social justice in some form is only mildly risky, especially when it does not violate the rule that such improvements come from above.[12]

Intuitively, then, a plausible case can be made that the developmental priorities of the elites reflect fundamental values. Certainly, such decisions are not taken through value-free debate. Furthermore, since two possibly different versions of elite agendas were elicited by way of the ranking item and the follow-up probe, the issue of how committed or opportunistic the various elite types are need not be left to speculation. While I consider the initial rankings given by the elites to represent their contingent priorities, their discursive responses were coded to retrieve the generic developmental models implied by the elites. If comparison of the two agendas reveals that the social reformers, for example, qualify their position by accepting the tenet that aggregate growth must reach some minimum before distribution becomes feasible, then there would be reason for skepticism about the primacy they accord social equity. Conversely, if there is hardly any change from the contingent to the generic priorities of the economists (or the politicians), a powerful case can be made for treating their developmental priorities as abiding values.

This is, in fact, my main hypothesis. By and large, the economists and

[11] The literature on the role of values in development is voluminous; see Leticia Vicente-Wiley, "Achievement Values of Filipino Entrepreneurs and Politicians," *Economic Development and Cultural Change* 27 (1979): 467-483, and the literature cited therein. The approach used here departs from most of these studies in that a simple ordering rather than a battery of items taps presumed value rankings. Compare Donald D. Searing, "Measuring Politicians' Values," *American Political Science Review* 72 (1978): 65-79.

[12] General Médici himself expressed concern over the social inequities exacerbated by economic growth in his widely publicized statement that "*a economia vai bem mas o povo vai mal.*" ("The economy is going well but the people are doing badly.") The flavor of authoritarian paternalism is captured by James M. Malloy, *The Politics of Social Security in Brazil* (Pittsburgh: University of Pittsburgh Press, 1979).

the politicians are uncompromising antagonists. The politicians tend to regard the economists as narrow-minded devotees of development-at-all-costs in whose worldview the rewards of national power more than compensate for the sacrifice of political freedom and social justice. For their part, the economists regard the politicians as useless and possibly subversive crackpots, bent on stirring up a usually apathetic citizenry with demagogic promises, when they are not scheming to do each other in out of personal spite. During the early seventies in Brazil, the economists and the politicians were poles apart. Neither considered the hegemonic ambitions of the other as legitimate, and there was little consensus and less communication between them.

The social reformers adopted a wait-and-see attitude. They aligned themselves temporarily with the economists because, as the Brazilian saying goes, their principal ideology is the budget. Many of the social reformers seem hugely indifferent to means and supremely committed to one end: the allocation of bread-and-butter benefits. They are less interested in economic or political power than in survival, their own and their clientele's. If the system falters, they are liable to switch sides. This is what gives them a pivotal role in determining the legitimacy of the regime.

It would be wrong, however, to characterize the social reformers simply as antiheroes. Just as the economists are not all true believers in military authoritarianism, not all the social reformers are humble supplicants bowing and genuflecting before the state. Some of the bishops, and a few of the labor leaders, for example, display a rebellious and often anarchist streak, and they are loath to concede legitimacy to the political powers of the moment.[13]

Organization of Analysis

It is not until Chapter Five that I specify and estimate a theory of the determinants of authoritarian legitimacy. This chapter is primarily concerned with variation in developmental priorities, in their own right, across the elite sectors. I am also interested in seeing how the at first glance shadowy phenomena of elite values relate to more specific orientations. Of these, two of the most important are evaluations of the performance of the government in concrete policy areas and satisfaction/dissatisfaction with the incumbent elites. Neither measure taps legitimacy as I define it. But their association with the developmental values of the elites provides a preliminary approach to validating the importance of elite values.

I deal, then, with two related but distinct tasks. The first is to understand

[13] For an analysis of elite orientations toward social justice in a politically more open setting, see Wendell Bell and David L. Stevenson, "Attitudes toward Social Equality in Independent Jamaica," *Comparative Political Studies* 11 (1979): 499-532.

how the developmental agendas of the elites tap their basic values. After charting the variation in priorities and developmental models across the elite sectors, I sift the discursive statements of the elites in order to capture, in the elites' own terms, the finely graded substance behind the "economic," "social," and "political" labels.

The second objective is to obtain a sense of where such values lead, of how they are translated into perspectives on specific issues. The idea is to bring the analysis of elite values down to earth and to establish their utility as well as their validity.

Variation in Developmental Agendas

The time-contingent priorities and the generic developmental strategies of the elites are unlikely to be exactly the same. By the early 1970s, it was credible to argue that Brazil was on the verge of economic take-off. Even if this view appeared overly optimistic, a strong brief could be presented for alleviating some of the social pressures engendered by wage restraints. A few of the elites whose fundamental values favor capital accumulation might be expected to flirt with social reform.

Inspection of the marginal distributions of first priorities supports this hunch. Comparison of the overall agendas yields the following percentages:

First Priority	Economic	Social	Political	All Equal	Total
Contingent	41	33	11	15	100 (250)
Generic	54	17	19	10	100 (249)

Most Brazilian elites rank national priorities along a hierarchy of needs, the foundation of which is the nation's economic might, with the luxury of politics in last place. For fairly obvious reasons, economic growth receives even greater priority in the generic than in the contingent agendas of the elites. The standard perspective is that the amelioration of social inequities depends on economic growth or, conversely, that untimely distribution would jeopardize economic growth. Because social distribution tends to be looked upon as an effect rather than a precondition of economic development, it ranks just below aggregate growth as a goal for the immediate future but falls to third place in the causal models of the elites.

Somewhat surprisingly, political development takes on greater importance in the generic agendas of the elites than it has in their timetables for the near future. In the long run, social reform may be more fundamental but it is also more ambiguous, and perceived in less zero-sum terms, than political change. Defined as liberalization, politics may consist only of a

far-off, innocuous goal. Defined as authoritative decision making, it becomes present at every stage of the developmental process and assumes
an active causal role even for some of the conservative elites.

In summary, comparison of the contingent and the causal agendas of
the elites suggests (1) that economic growth is accorded virtual majoritarian
priority in both versions; (2) that political development gains in priority
when viewed, apparently, as a decision-making process rather than as a
"stage"; and (3) that social reform, while considered a moderately desirable goal in the short to medium run, is not considered a prime mover of
either economic or political change.

All this is based on the simplest of comparisons. A clearer understanding
of the links between generic and contingent priorities can be gained by
tracing the shifts among the four major priorities, including the "all-good-
things-go-together" option. This is done in Table 4.1.

The tabulation is organized to highlight the relative stability of the
priorities. They are depicted from left to right, and from top to bottom,
in declining order of fixity, where "fixity" is indexed by the magnitude
of the percentages (the conditional probabilities) along the main diagonal.
The lower these percentages, the greater the movement away from a contingent (and possibly superficial) priority toward one that is held more
firmly.

Economic growth is plainly the core priority. Virtually all the elites who

TABLE 4.1
Relationship between Original and Revised Developmental Priorities

Original (Contingent) Priorities	*Revised (Generic) Priorities*				
	Economic	*Political*	*All Equal*	*Social*	*Totals*
Economic	97%	3%	—	—	100% (101)
Political	14	86	—	—	100 (29)
All Equal	17	17	66	—	100 (36)
Social	34	15	—	51	100 (83)
Totals	55 (136)	19 (47)	10 (24)	17 (42)	101 (249)

NOTE: "Original" = responses to question eliciting agenda for "next five years." "Revised"
= responses to follow-up probes. Row and column categories represent first priorities,
without regard to variation in second and third choices.

give it top priority over the next five years believe that it outranks the other goals in causal terms. The insistence of the economists on the continuing priority of accumulation in the foreseeable future reflects not only their sense of the conditional necessity of growth but also their fundamental commitment to this goal, even after the take-off is presumably well underway.

The proponents of political development are also persistent, although a few of them are apt to agree that in principle attention should be given to economic growth at the expense of democratic politics. Still, what is remarkable about the politicians is how few of them yield to the temptation of approving the conventional economicism of the period.

By contrast, there is considerable movement away from social welfare and from the "all-good-things-go-together" model when the elites express their fundamental priorities. For example, fully a third of those who advocate primary emphasis on social reform in the near future do so on the condition that it does not jeopardize economic growth.

The adamancy of the economists and the politicians, and the compromising inclinations of the social reformers, seem reasonably clear. The agendas of the economists and the politicians are virtually identical to their causal models, and this equivalence suggests that their models represent near-absolute values. The agenda of the social reformers is pliable to the extent that it departs from their causal theories of development. This does not mean that the social reformers are unscrupulous, but rather that many of those who abide by social well-being as a fundamental value probably consider it more as an end than as a means.

The official formula of economic development first, political development last, with social welfare in the middle, enjoys a plurality among the elites as a whole, but it is not a consensual paradigm. There is considerable intra- as well as intergroup variation in developmental agendas. The tendency is for conservative sectors, such as the businessmen and the state managers, to favor economic development, and for the more progressive groups, like the bishops and the labor leaders, to be less enthusiastic about this goal.

Table 4.2 presents the relevant data. The elite groups are arrayed from left to right in ascending order of the priority given to economic growth. The continuum corresponds roughly to intuitive notions about their placement on a conservative-progressive dimension. The MDB, the opposition party, stands on the left, as does the church. The position of the labor leaders is a bit less determinate, but there is no doubt that, compared to the state managers and the businessmen, they lean toward the left. With this rather obvious pattern in view, two further points are worthy of note:

the discrepancies between contingent and generic agendas and the variation within each of the elite groups concerning their priorities.

In some cases, the differences between the two versions of the rank-orderings are dramatic enough to alter the relative position of an elite group. For example, while a majority of the labor leaders give priority to social reform over the next five years, their generic models favor economic growth. The proportion of labor leaders opting for social reform is cut by more than half, from 57 to 23 percent, in the movement from contingent priorities to causation. Something like this drop-off was to be expected, since the social reformers are known to have the most changeable values. Yet changeability seems to be exceptionally high among the labor leaders, while it is not particularly common among the bishops, a majority of whom give top priority to social reform both times around.

The difference between the labor leaders and the bishops is not difficult to understand. The labor leaders are much more under the thumb of the government than the bishops. The government not only harasses the labor leadership on a regular basis but also has the dominant voice in deciding

TABLE 4.2
Development Priorities across Elite Sectors

Original (Contingent) Priorities	Elite Sector							
	Church	MDB	Labor	ARENA	Civil Service	Public Companies	Business	Totals
Economic	—	7%	28%	39%	41%	53%	57%	41%
Social	64	43	57	30	23	20	21	33
Political	27	29	9	12	15	—	8	12
All Equal	9	21	6	18	21	27	13	15
Totals	100	100	100	99	100	100	99	101
	(11)	(14)	(53)	(33)	(39)	(15)	(84)	(249)

Revised (Generic) Priorities	Elite Sector							
	Church	MDB	ARENA	Labor	Civil Service	Business	Public Companies	Totals
Economic	9%	21%	46%	49%	60%	66%	80%	54%
Social	55	29	18	23	8	13	—	17
Political	27	43	24	26	18	11	7	19
All Equal	9	7	12	2	15	11	13	10
Totals	100	100	100	100	101	101	100	100
	(11)	(14)	(33)	(53)	(40)	(84)	(15)	(250)

NOTE: Only first priorities are used to form row categories.

who should reach positions of leadership in the labor hierarchy. Furthermore, the syndical organizations are economically dependent on the government, since it is the ministry of labor that controls the allocation of union funds. The government is capable of making life difficult for the church, but it is reluctant to do so, and it has little influence over the appointment of bishops (as Franco had in Spain).

At first glance, the MDB seems to resemble the labor leadership. A near majority of opposition politicians assign first priority to social reform over the next five years. But unlike the labor leaders, a large proportion (43 percent) of the MDB senators and deputies give first place to political liberalization, instead of to economic growth, in their causal models. The MDB is clearly at odds with the dominant formula; indeed, it is the only one of the elite groups to make liberalization its modal priority.

As we turn to the right-hand panels of the tabulation, the shift in favor of economic development becomes evident. The supremacy of this goal is blatant among the directors of the state-owned corporations—a tendency that is not surprising, given their mandate to speed up industrialization. Groups like the state managers and the businessmen also favor the ''all-good-things-go-together'' option. This is the first empirical sign that such a model, far from being progressive, implies a conservative orientation.

A second major pattern entails the internal heterogeneity and homogeneity of the elite groups. As a rule, the sectors who attach greatest importance to economic growth are more clearly unanimous in their priority than those who favor political liberalization or social reform. Not only do the state managers and the businessmen give priority to economic development but they do so in overwhelming numbers: they are close to a consensus.

By comparison, groups like the MDB are internally divided. They disagree about whether political liberalization or social reform should take precedence. The only opposition group that gives majority support to a single goal is the church. Among the bishops, social well-being holds sway, and economic development quite clearly comes last. There is a faction within the church that puts political liberalization at the top of the agenda, but the dominant ecclesiastical concern is with social well-being—that is, with pastoral and presumably apolitical ministrations to the poor.[14]

[14] Although a cardinal tenet of liberation theology is that it is often impossible to draw the line between social concern and political activism, there is disagreement about the relationship between the two, within both the Brazilian church and the church at large. See the ambiguous statements made by Pope John Paul II during his visit to Brazil in July 1980, reported in "As Palavras de João Paulo II," *Isto É*, July 9, 1980: 27-29. Compare Thomas P. Fasse, "Bulwark-Catholics and Conciliar-Humanists in the Society of Jesus," *Sociological Quarterly* 21 (1980): 511-527.

Thus, the opposition seems in disarray. Most of the labor leaders and the bishops are less exercised than the MDB over explicitly political issues. The church is reluctant to intrude in the secular sphere, and the prevalent norm among the labor leaders seems to be one of cautious opportunism that promises some material payoffs.

To summarize. Three tendencies emerge from the examination of variation in developmental values across and within the elite groups: (1) the priorities of the elites follow a left-right pattern, with the MDB and the church, and the state managers and the businessmen, in opposing camps; (2) the economists on the right—the heads of the public companies being the most prominent example—engage in less flip-flopping from contingent priorities to causal theories than the politicians and especially the social reformers to the left; and (3) the economists are more united than the politicians and the social reformers—that is, groups such as the industrialists are more unanimous in their insistence on economic growth than the labor leaders, for example, are in their preference for social reform or political liberalization.[15]

Elite Interpretations of Developmental Priorities

So far the economists, the social reformers, and the politicians have suffered from the caricatural nature of all ideal types: the classification glosses over much of the substance and subtlety in the thinking of the elites. In particular, the orientations of the elites regarding the imposition of "order" from the top down—especially, the willingness of the economists to accept the curtailment of their own autonomy for the sake of aggregate growth—have yet to be analyzed in detail. Excerpts from the discursive responses of the elites help to capture these differences.

The Economists

While in some instances the distinctions are a matter of delicate shading, four subtypes of economists can be identified. Let us begin with the most single-minded.

---

[15] The perseverance of the economists also became evident when the Brazilian boom began to run down after 1973. If these men were thoroughgoing opportunists, they might have been expected to soften their accumulation-first policies. For the most part, this has not happened in the post-Médici period, although serious consideration to redistribution, and especially to an expansion of top-down social welfare programs with powerful elite backing, has begun to take shape. See "The Brazilian Gamble: Why Bankers Bet on Brazil's Technocrats," *Business Week*, December 5, 1977: 72-81, and "Oh, Brazil," *The Economist*, August 4-10, 1979: 1-22.

The Hard Core. One group within the economist camp is made up of those who are straightforward and even brutal in their insistence on the primacy of economic growth. An ARENA politician exemplifies this orientation:

Unfortunately, progress can only be made with a policy of belt tightening. We must get on with economic development, and then take care of people. Afterwards we can indulge in the luxury of politics. It is all a matter of survival.

The sentiment is echoed by an official in one of the economic ministries:

Given Brazil's current situation, we must build up the infrastructure of the country. The process of development is not peaceful. It can generate conflicts. But that's the way it is. Later we can attend to income distribution and social welfare generally.

In both statements, the need for economic expansion is viewed as sovereign and quite clearly at the expense of other goals, however desirable they may be in the longer run. Neither of the elites dwells on politics; it is either far in the future or stuck in the background, as the coercion required to manage conflict.

The Authoritarian Technocrats. This second group of economists resembles the hard core, except that they are even more explicit about the dictatorial implications of their model and more critical of those they consider outmoded and meddlesome dreamers. They do not apologize, even sarcastically. According to these men, the real thrust of political development is towards "administration." A Paulista banker expresses the position forcefully:

*Political development is foolishness (*besteira*). The entire world is headed toward a strong executive and toward economic centralization. In Brazil, when you talk about political institutions, people think of an opening at the level of the congress. So the politicians, instead of gaining competence in technical matters, make a profession out of politics, which is an anachronism.*

An industrialist from São Paulo also declares his belief that political development in the sense of liberalization is irrelevant to real problems:

Economic development comes first because that's what permits us to attain the most important thing: social welfare and the distribution of wealth. But it is only possible to distribute if we have the resources in the first place. Political development doesn't bring well-being to anybody, except for half a dozen people who are only concerned about their own selfish interests.

The gist of these and similar statements ("political development comes from the new laws and decrees that are designed to do away with demagogues and give prestige to those who are technically prepared to solve social problems,'' et cetera) is that development means political demobilization and the replacement of the antiquated and the inept by problem solvers. The authoritarian technocrats have little patience with textbook democracy even as a desirable end, much less as a means toward that end. Their definition of political development centers around a powerful and efficient state machine.

The Antidemagogic Paternalists. While these men do not have quite so explicit a vision of the positive state as the authoritarian technocrats, they have strong views about what political development should not be. The mass of Brazilians is perceived as uninterested in the political controversies that trouble the thin stratum of the university-educated, but they are also seen as gullible and easily misled by political agitators. The following are the words of the president of a multinational corporation located in São Paulo:

A prosperous economy facilitates the solution of social problems and permits appropriate political solutions. An underdeveloped people, without education, will have real social problems but false political solutions. We used to have strikes provoked by politicians who demanded salary increases that solve nothing. The government itself played with economic statistics in order to justify salary hikes. And instead of solving anything, it only made matters worse. You cannot have political solutions to economic problems.

This view is not the exclusive property of the businessmen; it runs through other elite groups as well. The president of a labor syndicate in São Paulo expresses his distaste for mass politics this way:

We cannot have social welfare without the country being economically strong. One of the worst evils of social development is inflation, because everybody suffers the consequences. We have had some very difficult times in the political development of this country that brought us to the brink of chaos. Argentina, Chile, and Uruguay are all examples of uncontrolled political development. It is nothing more than demagogic nationalism.[16]

The manager of a state-owned company is even more explicit about the differences between the needs of the benighted poor and the demands of the educated few:

In an underdeveloped country, the population is solely concerned with its own survival. It does not have the objective or subjective conditions

---

[16] The reference is to Peronist Argentina and to Chile and Uruguay of the early seventies.

to be worried about other things and to engage consciously in politics. Therefore, social and political development of the sophisticated kind, what you might call "political liberty" for the privileged classes, ought to be sacrificed temporarily, so that with economic development we can generate wealth, and overcome this phase.

None of these men suggests that political liberalization might not be a good thing in principle. But as a means toward development, it is foreclosed because it diverts the elites and stirs up the populace. Nevertheless, unlike the more overtly authoritarian of the economists, the antidemagogic paternalists are unwilling to give up on the liberal ideal altogether.

The Evolutionists. In this group are found elites who, even if they do not question the primacy of economic growth, at least make the point that democracy can and should be restored eventually. In the words of a leading bureaucrat in the ministry of agriculture:

By itself, economic development creates social welfare. As social conditions improve, and as we cultivate a more harmonious development, without "islands of progress" that leave out the rest, then we will attain a democracy in due course.

The same perspective is expressed by an ARENA politician in Aristolelean terms:

The philosophy of the government is that social welfare depends on economic development, since we don't believe in the possibility of distributing misery. And we can only take political development seriously as the outcome of a minimum of economic security and social development. There is no democracy without a large and stable middle class.

The developmental vision set forth in these remarks, which are a close paraphrase of General Geisel's statement, is linear and unclouded. Democracy in the North American and Western European mold will arrive once Brazil has attained the level of economic and social development of the industrialized nations.

Thus, the elites who are united in the belief that a moratorium must be placed on politics in order to get on with economic growth take diverse positions about the possibility and desirability of a democratic restoration. Some repeat the nostrum that democracy can and should be implanted once the economic and social groundwork is laid; it remains a respectable ideal, and it may even grow spontaneously, rather than having to be implanted. Others see representative democracy not only as dangerous for the here-and-now but also as worthless and perhaps pernicious in the long run. The professions of faith in democratic ideals on the part of the evolutionists invite cynicism, but their declaration cannot be dismissed as hypocrisy pure and simple. They imply a lingering deposit of liberalism that the advocates of economic growth by way of permanent technocracy and authoritarianism cannot erase completely.

The Politicians

A few of the politicians seem to be unabashed democrats, willing to give popular opinion free reign even if it fails to work responsibly. The president of a labor syndicate in São Paulo expresses this position:

> *What matters is that the people have the right to make their opinions known by direct vote, through democracy. If they choose badly, then they get the government they deserve. At least the choice is made from the bottom up and not decided by half a dozen people.*

But such a response is exceptional. Many of the elites who share the general position of the labor leader go on to suggest that changes in the political structure would promote economic development and social welfare. Politics is viewed as the means toward, rather than the result of, other goals. Still others claim that political repression is no longer necessary because the economy is going well. For these men, political liberalization depends to some extent on economic growth.

The first group I label the advocates of *politics as a cause*, in both the technical and the crusading sense of "cause," since the two were barely distinguishable under the conditions prevailing in Brazil during the early seventies. (Within this group, a further distinction can be made between those who view political development as an essentially liberating process, releasing social forces from the burdens of the centralizing state, and those who see it as strengthening the capacity of the state to accelerate growth along redirected lines.) The second group is composed of the *stage theorists*, who believe that economic growth has made possible a political reopening.

Politics-as-Cause. In the suffocating atmosphere of the Médici years, the claim that political liberalization might be a more efficient means than continued repression toward further growth took on an emotional as well as a theoretical significance. The passion comes through in this statement by an opposition deputy:

> *The essence of development is to raise the social and cultural level of the population. There can be an increase in the gross national product, but this is not development unless it is accompanied by improvements for the people. Without political development, without a minimum of freedom, none of this is possible. Democracy is not dessert.*

A bureaucrat in the ministry of transports states a similar causal chain in less dramatic terms:

> *What Brazil should resolve first is the political question. There are*

certain social tensions among Brazilians. Political development means trying to perfect political and juridical institutions so that internal peace can be maintained, so that we will gain respect in world opinion, and so that the rights of individuals and private businessmen are protected, too. These are the conditions without which, it seems to me, regular and continued economic growth is impossible.

The message here is not that political liberalization is a radical venture, an inference that can be drawn from the previous statement by the MDB deputy. Rather, political development should be designed to overcome the arbitrariness and uncertainty of authoritarian centralization. The rule of law should be reestablished so that individuals will know what to expect. In turn, this sense of security should encourage the initiatives that will sustain economic growth.

There is one significant variation on the theme of politics-as-cause, and it is diagnostic of the ambivalence in the Brazilian political tradition. In this view, politics means something different from a reversion to the liberal ethic. A politician of the MDB summarizes this approach:

Politics is the superstructure that takes charge of economic development. Without political direction, economic development and social well-being are impossible in the medium and long run. Without political leadership that works for economic development and social welfare, there can be civil war and bankruptcy. This happened in Germany and Italy. The concept of democracy includes the notion of economics. The political authorities should interfere in economic affairs. This is the modern meaning of democracy; it is not the same as laissez-faire. The government should control economic forces; it should restrain the abuses of economic monopolies; it should fight for those who are economically weak, for equal opportunities for all.[17]

Apart from the deputy's frankness in favoring an overtly political role for the bureaucracy and his avowal of progressive values, his vision of the importance of the state as an agent of development does not stray markedly from the centrality assigned to the government (though not to the politicians) by those who give primacy to economic growth. The problem for the deputy is that the wrong people, promulgating the wrong policies, are in power; but it is doubtful that he wants to revive a strictly parliamentary state.[18]

---

[17] The deputy's views are consistent with discussions of the "directive" state by Ted Robert Gurr, "Persistence and Change in Political Systems, 1800-1971," *American Political Science Review* 68 (1974): 1482-1504. Compare Samuel P. Huntington, *Political Order in Changing Societies* (New Haven: Yale University Press, 1968).

[18] For an extensive discussion of the weakness of the liberal-democratic tradition in Brazil, see Wanderley Guilherme dos Santos, *Ordem Burguesa e Liberalismo Político* (São Paulo: Livraria Duas Cidades, 1978).

The Stage Theorists. So far two variations on the primacy of the political have been exemplified: one that stresses the need for a more participatory and representative process and another that advocates the rationalization of state activism as a way to set Brazil on the proper course. The views are not completely contradictory, but neither are they the same. The other major reading of the primacy of the political relegates politics to a more contingent role. The causal chain begins with economic growth, but political factors intervene in the division of spoils. In the words of a top-level civil servant:

> *Political development has been held back by circumstances. It has been kept within bounds, in order to speed up economic growth. But now we can, and in fact we should, open up the political process. The revolution [of 1964] destroyed political values that have not been restored. We need a better distribution of income. Social welfare is very important, and it cannot be ignored any longer.*

This model does not reject the assumption that economic growth comes first. But it contradicts the regime's prescription that decisions about social development should be as antiseptic as the norms governing economic growth.

Despite these qualifications, the elites who push for the reintroduction of politics into national life are in a different camp from those who favor economic development at all costs. A principal concern of the politicians is with gaining some measure of autonomy for the interests, including their own, buried by the authoritarian system. Some argue this position out of exasperation; others contend that the authoritarian Leviathan no longer works and has become an obstacle rather than a guarantor of development.

At the same time, there exists a certain parallel between the economists and the politicians. Most of the economists maintain a view of politics as a harmless normalcy to be revived after serious economic and social problems have withered away, although some of them are skeptical about the utility of even decorative democracy for Brazil now and in the future. Their premise is that the state expands with the economy and that it will not vanish with the attainment of economic and social goals. Similarly, many of the elites with a greater sense of urgency about political development define it in the conventional way, as representative pluralism. Others, however, stress the need for strong and autonomous public authority. Sometimes the need is to control economic interests, to rectify the more extravagant abuses of social decency, or merely to assure that the process of economic growth can continue without the interruptions of dictatorial ukase. In any event, there is some reluctance to import democratic forms that may be of distinguished vintage, but obsolescent.

The Social Reformers

There are two kinds of social reformers among the Brazilian elites. One is formed by the men who argue, analogously to the economic evolutionists and the political stage theorists, that the time for dividing the pie has come. Distribution may even stimulate economic growth; in the least, it will not slow down or undo the course of development. It also promises to head off the political explosion that may result from continued inattention to social needs.

A second group does not justify distribution by a cost-benefit logic. Instead, they understand social well-being as elementary justice, an inviolable right that cannot be denied. I call these men the radical humanists. But they are not necessarily or even typically revolutionary. Just as the cost-benefit calculus is alien to their demands for social change, they rarely apply causal reasoning to the politics of righting wrongs.[19] Often, it is unclear whether their social fundamentalism implies rebellion or paternalism.

The Radical Humanists. Most of the social reformers are repelled by what the economists would term the "negative externalities" generated by exclusive attention to aggregate growth, but they are not convinced that solving these ills requires change in political leadership. Implicit in this view is a tendency to consider specific institutional arrangements as irrelevant to "real problems." In the words of one of the bishops:

Politics exists to promote social welfare, and so does economic development. Social welfare and economic development are more important than this or that form of government. Social welfare should always come first.

Although the commitment of the bishop to social welfare is unmistakable, he does not seem to care much about how this end is reached. The principal feature of his statement is the absence of a causal model of the developmental process. There is an evident dismay with the devotion to a crash program of industrialization, but there is no willingness to specify the relative importance of the means toward the goal of social welfare.

While other radical humanists are as unconciliatory as the bishop, they sometimes hint of a connection between social reform and political change.

---

[19] In some respects, especially in their ambivalence with regard to political form, the radical humanists resemble the advocates of what has come to be known as the basic needs approach to national development. See Norman L. Hicks, "Growth vs. Basic Needs: Is There a Trade-Off?" *World Development* 7 (1979): 985-994, and Hicks and Paul Streeten, "Indicators of Development: The Search for a Basic Needs Yardstick," *World Development* 7 (1979): 567-580. Compare Francine du Plessix Gray, *Divine Disobedience: Profiles in Catholic Radicalism* (New York: Alfred A. Knopf, 1970).

This statement by an MDB politician is somewhat elliptical, but it suggests a rather far-reaching overhaul of prevailing conditions:

We simply must overcome the present social disparities. Brazil imitates foreign models and has thus developed only technocracy and the exact sciences. It is necessary to turn more toward the human sciences, toward social and political development, to redress the dangerous imbalances we see nowadays.

Here again, the humanistic slant is evident. Yet it is difficult to retrieve a clear-cut model of development from the declaration. The deputy believes that economic disequilibria damage the poor, but he suggests that they are dangerous to the rich as well and that they ought to be rectified to avert a complete overthrow of the existing order.

Nevertheless, some of the radical humanists envision the effects of political action in less manipulative fashion, when they consider political factors at all. Here is another MDB politician:

First place must be given to social welfare, because in the last decade there has been a shocking increase in the number of poor people in this country. Economic growth has not been handled rationally, and so political factors must take priority in this area in order to improve social conditions.

The deputy, unlike most of his fellow radical humanists, has a developmental model at the same time that he is just as outraged as they are by the suffering ensuant on the official theory. The dominant paradigm is not only inhuman, it is inefficient ("irrational"). But on the whole, the radical humanists are a curious compound of advocates of extensive social change whose program of reform ignores politics. While there is no reason to doubt their instinctive anger, it is hazardous to predict the political form and content of their values or to estimate the probabilities of their allying with coalitions of the left or the right.

The Antipolitical Pacifiers. Most of the social reformers do not seriously question the general model of development promoted by the regime. They view aggregate growth as the base on which to build toward distribution and as a prerequisite for social harmony. The following statement by an ARENA politician is quite in accord with an indulgent reading of the regime's formula:

Social welfare does not exist without at least relative economic growth, and political development is the consequence of social welfare. A socially developed country is a politically developed country. Social well-being means perfect understanding between classes—for example, employers and employees are in agreement over wage levels. Rulers and ruled have the same objectives.

In other words, social development means political peace.

Another ARENA politician makes the case for the primacy of social welfare in terms that reflect even more clearly the belief that most Brazilians are not interested in politics:

People should be the principal objective. Political development comes after social welfare, because the people have a greater need to eat than to vote.

In none of these statements is there any evidence of a desire for a restructuring of the hierarchy of power. But the attitude of the social reformers, including most of the radical humanists, is not entirely Machiavellian. While many of them are disenchanted with the political class, the social reformers are also worried by the tunnel vision of the economists, both for the exploitation it involves and for the threat (the "dangerous imbalances") that continued neglect of domestic well-being poses to political order. After a while, it seems, the social reformers begin to lose interest in capital accumulation and probably find it indistinguishable from politically counterproductive and socially inefficient hoarding.

The All-Good-Things-Go-Together Model

This is not a model in any rigorous sense but rather a belief that developmental choices cannot and indeed should not be made. Only one of the elites, an MDB politician, agonizes over the difficulties of reconciling disparate goals, and in the end despairs of a resolution:

I cannot give priority to any of these goals. Political development fundamentally concerns the opposition, my party. But economic and social development, they are a matter of the survival of the Brazilian people.

The rest of the elites in this camp see no such problems. In the words of the manager of a public company:

There are no priorities. Industrial development produces social well-being, and political development lies within the global plan. These things cannot be isolated. Otherwise, imbalances would begin to appear. Brazil knows what it is doing.

The director of a large manufacturing corporation in São Paulo elaborates:

We should proceed simultaneously with the harmonious development of all three. The emphasis on economic growth should continue but without neglecting social and political development. Economic growth brings as a necessary result an increase in social welfare. As for political development, it doesn't derive so much from economic growth as from educational conditions, as more and more people become educated.

Behind the call for harmonious development, causal priority is assigned to economic growth, and political liberalization comes at the end of the sequence, after the spread of education has civilized the Brazilian populace.

The "all-good-things-go-together" model does not challenge the dominant strategy; the escape from the primacy of economic growth is verbal rather than logical. The ideal of integrated development represents both a denial of conflict and a yearning for consensus that is compatible with the authoritarian enforcement of social peace.

Developmental Values, Policy Performance, and Government Support

Variation in strategic priorities across the elite groups, with the businessmen and the state managers stressing economic growth more than the opposition politicians, the labor leaders, and the bishops, transmits a sense of the tensions and ambiguities in an authoritarian setting. The question remains regarding the extent to which the values of the elites affect their orientations toward the performance of the government and toward the government itself.

The two are not identical. Some of the elites might steadfastly oppose the government while giving it high marks for its conduct of economic policy. Others might be appalled by its social service programs yet give the government strong support. The regime may be applauded and criticized for different reasons. Much depends on what areas of economic, social, and political decision making the elites care about most: that is, much hinges on their priorities.

Let us begin with the connection between the priorities of the elites and their support for and opposition to the government. On the average, the economists should be the most satisfied with the regime, and the politicians the most distressed. The social reformers, considered the most ambivalent, should fall somewhere in between. If the social reformers were thoroughly alienated from the government, more so than the politicians, the idea of an authoritarian order based on cooptation as well as force would be meaningless.

Figure 4.1 substantiates the hypothesis. The economists and the adherents of the "all-good-things-go-together" model are more likely to be satisfied with the government than are the proponents of alternative agendas. The social reformers fall below the average level of enthusiasm for the government, and the politicians are the least supportive.[20]

Not only is it true that the economists and the politicians are in opposite

[20] It should also be noted that the contingent priorities of the elites are firmer indicators of conflict over developmental values than their generic causal models. This is most obviously the case for the politicians, whereas for the other types of elites the distinction between circumstantial and causal models makes essentially no difference regarding their satisfaction with the government.

FIGURE 4.1
Average Government Support by Developmental Priorities
(standard deviations in parentheses)

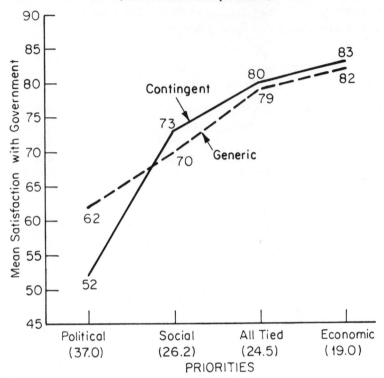

NOTES: "In general, how satisfied or dissatisfied are you with the policy (*a politica*) of the government?" The scale varies between 0 and 100.
ETA^2 (original) = .13
ETA^2 (revised) = .09

camps but it is also clear that the sharpest break in government support occurs between the politicians and all the rest.[21] This does not mean that

[21] One other feature of these results deserves mention. This is the tendency for variation in satisfaction/dissatisfaction with the government to increase as we move from the economists to the politicians. In Figure 4.1, associated with the average level of support for each developmental priority is the variation about this mean, indexed by the standard deviation. As the level of support declines, the variation in support/opposition goes up. The phenomenon is related to the risks involved in expressing outright opposition to the Médici government. Interviewers completed a form designed to check the quality of responses. Among the items measured was the degree of "hesitancy"—that is, circumspection—that the respondents showed during the course of the interviews. For the economists and the proponents of the "all-good-things-go-together" model, there is no correlation between "discretion" and the degree of support expressed for the government. For the politicians and the social reformers,

interelite conflicts in Brazil are devoid of policy substance or that social and political conflicts are wholly compartmentalized. It does suggest that tensions are most acute in controversies touching on the autonomy versus the subjugation of contending groups.[22]

With this basic relationship in mind, let us turn to an examination of factors that might influence more directly the orientations of the elites toward the government. Regimes that are both economically developmental and politically repressive may rely, in some measure, on the promise to restore democratic processes for legitimacy; they rarely disavow democracy as an ideal. But in practice, their bid for compliance depends on the achievement of pragmatic rather than political goals. If the authoritarian system fails to demonstrate a problem-solving capacity, it may resort to coercion, pure and simple, to defend itself.[23]

The connection between support for the government and its outputs, its perceived performance, is bound to be tight. In the imaginary world where the utilitarian calculus reigns, political support is a function of the production of the government and the allocation of this product. And in the world of Brazilian politics, this rule constitutes a fair approximation of reality.

---

however, the correlations are significantly positive: .29 and .32 respectively. For these elites, the self-reported indicators of support underestimate the true extent of disaffection. At one level, the results are discouraging. They show that the elites, or certain elites, are dissembling, at least a bit. But in retrospect they are not at all surprising, and it is useful to lay bare such problems early in the analysis, so as not to be startled by or simply unsuspecting of them later on. Furthermore, the difficulty is with the measure of satisfaction/dissatisfaction, not with the indicators of elite priorities. Their priorities stay the same, but the elites suffer diplomatic inhibitions in implementing them.

[22] The tabulation of satisfaction/dissatisfaction by elite groups (not shown here) backs up this inference. From left to right, the average levels of support on the 100-point scale are: MDB (31); bishops (50); labor leaders (73); ARENA (81); businessmen (84); and civil servants (87), with an eta-squared of .31. Again as the average degree of support decreases from the state managers to the MDB politicians, the variation within sectors also increases. The businessmen claim to support the government strongly, and they express this support in a single voice compared to the bishops, for example, who are less enthusiastic about the government but also less unified in their opposition. Correlations between hesitancy and satisfaction with the government were computed for each of the sectors, and the expected results were obtained. Within the MDB and the labor leadership, for example, the correlations are .23 and .28. Within the ARENA, the correlation is an insignificant .08, and among the businessmen − .07. The opposition is tainted with discretion, but the relative ordering of groups does not undergo distortion.

[23] This is essentially the route followed by the Pinochet regime in Chile. See Karen L. Remmer, "Public Policy and Regime Consolidation: The First Five Years of the Chilean Junta," *Journal of Developing Areas* 13 (1979): 441-461, and Remmer, "Military Rule and Political Demobilization in Latin America," paper presented at the annual meetings of the American Political Science Association, Washington, D.C., August 31-September 3, 1979.

Thus, there is not much suspense in testing the hypothesis that the elites support the government in the measure that it produces results. The problematic question has to do with how the values of the elites intervene in the assessment of how the government performs. The elites grant a bonus, or assign a handicap, to the government, to some extent regardless of what it does.

Authoritarian governments in Brazil have set multiple short- and medium-range goals. The primary one is economic expansion: sustained growth in the national product accompanied by successful management of other aggregate phenomena, principally inflation. The political corollary of this set of goals is the elimination of subversion, inclusively defined.

A second set of priorities takes in measures designed to ameliorate the disparities generated by economic growth. They concern not only social welfare programs but also efforts to reduce regional and rural-urban disequilibria. They have taken the form of indirect distributive mechanisms such as pension plans and other social security, medical, and educational projects.

In the early seventies, there were no immediate- or medium-term goals of political liberalization. Although all the military presidents since 1964 had promised to restore democracy before they left office, the settling-in of the authoritarian state made these vows less and less credible. At the time we conducted our research, the idea that democracy would be granted from on high was not taken seriously, and it made no sense to ask the elites about the progress of the regime toward meeting such a goal.

In order to assess the perceptions of policy performance, taking into account what the elites understood to be the objectives of the government, the elites were asked to estimate the success of the government in ten specific areas, almost all of them covering economic and social development. Table 4.3 gives the results.

The accuracy of the elites' judgments as absolute indicators of the performance of the government is not in question. What matters is the ranking of their perceptions. The government is judged most successful in increasing the rate of growth in the GNP and least successful in reducing the differences between rich and poor. Roughly speaking, the elites are objective.

The ratings can be divided into three tiers. In the "good" category are growth in the GNP, elimination of subversion, and control of inflation. These are the goals the government stressed and toward which it made progress. The first and the third are economic; the second is political. They capture the essentials of the Brazilian model of the early seventies.

The government is rated "fair" in four areas: extending social security protection to workers, increasing the efficiency of the public sector, re-

TABLE 4.3
Elite Evaluations of Governmental Performance in Ten Policy Areas

Performance Indicators	Mean	Standard Deviation
Increase Rate of Growth of GNP	82.0	19.8
Eliminate Threat of Internal Subversion	80.3	20.6
Reduce Rate of Inflation	76.5	19.6
Extend Social Security Protection to Majority of Working Class	66.7	23.9
Increase Efficiency of Public Administration	64.8	21.8
Reduce Proportion of Adult Illiterates	64.0	22.1
Increase Per Capita Income	62.8	27.6
Improve Living Conditions of Rural Population	51.6	26.6
Reduce Per Capita Income Difference between the Northeast and Center-South	47.2	26.2
Reduce Income Differences between Rich and Poor	36.4	26.8
Mean	63.3	—

NOTE: "The Revolution of 1964 set a series of national objectives to be met in the medium run. Can you give us your estimates, in percentages, of the degree of success obtained until now in meeting these objectives? The scale goes from 0 to 100, where 0 is 'no success' and 100 is 'complete success'."

ducing illiteracy, and increasing per capita income. All of these, even the last, are moderate goals. Below this level are three objectives: improving living conditions in the countryside, reducing regional income disparities and, last, reducing income differences between classes. The government did not bother to pretend, or occasionally protested too much, about its nonobjectives in these areas.

The elites do not accord the regime across-the-board success. There is greater consensus about the primary goals, like economic growth, than about those of secondary priority involving the splitting-up of the pie. Opponents of the government did not contest the reports of aggregate output, although by the early seventies they began to question the growing addiction of this output on foreign inputs. Instead, their quarrel was over the division of benefits. The opposition, and the government itself, saw that aggregate growth proceeded at the cost of distribution. They disagreed about the indirectly distributive, service-delivery pretensions of the official paradigm. While even supporters of the government admitted that the distribution of income suffered because of the drive for accumulation, they pointed to the beneficence of long-term investment in human capital and the short-term distribution of indirect benefits: welfare in the form of selective, discretionary services.

Thus, while some of the government's goals are perceived as contradictory, others have a less either-or connotation. Moderate social reform does not violate the precepts of authoritarian development; it has both a paternalistic and an investment component. The question is how finely the elites themselves distinguish between the economic and social programs of the government or, conversely, how closely they are associated in their minds. Again, if it turned out that the elites differentiated sharply between the two types of programs, there would be reason to question the political significance of the social reformers' flirtation with the developmental ideology of the economists.

Table 4.4 provides the answer. The elites divide the policy outputs of the government into two areas, economic and social, but the dimensions of evaluation are closely related. This is most obvious in the case of the program (MOBRAL) mounted by the government to reduce illiteracy among adult Brazilians. Education is seen as both an economic investment and a social service.

Other objectives overlap as well. Increasing the efficiency of the public

TABLE 4.4
Normalized Loadings, Oblique Factor Rotation, on Ten Performance Indicators

| | Factors | | |
| | I | II | |
Performance Indicators	(Social)	(Economic)	Communalities
Reduce Income Differences between Rich and Poor	1.10	−.15	1.23
Reduce Per Capita Income Difference between the Northeast and Center-South	1.09	−.14	1.20
Improve Living Conditions of Rural Population	1.03	−.05	1.07
Extend Social Security Protection to Majority of Working Class	.81	.25	.73
Reduce Proportion of Adult Illiterates	.49	.60	.60
Increase Efficiency of Public Administration	.40	.68	.63
Eliminate Threat of Internal Subversion	.34	.74	.66
Increase Per Capita Income	.26	.81	.72
Reduce Rate of Inflation	−.13	1.09	1.20
Increase Rate of Growth of GNP	−.32	1.19	1.53
Sum of Squares	4.83	4.72	

NOTE: Correlation between factor scores = .68.

bureaucracy is a laudable and neutral objective, and extending social security coverage to workers is also perceived, to some extent, as complementary to economic development. The government is rated not only as successful in "eliminating the threat of subversion." The policy itself tends to be viewed as fairly consensual, though not quite so benign as "reducing illiteracy" or "increasing the efficiency of public administration." The important point is that the "war against subversion" is not linked as intimately as it might be to policies promulgating economic growth in the aggregate. The accumulative and the coercive drives, in the view of the elites, are partially distinct.

Only with the measures aimed at capital accumulation versus direct income redistribution does the perception of an increasingly harsh trade-off appear. Boosting the rate of growth in the GNP and cutting inflation are seen as objectives that have little to do with, and that have indeed been realized at the cost of, whatever efforts have been made toward the direct and immediate rectification of social inequities.

But most policy trade-offs are seen in relative terms. There are at least two partially overlapping criteria for evaluating the performance of the government. Although the elites view the record of the government in promoting economic growth as a good obtained in detriment to social redistribution, they do not see the goals in black-and-white terms. Several intermediate policies serve both ends. These are what the government calls "impact projects" (*projetos de impacto*): programs like adult education and straightening up the bureaucracy that are difficult to oppose on ideological or technical grounds, that are tangible to many citizens, and that engage the righteousness and rationalizing impulses of many of the elites.

Thus, for the elites, while the class division in government policy is fundamental, it also seems manageable. The spectrum of alternatives in social policy is fairly broad, permitting selective distribution rather than radical redistribution. It is this intermediate set of indirect reforms that masks the class bias of policy.

Not all the elites perceive the government's performance in the same way. For example, the MDB politicians cannot be expected to rate the performance of the government in the economic, much less the social, areas as positively as do the businessmen, because the opposition tends to downgrade the primacy of economic growth itself. On the other hand, the industrialists, the bankers, and the ARENA politicians are favorably disposed to the government's priorities, and this in turn should cause them to be generous in their ratings, at least in the economic area. The labor leaders are liable to be critical of the concern of the government with economic development per se not only because the model of aggregate

growth postpones distribution but also because they are largely indifferent
to the macro-economics of expansion.

Figure 4.2 traces the variation in factor scores on the two evaluative
dimensions, economic and social, across the elite groups. The groups are
aligned from left to right in ascending order of their rating of the government's success in meeting its social goals. This is a slightly more subtle
and ambiguous area of public policy than the economic arena, where the
intentions of the government are manifest. Nevertheless, evaluations of
the government's economic performance are very close to those on the
distributive dimension. On the whole, the MDB politicians, the bishops,
and the labor leaders give the government low ratings on both counts. The
businessmen, the state managers, and the ARENA politicians are generally
pleased with the economic and social policies implemented since 1964.

FIGURE 4.2
Standardized Factor Scores on Social and Economic Performance of Government,
by Elite Sector

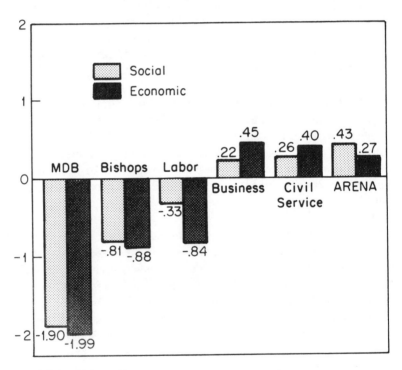

NOTE: ETA² (social) = .21
          ETA² (economic) = .30

Two related features of these results are of interest. First, the most simplistic of expectations about the bias in policy evaluations is plainly untrue. The labor leaders are not at the extreme left, nor are the businessmen on the extreme right. Indeed, the syndical elites turn out to be closer than either the bishops or the opposition politicians to the industrialists and the bankers. Class polarization around the performance of the government is muffled by a more visible, political cleavage, formed by the ARENA and the MDB politicians.

Second, the key to the muting of the class dimension is the ambivalence of the labor leadership. The bishops and especially the MDB politicians rate the performance of the government in both the economic and the social areas quite negatively. But the labor leaders, while they are not at all happy with the government's stress on economic grandeur, assign an only moderately negative rating to the government for its conduct of social welfare policy.

Most of the labor leaders, being social reformers of the mild variety, are not wrought up about politics. They attempt to play a protective role vis-à-vis their constituents, rather than adopt a confrontational stance vis-à-vis the government. They give the government below-average ratings in the social and the economic areas. But they are the only elite actors to make a significant distinction between economic and social performance, with social policies coming out on the high side.[24]

Analogous, although weaker, distinctions can be detected in the other elite sectors. The businessmen are high on the economic policies of the government but they are only *pro forma* positive about the government's social programs. They do not disapprove of social reform as implemented by the government, but they are not enthusiastic about it.

The ARENA politicians seem a bit more concerned with making friends. They are the strongest supporters of the social policies of the government, while they see less political return in an almost exclusive emphasis on economic growth. Even if they are conservative, the ARENA senators and deputies are still politicians. The state managers and the businessmen apparently feel that they can afford to be less politic.

The proximity of the labor leaders and the businessmen, as they rate the regime, is only mildly paradoxical in the Brazilian context. Among the progressive elites, the labor leaders are the most dependent on the government, and on the conservative side, the businessmen are the least dependent. In Brazil, the state has often been thought to be relatively autonomous from social classes. It has been noted less often that some classes

---

[24] Compare Luis Werneck Vianna, *Liberalismo e Sindicato no Brasil* (Rio de Janeiro: Paz e Terra, 1976).

are more autonomous from the state than others. In this respect, the capitalists enjoy a clear advantage over the labor organizations.

In summary, two important findings have emerged from the analysis of elite evaluations of the government's performance. First, despite some discrimination between the economic and social parameters of such programs, the two domains are perceived as strongly related. This is not surprising in light of earlier evidence that elite perspectives on social reform tend to be moderate and distributive rather than radical and redistributive and given the assumption of many of the social reformers that welfare depends on the generation of an aggregate surplus.[25]

Second, the polarization between the class elites—between the labor leaders and the businessmen—is submerged, compared to that between the labor leaders, the businessmen, together with the state managers and the ARENA politicians, and on the other hand the bishops and the MDB politicians. The sharpest cleavage within the establishment is political rather than vulgar materialist. Corporatist organization dulls cleavages among leadership cadres that have a potential for mobilizing groups according to class divisions. While the labor leaders do not give the government wholehearted support, neither are they permitted to assume a strenuously adversary position.[26] This is left both to the opposition party, whose role during the Médici period was restricted to verbal criticism, and to the church, whose penetration of Brazilian society is limited.

The results also raise an intriguing question. On the one hand, the evaluations made by the elites are about as close as we can expect to come to hard measures of elite attitudes. They concern real outputs, and in this sense they differ from the presumably broader values of the elites. In fact, the elites do not grossly distort the overall performance of the government. Not even the state managers or the ARENA politicians argue that the government has done a better job in redistributing income than in promoting an accelerated rise in the domestic product.

On the other hand, given this reality constraint, it is also clear that the

---

[25] Because they are so closely associated, I combine the two dimensions into a single index of perceived economic and social policy performance in subsequent analysis (see Figure 4.3). The loss of information and predictive power is negligible. The index, which varies between 0 and 100, is the mean of the 10 performance ratings. The correlation of the first factor with the index is .95; the correlation of the second factor with the index is .89. Compare Kent W. Smith, "Forming Composite Scales and Estimating their Validity Through Factor Analysis," *Social Forces* 53 (1974): 158-180, and Richard Zeller and Edward Carmines, "Factor Scaling, External Consistency, and the Measurement of Theoretical Constructs," *Political Methodology* 3 (1976): 215-252.

[26] For a detailed analysis of the pressures suffered by labor leaders in Brazil, see Argelina Cheibub Figueiredo, "Política Governamental e Funções Sindicais," Master's thesis, Universidade de São Paulo, 1975.

elites raise and lower their estimates of governmental performance, depending (a) on their general disposition to applaud or condemn the government and (b) on the differential importance that they attach to economic and social goals. If the politicians are ideological in their yearning for liberalization, so too are the businessmen and the bureaucrats in stressing economic growth at all costs. Thus, although the outputs of the government may be "hard," and although the perceptions of the elites are far from capricious, their evaluations of the government cannot be called strictly objective.

There is an intuitively appealing way to substantiate this point. Figure 4.3 maps the connection between performance evaluations and governmental support for the economists, the social reformers, and the politicians separately. The results confirm the fact that the level of support dips dramatically among the politicians and that it tends to be much higher among the economists and the social reformers.

The fresh information is revealed in the differing forms of the relationship between evaluation and support. Not only is the level of support higher among the economists; variation in support is also less sensitive to perceived improvements or failures in performance than is the case among the advocates of social and political change.[27] While the elites who are mainly committed to economic growth respond positively to the performance of the government, their assessments are not linked so tightly to their support for the government as those of other elites.

On the average, the advocates of social reform also appear to be rather satisfied with the government. At the same time, their support varies more closely with their perceptions of the effectiveness of the government. The politicians, too, follow the ups-and-downs of the government closely, even though they are not well-disposed to the government and its goals to begin with. But the most striking result lies in the tendency for the economists to be more steadfast—less rational and pragmatic about the efficiency of the government—than interpretations based on the dichotomy between normative and utilitarian compliance might suggest.

This outcome is puzzling only if we credit the image of the economists as dispassionate technocrats. Yet the stress on economic growth implies a righteous sort of social engineering and a political intolerance, a "damn-the-torpedoes-full-speed-ahead" developmentalism, that is unlikely to be deterred by temporary setbacks. The data hint of a coercive utopianism

---

[27] The curves in Figure 4.3 were drawn by plotting the mean support for the government for each quartile ranking of performance, within the developmental agendas. Thus, the lines are not linear regression estimates but empirical slopes. The least-squares parameters are given at the bottom of Figure 4.3.

FIGURE 4.3
Relationship between Government Support and Performance Evaluations, Controlling for
Developmental Priorities

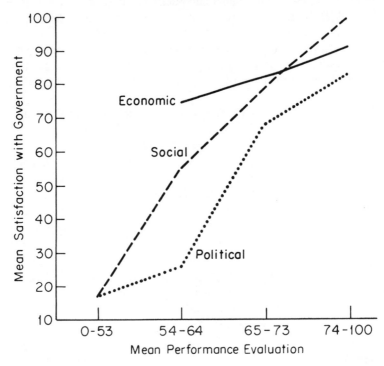

Priority	Mean Support	Slope	Correlation
Economic	83.3	.53	.37
Social	72.4	1.08	.73
Political	49.8	1.32	.77

NOTE: Elites with agendas in which all priorities are tied are omitted because the number of observations is too small for statistical analysis.

among the economists that makes the promoters of social reform seem sensible opportunists by comparison.

The economists are not unconcerned with the actual performance of the government. Many of them—the state managers, for example—have operational responsibility for the developmental effort. But their commitment to the government seems less likely to be influenced by short-term fluctuations in its performance than happens among the elites whose devotion to economic growth is less persistent.

The orientations of the social reformers seem more tactical, guided by the allocation of short-run benefits and sanctions. But there is also a suggestion of susceptibility to extremes among the social reformers. Those who rate the performance of the government at the very top also claim to support it totally, while those who rate its performance at the bottom are thoroughly dissatisfied with the government itself. The social reformers are not generally given to extremes. But they are the most wildly heterogeneous of the elites, a compound of radical fundamentalists and ingratiating survivors. As a group, they are less predictable than either the economists or the politicians.

The politicians themselves are clearly least supportive of the government. They respond in a linear way to its performance, or to their perceptions of it, by translating these evaluations into satisfaction/dissatisfaction with the government.

Although it is clear-cut in an after-the-fact way, such a tendency is not inevitable, and it is useful to contrast it with another equally plausible but in the present case hypothetical pattern. Among the politicians, the connection between perceptions of performance and attributions of support might have turned out to be much weaker, as it is among the economists. The slope in Figure 4.3 might have been essentially flat, with minor fluctuations around a low average level of support. And indeed the average level of support among the politicians is low. Moreover, even the politicians who are most enthusiastic about the performance of the government do not give the government a blank check, as some of the social reformers do. Yet despite this restraint, the politicians respond to the outputs of the government. The form of the relationship between performance and support is livelier—that is, steeper—among the politicians than the economists.

Thus, the politicians, like the social reformers, are subject to the interplay of cooptation and coercion. Yet as we saw in examining their developmental values, they are nearly as adamant as the economists. The present analysis does not refute this conclusion, but it suggests that the parallelism between the economists and the politicians is far from neat and that we will have to look elsewhere for evidence about the ways in which the politicians withold legitimacy from the regime.

To sum up, the developmental values of the elites bias their perceptions of the government. The impact of the bias is statistically modest. Nevertheless, the priorities of the elites contribute, at the margin, to a systematic inflation and deflation in satisfaction/dissatisfaction with the government. Although I have yet to demonstrate exactly how, it appears that elite values operate to some extent independently of circumstantial and specific factors and that they affect the legitimacy of the authoritarian system.

Although Brazilian elites consider economic growth to be of fundamental importance, many of them are disturbed by the social inequities accompanying the process and by the concentration of political power that some of the military, the technocrats, and the businessmen claim is dictated by the imperative of rapid industrialization. During the Médici years, the ruling coalition had the advantage not only of a monopoly of power but also of focusing on a determinate goal. The members of the coalition exhibited a remarkable unity in their commitment to this goal, perhaps because it was inherently less ambiguous than social or political development. An expansionary world economic climate made their position seem virtually unassailable.

Having fixed their priorities, the economists contend that alternative agendas are unrealistic and unviable. Political liberalization is put off to a becalmed future, after the problems of economic growth and the strains of social imbalance have been resolved. In placing economic growth first and political development last, the official agenda polarizes economists and politicians.

The conflict between economic development and political liberalization is seen as less manageable, if not more severe in objective terms, than that between accumulation and distribution, because rapid growth tends to be associated (although imperfectly) with authoritarian rule. The fear is that political relaxation will undermine control of demands for distribution and will upset the paternalistic mode of selective cooptation. This, in turn, may subvert economic growth.

In retrospect, it has become common to argue that the very concentration of resources dictated by the regime's economic plan, rather than any untoward redistribution, led to the decay of the Brazilian miracle by way of an atrophied domestic market, an extravagant habituation to foreign loans, and so forth. However this may be, a case can be made that the economists are not so simplistically enthralled by growthmanship as they may seem. As the record of preemptive social programs initiated by the post-1964 regime suggests, the economists are also concerned with staying in power—in practice, with anticipating the politicians in their competition for the loyalties of the social reformers.[28]

Many of the elites, including some who identify with the opposition, sense that a large part of the Brazilian public may be as unconcerned with political debate as with economic development in the aggregate. The former is "ideological," and the second is boring, apart from an occasional surge of patriotic pride for *Brasil grande*. Social well-being is a tangible good, even when doled out from above. The elites who place social welfare first

[28] See Wanderley Guilherme dos Santos, *Cidadania e Justiça: A Política Social na Ordem Brasileira* (Rio de Janeiro: Editora Campus, 1979).

on their agenda do not generally express serious opposition to the government. But neither are they devoted to it in principle, as the economists. For them, the government is neither legitimate nor illegitimate. Or if it is, this matters less than what the government gives to whom, here and now.

The economists are not so opportunistic as their supposed devotion to the utilitarian calculus might indicate. Many of them seem obsessed rather than truly pragmatic. Their agreement with the basic thrust of a government that places economic growth first seems as important as their evaluation of specific policies in preserving their allegiance to the system. Their resolution is not likely to be deflected by presumably ephemeral downturns in the economy, although one can imagine their draping themselves in democracy if, after a series of economic failures, politics came back into fashion as a second-best solution to economic collapse. After all, their fundamental commitment is to accumulation and investment for production.[29]

The politicians are the least satisfied with the regime, yet they show a good deal of variation in their judgments of the performance of the government. Despite their inclination to withold support from the government, as a group they are fragmented in their assessment of particular programs. They are not so unified in their opposition to the government as the economists are in their support of it.

The heterogeneity of the politicians derives in part from an understandable wariness about expressing their opposition and in part from a genuine uncertainty about the form and substance of liberalization in a historical context where economic growth and social reform have strong claims to priority. Some of them are ambivalent about the return to conventional democracy as a solution to the economic and social problems facing Brazil. They are searching for a means to control the arbitrariness of the state machine, without jeopardizing economic growth. This is a complicated venture involving decisions about the redistribution of power as well as the allocation of material resources and benefits. And lurking behind this is the specter of a more radical rethinking of the capitalist model of development itself, with the attendant questions of political control over economic power and the assimilation of the politically excluded.

It is this hidden agenda that gives the complaints of the politicians a simultaneously superficial and critical connotation. Their concern with taking power themselves may have deeper repercussions than the customary *opera buffa* of elite posturing, to the extent that the struggle engages contradictory values and rival models of development.

[29] See Euríco de Lima Figueiredo, "Abertura Política: Processo de Conservar o Ontem," *Jornal do Brasil*, September 30, 1979: 7, and Richard Rose, "Dynamic Tendencies in the Authority of Regimes," *World Politics* 21 (1969): 602-628.

By contrast, the unity of the economists stems from their disinclination even to attempt to reconcile disparate goals except in the very long run. The near consensus of the economists is not so stable as it may seem, however. The logic of their developmental model requires movement toward redistribution and liberalization as the economy expands. Some, though not all, of the economists are unwilling to give up on the democratic ethic. The ideal is bland and respectable, but its presence lends a curiously dialectical quality to the otherwise linear evolutionism of the economists: the faster the progress toward economic growth, the less rational it becomes to postpone political change. Conversely, if growth rates were to fall over a prolonged period, or if they were to remain simply at modest levels, the "unfortunate necessity" of repression—the perceived causal link between authoritarian politics and economic take-off, which seemed self-evident during the Médici years—would come increasingly into question.

Thus, by its own logic, either way it goes, the authoritarian solution—or rather, the legitimacy of the authoritarian solution—is precarious. The elites may grant the state a primary role in the drive toward development, accepting it as a fact of life of the twentieth century and not without precedent in the history of Brazil. But for many of the elites it is disagreeable and muscle-bound. The regime has many apologists but few ideologists. I explore this latent contradiction in the following chapter.

FIVE

Ideologies and the Limits of Legitimacy

> . . . the Revolution does not seek to legitimate itself through Congress.
> It is the latter that receives its legitimacy from this Institutional Act,
> resulting from the exercise of the constitutent power inherent in all rev-
> olutions.[1]

> All power emanates from the people and it will be exercised in their name.
> No matter how patriotic, honest, hard-working and wise he may be, a ruler
> is not, and will never be, a god on Olympus; nor can a nation of 113
> million have her fate decided by 13 people.[2]

If political legitimacy has any meaning at all, it goes beyond the short-
term, group-specific interests of powerful actors and establishes the ground
rules by which they are to live with one another in the midst of inevitable
conflicts. Legitimacy does not derive from or necessarily produce agreement on policy issues; this is a phantasmagoric and apolitical standard
even in authoritarian systems. Instead, it stems from an understanding
among the principal rivals for power regarding permissible gains and tolerable losses.

These premises have several implications. First, the question is not
whether the authoritarian regime in Brazil is legitimate; I assume that its
legitimacy is gravely flawed. The problem is to identify the standards by
which the legitimacy of the regime is undercut.

The second point, and the substance of my argument, is that of the three
major camps among the elites—the economists, the politicians, and the
social reformers—it is the third group that holds the decisive vote on the
legitimacy of the system. The economists and the politicians represent
adamant extremes. The former grant the system legitimacy; the latter do
not. The social reformers, who care relatively little about either "politics"
or "economics," are in the middle, wavering.

Somewhat ironically, the legitimacy of the regime is in the hands of

---

[1] From the First Institutional Act, promulgated by the Brazilian military in 1964. Quoted
by Ronald M. Schneider, *The Political System of Brazil: Emergence of a "Modernizing"
Authoritarian Regime* (New York: Columbia University Press, 1971), p. 126.

[2] From a manifesto, probably apocryphal, attributed to captains attached to the School of
Command and General Staff of the army. Quoted in *Isto É*, August 9, 1978: 11.

elites who are neither very powerful nor much concerned with principles and ideological abstractions. On the whole, the social reformers are not blessed with the rarefied cunning of long-term thinkers. But they are gifted with a shrewdness that goes with a lack of illusions about the extent of their own power. They resemble large portions of the Brazilian public, apparently deferent and politically indifferent but not infinitely patient.[3]

It is when the social reformers lose patience that whatever legitimacy the authoritarian system has breaks down. For a variety of reasons—a comparative insensitivity to problems involving civil liberties, an appreciation of the costs entailed in confronting the military relative to the security of subordination and cooptation, a traditional suspicion of *políticos* and intellectuals—the social reformers are reluctant to pull out of their one-sided alliance with the economists. They do not part company with the economists on the controversies that might seem to concern them most, the distributive, bread-and-butter issues, even though they never see eye-to-eye with the economists on these issues. It is on the policies that imply their continued subjugation to the state, even when this subjugation is

---

[3] This characterization of the social reformers raises the question, which I do not consider at length, of the level of their ideological consciousness, as compared to that of the economists and the politicians. The men I call social reformers are concentrated among (although not confined to) the labor leaders. Amaury de Souza has shown that, by the standard of cognitive consistency, many of the labor leaders are not fully ideological, even though they rank way above most of the rank-and-file on this score. See "The Nature of Corporatist Representation in Brazil," Ph.D. dissertation, Massachusetts Institute of Technology, 1978.

There have been some recent attempts, all of them drawing on neo-Marxist theories of the state, to deal with the levels-of-ideology problem among elites. A common contention is that those who run the government, supposedly because they are not caught up, as private enterpreneurs are, in the daily scramble of capital accumulation and competition, are better able to grasp "the big picture"—that is, to develop something very close to a strategic vision of where the best interests of the capitalist system lie. A slightly different version of the same argument is that such an awareness is most likely to arise among key elites, members of the inner circle by reason of their stewardship of mammoth organizations, regardless of whether these institutions are called public or private. Critical variations on this theme are Fred Block, "The Ruling Class Does Not Rule: Notes on the Marxist Theory of the State," *Socialist Revolution* 7 (1977): 6-28; Block, "Class Consciousness and Capitalist Rationalization: A Reply to Critics," *Socialist Review* 40-41 (1978): 212-220; and David Vogel, "Why Businessmen Distrust Their State," *British Journal of Political Science* 8 (1977): 45-78. The single empirical attempt to test the hypothesis failed, in part because the data were of the customary closed-ended questionnaire type. See Michael Useem, "The Inner Group of the American Capitalist Class," *Social Problems* 25 (1978): 225-240.

My position is that the deepest ideological demarcation among the Brazilian elites is not that between the tacticians and the strategists—what might be called "the-best-and-the-brightest" model of political management—but instead between those with tunnel vision and those with peripheral vision: between the obsessive (many of the economists and politicians) and those who, even though they might not see very far very clearly, have a more labile view of the political world around them.

relatively benign, that the social reformers move closer to the politicians. The economists are thereby left to fend for themselves, or rather are faced with the option of calling on their allies in the military to protect them. In Brazil, it is difficult to keep this up for long.

Thus, political legitimacy is less a function of common priorities, much less of shared opinions on particular issues, than it is the outcome of the capacity of elites with different values to put up with one another. The economists and the politicians do not have the same priorities, and they do not get along. But such a test of legitimacy is simplistic inasmuch as it requires a near-perfect consensus that no political system is likely to sustain. For this reason, I inject a third criterion besides the economic and the political—roughly, social equity. It is the coalition, not consensus, between two of these three types that lends a working, albeit imperfect, legitimacy to the system. When in an authoritarian situation the social reformers split from the economists, even this threadbare legitimacy is gone.[4]

The gist of the theory, then, is that legitimacy/illegitimacy in Brazil is rarely a matter of heaven or hell but more typically a sort of purgatory, regulated by the vacillations of the social reformers. Because an overarching consensus among the proponents of the three developmental priorities is most improbable, and because coalition partners need not agree on a positive political alternative, it may be more appropriate to consider the argument as a theory of tenability rather than legitimacy. In any event, while it may have applications elsewhere, the theory is directed at the classic authoritarian situation in which no one group is considered powerful enough to rule alone.

In schematic form, these ideas are straightforward, though more elaborate, than red-versus-expert constructions of legitimacy. The problem is to test them: to observe how the values of the elites condition the viability of the system. It is one thing to describe the fundamental values of the elites in terms of their development priorities. It is another to demonstrate that these values affect the legitimacy of the regime as I have defined it— that is, as commitments to the norms of interelite accommodation and competition. The following sections set forth the plan of analysis.

Progressives and Conservatives

Although many indicators of elite opinion have been dissected, one variety remains to be examined. This is made up of the policy preferences of the

[4] Compare William M. Sullivan, "Shifting Loyalties: Critical Theory and the Problem of Legitimacy," *Polity* 12 (1979): 253-272.

elites on specific controversies, their attitudes pro and con on the issues of the day.

While we already have a reasonably clear notion of the ideological leanings of the elite groups, it is uncertain how the gradations between conservatives and progressives hold up across a battery of policy disputes. The task is to clarify where the elites stand, and how they shift around, on the issues that form the subject of political discourse in Brazil.

The Dimensionality of Elite Ideologies

There is no reason to assume that elite opinions are organized along a single gradient, and there are good reasons to suspect that the belief systems of Brazilian elites are structured along at least two and probably three coordinates. One reason is that the elites, being cognitively sophisticated, are able to integrate various dimensions of public controversy, as well as to keep them separate when in fact the lines of conflict tend to be distinct.

Another reason has to do with the notion that in authoritarian systems purely ideological cleavages, in the classic left-right sense, tend to be blurred. The progressive-conservative split is not foggy; we shall see that it is the clearest dimension of conflict among Brazilian elites. But it is not the only line of battle. Instead of being diffuse, elites ideologies in Brazil are multidimensional.

This organized complexity becomes most evident with the special position of what I call the moral issues—birth control, divorce, and so on—preferences that cannot be fitted within the same frame of reference as those involving the standard left-versus-right controversies. A further twist is added by the differential polarization intrinsic to the left-right cleavage. Some issues that fall in this general domain are more conflict-laden than others; altogether, they constitute an escalating scale of controversies.

As for the moral issues, they may not be the only ones that fail to fit on a progressive-conservative axis. One can imagine items tapping regional or ethnic cleavages that could not be superimposed on the vocabulary of left versus right, although this line of conflict is probably more salient in a country like Spain than in Brazil. Nevertheless, consideration of a set of issues that is distinct from the divisions between left and right confirms the multidimensional nature of elite ideology in Brazil.

But the virtual independence of the moral issues from other lines of conflict tells us more about Brazilian politics than that the ideologies of the elites are complex—a discovery that, after all, comes as a surprise only if we stick to the notion of ideology as a rather simple-minded polarization between two opposites, with perhaps a few intermediate positions along a single continuum.

On the one hand, the moral issues are relatively unimportant in Brazil;

they do not directly affect the legitimacy of any regime. On the other hand, they point to a practically irretrievable but, I believe, extremely important aspect of legitimacy in Brazil that is not captured by the interplay between positions on socioeconomic issues like agrarian reform (the accumulation/distribution axis) and positions on the even more conflictive issues, such as the control of labor organizations by the government (the order/liberty axis).

The moral issues are freighted with overtones of political community. In a way, the fact that the issues of family planning, divorce, and abortion cluster around the moral axis is circumstantial, although the separation of preferences on these issues from the remaining cleavages is not. The essence of the moral axis is a split between private and collective, or parochial and collective, orientations. Hence, the analogy between these issues in Brazil and regional and linguistic cleavages elsewhere has a certain validity, with the crucial qualification that the moral dimension is fairly weak in Brazil.

Consideration of the moral issues, then, fills a gap in the analysis of elite ideology and political legitimacy left vacant by examination of the accumulation-versus-distribution and order-versus-liberty issues. On the assumption that no single ideological current can gain hegemony in Brazil, any settlement among rival priorities will involve a delicate and—to some—vacuous pluralism of toleration. Even though it may be the next best thing, this is not quite the same as a sense of political community or, if it is, it is unfamiliar and disenchanting.

Routine (Accumulation versus Distribution) versus Rules-of-the-Game (Order versus Liberty) Issues

Establishing the conflict-potential of issues that fit on the left-right cleavage is a more complicated venture than proving the distinctiveness of moral controversies in Brazil. It is a problem that I do not really tackle until the next chapter, when the chasm between what the elites say they believe and where they say their colleagues stand is charted issue by issue. For the present purpose of seeing what it is about certain features of the ideologies of the elites that might be associated with the legitimacy of the regime, a simpler procedure suffices.

The search for the ideological determinants of legitimacy follows two stages. The first involves a distinction between two kinds of issues, both of which form part of the progressive-conservative split. One package of controversies I refer to as routine issues. The term is meant to designate policy questions on which the positions of the elites can be regularly predicted as a function of their membership in nominally progressive or conservative sectors.

The issues themselves may be far from routine. The question of income redistribution, for example, is explosive, and the elites hold quite discrepant views on the matter. But it is also an issue on which the preferences of the elites can be categorized satisfactorily with reference to their group and partisan interests. While the connections are not always transparent, there is little mystery about where the MDB politicians as compared to the businessmen, for example, stand on income redistribution, labor-government relations, and so forth.

However, my treatment of legitimacy centers on the notion of supragroup norms that set the terms of intergroup behavior. We must identify, therefore, a subset of issues on which elites who are usually at odds manage to pull together.

One such issue involves the question of the participation of the Brazilian military in politics.[5] This is the touchiest, if not the deepest, controversy in Brazilian public life. It bears directly on the rights of the elite estates, especially on their ability to retain some autonomy and to protect their interests under limited pluralism. The implications of such controversies, which I call rules-of-the-game issues, are broader than the defense and cultivation of the special aims of particular groups. This kind of issue evokes the common interests of the elites—at least, of the social reformers as well as the politicians—in fending off the intrusions of the authoritarian state and in safeguarding, if not expanding, their separate turfs.

The distinction between routine and rules-of-the-game issues is plausible but, up to this point, purely taxonomical. The second stage in the search for the determinants of legitimacy involves the pivotal role played by the social reformers. The essential idea is that the usually forebearing social reformers break with the economists precisely on those matters in which whatever shreds of autonomy and control over patronage they have left are threatened with annihilation by the state. They abandon the economists and approach the politicians in their disaffection from the workings of the authoritarian system.

In order for this to happen, the social reformers must look a bit beyond their group-specific concerns and come to terms with the politicians, whom they distrust, rather than with the economists, whom they dislike but accept as the best of a bad bargain. The social reformers are pushed in this direction by the continued and seemingly endless suspension of their right, as elites, to bargain for power and privilege at the hands of the authoritarian bureaucracy.

[5] The question reads: "To what extent do you oppose or favor the participation of the military in national politics?" The elites were presented with a 100-point scale, with the midpoint labelled "indifferent" and the upper and lower ends representing varying degrees of agreement and disagreement.

In summary, the rules-of-the-game issues cut to the quick of the authoritarian compromise among Brazilian elites. The routine issues, although volatile in varying degrees, do not. On the latter, the elites may be bitterly divided, but they do not question directly the rules by which outcomes on these issues are settled. In the former case, latent allies overcome their group differences. The social reformers coalesce with the politicians in defiance of the authoritarian state.

Ideologies

The Distribution of Policy Preferences

Restrictions on political debate during the Médici era were severe. The printed media as well as radio and television were censored, and the universities were purged of outspoken dissidents. Nevertheless, while open discussion was stifled, there were no sustained attempts at indoctrinating the elites. Provided they did not air their views to a large audience or try to mobilize groups for action, the elites were entitled to their opinions. It was understood that a demarcation existed between what could be professed in public and what might be entertained in private.

The range of issues discussed in elite circles is broad. Controversies vary from the global ("foreign investment," "agrarian reform," and the like—in effect, bundles of issues) to the pedestrian ("unionization of domestics," a matter involving the extension of minimum wage laws and social security protection to maids). They include issues such as income redistribution, which toward the end of the Médici period came to be debated in newspapers and specialized publications, as well as practically forbidden topics, such as the enfranchisement of illiterates. Much interelite polemic also revolved around issues that, at the time, did not seem to arouse most Brazilians: the possibility of creating a third party, amnesty for political prisoners and exiles, the restoration of *habeas corpus*—the gamut of civil rights controversies.[6]

Table 5.1 provides a breakdown of the preferences of the elites on twenty-three issues, many of which continued to be objects of contention through the Geisel (1974-1979) and Figueiredo governments (1979-).[7]

[6] Preferences on the issues mentioned in this paragraph were measured on 100-point scales. The midpoint for most is "indifferent," as for the question about the role of the military. The midpoint for the foreign investment is "the situation in Brazil nowadays," and the alternatives signify preferences for greater and lesser amounts of foreign capital relative to this point. See footnote 8 for the phrasing of the income distribution item.

[7] For any single issue, there is likely to be some uncertainty about the empirical results as valid indicators of elite opinion. The broader the question, the more open it is to multiple interpretation. See Howard Schuman and Stanley Presser, "Question Wording as an Inde-

The responses vary along 100-point scales, with the higher values representing progressive opinions.[8]

The elite sectors are ranked from left to right in progressive-conservative order. The MDB politicians are at the left and the businessmen at the right; the labor leaders stand toward the center-left.

The issues are ranked from top to bottom in descending progressive-conservative order. The elites are most progressive on the issue of the restoration of *habeas corpus*; they tend toward conservative positions on matters like subversion. The commitment of the elites to the writ of *habeas*

---

pendent Variable in Survey Analysis," *Sociological Methods and Research* 6 (1977): 27-46. However, since potential bias operates uniformly across the elites as a function of the way in which questions are phrased, it does not obscure the relative differences among the elite groups. Even though the average of elite opinion on some questions may sound overly enlightened, the progressives still incline toward a more leftist position than the conservatives. A detailed presentation of the discursive responses to a sample of four major questions—foreign investment, income redistribution, government-labor relations, and government-opposition relations—is given in the Appendix.

[8] All questions were posed with 100-point response scales, and most used the "To what extent do you oppose or favor . . ." format. The exceptions are: redistribution of income, political opposition, autonomy of labor organizations, birth control, and the previously cited question of foreign investment. The midpoint for this subset is "the situation nowadays in Brazil." Most questions read: "To what extent do you oppose or favor . . .": (1) the re-establishment of *habeas corpus*; (2) agrarian reform; (3) the death penalty; (4) the participation of rural workers in national politics; (5) the unionization (*sindicalização*) of maids (*empregadas domésticas*); (6) the participation of students in national politics; (7) the legalization of divorce; (8) a greater degree of autonomy for the state governors; (9) the organization of a third party; (10) censorship of the media (*meios de comunicação*); (11) indirect elections for governor, in principle; (12) amnesty for persons who have had their political rights taken away (*para pessoas que tiveram os seus direitos políticos cassados*); (13) the involvement of the church in social and political issues (*questões*); (14) the participation of the military in national politics; (15) the legalization of abortion; (16) voting rights (*o direito de voto*) for illiterates; (17) a greater fight (*um maior combate*) against internal subversion; and (18) the leadership of Brazil in Latin America.

The other questions were worded as follows: "Keeping in mind the situation nowadays in Brazil, where would you place yourself with respect to income redistribution policy on this scale?" The 100-point scale runs from "much less rapid" to "much more rapid." The political opposition question is: "In comparison with Brazil nowadays, on the matter of limits on opposition against the government (*limites à oposição ao governo*), where do you place yourself?" The scale runs from "much less limits on the opposition" to "much greater limits." The labor question is: "In comparison with the present situation, where do you stand on the question of the degree of governmental control of the labor syndicates?" The scale goes from "much less control" to "much more." The birth control question is: "In comparison with Brazil nowadays, on the matter of the extent of birth control (*controle de natalidade*) as government policy, where do you place yourself?" The five alternatives are: "total prohibition of birth control"; "a more active policy against birth control"; "current policy"; "some governmental incentives for birth control"; "much greater governmental incentives for birth control."

TABLE 5.1
Average Preferences on Twenty-Three Issues, by Elite Sector
(standard deviations in parentheses)

Issue	MDB	Church	Labor	ARENA	Civil Service	Business	Mean	ETA^2
Habeas Corpus	100 (—)	100 (—)	87 (23)	81 (25)	83 (25)	83 (28)	85 (25)	.04
Agrarian Reform	95 (10)	99 (3)	94 (12)	89 (21)	80 (27)	74 (30)	84 (25)	.13
Abolition of Death Penalty	80 (39)	99 (3)	79 (31)	85 (30)	77 (34)	72 (38)	78 (34)	.03
Participation of Peasants	96 (9)	87 (17)	82 (24)	81 (24)	73 (32)	73 (28)	78 (28)	.05
Unionization of Domestics	88 (29)	89 (17)	92 (21)	66 (29)	71 (33)	73 (32)	77 (30)	.10
Redistribution of Income	90 (16)	89 (14)	84 (19)	71 (22)	71 (15)	67 (17)	74 (19)	.17
Political Participation of Students	92 (27)	76 (23)	79 (30)	80 (30)	67 (32)	59 (38)	70 (34)	.09
Political Opposition	96 (13)	89 (16)	66 (24)	69 (24)	69 (20)	65 (23)	69 (23)	.13
Autonomy of Labor Organizations	86 (27)	88 (17)	73 (27)	56 (16)	60 (16)	58 (19)	64 (22)	.18
Legalization of Divorce	75 (40)	2 (8)	74 (34)	43 (41)	68 (35)	73 (35)	64 (39)	.19
Autonomy of Governors	98 (8)	64 (16)	65 (27)	70 (26)	54 (28)	54 (34)	61 (31)	.12
Birth Control	55 (29)	40 (27)	53 (30)	56 (23)	62 (21)	65 (25)	59 (26)	.06
Third Party	88 (28)	69 (33)	70 (33)	64 (36)	45 (31)	50 (38)	58 (36)	.11
Relaxation of Censorship	96 (13)	74 (36)	56 (33)	57 (30)	55 (37)	51 (34)	57 (35)	.10
Direct Gubernatorial Elections	89 (27)	63 (32)	62 (41)	61 (40)	47 (37)	42 (39)	54 (40)	.10
Political Amnesty	95 (10)	82 (25)	56 (36)	39 (34)	51 (32)	42 (35)	51 (36)	.16
Political Participation of Church	74 (33)	84 (24)	48 (35)	49 (31)	45 (33)	40 (32)	48 (34)	.11
Political Participation of Military	51 (43)	72 (27)	44 (30)	36 (32)	33 (27)	36 (33)	39 (32)	.06
Legalization of Abortion	58 (41)	0 (—)	34 (38)	21 (37)	44 (39)	45 (40)	38 (40)	.09

TABLE 5.1 (*cont.*)
Average Preferences on Twenty-Three Issues, by Elite Sector
(standard deviations in parentheses)

				Elite Sector				
Issue	*MDB*	*Church*	*Labor*	*ARENA*	*Civil Service*	*Business*	*Mean*	*ETA²*
Reduction of Foreign	57	67	44	43	34	27	38	.16
Investment	(21)	(29)	(27)	(22)	(21)	(23)	(26)	
Enfranchisement of	79	56	30	23	23	22	29	.14
Illiterates	(29)	(44)	(39)	(31)	(33)	(36)	(38)	
Subversion	39	82	24	22	32	25	28	.10
	(42)	(26)	(36)	(30)	(31)	(32)	(34)	
Leadership of Brazil	40	45	18	13	23	33	26	.09
in Latin America	(41)	(30)	(27)	(25)	(30)	(29)	(30)	
Mean	79	71	61	55	54	52	57	.25
	(12)	(11)	(13)	(11)	(11)	(12)	(14)	

NOTES: 0 = conservative, 100 = progressive.
An ETA² of .05 or greater is significant at the .01 level.

corpus is believable, since it is one of the fundamental bourgeois decencies. Most of the elites take a nationalistic position with respect to the destiny of Brazil as a world power. They are not fond of sedition. The top-to-bottom ranking of issues, while it cannot be taken seriously as a set of absolute estimates, provides a rough ordering of elite preferences.

The principal interest, however, lies in the relative differences among the elite sectors rather than in the numerical scores themselves. For example, even though the overall drift of opinion on agrarian reform appears excessively leftist, interelite polarization on the issue is considerable.[9]

[9] "Agrarian reform" is another bundle of issues. We did not elicit open-ended responses from the elites on this issue, but we did ask them how much importance they would give to each of eight different measures for the promotion of agricultural development (*medidas para a solução do desenvolvimento agrícola*). In order of presentation in the interview, these measures are: (1) colonization of the virgin areas of the Amazon; (2) more direct credit facilities to landowners (*fazendeiros*); (3) mechanization (*racionalização e inovação tecnológica*) of agricultural production; (4) incentives to the formation of agrobusinesses (*empresas agrícolas*); (5) creation of industries in rural areas; (6) redistribution of large rural holdings (*propriedades*) of low productivity; (7) incentives for peasants (*camponeses*) to migrate to industrial centers; and (8) elimination of small holdings (*minifúndios*). The elites could then rate the measures as "very important," "more or less important," or "without importance."

One way to understand what the elites mean by agrarian reform is to correlate each of these indicators with the pro-con item on agrarian reform. The results are: redistribution of large rural holdings of low productivity ($r = .46$); colonization of the Amazon region (.30); elimination of *minifúndios* (.18); mechanization (.14); industries in rural areas (.13); incentives to agrobusiness (.13); direct credit to landowners (.06); and incentives to migration (.02).

Similarly, while on the average the elites do not favor giving the vote to illiterate Brazilians, the issue provokes a real split among them, dividing the MDB politicians and the bishops from the rest.

Several other patterns can be discerned. There are scarcely any significant differences within the conservative ranks. Occasionally, as with the question of the legalization of divorce, the ARENA politicians assume a more reactionary stance than the state managers and the politicians.[10] On other controversies, such as those over the creation of a third party or over the regional autonomy to be granted to the governors, members of the government party are inclined to be more liberal. Their professional interests come into play, undercutting their identification with the antipoliticism of the regime. As politicians, the members of the ARENA betray antitechnocratic yearnings; but between the state managers and the businessmen there do not appear to be any major quarrels.

By comparison, differences on the left are substantial. On most of the political issues—for example, on the questions of party opposition, amnesty, and censorship—the labor leaders are closer to the businessmen and the civil servants than they are to the church or the MDB. It is mainly on the social issues, like income redistribution, that the labor leaders close ranks on the left. Even on the issues of presumably greatest centrality to them, the freedom of the workers' syndicates, the labor leaders are prudent. They owe their jobs to the government, and the issue is fraught with confrontation. In general, the labor leaders are not political liberals, although they can be counted on to be less reactionary than the state managers and the businessmen.

The MDB politicians are the most consistently progressive of the elites. The primary exception occurs on the issue of "subversion." The opposition party has an interest in not being labelled subversive itself.

The bishops claim to be enlightened on the subversion issue for two reasons. First, in a Catholic country, it is virtually unthinkable to accuse the ecclesiastical hierarchy of treason. Second, the bishops became increasingly concerned about the violations of human rights, some of them at the expense of priests, committed in the name of the "war against subversion." The humanism of the bishops is also reflected in their over

---

It is clear that the more the elites declare themselves in favor of agrarian reform, the more they have in mind a structural solution entailing land redistribution. However, this is not the only solution they contemplate. They also tend to look favorably on expansion into the open spaces of Brazil ("colonization of the Amazon"), and they favor the consolidation of presumably inefficient small holdings as well.

[10] Divorce was legalized in Brazil in 1976, after a long campaign led by Senator Nelson Carneiro of the MDB. One factor that encouraged the ARENA politicians to support this legislation, despite their moralism on the issue, was their resentment at what they considered the meddling of the church. The executive branch also supported the legislation, partly as a way of putting the church in its place.

whelming rejection of capital punishment for political crimes.[11] Their nativism and distaste for the secular vulgarities of modernization are reflected in their radical stand on the question of foreign investment.[12]

Otherwise, the MDB politicians have a liberal edge over the bishops. They are more favorable to direct elections, to political amnesty, to increased political participation, to freedom of the press, and so on. As opposition politicians, members of the MDB are extremely sensitive to matters of political liberties. Their progressive stance on the issue of the enfranchisement of illiterates suggests a commitment to wider political involvement, to the possibility of mobilizing and forming alliances with groups outside the elite system.

The quasi-populism of the MDB politicians sets them apart not only from the conservative elites and from the syndical leaders but from the bishops as well, whose mildly progressive stance on the issue of the extension of the franchise is the result of considerable internal division. The paternalistic strain in the humanism of the bishops makes them ambivalent. Like the military, the ecclesiastical corporation has a strong sense of hierarchy.

Yet, whatever their pastoralism regarding popular movements, the bishops, unlike the MDB, are not fearful of confronting the authorities on matters in which other opposition groups have much to lose. This is evident in their forthrightness about denying the military an active political role, a question on which the MDB politicians are understandably circumspect.

It is on the moral issues—legalization of divorce and abortion and government involvement in birth control programs—that the bishops turn to the right. On these issues, their views are dictated by church dogma. But this is not the only consideration drawing the bishops to the right of the MDB. They are not so concerned as the MDB with issues of political form (amnesty, multipartism, censorship, direct-versus-indirect elections), nor are they as enthusiastic about mass participation. The social fundamentalism of the bishops is ambiguous and cannot be categorized with certainty as radicalism of the left or the right.[13]

[11] The death penalty was abolished in Brazil in 1979, after having been instituted by the Médici government.

[12] The orientations of the bishops regarding foreign investment resemble those of many on the Brazilian left, although their motives differ a bit (somewhat as the church and the secular left tend to agree, for slightly different reasons, on birth control policy). The bishops, like the left, are appalled by the simultaneous consumerism and pauperism they associate with the penetration of North American, Western European, and Japanese capitalism. But the indignation of some of the bishops stems at least as much from traditional Christian scruples about profit making and commercialization as it does from a secular critique of materialist degradation and from belief in a socialist alternative. Many of the bishops are precapitalists rather than secular radicals.

[13] The willingness of the Brazilian church to defy the military on questions on civil liberties,

The progressives, then, are disunited. The labor leaders are cautious on political liberties; they are more worried about economic and social benefits. And except for their outrage at the policies enacted to liquidate subversion and their hostility to the presumption of the military, the dissidence of the bishops is tempered. The MDB politicians are the most thoroughgoing progressives.

Overall, despite these differences, the tendency is for elite opinion to tilt in a liberal direction. To be sure, there are certain issues, like the enfranchisement of illiterates and subversion, on which preferences are skewed to the right. Nothing reveals the exclusionary, antipopulist leanings of the elites more strikingly than their refusal to admit nearly a third of the adult population to first-class citizenship.

Yet it is difficult to isolate an extreme right in the sense of a sizeable proportion of blatant antiliberals. By default, liberal-democratic ideals maintain a hold. That these ideals may exist mainly in words, and that they may be limited to a world that keeps much of the population from effective participation, are compelling possibilities, especially in light of the long-standing ambivalence in Brazilian politics over elitism, liberalism, and mass mobilization. Nevertheless, the ambiguity of the elites constitutes an important fact. The detritus of liberalism is an ideological embarrassment that impedes the institutionalization of reactionary programs.[14]

---

so that conservative and progressive clergy stand virtually as one against the state's meddling in religious affairs, broadly defined, does not imply that the bishops as a body have uniform views about either social justice or mass political participation. The following statement made by Cardinal Paulo Evaristo Arns of São Paulo, a leader of the progressive wing of the Brazilian church, is one to which many conservative prelates would subscribe: "You shall not kill. . . . It is impossible to pray in peace when dignity is being trampled on and ignored. The lack of respect for legal guarantees means social insecurity, for the people who have been imprisoned and subjected to harsh treatment on the basis of mere suspicion or even by mistake; for families in which one of the members has suddenly disappeared; and for a society that ends up losing faith in those responsible for its protection." Quoted by Penny Lernoux, "Latin America: The Revolutionary Bishops," *The Atlantic* 246 (July 1980): 12. See also Dom Paulo Evaristo Arns, "Deus o Acompanhará," *Veja*, November 5,1980: 146.

By contrast, the heterogeneity of the bishops regarding political participation, like their unity with respect to the defense of a community beyond the reach of the state, has traditional as well as radical roots. This is true, for example, with regard to the exercise of the vote, about which the church has been ambivalent for at least two reasons: it may be used "irresponsibly" (for example, to pass laws favoring changes in what for the church are practically non-negotiable issues, such as abortion); or it may not promote what the bishops consider genuine change in the area of social justice. For at least some of the bishops, the question of expanding the franchise may also represent a diversion toward what some Marxists would call "electoralism"—an inordinate stress on the political process without corresponding returns in the alleviation of mass poverty.

[14] For at least one issue, the "unionization of domestics," the progressivism of the elites is not illusory. Early in 1973, when about half of the elite interviews had been completed, President Médici signed into law a decree extending social security benefits to maids, and

There is also a good deal of intrasector heterogeneity on the issues. The averages yield significant differences among the elite sectors. The progressivism of the MDB is unmistakable, and so is the conservatism of the businessmen. Yet the elites do not form uniform blocs. Individual variation in political opinions is not at all surprising under authoritarian conditions, for behavior is more circumscribed than thought.

A finer and more consequential pattern can be detected in the internal heterogeneity of the elite groups. Extremely sensitive issues, like subversion and the political role of the military, provoke considerable division within the MDB. These are dangerous questions for any of the elites to take advanced positions on. There is an evident tension on the left between adherence to principle and the need for discretion.[15]

On the other hand, on less touchy but still controversial issues, such as the autonomy of the governors, political amnesty, party opposition, direct-versus-indirect elections, and the like, the progressive sectors actually tend to be more unified than the state managers and the businessmen. Within the latter groups, there are more or less liberal and more or less reactionary strands. The general positions of the state managers and the businessmen are clear: they can almost always be expected to adopt a harder line than the bishops and the MDB politicians. But, given this tendency, the conservatives also show substantial variegation.[16]

For all this, the lines of conflict are more sharply drawn on some issues— income redistribution, the enfranchisement of illiterates, the autonomy of labor, and so on—than on others. The conservatives loosen up on many of the "merely political" issues, like multipartism, electoral procedures, and censorship. Here the countercurrents of hard-nosed developmentalism and liberal-democratic ideals produce appreciable intragroup variation.

These patterns seem realistic. The conservatives are not sympathetic to a return to what they consider a populist rampage, but they are attracted

the possibility of such a regulation had been discussed in elite circles before that time. Thus, the progressivism of the elites on this issue is not daring. Nevertheless, it is interesting to note that the distribution of opinion on the issue follows the usual left-right pattern.

[15] The correlation between the left-right index and interviewer-assessed "hesitancy" is −.22, indicating that the greater the discretion of the elites, the more conservative their statements of opinion. The association is only moderate, but it is fairly constant across the elite sectors. The effect of this fear-factor is to make the drift of elite opinion slightly less progressive than it would be if the elites felt they were speaking in utter confidence.

[16] One of the reasons for the heterogeneity of the conservative elites on certain political issues is that they are closer to the midpoints of the preferences scales, where considerable variation is possible. The progressives, on the other hand, position themselves toward one extreme of the scales. Thus, a ceiling effect sets in, restricting variation about their "extreme" position. This is, of course, a substantively meaningful fact and not merely a statistical problem.

to a political opening that will get the state off their backs. The progressives, particularly the MDB, want more popular involvement, but they are rather timid when it comes to facing down the military.

The more paternalistic bishops show the reverse syndrome. They are willing to take on the military, but they prefer a flock that can be ministered to, instead of an unruly crowd.

The labor leaders stand between the progressives and the conservatives. They are patriotic, moralistic, and often imitative of their superiors, as their opinions on the role of Brazil in Latin America, on censorship and political amnesty, and the enfranchisement of illiterates suggest. But on the bread-and-butter issues, particularly income redistribution, they come down on the progressive side.

The Dimensionality of Policy Preferences

It is easy to slip into the vocabulary of left versus right when describing the results presented in Table 5.1, because the overall distribution of elite opinion does in fact follow that division. But there are signs that this is not the only cleavage dividing the elites.

For example, the ARENA politicians are roused from their customary solidarity with the government when their rights as politicians seem threatened. They are not enchanted by the total subjugation of the governors to the central authorities, and they favor the formation of a third party—one that, unlike the MDB and the ARENA itself, would not be a creature of the government. The usually progressive bishops become quite conservative on issues like abortion and divorce. And the labor leaders are at most cautiously liberal on the political-opening issues.

It seems, then, at least for the bishops, that the moral issues have a special meaning setting them apart from the other controversies. Moreover, the generally progressive and conservative elites respond to the left-right issues in a selective way. Some—the labor leaders provide the most conspicuous example—are socially progressive (though distinctly unradical) and politically moderate rather than conservative.

In order to specify these ambiguities, the positions of each of the elites on each of the issues can be correlated with his average inclination toward the left or right. This enables us to estimate the degree to which an issue is strongly or weakly cast in left-right terms, for each of the elite groups. The stronger the association between a policy preference and the overall measure, the sharper is the division between progressives and conservatives on that issue.

In Table 5.2 the issues are listed from top to bottom in descending order of the strength of the association between the elites' position on them and their average left-right position. Calculations were also performed for the major sectors separately. Occasionally, as will be noted, the sector-by-sector results diverge from the pattern for the entire sample.

Let us focus first on the general tendencies. A clear distinction emerges between political issues generally and moral dilemmas: abortion, divorce, and especially birth control. Preferences on the latter three issues are not very closely related to the average conservative-progressive propensities of the elites.

The major exception occurs among the bishops. The more progressive

TABLE 5.2

Correlations of Twenty-Three Policy Preferences with Left-Right Index,
by Elite Sector

				Elite Sector			
Issue	*All Elites*	*MDB*	*Bishops*	*Labor*	*ARENA*	*Civil Service*	*Business*
Political Amnesty	.65	.36	.83	.59	.47	.60	.61
Autonomy of Labor Syndicates	.64	.83	.69	.40	.62	.72	.57
Direct Gubernatorial Elections	.59	.67	.68	.67	.54	.50	.49
Political Opposition	.58	.65	.60	.55	.14	.56	.61
Relaxation of Censorship	.57	.32	.58	.56	.30	.56	.55
Political Participation of Church	.54	.88	.85	.40	.46	.42	.48
Income Redistribution	.52	.77	.38	.42	.57	.30	.42
Enfranchisement of Illiterates	.50	.15	.87	.58	.22	.43	.26
Subversion	.45	.46	.45	.66	.14	.40	.43
Creation of Third Party	.44	.22	− .23	.52	.21	.45	.36
Political Participation of Students	.42	.35	.24	.42	.23	.02	.57
Abolition of Death Penalty	.42	.58	.48	.42	.67	.28	.46
Habeas Corpus	.41	—[a]	—[a]	.43	.45	.36	.37
Unionization of Domestics	.40	.11	.62	.32	.44	.28	.44
Political Participation of Peasants	.39	.47	.57	.48	.46	.13	.38
Agrarian Reform	.39	.44	.47	.28	.46	.22	.36
Political Participation of Military	.37	.50	.75	.39	.02	.45	.23
Reduction of Foreign Investment	.36	.42	.68	.49	.19	.23	− .01
Autonomy of Governors	.36	.69	.37	.17	.55	.11	.29
Brazil in Latin America	.31	.49	.43	.53	.30	.15	.28
Legalization of Abortion	.30	.73	.27	.19	.44	.50	.34
Legalization of Divorce	.17	.25	.27	.04	.50	.45	.24
Birth Control	.08	.43	.70	.05	.01	.21	.26

NOTE: Index = mean of 23 policy preferences.

[a] No variance (see Table 5.1).

bishops tend toward a sweeping liberalism, and that includes a permissive attitude toward family planning. But even the progressives are not carried away with enthusiasm for the legalization of divorce and abortion, matters that threaten the little public power that the Catholic church in Brazil enjoys.

On the whole, then, the moral issues lie apart from the controversies usually associated with progressive and conservative positions in political debate. These results reflect the contradictory nature of polemics about population planning and related issues in Brazil and other parts of Latin America. An enlightened position by some standards (antinatalism) may be looked upon as retrograde, superficial, or immoral by others (by many communists as well as devout Catholics).

Among the political issues, a few seem to have strongly polarizing properties. Toward the top of the list are the controversies that center around interelite competition: political amnesty, direct gubernatorial elections, freedom of party opposition, the political involvement of the church, and so on. These issues touch on the question of the autonomy of significant actors vis-à-vis the authoritarian state.

Although the outlines of a left-right gradient are visible, escalating from the less to the more explosive issues, several factors cloud the connection of specific issues to the progressive-conservative dispositions of the elites. On some issues there is so little disagreement that the magnitude of the correlations is forced down. The restoration of *habeas corpus* is one such issue. Even the most conservative elites support the measure, and the bishops and the MDB politicians back it 100 percent. On this rule-of-law issue there exists virtual consensus.

A second consideration qualifies any sweeping generalizations about "the elite." At times, the associations derived from viewing the elites as a whole change when viewed sector by sector. For example, the mild overall association between preferences about the participation of the military and the summary left-right measure results in part from the absence of any correlation whatsoever within the ARENA. In this case, the men assigned to gather support for their masters are ambivalent. But even elsewhere, among the labor leaders and the state managers, the corresponding correlations, while positive, are not overpowering.

On this issue, the response of all but the most reckless and genuinely courageous of the elites, the bishops, are contaminated with prudence. Many of the elites who vouchsafe their liberalism on less delicate issues tone down their views on the role of the military. Fear weakens the strength of the association between elite opinions about the political role of the military and their generic left-rightism.[17]

Third, a few issues behave differently from sector to sector not because some elites are more forthright than others but because the issues produce genuinely conflicting views among elites with otherwise predictably conservative or progressive positions. The most striking example of this tension occurs within the business community on foreign investment policy. The lack of a strong association between preferences on this issue and the general left-right measure does not stem from differences among the heads of multinationals, the banks, and private domestic industry. The business community as a whole is genuinely torn between the attractions of another source of capital and the loss of autonomy at the hands of foreign capitalists.[18] Hence, it is impossible to characterize with much accuracy where the typically progressive or conservative businessman stands with regard to the complex issue of foreign investment. Above all, he is liable to be ambivalent.[19]

In summary, the most forceful cleavage among the elites is a progressive-

[17] A revealing way to estimate the touchiness of an issue is to correlate preferences on it with interviewer-assessed hesitancy. In footnote 15, I indicated that the correlation between hesitancy and the overall left-right index is $-.22$. When correlations are computed issue by issue, the three controversies that have the strongest associations with the hesitancy measure are *habeas corpus* ($r = -.20$), political participation of the military ($-.18$), and creation of a third party ($-.18$). The lowest correlations occur for the "moral" issues: birth control ($-.03$), divorce ($.01$), and abortion ($-.08$). The results vary a bit from sector to sector, but in general they are quite in line with expectations drawn from observation of elite politics during the Médici era.

[18] There is no contradiction between the elites' essentially moderate position regarding foreign investment and their resentment, documented in Chapter Four, of foreign capitalists. Most of the elites prefer order over anarchy, but they resent the military for continuing to impose it. Similarly, most of them are not acutely worked up over the foreign investment in general, but they harbor deep hostility against the privileges granted to foreign firms. For a sensitive analysis of this balancing act, see Nicholas Asheshov and Cary Reich, "Has Delfim Worked his Last Miracle?" *Institutional Investor*, August 1980: 174-193.

[19] This pattern merits more explanation, for it is natural to expect some differences among the directors of national and foreign-owned enterprises. In Table 5.1, the position of the businessmen as a whole is a conservative 27. On the average, they are the most receptive of the elites to foreign capital. When the business community is divided into its component sectors, certain differences emerge, but none is significant. Thus, the average position of the executive officers of national private industries is 28, of national private banks 22, of multinational corporations 29, of the leaders of business associations 27. Furthermore, when correlations between preferences on foreign investment and the left-right index are computed within each of these subsectors, they turn out to be about the same as the -.01 correlation for the businessmen as a whole. One explanation for this apparent anomaly is that the businessmen are the closest of all the elites to this issue and that they are therefore less likely to take stereotypical positions on it. They distinguish between foreign capitalists as individual holders of power and foreign capital as a source of investment.

conservative one. The issues that clearly can be dissociated from this line of conflict are moral controversies that have traditionally created odd alliances in Brazil—in the pronatalist camp, among adherents of the Catholic interpretation of natural law, among leftists who argue that population planning skirts the deeper issue of social inequality, and among nationalists bent on increasing the power of the country on the backs of a large labor force.[20]

This sketch of elite ideology is blurred somewhat by variations across the groups. Certain issues, like foreign investment, stir cross-currents among elites with an ambiguous relation to the stakes involved. The relationship of preferences on such issues to an average left-right position thereby becomes attenuated.

There is a tendency for the issues involving the relative autonomy of the elite estates to produce strong preferences, in the sense that opinions on these issues assume a sharp left-right flavor. But this is not always the case. Some such issues bear only a modest relation to the left-right continuum because of what appears to be a compound of discretion on the part of the progressives and resentment on the part of the conservatives at their usurpation of their prerogatives by the bureaucratic state. These issues have the power to draw together in common opposition elites who in other areas remain far apart.

Since there are so many issues, it is difficult to condense the major ideological patterns in coherent form. Furthermore, the analysis conducted so far fails to distinguish clearly among the controversies that cling to the left-right continuum: between those that are "routine," the standard fare of political debate in Brazil, and those that touch a deeper nerve, bearing on the delicate question of elite autonomy vis-à-vis the state, on the rules of the interelite game, and thereby, on the legitimacy of the regime.

Table 5.3 brings us closer to an understanding of the multidimensional nature of elite ideologies in Brazil. It gives the results of a factor analysis of sixteen representative issues; three principal cleavages emerge.[21]

The most readily interpretable cleavage is the third and least powerful, that involving the issues of birth control, divorce, and abortion. Preferences on these issues are almost wholly unrelated to positions on other contro-

---

[20] Compare Neil W. Chamberlain, *Beyond Malthus: Population and Power* (Englewood Cliffs, N.J.: Prentice-Hall, 1972); Nicholas J. Demerath, *Birth Control and Foreign Policy: The Alternatives to Family Planning* (New York: Harper & Row, Publishers, 1976); Bonnie Mass, *Population Target: The Political Economy of Population Control in Latin America* (Brampton, Ontario: Charters Publishing Company, 1976); and Ronald L. Meek, ed., *Marx and Engels on the Population Bomb* (Berkeley: Ramparts Press, 1971).

[21] Six of the twenty-three preference measures have been omitted because their communalities in a factor analysis of all the measures turned out to be inadmissably low. This is the result of the restricted variance of some of the measures—for example, *habeas corpus*.

versies. The moral issues do not lend themselves to classification according to the parameters of accumulation versus distribution or repression versus liberation.

Although they are dissociated from the moral cleavage, the first two dimensions of elite ideology are themselves correlated. One captures what,

TABLE 5.3
Normalized Loadings, Oblique Factor Rotation, on Sixteen Issues

	Factors			Commu- nalities
	I	*II*	*III*	
Political Participation of Military	1.15	.45	.01	1.53
Relaxation of Censorship	1.05	.17	−.23	1.20
Subversion	1.05	.15	.15	1.15
Political Opposition	.97	−.04	−.18	.98
Direct Gubernatorial Elections	.93	−.12	.03	.88
Autonomy of Labor Syndicates	.84	−.27	−.14	.79
Foreign Investment	.80	−.10	.47	.87
Political Amnesty	.73	.40	.20	.73
Income Redistribution	.68	.44	−.13	.67
Political Participation of Students	.02	.97	−.13	.95
Unionization of Domestics	.05	1.02	.25	1.11
Agrarian Reform	.12	1.06	−.01	1.13
Political Participation of Peasants	.25	1.10	−.02	1.28
Birth Control	.10	−.03	.98	.98
Legalization of Divorce	−.14	−.09	.99	1.00
Legalization of Abortion	−.12	.14	1.00	1.03
Sum of Squares	7.93	5.64	3.44	

Correlations between Factor Scores

	I	II	III
I	—		
II	.51	—	
III	.05	.12	—
	I	II	III

during the early seventies, were almost exclusively interelite concerns (the political participation of the military, the freedom of political opposition, and so on). The other taps issues, like agrarian reform, the political participation of peasants, and the unionization of domestics, with extraelite, elite-mass overtones and welfare, social-reform connotations.

It bears emphasis that, while these two dimensions of ideology are related, they are not identical. Issues involving elite and mass politics in

Brazil cannot be packaged in entirely separate compartments. At the same time, the elites themselves make a partial distinction between expressly political controversies, entailing conflicts over their own ability to organize and compete more or less autonomously, and those that touch them less directly, even if they might be of fundamental importance to the majority of Brazilians.

Some issues span both dimensions. The controversy over income redistribution, for example, is at once a mass issue and of great significance to the elites themselves, because it is tied to the question of the autonomy of the labor syndicates.

The foreign investment issue, however, seems the most curious of all. On the one hand, the elites tend to perceive it as a political matter, involving the threat to their own power posed by the multinationals; none of this is startling in light of the sentiments of the elites toward the multinationals. On the other hand, the elites are also inclined to place the controversy over foreign investment alongside the moral issues not because it evokes the same or even similar private-versus-public orientations but because the controversy, like the moral issues, is profoundly ambiguous. Only in part is it a left-right issue. In the view of many of the elites, the management of foreign capital demands a high-risk, high-benefit strategy. To exclude it altogether would be retrograde, given a developmental model that does not contemplate mercantilist withdrawal; to allow its unconditional entry would lead to further denationalization of the developmental model.

Thus, the issue of foreign investment is itself two-dimensional. In one respect, the elites view it as a decomposable series of challenges, to be dealt with incrementally. At the same time, the stakes are very high, engaging the cultural and economic identity of the nation. The first aspect of the issue may be negotiable; the second is less so.

In sum, three distinct cleavages underpin the ideologies of Brazilian elites: a political rules-of-the-game, interelite dimension; a dimension cast more in the direction of mass politics, toward questions of popular participation, distribution, and welfare; and a third dimension related to moral issues such as divorce and abortion. The remainder of this chapter is devoted to a comparison of the effects of these cleavages on the legitimacy of the regime.

Bureaucratic-Authoritarianism versus Interest-Representation

One of the reasons for the liberal tilt to the preferences of the elites on policy issues is the same as that which inflated their perceptions (and preferences) about the attention paid and to be paid by the government to contending interests. When faced with a list of more or less desirable items, and when budgetary constraints and other limitations are not explicit, the temptation is to maximize all good things, whatever the unrealities of such a decision-rule.

In effect, the difference between ends and means get lost. Even the conservatives find it hard to oppose the "political participation of peasants" in the long run, in principle or as some agreeably distant goal. The elites are not forced to establish priorities.

Such results are not utterly misleading. The relative differences among the elites stay intact. There is seldom any doubt regarding the position of conservative and progressive sectors, even if the elites as a whole appear to have been pushed slightly to the left. Yet the pattern lacks bite. A firm standard, something approaching an absolute scale against which to evaluate the liberal-sounding displacement of opinion, is elusive.

No such standard exists, but we can come fairly close. The elites were drawn into clear-cut comparisons between alternative, though not mutually exclusive, routes to the same end. The approach resembles that used in assessing the developmental priorities of the elites.[22] They were asked:

> There exists ample agreement about many of the general objectives of national politics. But there also exist fundamental differences of opinion about the best ways to reach such objectives. For example, there are at least two ways to promote political development. On a scale going from zero to 100, what value would you give to each of these two means: strengthening the executive, and strengthening the representation of interests?

The question sets up a clear comparison. The alternatives are broad, and they are not contradictory. But the elites are confronted with two alternatives, and the sense of choice is present.

The pair of items touches a nerve in Brazilian elite politics. Discussions of political legitimacy in Brazil make reference to several interconnected dilemmas: to the role of the military, to the succession problem, to the restoration of the rule of law, to the functions of political parties, and so forth. If the basic issue were expressed in its simplest form, it would probably hinge on the trade-off between two fundamental factors: the power of the central bureaucracy, on the one hand, and the freedom of representation, on the other.

Certainly, there are other ways of posing the problem. The notion of interest representation, for example, is indefinite concerning the limits set on mass participation. Nevertheless, it connotes a more participatory mode

---

[22] Compare James R. Bettman, "Measuring Individuals' Priorities for National Goals: A Methodology and Empirical Example," *Policy Sciences* 2 (1977): 373-390.

of politics than that which prevailed under the Médici government. "Representation" also draws attention to institutional, organized forms of participation, and in this respect it is more specific than "inclusion" or "mobilization." Moreover, even the most progressive of the elites are not anarchists. The issue is not so drastic as repression versus revolution. The elites tend to view the trade-off between a strong executive and freedom of representation as a problem involving the balance of powers. This is a problem that concerns them deeply and directly.[23]

When the responses are tabulated for each question separately, all the elite groups assign greater priority to interest representation than to strengthening the executive. This is hardly amazing, since there is a natural tendency to redress the overwhelming dominance of the state bureaucracy. Even among the conservatives, vestiges of the liberal-democratic faith prevail.[24]

But the meaningful datum is the weight assigned to one mechanism relative to the other, and this is the information on display in Figure 5.1. The bishops and the MDB politicians again turn out to be the distinctively progressive sectors. For obvious reasons, the opposition politicians feel that they have a great deal to gain from a liberalization of the representative process. Conversely, the state managers have the most to lose, and they are not enthusiastic about a loosening-up of the political system. Neither

[23] It is also one that continues to absorb the elites, even after the post-Médici liberalization, and that has as well its mirror-image in the pre-1964 era. With the sudden departure of Jânio Quadros from the presidency in the early sixties, the military permitted Vice President João Goulart to assume the office on the condition that the political system be changed from presidential to parliamentary. This was done; later, Goulart called a referendum that changed the system back again. It was Goulart whom the military deposed in 1964. As for more recent times, despite its liberalizing gestures, the government still refuses to grant the congress power over the purse, to grant more than a month and a half for the discussion of executive legislation, to recognize parliamentary immunity, or to allow secret (anonymous) congressional voting in attempts to veto presidential proposals. See the article entitled "Negociar É Possível," *Veja*, June 11, 1980: 20-22. The following excerpt is characteristic: "The decisions taken by the Political Development Council [a presidential advisory group] and the reaction of the Planalto [equivalent to the White House] to congressional speeches given in a defiant tone suggests that the government wants to negotiate—but only with those who accept negotiation. 'The political game can only be played by political professionals,' reminded Deputy Thales Ramalho. 'Like poker or chess, it's a matter for professionals. Congress is not the place for people with fixed ideas.' "

[24] There is not much of an association between either of these items and interviewer-assessed hesitancy. Across the entire sample, the correlation between "strengthening the representation of interest" and hesitancy is $-.01$; between "strengthening the executive" and hesitancy the correlation is .15. The latter result suggests that the more "confident" the elite, the more likely he is to assign a high value to strengthening the executive. However, this association tends to wash out when examined sector by sector. In brief, on this pair of items, the responses of the elites are not contaminated by discretion.

FIGURE 5.1
Difference between Emphasis Given to Strengthening Representation and Strengthening
Executive, by Elite Sector
(standard deviations in parentheses)

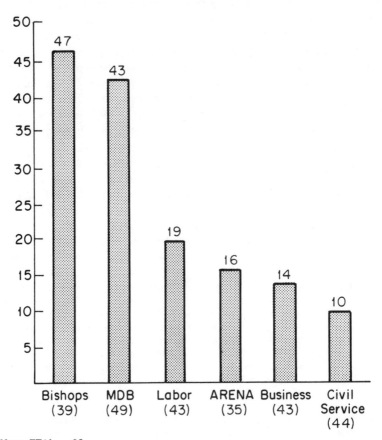

NOTE: ETA^2 = .05

are the businessmen. All of the conservatives would like to see the government become a bit more flexible, but not much more. The labor leaders do not differ significantly from the conservative elites in their reluctance to give "too much" freedom to the play of contending interests. The traditional dependence of Brazilian labor organizations on the state weighs heavily.

In the Brazilian context, all of this is familiar. But the key argument is that the group interests of the elites do not provide the primary explanation for the opinions of the elites on certain basic issues, among which the trade-off between representational autonomy and bureaucratic control figures prominently. And in fact, while the elites' group affiliations influence their preferences on this issue, the association is pretty feeble. There is substantial division of opinion within the elite sectors about the importance to be given to consolidating the executive as compared to allowing interest representation a free hand, even though on the average the elite groups line up along the expected progressive-conservative continuum.

The hypothesis is that preferences on basic, rules-of-the-game issues are not reducible to the interests of disparate groups. The developmental priorities of the elites, their presumably deepest values, are activated in the face of the common jeopardy to which the social reformers as well as the politicians are exposed by the persistent encroachment of the authoritarian state.

Figure 5.2 plots the differences between the emphases given to representation and bureaucracy across the developmental priorities of the elites. The impact of these values, although modest, appears to be greater than that of sectoral affiliation.

The economists are not willing to let the representation of diverse interests hold much sway over the imperatives of centralized rule; a free market in politics is not to their liking. The dispossessed politicians want to tame the bureaucracy. While many of them favor a strong executive, and few of them are fervent populists, they favor even more allowing a relatively free reign to contending interests.

The proponents of the all-good-things-go-together model, as well as those who advocate greater attention to the distribution of social benefits, fall in between. But this pattern differs in a crucial way from the one reported in Chapter Four, where the social reformers and the all-good-things-go-together types were shown to be practically indistinguishable from the economists in their satisfaction with the government. It is the turning-away of the social reformers from the economists on issues involving the rules of the game that is the telltale sign of the fragility of authoritarian domination.

Even the economists have a net preference, minimal as it may be, for the development of representative institutions over the strengthening of the state bureaucracy, although by a wide margin they remain the least progressive of the elites. The elite culture does not permit the representative ideal to vanish. The conservatives could have accorded the state a normative status higher than that which they give to representative bargaining, and it is undeniable that most of them do just this in practice. But the representative ideal enjoys respectability, while the authoritarian state does not.

Although the evidence is encouraging, none of this proves that the

FIGURE 5.2
Difference between Emphasis Given to Strengthening Representation and Strengthening
Executive, by Elite Priorities
(standard deviations in parentheses)

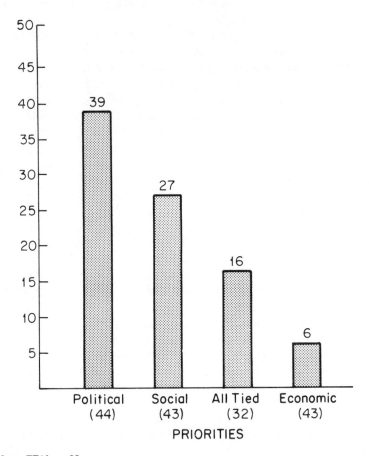

NOTE: ETA^2 = .08

developmental values of the elites play a special role in the determination
of the legitimacy of the regime. For one thing, analysis has been confined
to bivariate associations. I have yet to establish the importance of elite
values above and beyond (controlling for) the group interests of the elites.
For another, the argument so far hangs on the consideration of a single,
albeit critical, issue. Let us now gauge the validity of these preliminary
results.

The Limits of Authoritarian Legitimacy

The preferences of the elites about changes in the structure of power reflect not only their immediate group interests but also, at least implicitly, their generic orientations toward the system of interelite competition. As politicians, members of the ARENA and the MDB exhibit a corporate solidarity vis-à-vis the *continuista* pretensions of military-technocratic rule. In addition, all of the elite sectors favor some reduction in the power of the military, the technocrats, and the multinationals.

My principal thesis is that political legitimacy among Brazilian elites derives from a consensus not about specific policy issues or about the benefits and sanctions for particular groups but rather about the procedures governing elite interaction. Are such abstractions detectable among the elites, and can they be linked to the problem of authoritarian legitimacy?

The answer to the first question is yes. The elites can be categorized according to the priorities they assign to economic development, social well-being, and political liberalization. The problem is to determine whether what I have called developmental values explain anything of consequence. Specifically, it is necessary to determine the extent to which the developmental priorities of the elites exert an influence on their preferences about crucial issues that surpasses their immediate group interests.

The test is strict. It may produce negative results in two circumstances, and only one type of positive result is valid. The theory of limited legitimacy would clearly be refuted if the putative effects of developmental values on certain policy preferences disappeared, or left only a chemical trace when the influence of sectoral affiliation is simultaneously taken into account. In this case, the most that could be claimed for the developmental priorities is that they exercise an indirect and fairly negligible influence on the policy preferences of the elites.

The other circumstance in which the theory would prove a failure would arise if the developmental values emerge as strong predictors of elite preferences on the wrong issues. For example, if it happens that the developmental values of the elites actually have a stronger impact than their sectoral affiliation on opinions about income redistribution or agrarian reform, this would constitute a finding of high interest but one that would be thoroughly anomalous from my theoretical perspective. These issues are fraught with conflict, but they do not serve to unite the usually acquiescent with the traditionally dissident elites in a common front against the authoritarian state.

Thus, if the developmental priorities of the elites have any effect at all, it should appear for those issues tapping orientations toward interelite relations. Any substantial impact of these values on issues that mainly concern one or two rather than all major actors would also be problematic. The "political opposition" issue is a good example of this type of inter-elite but particularistic controversy. It is too closely identified with the special interests of the MDB. It serves to fragment and narrow the potential opposition.

The sole outcome validating the theory, then, is one in which the strategic priorities of the elites influence opinions on rules-of-the-game issues independently of the group-specific interests of the elites. The political participation of the military and the balance of power between the state and contending interests seeking representation are just such issues.

But how do the values of the elites overcome the short-term interests of the elite groups and their propensity for infighting that, while tumultuous, do not threaten the authoritarian state? Everything depends on the social reformers, who are concentrated among the labor leaders and the bishops but who are also scattered across the other elite sectors. By and large, these men are not anxious to challenge the authorities—any authorities. While they are not so enthusiastic about the feats of the technocracy as the economists, they do not display what used to be called character so openly as the politicians. Precisely because of their reluctance to condemn authoritarian rule even when they cannot maximize their gains under it, the defection of the social reformers from the economists and their movement toward the politicians must be viewed as a severe blow to the viability and precarious legitimacy, the tenability, of the regime. The core contention of the theory is that the developmental values of the elites assume vital significance when the social reformers, and not the already alienated politicians, become exasperated with restrictions on their right as elites to bargain and compete for power.

The method for testing the theory is a set of multivariate analyses, one for each of the twenty-four issues examined so far. The predictors are the same for all issues: elite sector and developmental values. The crucial indicators are the net impact of the developmental values, as compared to that of sectoral affiliation, on the distribution of elite preferences and the proximity of the social reformers to the politicians (and their distance from the economists) on issues concerning the canons of interelite accommodation and conflict.[25]

Of all the issues submitted to this test, only two show a stronger relation with developmental priorities than with sectoral affiliation. One concerns

[25] Since neither elite sector nor developmental priorities, the two predictors, have interval-scale properties, the technique used to separate their effects is multiple classification analysis (MCA). The technique is analogous to multiple linear regression, with the added capacity to handle nominal scale predictors. See Frank M. Andrews et al., *Multiple Classification Analysis* (Ann Arbor: Institute for Social Research, 1973).

the political participation of the military, the other the trade-off between executive power and the representation of interests. Unlike preferences on controversies that are routinely predictable from the group membership of the elites, opinions on these two issues can be traced squarely to the fundamental values of the elites, and the issues directly involve the rules of interelite competition.

The results for the two issues just noted are displayed in Table 5.4, together with those for another issue, the controversy over the creation of a third party, that comes very close to satisfying the test outlined in the preceding paragraphs.

The key statistics are the beta coefficients, which estimate the relative effects of the two predictors. For example, the coefficient associated with "priority" on the issue of the political participation of the military is .28, while the corresponding weight for "elite sector" is .18. The impact of group interests does not disappear, but it is secondary to that of the developmental values.[26]

On this issue, the social reformers side with the politicians, leaving the economists with the less-than-reliable proponents of the all-good-things-go-together model. Evidently, the social reformers feel that their ability to influence policy and to receive credit for policy outputs—to receive their due—is crippled by the continued presence of the military. For this reason, the cooptative attractions of the system wane.[27]

A similar process occurs with the controversy over the emphasis to be given to interest representation versus executive centralism. Again, the social reformers come closer to the politicians than to the economists.

On the debate over the creation of a third party, even the upholders of the all-good-things-go-together model turn against the economists. The two-party system was fabricated by the military in 1965. The movement to abolish this artifice was initiated by Pedro Aleixo, vice-president under

[26] It would be cumbersome to present the full array of results for all twenty-four issues, but the following figures give an indication of what happens with the "routine" issues. The average beta coefficient associated with elite sector for the twenty-one issues not shown in Table 5.4 is .30; for the same issues, the average beta coefficient associated with developmental priorities is .11. Elite sector rather than developmental values is the better predictor of attitudes on such issues. It is worth noting, in addition, that while most of the variance in the dependent variables remains unaccounted for (as might be expected with data of this sort), the relative effects of the predictors support the substantive model. See Robert Rosenthal and Donald B. Rubin, "A Note on Percent Variance Explained as a Measure of the Importance of Effects," *Journal of Applied Social Psychology* 9 (1979): 395-396.

[27] Usually the social reformers are only about 10 points to the left of the economists on the 100-point opinion scales. It is when the distance between reaches 15 or 20 points that the split becomes serious and the developmental priorities of the elites take on more significance than their group interests.

TABLE 5.4
Multiple Classification Analysis of Preferences on Three Issues,
by Developmental Agendas and Elite Sector

	Dependent Variables					
	Political Participation of Military		*Representation-State*		*Creation of Third Party*	
Predictors						
Priority	*Unadjusted Mean*	*Adjusted Mean*	*Unadjusted Mean*	*Adjusted Mean*	*Unadjusted Mean*	*Adjusted Mean*
Economic	32	33	6	7	45	48
All Tied	26	27	15	16	64	66
Social	50	48	27	26	68	65
Political	54	51	39	37	67	65
beta	.28		.24		.23	
Elite Sector						
MDB	51	47	43	34	88	81
Bishops	72	64	47	38	69	62
Labor	44	40	19	16	70	68
Business	36	38	14	18	50	53
Civil Service	34	36	12	14	45	45
ARENA	36	36	16	15	64	64
beta	.18		.14		.27	
R²	.11		.06		.13	

NOTES: The higher the score, the more progressive the opinion; scores vary between 0 and 100. For example, those who give priority to political liberalization hold more progressive views about participation of the military than those who give priority to economic development. The scores are means of the dependent variables within categories of the predictor variables.

The *unadjusted means* are the scores resulting from a simple bivariate relationship between one predictor and a dependent variable. The *adjusted means* take into account the influence of a second predictor and give the values of the dependent variable after the other predictor has been controlled for. Thus, the scores in the higher rows give the effect of "priority" on three dependent variables, first in bivariate form and then controlling for elite sector. The scores in the lower rows give the values of the dependent variables by "elite sector" and then by "sector" controlling for "priority."

the general who preceded President Médici and a man with impeccably conservative, but civilian, credentials. His campaign was looked upon as a crusade to restore some semblance of the liberal creed. The military established the loyalist and opposition parties in order to gain an aura of legitimacy. But bipartism itself tends to be regarded as illegitimate in Brazil, at least insofar as it is foisted on the civilian elites by the military.

What do these issues have in common that renders them so sensitive to the influence of the basic values of the elites? In particular, what is it about them that mobilizes the shrewd and normally nonassertive social reformers? They bear on the fundamental rules, the minimal equity, of elite interaction.[28] Military intervention and bureaucratic heavy-handedness have long been familiar in Bazil and other parts of Latin America. But their chronic re-occurence makes them neither venerable nor legitimate.

Occasional rescue operations and surgical strikes on the part of the military do not throw the elites into shock, so long as it is understood that control returns to civilians. It is this understanding that the Brazilian military rejected. In doing so, they lost legitimacy. It is the hegemonic pretensions of the military, and the sustained intrusion into the bases of power and patronage formerly controlled by nonmilitary estates, that the elites find unacceptable. The military can save ·the bourgeoisie; they may not rule them.

Consideration of the developmental priorities reveals that the elites have more in common on the legitimizing issues than might be expected if their group labels were taken as the final word on their political preferences. This suggests a communality of interest among otherwise diverse actors vis-à-vis the encroachment of the military-bureaucratic state. The social reformers and the politicians have a joint stake in gaining room for maneuver, even though this goal does not overcome completely the differences between them that are due to separate and sometimes conflicting institutional positions. The developmental agendas therefore constitute a latent basis for resistance against arbitrary and sustained military rule.

Between *Arbítrio* and *Autonomia*[29]

The opposition of the elites to the dominance of the military and their protégées reflects not only the resentment of the elites at the invasion of their separate turfs but a generalized withdrawal of legitimacy from the extension of despotic militarism. It derives from the breakdown of the "agreement between certain established elites to treat each other in a civil

[28] Certain issues that qualify as rules-of-the-game controversies are not very strongly associated with the developmental values of the elites. The *habeas corpus* and amnesty issues are examples. As previously mentioned, variation on the issue of *habeas corpus* is so small that it does not lend itself to statistical analysis. As for the political amnesty issue, preferences on it seem to be very much a function of group interests—in particular, of the MDB and the bishops. However this may be, the developmental values have a powerful direct influence on at least two of the rules-of-the-game issues and on none of the routine issues.

[29] "Arbitrariness" and autonomy.

fashion."[30] The system may be tolerable for some time. It may be structurally induced by historical circumstances. But it is not particularly legitimate. The prolongation of military authoritarianism violates the norm of restricted, interelite pluralism—that is, the convention of the elites that there should be honor even among thieves.

Relations between civilian and military elites have been unsettled for long stretches of Brazilian history. It is not surprising that the civilians, while granting the military a function as political guardians, do not accept them as overlords. But the problem of authoritarian legitimacy goes beyond the institutional role of the military. It involves the threat posed by the state itself to the system of interelite relations.

These findings also suggest that the notion of authoritarian mentalities is mistaken, at least inasmuch as such dispositions are supposed to be unideological and peculiar to elites in authoritarian regimes. The most authoritarian of the elites, the economists, are every bit as driven as the politicians. It is not only their commitment to forced-draft industrialization that makes the economists ideological. They have a coherent theory of development, however wrong it may be.

Most of the elites are ideological by the standard of internal cognitive consistency. But they are not unidimensional thinkers. Even though left-right differences compose the most salient line of conflict, at least one other cleavage divides the elites. This is a moral axis on which opinions about population planning are aligned. Many of the elites are fond of proclaiming their a-politicism and their abhorrence for ideology. It is difficult to credit such denials when the links between their preferences on various issues are examined systematically.

Theories of legitimacy based on the dichotomy between governmental effectiveness and mythic beliefs also fail to capture the subtlety of elite thinking.[31] The tolerance of the elites for one another is probably always limited, so that total legitimacy may be an illusion. Solid hegemony seems an impossible standard by which to judge complex political systems. The question is not whether the regime is both effective and ideologically sound but whether, given diversity in the values of the elites, tenable coalitions can be formed that avert recurrent hegemonic crises.

The theory of political tenability developed here holds to a distinction, at least among elites, between the incumbents of the moment—in Brazil, this or that general and his entourage—and what Brazilians call *o sistema*, the system. I define the system normatively, as the rules of the game, the

[30] Charles W. Anderson, *Politics and Economic Change in Latin America* (Princeton: D. Van Nostrand, 1967), p. 102.

[31] Compare Seymour Martin Lipset, *Political Man* (New York: Doubleday & Company, Inc., 1969), pp. 65-86.

chief one of which is limited pluralism. Added to this is the concept of multiple criteria, or ideologies, of legitimacy, which the elites have not been able to reconcile.

For some time after 1964, the Brazilian regime met with success. The reigning coalition was based not on force alone but on a combination of ruthless repression, economic growth, and selective pay-offs or the promise of them. The costs of resistance were so high, and the memories of populist turmoil so vivid, that the social reformers came to terms with the economists. Underlying their complicity was the intuition that the politicians, as a whole, were neither effective nor popular.

But the very logic of this compromise leads to its dissolution. If the arrangement cannot deliver, the social reformers have no incentive to join with the economists and the economists, in turn, may rely on force more than they would like to. Over the long term, this is probably not cost-effective. If the arrangement does succeed in driving up the national product, then there would seem to be little sense in continuing to postpone social distribution and political liberalization, to comply with the dominance of the military and the technocrats, and to accede to the privileges granted to the multinationals.

Unlike classical polyarchies on the one hand and totalitarian systems on the other, authoritarian regimes such as the Brazilian seldom make themselves out to be permanent arrangements: they are something more than transitory coups but something less than abiding solutions. Possessed of an uncertain legitimacy, the regime must prove itself through its performance. But, as the economic-social-political development paradigm of the system implies, the better the performance of the regime, the more appropriate it becomes for the elites to turn their attention to questions of political legitimacy. In addition, the developmental policies of the elites serve to expand the size of a proletariat that must somehow be dealt with. Both when it fails and when it succeeds, the system generates ideological and structural tensions.

Several emendations should be made to this diagnosis. First, if political legitimacy among Brazilian elites is a partial phenomenon, involving temporary coalitions rather than consensual support, it is also true that illegitimacy is rarely a total condition igniting thorough opposition. Many of the elites, including some of those who deny the regime legitimacy on political grounds, do not quarrel radically with its economic and social policies. They condemn *o capitalismo selvagem*—savage, jungle capitalism; but there is little evidence that they condone revolutionary alternatives.

In technical terms, then, legitimacy as understood by Brazilian elites is a continuous valuable rather than an all-or-nothing state. More accurately, legitimacy is the outcome of judgments based on multiple criteria, and the elites resort to these standards in a selective manner. A regime that gains support for its perceived success with economic policy may still be considered unacceptable for political reasons, and vice versa.

Second, the defection of the social reformers and the ensuing legitimacy crisis of the regime did not lead to its collapse, even if the military and the technocrats could no longer govern in the same high-handed way. In part, this twilight situation follows from the fact that the legitimacy/illegitimacy of the regime is contingent and restricted. It evokes neither blanket condemnation nor unquestioning loyalty.

A related factor behind the regime's persistence, however modified its polities, can be traced to the multidimensional quality of the belief systems of the elites—that is, to the cross-cutting nature of cleavages in Brazilian elite politics. Not only are rules-of-the-game and socioeconomic controversies partially separable; it is also the case that religious-moral issues are in large measure separate from secular conflicts. This segregation of the lines of conflict makes for experimentation rather than polarization. It helps account for both the comparative absence of violence in Brazilian politics and for its unideological appearance.

Third, while I have emphasized the pivotal role of the social reformers, divisions and defections among the economists have also undermined the tenability of the regime. As a whole, the economists are an extremely determined lot, conceding the occasional short-term battle but unswerving from their larger, long-term goals. And yet, not all of them have a bunker mentality, and some of them—the "evolutionalists," for example—retain traces of the democratic ethic.

It is tempting but, I believe, inaccurate and unfair to patronize this sentiment. The tragedy of the economists is that a political opening, however small, that they vaguely entertained as the outcome of aggregate growth now seems less feasible, along their own guided, pacific lines, during the economically depressed decade of the eighties than it was during the boom of the sixties when, at least in retrospect, they missed their chance. In any event, the ambivalence of some of the economists has also tempered the style of political conflict among the elites.[32]

The problem, however, is not simply a case of political shortsightedness

[32] The ambivalence of the economists usually means the preemption of the demands of the social reformers—for example, through the launching of compensatory programs aimed especially at the marginal and unorganized poor and the invocation of force to squash autonomous mobilization on the part of the politicians. Compare Regis de Castro Andrade, "Política Salarial e Normalização Institucional no Brasil," mimeograph (São Paulo, CEDEC, 1980); José Márcio Camargo, "A Nova Política Salarial, Distribuição de Renda, e Inflação," mimeograph (Rio de Janeiro, Pontifícia Universidade Católica, 1980); and Robert W. Jackman, "Politicians in Uniform: Military Governments and Social Change in the Third World," *American Political Science Review* 70 (1976): 1078-1097.

and economic bad luck. No doubt a few of the military would be willing to relinquish power, at least for a time, and the slow-down in real growth makes it difficult to reconcile mounting and conflicting demands. Nevertheless, the military and their allies have constructed a state machine of such concentrated power that some of them must fear the consequences of its use in hands other than their own. Similarly, the centralization of political power has been accompanied by a concentration of economic resources within an infinitesimal fraction of the population. These structurally entrenched interests are not self-liquidating.

While a myriad of fresh alliances is possible, it is virtually inconceivable that the sheer size and scope of the government will be reduced no matter which groups follow the military into office. The military may depart or be overthrown, temporarily, but not the state. It is less inconceivable, though still unlikely, that the machine might be turned against its creators. This, together with a certain immobilism among those who have gained extravagantly from the Brazilian model and have a stake in holding on to their fortunes, is what makes negotiating the unnegotiable so delicate.

But, finally, these are not the only factors conditioning the tortuous transition away from authoritarianism. I have stressed that no single ideological current dominates Brazilian politics even though, institutionally, the state holds sway. The absence of hegemony, not to mention consensus, is not necessarily a disadvantage: contrast this uncertainty with an utter lack of toleration and respect for dissident views. It may even encourage a kind of political patience and a respect for piecemeal, zigzag innovation. This is the benign side of the comparative "immoralism" of Brazilian politics. Even if they are unaccustomed to dialogue, most of the elites are not enthusiasts of final solutions.

Yet this amorphous condition also eats away at the sense of political community and perhaps at the capacity of the elites to translate justifiable ideological differences into legitimate institutional forms. Nothing in the interaction between the imperatives of accumulation and distribution, or between order and autonomy, guarantees an overarching consensus of this type, even if a truce is reached among contending forces. It is this fear of what many of them view as a hollow, centrifugal pluralism that makes the elites suspicious of permitting the tangible organization of diversity. Peter Gay described the Weimar Republic as "an idea seeking to become reality."[33] Brazilian authoritarianism may be termed a reality in search of an ideal.

[33] Peter Gay, *Weimar Culture: The Outsider as Insider* (New York: Harper & Row, Publishers, 1968), p. 1.

SIX

Mutual Perceptions

We are each nested in a cacophony of relations with other actors in society. . . . With the growth of technology and its concomitant division of labor, the determination of actors in a society as a function of their relations with other actors is likely to increase rather than decrease.[1]

. . . because it has grown in such a disorganized way, at the mercy of impulse, the machine has lost its machine-like qualities. It has split into a thousand disconnected pieces which operate on their own, without any type of functional structure. . . . Whatever the ministry or secretariat, there is only one word to describe what goes on inside: chaos. The bureaucrats . . . don't understand one another, they know that they don't understand one another, and they admit that they don't understand one another to anyone with the time and patience to listen to their endless lamentations.[2]

Theories of political change are replete with references to coalitions between vast elite estates—between landlords and industrialists, between technocrats and the military, and so on—just as they abound with analyses of the conflicts between these groups and their opponents—between industry and labor, between bureaucrats and politicians, and the like. The imputation of broad motives to a series of more or less homogeneous collectivities can be useful to block in major lines of conflict, and heuristic simplification is an acceptable device in attempting to construct theories of long-run transformation.

At the same time, elite perceptions (of the populist peril, for example) play an important role in reconstructing the rationale behind authoritarian demobilization. Information about the magnitude of large-scale events—say, the rise of mass participation—is likely to be fragmentary. Even in the unlikely case of reasonably consistent perceptions about "what is out there," variable evaluations of this supposed reality are liable to engender distortions among elites with differing perspectives. So, the absence of

[1] Ronald S. Burt, "Positions in Networks," *Social Forces* 55 (1976): 93.
[2] Carlos Estevam Martins, "Reflexões de um Cidadão Mal Informado," *Escrita* 2 (1977): 11.

information about the perceptions and evaluations of key actors makes it difficult to get beyond schematic statements about coalition and conflict.[3]

Such attitudinal information is not a panacea. On the one hand, the tone of elite opinion, of their self-declared preferences, is pitched in a suspiciously liberal key—not by much, perhaps, and never by enough to make conservatives like the ARENA politicians sound more progressive than their colleagues in the MDB. On the other hand, the elites' perceptions of others are likely to be no more accurate than declarations of their own preferences. Although the elites do not distort the political world at random, they do try to make it conform to their predilections.[4]

The question has to do not only with accuracy of elite perceptions but with the confusion and "gratuitous" conflict that misperception might precipitate. The perceptions of the elites constitute an important element of the policy environment—that is, the structure of expectations that may block or facilitate initiatives on certain issues.[5] Although elites in an authoritarian situation are under no obligation to respond to public opinion, they would be foolhardy not to take into account and to anticipate the opinions, or what they believe to be the opinions, of their colleagues and rivals for power.

Sometime after the elites gave their own opinions on a battery of controversies, they were asked to assess for each of five issues—birth control, foreign investment, income redistribution, government-labor relations, and government-opposition relations—the general positions of all elite groups except their own.[6] When the preferences of the elites are compared with

[3] Some of the confusion in the debate over the origins of authoritarianism can be traced to the failure to distinguish presumed increases in popular mobilization from the perception of this as a threat on the part of elites. See the essays in *The New Authoritarianism in Latin America*, ed. David Collier (Princeton: Princeton University Press, 1979).

[4] At least two types of misapprehension may occur: (1) pluralistic ignorance that opinions on issues converge when the elites assume that they are discrepant, and (2) false consensus, the assumption of interelite agreement when preferences are in fact divergent. See Hubert J. O'Gorman with Stephen L. Garry, "Pluralistic Ignorance—A Replication and Extension," *Public Opinion Quarterly* 40 (1976-1977): 449-458, and Lee D. Ross, David Greene, and Pamela House, "The 'False Consensus Effect': An Egocentric Bias in Social Perception and Attribution Processes," *Journal of Experimental Social Psychology* 13 (1977): 279-301.

[5] See Mark Snyder, Elizabeth Decker Tanke, and Ellen Berscheid, "Social Perception and Interpersonal Behavior: On the Self-Fulfilling Nature of Social Stereotypes," *Journal of Personality and Social Psychology* 35 (1977): 656-666. For early attempts to investigate the effects of mutual perceptions in worsening or stemming conflicts, see the essays in Gabriel A. Almond, Scott C. Flanagan, and Robert D. Mundt, eds., *Crisis, Choice, and Change: Historical Studies of Political Development* (Boston: Little, Brown and Company, 1973).

[6] In general, with *n* groups, there are n(n - 1) mutual perceptions multiplied by the number of issues to give the total number of perceptions. In the present case, there are five issues and seven elite groups; the total number of mutual perceptions is therefore 210. The seven perceived and perceiving groups are MDB politicians, ARENA politicians, labor leaders,

those attributed to them by their peers, one striking pattern emerges. Almost always, the elites spot one another as more conservative than they themselves say they are. The only exception occurs with the labor leaders, who are thought to be more progressive than they admit to being.[7] Before I elaborate and test a model of elite perception, it is helpful to get a closer look at the nature of the "misunderstanding" that needs to be explained.[8]

The Lay of the Data

In order to visualize the magnitude of the gap between the preferences and the perceptions of the elites, let us consider the two in simplified form. Figure 6.1 gives a highly abbreviated view of the rightward drift in perceptions as compared to avowed preferences. To make the introductory point, I have aggregated the perceiving groups and averaged their attributions; avowed opinions over the five issues have been averaged, too.

bishops, top civil servants [*altos funcionários públicos*], industrialists, and bankers. The businessmen were divided into industrialists and bankers on the guess that the elite respondents might feel uncomfortable at being asked to lump these nominally disparate groups together. However, the elites perceive bankers and industrialists virtually as a single group, and bankers and industrialists themselves do not differ markedly in their perceptions of their fellow elites. I maintain the distinction between bankers and industrialists throughout the chapter mainly to prove this point. It should also be noted that measures of reflexive perceptions—for example, estimates by an ARENA politician of the preferences of members of his own party—were not obtained principally so as to avoid fatigue on the part of respondents, each of whom was asked to state the positions of seven groups. Thus, I start with six perceptions, to which are added the opinions attributed to a seventh estate, the military.

[7] Perceptions were measured on the same 100-point scales as preferences, with identical reference points. The foreign investment item exemplifies the procedure: "Now we would like you to compare the positions of some groups. For example, on the question of foreign investment, certain groups have more or less similar or different positions. Where would you place _____ on this scale?" The respondent was given a card with decile and quartile values and asked to estimate the position of each of seven elite sectors other than his own. For example, ARENA politicians estimated the positions of MDB politicians, labor syndicate leaders, large industrialists, large bankers, the higher military, the bishops, and the top civil servants.

[8] Even at this stage, however, the data do not speak for themselves. The general orientation brought to the description of the basic findings is drawn from attribution research. For a coverage of the state of the art, see the papers collected in John H. Harvey, William John Ickes, and Robert F. Kidd, eds., *New Directions in Attribution Research*, Vol. 1 (Hillsdale, N.J.: Lawrence Erlbaum Associates, 1976). See also Lee D. Ross, "The Intuitive Psychologist and his Shortcomings: Distortions in the Attribution Process," in *Advances in Experimental Social Psychology*, ed. Leonard Berkowitz (New York: Academic Press, 1977); Ross, "Problems in the Interpretation of Self-Serving Asymmetries in Causal Attribution," *Sociometry* 40 (1977): 112-114; and Mark Snyder and William B. Swann, Jr., "Behavioral Confirmation in Social Interaction: From Social Perception to Social Reality," *Journal of Experimental Social Psychology* 14 (1978): 148-162.

What remains is the distribution of mean opinions stated by the elites paired with the distribution of opinions attributed to them.[9]

All of the groups save the labor leadership are viewed about ten points to the right of where they claim to stand. The labor leaders tend to be viewed to the left of their self-declared positions—just as would be expected from accounts of the elites' propensity to view popular, class-based movements with alarm. The cleavage between classes in Brazil may not be so volcanic as is sometimes supposed, but it is powerful all the same.

The ostracism of the labor leaders is not difficult to explain. Despite purges of the syndical cadres and the repression of labor militancy since 1964 and on through most of the seventies, members of the establishment

FIGURE 6.1
Mean Preferences and Perceptions of Seven Elite Groups

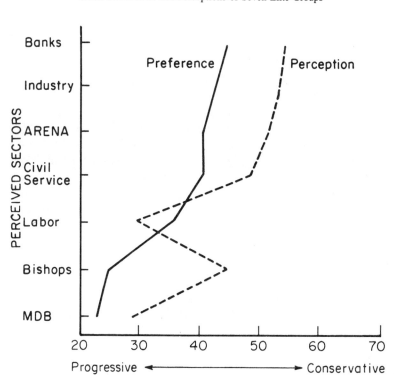

[9] In this figure and throughout the chapter, the scoring conventions used so far are reversed. A low value on the 100-point scales now represents a leftist position and a high value a rightist position. The change is merely for illustrative purposes, so that a low score (progressive preference or perception) appears toward the left in the graphs.

during the Médici regime continued to see the labor leaders in outright opposition to the policies of the government. The image of labor radicalism persists for a variety of reasons, one of which is simply that most of the elites have no contact with the syndical representatives.[10] The challenge is not to figure out why the labor leaders are perceived to the left but instead to understand why the rest of the elites, who are in fairly regular contact, insist on labelling one another to the right.[11]

Figure 6.2 provides a complementary perspective on the gap between avowed and attributed opinion, this time by issues rather than groups. I have ignored between-group differences and have computed the average avowed and attributed preferences for each of the issues.

The single exception to the tendency for the elites to place one another toward the right occurs with the issue of foreign investment. On the average, the elites locate their peers at around the midpoint of the foreign investment question—at the status quo as of 1972 and 1973, when the amount of foreign capital in Brazil was already large. The public norm seems to be mildly nationalistic, even though the elites themselves assert that a bit more foreign investment is needed, or at least acceptable.

More generally, there is a tendency for the perceptions of the elites to show a regression toward the middle, and in this respect the issue of foreign investment is no exception. The elites tend to place their colleagues within a narrow band around the "as is" position. In the absence of definite information about the opinions of others, and given the repressive conditions prevailing in Brazil, this is probably the safest course.[12]

The evidence presented so far documents the inclination to rightward

[10] Another reason for the leftist image of the labor leaders, even during the quiescent times of the early seventies, is that many of them were treated badly by the government, and the elites naturally suppose that this would reinforce their progressive and opposition leanings. As will be shown, what is remarkable about the elites' perceptions of labor is that they place the syndical leaders to the left on all issues. The pattern is basically the same as that discussed in Chapter Three, where the indicators of governmental "attention paid" and "attention owed" were analyzed. It is worth recalling that members of the elite establishment placed the labor organizations farther to the left than did the syndical leaders themselves.

[11] The absolute difference between avowed and attributed opinions was examined as a function of contact for each pair of perceiving and perceived sectors, for each issue. Contact was measured in three ways: as kinship, friendship, and working ties. Less than 5 percent of the analyses of variance yielded statistically significant results.

[12] The regression-to-the-middle phenomenon has been noted in perceptual studies by Charles Korte, "Pluralistic Ignorance about Student Radicalism," *Sociometry* 35 (1977): 576-587. However, when the data are disaggregated further, as in Table 6.1 below, it becomes evident that this tendency is not constant across issues. We must then account for the differential gap between attributed and avowed opinions, which the general regression-to-the-middle pattern cannot explain.

FIGURE 6.2
Mean Preferences and Perceptions for Five Key Issues

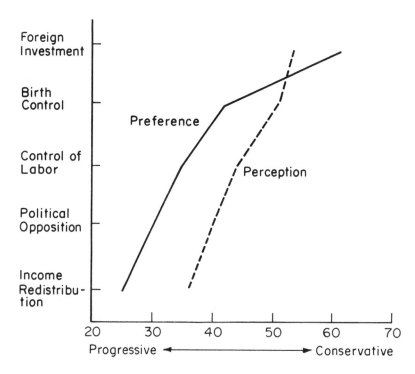

perception on the part of the elites.[13] But because the data have been subjected to considerable averaging, they conceal one crucial feature of the gap between perceptions and preferences. This is the tendency for the gap to widen on the presumably more conflictive issues such as government-opposition relations.

Table 6.1 brings this tendency to light. It portrays the average preferences of the elites, along with the opinions attributed to them, for each of the five issues.[14]

At first glance, the array might seem only to confirm what we already know—namely, that with the exception of the labor leaders, the elites

[13] Conservative bias in perceptions has been documented elsewhere, for example, by James M. Fields and Howard Schuman, "Public Beliefs about the Beliefs of the Public," *Public Opinion Quarterly* 40 (1976-1977): 427-488, and Philip E. Converse, "Some Mass-Elite Contrasts in the Perception of Political Spaces," *Social Science Information* 14 (1975): 49-83.

[14] The array still represents a simplification. It does not distinguish among perceiving groups, and variation around the means is not shown.

TABLE 6.1

Mean Avowed (A) and Perceived (P) Opinions of Elite Sectors, by Issue

			Issues									
Perceived Sectors	*Birth Control*		*Foreign Investment*		*Income Redistribution*		*Labor Control*		*Political Opposition*		*Mean*	
	A	P	A	P	A	P	A	P	A	P	A	P
MDB	45	51	43	36	10	21	14	24	4	13	23	29
Bishops	60	88	33	46	11	25	12	35	11	33	25	45
Labor	47	56	56	35	16	19	27	17	34	24	36	30
Civil Service	38	42	66	59	29	39	40	53	31	50	41	69
ARENA	44	47	57	66	29	40	44	52	31	53	41	52
Banks	35	35	78	71	35	54	45	62	24	54	45	54
Industry	36	41	71	60	33	55	41	63	33	53	43	54
Military	—	48	—	61	—	38	—	59	—	58	—	53
Mean[a]	42	51	62	53	25	36	35	44	30	40	36	45

NOTE: Low score = progressive opinion.

[a] Does not include military.

claim to be more progressive than they are perceived to be. For example, the opposition politicians have an average position on the question of the control/autonomy of labor to the left of the position attributed to them.

On closer inspection, however, it becomes evident that the gap between preferences and perceptions varies not only from issue to issue but also from one perceived group to another. First, while almost all elite groups are perceived to the right of where they say they stand, the tendency is to perceive the supposedly progressive groups, like the MDB, about ten points to the right of their avowed positions, and to perceive the conservative groups, like the bankers and the industrialists, even further to the right, by about twenty points.

Second, the discrepancy between avowed and attributed opinions widens on the more controversial issues: income redistribution, labor control, and political opposition. On the question of birth control, for example, the industrialists are thought to hold a position only slightly more to the pronatalist side than they admit to having. The distance between perception and preference is on the order of only five points. But on the touchier issues of political opposition, the industrialists, as well as the ARENA politicians and the civil servants, are thought to be fully twenty points to the right of their declared positions. Similar misperceptions can be detected for the income redistribution and labor control controversies.

Finally, the military are not viewed as being extraordinarily reactionary compared to the civilian conservatives. On the question of income redistribution, they are seen as somewhat less antediluvian than the businessmen, and their image is slightly more liberal than that of the industrialists and the bankers on the issue of the control of labor.

However, when the elites state their perceptions of the opinions of the various groups with respect to political opposition, an issue with a pronounced repression-versus-liberalization ring, the military are rated as the most conservative of all. As we move across the issues from left to right, toward those in which the freedom of definite groups is explicitly involved, the position of the military is seen as increasingly defensive and conservative.

These, then, are the preliminary findings. As a rule, the elites view one another to the right of the positions they claim to hold. In addition, the conservative drift in perception becomes pronounced on issues whose conflict-potential is great. The task now is to explain the fluctuating gap between the perceptions and the preferences of the elites.

A Model of Interelite (Mis)Perception

My model of interelite perception derives primarily from a consideration of two elements: the polarizing potential of different issues and the distinction between public and "private" opinions. A third factor—the differential proclivity of groups to perceive others more or less accurately for political reasons, regardless of the issues—will also be considered. However, since it is difficult to take all three elements into account at once, I will stress the first two, and treat the third as a means of tying up loose ends.

Issue Effects[15]

Two contradictory yet equally plausible hypotheses come to mind in speculating about the effects of issues on elite perceptions. One is that the gap

[15] This part of the model draws on assimilation—contrast theory, originally formulated by Muzafer Sherif and Carl Hovland, *Social Judgment: Assimilation and Contrast Effects in Communications and Attitude Change* (New Haven: Yale University Press, 1961). For an updating and critique of this approach, see Chester A. Insko, *Theories of Attitude Change* (New York: Appleton-Century-Crofts, 1967). For applications by political scientists, see Donald Granberg and Richard Jenks, "Assimilation and Contrast Effects in the 1972 Election," *Human Relations* 30 (1977): 623-640; Donald R. Kinder, "Political Person Perception: The Asymmetrical Influence of Sentiment and Choice on Perceptions of Presidential Candidates," *Journal of Personality and Social Psychology* 36 (1978): 859-871; and Michael King, "Assimilation and Contrast of Presidential Candidates' Issue Positions, 1972," *Public Opinion Quarterly* 41 (1977-1978): 515-522. Where my model differs from most other approaches is in its stress on the issues themselves—specifically, on the variable polarizing nature of issues and on the effects of this quality of issues on the propensity to misperceive. For a perspective that emphasizes the properties of perceived and perceiving groups rather

between avowed and attributed opinion should be smallest on the most controversial issues, because preferences on them tend to be clearly defined. Conversely, misperception should be most frequent on the less polarized issues, insofar as they are not very salient and positions on them are correspondingly equivocal. The vaguer the issue, the greater the likelihood of misperception. With little information to go on, or with conflicting signals from others, the elites may tend to project their views on others.

But it is also possible to argue the other way around. Perceptual distortion may be most common with regard to the conflictive issues precisely because the elites have a stake in stereotyping those whom they consider their opponents. Furthermore, it may be comparatively rare on the low-key issues that do not arouse the antagonistic propensities of the elites. A countertendency for the elites to place others at a distance from themselves may increase with the polarization of issues, and ideological stereotyping may increase the probability of misperception.[16]

Conceivably, both factors—uncertainty on the less controversial issues and stereotyping on those that are more polarized—work to broaden the gap between the perceptions and preferences. On a priori grounds, there seems to be no way to settle the question, and it is for this reason that I turn to a second factor, the split between public and private opinion.

Public versus Private Opinion

Progressive ideals are not forbidden in authoritarian systems like the Brazilian, where powerful actors may declare themselves in favor of eventual social reform and political liberalization ''in principle.'' If the discrepancy between the operational code of authoritarianism and democratic-sounding ideals surfaces in the public declarations of the elites, it should be all the more apparent in the anonymity of confidential interviews. Authoritarian regimes are more concerned with controlling overt behavior than with monitoring the private thoughts of individuals.

This distinction provides a key component of the model of perception. So far I have argued that elite perceptions are subject to two types of distortion: (1) a tendency for the elites to *project*—to assume that the preferences of others are similar to their own, and (2) a propensity for the elites to *stereotype*—to contrast their own views against those they impute

than issues, see David A. Wilder, ''Reduction of Intergroup Discrimination through Individuation of the Out-Group,'' *Journal of Personality and Social Psychology* 36 (1978): 1361-1374.

[16] Compare Joop Van Der Pligt and Jos A. Van Dijk, ''Polarization of Judgment and Preference for Judgmental Labels,'' *European Journal of Social Psychology* 9 (1979): 233-241, and Clark McCauley and Christopher L. Stitt, ''An Individual and Quantitative Measure of Stereotypes,'' *Journal of Personality and Social Psychology* 36 (1978): 929-940.

to others by labelling others as reactionary or, less frequently in the Brazilian case, radical. I have also suggested that projection should be more common on the less well-defined issues, like birth control and foreign investment, and that stereotyping should come into play on the conflictive issues, like government-labor relations.

But the question remains concerning which tendency might cause greater misperception. In general, I expect stereotyping rather than projection to increase the gap between avowed and attributed opinion. Because the elites are privately more progressive on most issues than they imagine one another to be, the projection of their own opinions on their colleagues will enhance the correspondence between avowed (private) and attributed (public) preferences. To the degree that the elites have little hard information about the views of others, uncertainty will cause them to project their own preferences and thereby make reasonably, if inadvertently, sound estimates of the views of their colleagues.

A different mechanism comes into play as the issues become polarized. Elites who in the privacy of confidential interviews vouchsafe their liberalism are likely to see their colleagues as conservative and to be labelled conservative in turn when the issues entail sharply defined progressive-reactionary alternatives. The gap between avowed and attributed opinion should be wider on the conflictive than on the fuzzy issues because the incentive structure of perception encourages stereotyping rather than projection as the issues engage the combative inclinations of diverse groups.

Misperception as a Function of Stereotyping and Projection

Uncertainty and Projection

One of my primary arguments is that the tendency to project should increase on the fuzzier issues as a function of uncertainty. The simplest way to estimate the degree of perceptual uncertainty for an issue is to calculate the incidence of "don't knows" given by the elites when they were asked to gauge the opinions of others. The variation in "don't knows" suggests the differential clarity of the issues: birth control (14 percent), foreign investment (9 percent), government-labor relations (8 percent), income redistribution (7 percent), and government-opposition relations (7 percent). Birth control is the most ambiguous of the questions facing the elites, dissociated from the conventions of left versus right, and the issue of foreign investment is also freighted with ambivalence. Once past these two questions, uncertainty declines markedly.

The next step is to determine whether the probability of projection rises with the uncertainty of the issues. Correlations between the elites' own opinions and the opinions they attribute to others were computed for each of the issues. A positive correlation indicates a tendency for the elites to superimpose their preferences on others.

Again, the results are as expected. In descending order: the number of significant positive correlations between preferences and perceptions on birth control is 18 percent, on foreign investment 15 percent, on income redistribution 9 percent, on government-opposition relations 8 percent, and on government-labor relations 4 percent. The fuzzier issues, like birth control and foreign investment, are much more likely than the conflictive ones to cause the elites to project their views on others.[17]

However, the link between uncertainty and projection does not establish a connection between projection and misperception. Testing for projection involves correlating two variables: the elites' own preferences and their perceptions of others. Nowhere in this procedure have the actual preferences of others been entered.[18] Indeed, given the distinction between the public and private opinions of the elites, projection may not detract from and may even enhance the accuracy of elite perceptions. Let us examine this nonobvious tendency.

Stereotyping and Misperception

The indicated measure of the discrepancy between avowed and attributed opinion is the size of the discrepancy between the two. Not every discrepancy, however slight, need be counted as misperception but only those in which the distance between the two variables is significant.[19]

---

[17] Conversely, the number of significant negative correlations between preferences and perceptions increases on the more conflictive issues. Only one such correlation occurs for the birth control issue; for the political opposition issue, the figure reaches four. An inverse association between preference and perception indicates the presence of "reverse projection," the tendency to assume that the views of others are opposed to one's own. In my terminology, this is equivalent to stereotyping. By the way, significant reverse projections, which total eleven, are much less common than positive projections (total = fifty-four). This suggests that the elites are more inclined than not to assume that their peers agree with them. But, as we shall see, correlations are sometimes unreliable measures of concordance; in fact, the extent of disagreement is greater than indicated by the incidence of "reverse projection."

[18] See Christopher H. Achen, "Measuring Representation: Perils of the Correlation Coefficient," *American Journal of Political Science* 21 (1977): 805-815; Aage R. Clausen, "The Accuracy of Leader Perceptions of Constituent Views," paper presented at the annual meetings of the American Political Science Association, Washington, D.C., September 1-4, 1977; and Edward O. Laumann, "Friends of Urban Men: An Assessment of Accuracy in Reporting Their Sociometric Attributes, Mutual Choice, and Attitude Agreement," *Sociometry* 32 (1969): 54-69.

[19] The fact that the elites' own opinions and their perceptions of others tend to be correlated (through projection) presents a technical obstacle to discovering "misperception." The detection of discrepancies between avowed and attributed opinions is confounded by the lack of independence between the two measures. The acid test of such discrepancies is the statistical

When these differences are calculated across the five issues, the results turn out to be practically the reverse of those obtained in examining projection. Misperception is lowest for the issues on which the elites project the most and highest for the issues on which they project hardly at all. Of the total of forty-two attributions made for each of the issues, only one statistically significant misperception emerges for the birth control controversy, six for foreign investment, fourteen for income redistribution, sixteen for control/autonomy of labor, and twenty-three for political opposition.[20] As the polarization of the issues increases, so, it would appear, does the inclination of the elites to stereotype their colleagues, with the result that the incidence of misperception soars.

Inspection of the detailed results for two representative issues helps in understanding the link between stereotyping and misperception. Tables 6.2 and 6.3 give the average differences between avowed and attributed opinions, group by group, for one issue that is only moderately polarized (foreign investment) and another that is extremely politicized (government-opposition relations).

The issue of foreign investment, we know, is the only one on which the elites are inclined to see their colleagues as a bit more progressive—that is, nationalistic—than they claim to be. But the extent of misperception

---

significance of the difference between the mean preference of an elite sector and the mean position attributed to it by another. But the correlations between avowed and attributed opinions encountered in analyzing projection violate the assumption of independence on which difference-of-means tests are based. Serial comparisons of means for each of the 210 pairwise combinations of perceived and perceiving sectors are therefore inappropriate.

The problem can be circumvented by a two-step procedure. First, instead of the conventional t, Hotelling's T^2 statistic is used. See Donald F. Morrison, *Multivariate Statistical Methods*, 2d ed. (New York: McGraw-Hill, 1976), pp. 128-169. (For an application of a somewhat different method to the same problem, see David A. Wilder, "Perceiving Persons as a Group: Effects of Attributions of Causality and Beliefs," *Social Psychology* 41 [1978]: 13-23.) The T^2 statistic tests for the significance of differences between vectors rather than pairs of means while taking into account the possibility of correlations between the measurements.

However, the method does not indicate how many and which of the issues may be contributing to the discrepancy between the vectors. The second step is thus to compute confidence intervals for each of the differences, issue by issue, simultaneously correcting for possible correlations between avowed and attributed preferences. The method for estimating the simultaneous confidence intervals, developed by Roy and Bose, is also reported in Morrison, *Multivariate Statistical Methods*. If avowed and attributed opinions are correlated, the Boy-Bose confidence intervals will have widths different from those resulting from individual t-tests, and this information permits me to evaluate the significance of differences between avowed and attributed opinion when the two variables are correlated.

[20] With each of the seven elite groups making attributions to all groups except their own, a (7) (7-1) perceivers/perceived matrix is generated; hence, the forty-two mutual perceptions for a single issue.

TABLE 6.2

Mean Differences between Avowed and Attributed Opinions on Foreign Investment,
by Elite Sector

	Perceiving							
Perceived	MDB	Labor	Bishops	Civil Service	Banks	ARENA	Industry	Mean
MDB	—	2	10	13	11	10	4	7
Labor	38*	—	28	25*	21*	14	15*	21
Bishops	8	−17	—	−10	−18	−18	−11	−13
Civil Service	13	11*	−3	—	9	9	5	8
Banks	−5	10	−5	7	—	15	3	7
ARENA	−7	−13	−15	−7	−7	—	−6	−9
Industry	10	16*	2	10	11	13	—	12

NOTE: A negative difference indicates that perceptions are more conservative than preferences.
* Significant with p ≤ .10.

TABLE 6.3

Mean Differences between Avowed and Attributed Opinions on Government-Opposition
Relations, by Elite Sector

	Perceiving							
Perceived	MDB	Labor	Bishops	Civil Service	Banks	ARENA	Industry	Mean
MDB	—	−15	1	−8	−9	−9	−7	−9
Labor	24*	—	17	10	10	10	6	10
Bishops	−9	−28*	—	−21*	−27	−28*	−17	−22
Civil Service	−9	−18*	−27*	—	−28*	−14*	−22*	−19
Banks	−21	−18*	−23*	−21*	—	−9	−27*	−20
ARENA	−16	−26*	−23*	−17*	−25*	—	−24*	−22
Industry	−22	−30*	−43*	−21*	−25*	−23*	—	−26

NOTE: A negative difference indicates that perceptions are more conservative than preferences.
* Significant with p ≤ .10.

is very slight, and most of it focuses on the supposedly leftist labor leaders. The MDB politicians place the labor leaders nearly forty points to the left of where they actually are. This is one instance in which projection—that is, wishful thinking—on the part of a leftist group leads to misperception.[21]

[21] In Table 6.2, it may seem anomalous that the average perception of the bishops by the

But on a truly explosive issue, like government-opposition relations, the reverse tendency sets in. Except for the persistent supposition of the MDB politicians that the labor leaders lean toward the far left on the controversy, most of the elites look upon one another as conservatives or cautious moderates. They stereotype one another to the right, and the frequency of misperception climbs. On such an issue, the elites get locked into an "everybody-is-a-fascist-except-me" syndrome. Avowals of enlightenment go hand-in-hand with condemnation of the authoritarian urges of fellow elites.

A Note on Group Effects: Perceivers versus Perceived

One of the most consistent findings that has emerged from studies of social perception is the tendency for individuals to perceive others as more conservative than they themselves claim to be.[22] With the exception of their view of the labor leaders, the Brazilian elites roundly confirm this tendency. They distrust one another, especially on the polarized issues.

This fact has other repercussions. For example, it is well established that whites perceive their fellow whites as more conservative in racial matters than they say they are. In addition, however, those who are conservative on racial issues are more likely than liberals to believe that others share their views, while liberals are inclined to reverse projection, imputing segregationist views to others. The net result is a distribution of perceptions far to the right of public opinion as conventionally defined.[23]

What has this got to do with Brazil? It seems that liberals and conservatives exhibit differential perceptual inclinations. In a cross-national study of parliamentarians, Putnam reasons that

> the left, attacking an established social order, finds the origin of injustice in conflicting interests. The right, defending the existing order, argues that no one is "really" disadvantaged by that order and that issues must be resolved, not by conflict, but "on their merits." It is obviously no accident that Burke, the great conservative, extolled social harmony, while Marx, the great revolutionary, stressed social cleavage.[24]

---

bankers and the ARENA politicians is off by eighteen points, yet is not significant, while the perception of the civil servants by the labor leaders, off by eleven points, turns out to be significant. One reason for this is that some elite groups, like the labor leaders, are larger than others, so that a smaller discrepancy between attribution and preference qualifies as statistically significant misperception.

[22] Besides the studies cited in footnote 13, see O'Gorman with Garry, "Pluralistic Ignorance—A Replication and Extension," pp. 449-458.

[23] Fields and Schuman, "Public Beliefs about the Public," and O'Gorman with Garry, "Pluralistic Ignorance—A Replication and Extension."

[24] Robert D. Putnam, *The Beliefs of Politicians* (New Haven: Yale University Press, 1973), p. 107.

The characterization of the evasive conservatives is reminiscent of the *homen cordial*, the diplomat of Brazilian politics. More generally: the tendency for Brazilian elites to view others in agreement or disagreement with themselves may vary with their ideological predispositions. If the political styles of the elites affect their perceptions in this way, the MDB politicians and the bishops can be expected to be less agreeable than the ARENA politicians, the businessmen, and the state managers.[25]

So it appears that conservatives are prone to project, to convince themselves that the opinions of others resemble their own. Progressives are likely to stereotype, to imagine that the opinions of others are opposed to their own and are, therefore, reactionary. The psychological mechanisms differ, yet they reinforce each other in the aggregate. Their combined result is a profile of perceptions with a strongly conservative cast.

The argument implies that the elites are ideologically predisposed to view their colleagues in biased ways irrespective of particular issues. This cannot be completely true, of course. But it is plausible enough to warrant a test. The impact of any single issue in reducing or increasing the gap between avowed and attributed opinion can be held constant, in effect, by forming an index that estimates the correspondence between self-declared and perceived preferences for pairs of elite groups across all five issues.

The measure of concordance is the correlation, computed for each individual elite, between the attributions of preferences to an elite group and the mean self-declared preferences of the group on the same issues. For example, in estimating the opinions of the industrialists, an ARENA politician produces five scores, one for each issue, which can be correlated with the actual mean opinions of the industrialists on these issues. Each one of the elites does this for all groups except his own so that, discounting the military, for whom self-declared opinions are unavailable, he generates a total of thirty attributions: five issues by six groups.

Although the number of observations on which a single individual-level correlation is based is only five (the number of issues), the instability of the coefficients is reduced by averaging them over an elite sector. Thus, we arrive at a set of measures for gauging the fit between avowed and attributed opinion, between perceived and perceiving pairs of elite groups, across the five issues. The higher the correlation, the closer the corre-

---

[25] It may not be ideology alone that makes elites the likes of the MDB politicians critical of their peers but rather, or also, their subordinate position in the power structure. Some of the elites remain in opposition because they are determined leftists; others sound leftist because they are denied entry into the establishment. This dialectic between the *situação* and the *oposição*, between the ins and the outs, is a commonplace of Brazilian politics.

spondence between self-declared and perceived preferences.[26] Table 6.4 gives the results of the calculations.

The rows are formed by the perceived groups, who are listed in descending order of the average degree of accuracy with which they are perceived. The arrangement of the groups from top to bottom follows an approximate left-right ordering, with the MDB politicians at one end and the industrialists at the other.

There is no doubt that the conservative elites are more likely than the progressives to be "misunderstood." It is with the civil servants, the bankers, the ARENA politicians, and the industrialists that the relationship between their avowed opinions and those attributed to them becomes most attenuated. Their colleagues perceive them as reactionary, while they consider themselves enlightened conservatives. For example, the average correlation between the opinions that the industrialists claim as their own and those that their peers think they have is zero, and the figures for the

TABLE 6.4

Mean Individual-Level Correlations between Perceptions and Actual Opinion of Seven Elite Groups, by Elite Sector

	Perceiving							
Perceived	*MDB*	*Labor*	*Bishops*	*Civil Service*	*Banks*	*ARENA*	*Industry*	*Mean*
MDB	—	.68	.70	.88	.81	.81	.80	.78
Labor	.75	—	.53	.78	.82	.89	.73	.77
Bishops	.57	.46	—	.63	.44	.50	.54	.53
Civil Service	.36	.19	.05	—	.17	.43	.33	.28
Banks	.21	.07	.34	.35	—	.36	.24	.25
ARENA	.26	.05	.01	.43	.26	—	.27	.23
Industry	.08	−.18	−.02	.10	.01	.11	—	.00
Mean	.37	.21	.27	.53	.42	.52	.49	.47

NOTE: "Actual" opinion = mean avowed opinion of group. N on which individual-level correlations are based is 5 ($= n$ of issues). Note that the correlations in the upper-right side of the matrix tend to be larger than those in the lower-left side. This pattern facilitates interpretation of the results. In general, perceiving groups toward the left (MDB, labor, et cetera) attribute opinions to other groups, especially the conservative ones, that are at variance with the "actual" opinions of these groups. Perceiving groups toward the right (ARENA, industry, et cetera) attribute opinions that are more in accord with those actually expressed by other groups.

[26] Compare Susan B. Hansen, "Participation, Political Structure, and Concurrence," *American Political Science Review* 69 (1975): 1181-1199.

government politicians, the bankers, and the civil servants are not much better. The conservative sectors do not put forth a credible progressive image.

By contrast, the gap between the opinions of the progressive elites and those imputed to them tends to be smaller. The MDB politicians and the labor leaders are regularly perceived as leftist and, although somewhat less regularly, so are the bishops. While the labor leaders are tagged a bit more to the left than they admit to being, and the MDB politicians are placed to the right of their avowed positions, their fellow elites do not misjudge them grossly. The labor leaders and the members of the MDB are viewed as staples of the opposition, an assessment that is more accurate for the latter than the former; nevertheless, the elites are not far wrong in viewing the syndical cadres to the left. The bishops make up a more ambiguous object of perception, and the attributions made about their positions on the issues are a bit further off the mark.

Table 6.4 also brings to light the contrariness of the progressive elites—that is, their inclination to perceive their colleagues in terms of their public positions and thereby to attribute to them opinions at odds with the enlightened self-image of the conservatives. Columnwise inspection of the matrix reveals that the attributions made by the MDB politicians, the bishops, and the labor leaders have little to do with the self-avowed preferences of their fellow elites, in particular, with the protestations of liberalism on the part of the state managers, the businessmen, and the ARENA politicians. For example, the average correlation between the labor leaders' perceptions of the industrialists and the industrialists' own preferences is $-.18$.

On the other hand, the conservatives perceive their peers with greater "accuracy," because they are reluctant to view others in an adversary role. Instead, they are inclined to project their private opinions on others, with the result that they come fairly close to the hidden liberalism of their colleagues.

Yet the conservatives are not so given to wishful thinking as to overlook completely the hidebound image of their own kind. The correlations between the ARENA's perception of the bankers and the bankers' private views (or, for that matter, between the bankers' perception of the ARENA politicians and the ARENA politicians' own views) are very low. The conservatives put more faith in the liberalism of the genuinely progressive elites than in the closet progressivism of their conservative peers.

Are Stereotypes Misperceptions?

More for reasons of linguistic convenience than analytical precision, the gap between elite preferences and perceptions has been termed "misperception.'' Yet a strong case can be made that in the Brazilian context the opinions that the elites attribute to one another are quite accurate estimates of their public positions, of what they do rather than what they claim to be, and that they dissemble in a painlessly liberal direction when speaking off the record.

The argument is sensible, but it suffers from the fallacy of truth by definition. Since there is no systematic evidence about the behavior of individual elites, the case against them—that is, against their professed liberalism—is a compound of the circumstantial (what ''everybody knows'' about Brazil) and the testimony of expert witnesses (the elites themselves). In the absence of behavioral indicators, it is difficult to settle the question. Nevertheless, some evidence can be marshalled which indicates that the progressivism of the elites is not hypocrisy pure and simple.

The ''hesitation'' that the interviewers estimated the elites showed during the course of the interviews was correlated with their avowed preferences. This provides a check on the possibility that the greater the circumspection of the elites, the more likely they are to shade their responses conservatively, presumably because of caution about divulging inordinately progressive views.

In fact, most of the correlations go just this way, and the few that attain significance do so on the most delicate issues.[27] For example, the more hesitant MDB politicians give comparatively moderate answers; so, too,

TABLE 6.5
Correlations between Elite Preferences and Interviewer-Assessed ''Hesitation,''
by Issue and Sector

Elite Sector	*Issues*				
	Birth Control	*Foreign Investment*	*Income Redistribution*	*Control of Labor*	*Political Opposition*
ARENA	.04	.21	−.21	−.37*	.10
MDB	.29	−.23	−.39	−.56*	−.68*
Church	.45	.10	.12	.15	.31
Labor	.00	−.04	−.18	−.22	−.17
Civil Servants	−.09	−.03	−.16	−.14	−.11
Banks	.02	−.21	.06	.01	−.23
Industry	−.11	−.11	−.05	.10	−.11
All Elites	−.01	−.05	−.16*	−.17*	−.15*

*p ≤ .10.

[27] Given the scoring conventions, a negative correlation indicates that hesitancy decreases with the liberalism of the elites' preferences and that it increases with their conservatism. In other words, an inverse association means that the greater the hesitancy of the elites, the more conservative their responses.

do the ARENA politicians on the issue of government-labor relations. The inverse connection between discretion and liberalism suggests that many of the elites refrain from identifying themselves as full-fledged progressives out of fear. If the elites felt absolutely secure about revealing their opinions, the tone of the interview would probably be even more progressive.

This does not prove that the elites are wholly sincere in their progressivism, much less that there is no gap between their declarations of liberalism and their actual behavior. It is easier for elites to indulge in verbal liberalism than to act on these principles, in Brazil and most everywhere else. Yet the fact that, even in private, the conservatism of the elites is tainted with caution suggests the weakness of authoritarian norms. The tendency for the progressive remonstrations of the elites to have a self-serving ring does not demonstrate the opposite: namely, that they believe in the rightness of what they do. This, in turn, suggests the latent legitimacy of reformist impulses within the establishment. It is this reservoir of liberal-democratic idealism that seems to have bolstered elite receptivity to the limited political opening of the post-1973 period in Brazil.

Are stereotypes, then, misperceptions? Yes and no. While there is a self-serving component to the professions of liberalism on the part of the elites, a similar motivation no doubt enters into the conservative labels they foist on their colleagues. Neither the private nor the public opinions of the elites are necessarily "true"; nor does it follow that "true" opinion lies somewhere between avowed and attributed preferences. There may be no third term in the dialectic of preference and perception, or any happy medium, but instead two irreconcilable dimensions of "the truth," one private and the other public.

> . . . while in the manner of all disciplined organizations the corporation denies liberty of expression to quite a few people . . . repression [also] operates against the important participants in management. In all public utterances they are well advised to reflect an institutionally acceptable viewpoint, what is often called even in noncommunist countries the party line. Very often they are required to say what the guardians of the official truth, the public relations executives, have written out for them. . . . And the sanctions for speaking in conflict with the corporate perceptions of truth, if subtle, are severe: those so disposed may be praised for their character but they are not promoted. That over time becomes expensive.[28]

[28] John Kenneth Galbraith, "A Hard Case," *New York Review of Books* 25, April 20, 1978: 6.

In estimating the political positions of their peers, Brazilian elites respond in terms of nomothetic presumptions of where progressive and conservative actors are supposed to stand as public figures.[29] When the labor leaders are not overtly militant, then (so the elites believe) they nurse their leftism in secret. As for the members of the establishment, they benefit in varying degrees from the authoritarian situation, and they must therefore be conservative.

The generalizations made by the elites about one another are also conditioned by the nature of the issues. As controversies become polarized, taking on a clear left-versus-right, us-versus-them meaning, the gulf between avowed declarations of liberalism and attributions of conservatism widens. Conversely, the tendency for the elites to project their views on their colleagues is most frequent in controversies where policy alternatives are difficult to cast in purely left-right terms and where uncertainty is correspondingly great. Birth control is the prime example of such an issue.

Somewhat paradoxically, projection does not lead to misperception. Avowed and attributed opinions are most likely to coincide on the two issues, birth control and foreign investment, for which a crisp left-versus-right labelling is doubtful and on which projection is most common. But where left-right cleavages are manifest, and where group interests are incontrovertibly antagonistic, the temptation for the elites to identify themselves as progressive by stereotyping their colleagues as reactionary is strong. On such issues, the elites make a clear distinction between ''our'' liberalism and ''their'' intransigence.

What are the political implications of the tendency for the elites to stereotype one another? The result of stereotyping the labor leaders to the left and the rest of the elite groups to the right is to exacerbate the extent of conflict between them. The differences separating the elites are real enough: their private opinions are discrepant, and interelite antagonism is not simply an illusion that would disappear with an opening in the channels of communication. Yet stereotyping increases antagonism by decreasing the room for compromise. To some extent, interelite conflict in Brazil is self-generated.

The crucial point is that this tendency is not uniform; it changes regularly across issues. In fact, over the course of military government since 1964, the issues found to be politically less stressful, in the eyes of the elites, are those on which considerable movement, reform, and much-vaunted Brazilian pragmatism can be detected, whereas the polarized issues have proved less tractable.

[29] Compare Daryl J. Bem and A. Allen, ''On Predicting Some of the People Some of the Time: The Search for Cross-Situational Consistencies in Behavior,'' *Psychological Review* 81 (1974): 506-520.

The chronicle of the simultaneously gradual and erratic dissolution of authoritarianism in Brazil suggests that it began, although it could scarcely be known at the time, with the easiest issues: with the legalization of divorce and the relaxation of the government's traditional pronatalist stance, in the mid-seventies. None of these reforms threatened the authoritarian compromise. But even though changes were dispensed from above, the polemics surrounding them incited an experimental mobilization of previously quiescent interests, and the experience was not lost.

By virtual assent, foreign investment and income redistribution are more serious issues. Yet here, post-1964 (or more accurately, post-1973) governments in Brazil have scrambled and negotiated. The fundamental bet—that continued growth makes both increasing indebtedness and some movement toward redistribution feasible—has remained about the same.[30] This constancy has an empirical as well as a grandiose streak to it. The country is immense, and even pragmatists in Brazil deal in broad and unexpected gestures, and in sheer bluff. Redistribution by decree and the servicing of a monumental short-term debt may bring all the contradictions of capitalism inexorably to bear on a small, resource-poor nation. In Brazil the angle of vision and the flare for risk are, by comparison, Olympian.[31]

Although it is impossible to reconstruct here the complexity of the bargaining and decision-making process that has gone into the shift away from sheer authoritarianism on these economic and social issues, consultation among key figures has been extensive. Getting the ear of a powerful general or minister may suffice to shift policy a bit on the less conflictive issues, like birth control, although even here the regime has taken pains to negotiate with the bishops. Change does not come so easily on weightier issues, like income redistribution. More interests have to be sounded out and their will to resist contrary policies anticipated.

The expressly political issues—the autonomy of the labor organizations, the freedom of political opposition, and similar questions involving the nature of the constitutional order—have proved less tractable. A civilian superminister, like Delfim Netto, may wield colossal power and have exceptional discretion in setting economic and social policy. But civilians have been forced to bow to the military in matters touching on the rules of political conflict and competition. Even if they cannot run the economy

[30] Compare Charles S. Maier, "The Politics of Productivity: Foundations of American International Economic Policy After World War II," *International Organization* 31 (1979): 607-633.

[31] See "Will Foreign Bankers Blow the Whistle on Brazil?" *Business Week*, November 19, 1979: 56-63. To the surprise of many, including the authorities themselves, the real growth rate of the Brazilian economy in 1980 was 8 percent, despite an inflation rate hovering around 100 percent.

by themselves, the Brazilian generals are scarcely figureheads. They retain the final word about political restrictions and permissiveness.

The policy environment is charged and volatile on issues that do not readily lend themselves to incremental and technical solutions. Either the unions and the political parties are autonomous agents, or they are not; either the military have the right to run the country, or they do not. Intrinsically, such issues have a more confrontational substance, involving the fate of specific groups, than do controversies about foreign investment, income redistribution, and birth control for which fine-tuning or less than drastic options seem comparatively abundant. It is precisely in the area of the eyeball-to-eyeball issues that the authoritarian regime has postponed changes for the longest time.

The stereotypes with which Brazilian elites label one another are therefore not psychological quirks. They represent a magnification of dilemmas rooted in an institutional impasse. They serve as clarifying mechanisms for organizing lines of conflict in a situation where antagonistic passions are high but where the institutions of conflict-processing are nebulous, untrustworthy, rumor-ridden, and subject to a "reign or error."[32]

Thus, interelite perceptions, while they are distorted, are distorted systematically. "Misperception" is stylized rather than chaotic. Although the distances between conservatives and progressives are inflated, the relative ordering of elite actors is never seriously misconstrued. The ARENA politicians, for example, are not perceived as more liberal than members of the MDB; nor are the labor leaders viewed as more reactionary than the industrialists. While stereotyping promotes neither accuracy of perception nor consensus, it helps structure implicit coalitions and demarcate combatants on each of the issues.[33]

This can be driven home by correlating the perceptions of the elite groups for each of the issues and submitting the matrix of coefficients to a data-reduction technique like smallest-space analysis. For any given issue there are eight variables corresponding to the elite groups, including the military, to whom positions are attributed. The configuration of coalition

---

[32] Robert K. Merton, *Social Theory and Social Structure*, rev. ed. (Glencoe: The Free Press, 1957), pp. 421-436.

[33] The simultaneous distortion-clarification that stereotyping brings about may be more common in loosely institutionalized political systems, whether authoritarian or not, than in polities where the match between opinions and organizations is closer. In a study of mutual perceptions among elites in the Netherlands, where the organizational repertoire for expressing ideological differences is vast, Rochon found almost no cross-groups misperception, even on strongly polarized issues. See Thomas R. Rochon, "Local Elites and the Structure of Political Conflict: Parties, Unions, and Action Groups in the Netherlands," Ph.D. dissertation, University of Michigan, 1980.

and conflict, as perceived by the elites themselves, are displayed for the five major issues in Figure 6.3.

The diagrams are strikingly consistent with what has already been learned about the ideological disposition of the elite estates. For example, the bishops are perceived far to the right on the issue of birth control, and the bankers and industrialists are seen as antinatalists, which they are. The relative alignment does not violate the ranking of elite groups by their self-reported opinions, even though the bishops are spotted farther toward the pronatalist extreme than they admit to being. In effect, the perceptions of the elites transport the whole ideological spectrum several paces in a conservative direction and stretch the labor leaders to the left, without disturbing the positions of the elite actors vis-à-vis one another.

Much the same can be said about the remaining coalitional spaces, with one important modification. As the polarization of the issues increases, the elite sectors tend to be perceived as either of the left or of the right, with fewer intermediary positions. On the controversy over the autonomy of labor organizations, for example, the military begin to lose the centrist position they hold on the fuzzier issues and are placed way toward the right. And no groups, except perhaps the bishops, are seen as occupying a moderating role on the issue of political opposition. The center empties out on the confrontational issues, and opponents are seen as less and less reconcilable. This void in the political middle, specifically regarding controversies that bear on the vital interests of elite groups, helps explain why incremental, gradualistic changes in these areas have been painful in authoritarian Brazil.[34]

Of course, the less polarized issues may be objectively no more manageable than the explicitly political ones. Fine-tuning foreign investment policies does not guarantee the desired results; Brazil does not control the world market. Yet perhaps because the elites sense that the more narrowly political issues are more susceptible to purposeful solution, just as problems of political order and autonomy tend to be seen as man-made, tensions on such issues are exceptionally acute. The villains are visible, and blame can be laid unequivocally.

---

[34] It may be asked what the apparently complex presentation in Figure 6.3 adds to the results based on average perceptions given in Table 6.1. Although the two sets of data are roughly the same, the graphic representations take into account the variation around these averages. The fact that all the smallest-space solutions are two-dimensional reflects the "noise" in the elites' perceptions of one another.

FIGURE 6.3
Two-Dimensional Smallest-Space Diagrams for Perceptions of Elite Sectors on Five Issues

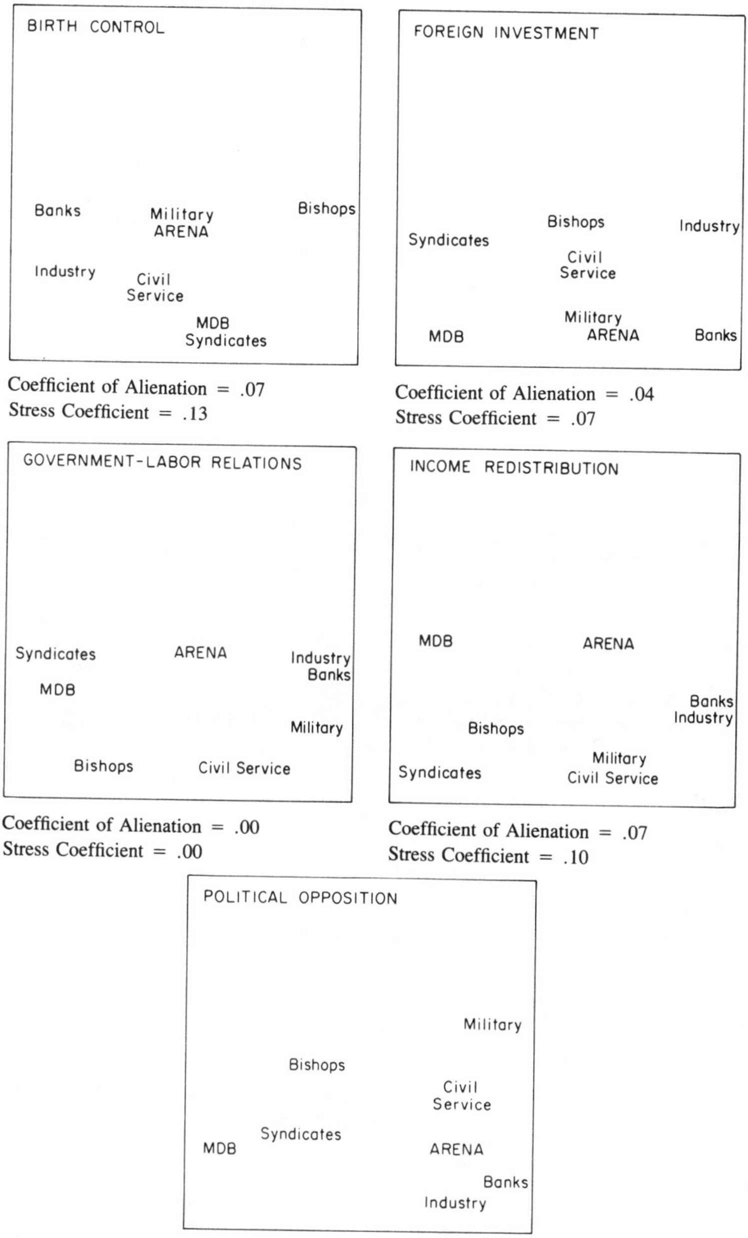

BIRTH CONTROL

Banks   Military   Bishops
             ARENA

Industry   Civil
         Service

         MDB
         Syndicates

Coefficient of Alienation = .07
Stress Coefficient = .13

FOREIGN INVESTMENT

         Bishops   Industry
Syndicates
        Civil
        Service

        Military
MDB   ARENA   Banks

Coefficient of Alienation = .04
Stress Coefficient = .07

GOVERNMENT-LABOR RELATIONS

Syndicates   ARENA   Industry
MDB   Banks

               Military

Bishops   Civil Service

Coefficient of Alienation = .00
Stress Coefficient = .00

INCOME REDISTRIBUTION

MDB   ARENA

                  Banks
    Bishops   Industry

Syndicates   Military
         Civil Service

Coefficient of Alienation = .07
Stress Coefficient = .10

POLITICAL OPPOSITION

          Military

   Bishops
        Civil
        Service

   Syndicates
MDB   ARENA
           Banks
     Industry

Coefficient of Alienation = .05
Stress Coefficient = .08

CONCLUSION

The great question now is to find a political-institutional formula that unites liberalism with democracy—or rather, unites the demand for freedom in purely political terms with the demand for social equality. . . . In Brazil it is no longer possible to force a pact among elites that is mere sophistry. . . . The great problem, in fact, is how to find an institutional space for the workers, a solution that will involve the creation of a new left and a new liberalism. . . . We have to escape from the alternatives we have lived with since the sixties, between popular governments without power and powerful governments without legitimacy.[1]

Organizations change in response to their environments, including their managements; but they resist doing exactly what they are told. As a result, they rarely change in a way that fulfills the intentional plan of a single group of actors. . . . Contemporary history is testimony to the proposition that if leadership wants to make arbitrary changes, neither bureaucracies nor armies are notably easier to control from the top than is a populace of unorganized citizens.[2]

The Planalto Palace has decided to take a new attitude toward the proliferation of guess-work and fantasy about how the government operates. Instead of denying erroneous reports in the news, it will ignore them and let them evaporate on their own. Denials, the government thinks, only encourage the production of nonsense.[3]

At one level, this has been a study of the organization and ideology of Brazilian elites. It has been less an examination of how the elite fraternity operates than an analysis of how the elites themselves think they and their allies and their rivals maneuver within and against the authoritarian system.

On another plane, I have concentrated on some of the factors contributing to the undoing of authoritarianism in Brazil, as well as on the elements that have made this decline so protracted and uncertain. The analysis of what happened in the minds of elites to diminish the legitimacy of the regime while enabling it to hang on, even after it had fallen from grace, raises questions not only about what has by now gone into history but also about the future course of Brazilian politics and the broader implications

[1] From an interview with Francisco Weffort, "Por um Novo Pacto Social," *Veja*, June 29, 1977: 3-6.

[2] James G. Marsh, "Footnotes to Organizational Change," unpublished paper, Stanford University, 1980.

[3] "Planalto Não Desmentirá Boatos," *Veja*, June 4, 1980: 31.

of studies of this type for the understanding of elite politics. In order to place these questions in perspective, it is helpful to review the parts of the study that have empirical backing, and then move on to speculation.

The contours of elite institutions and elite ideology in Brazil resemble one another. By every indicator examined—kinship, friendship, working ties—most of the elites are separated from the leaders of urban labor. The elites are divided internally as well. On the whole, those who run the Brazilian bureaucracy, the military and the civilian technocrats, have been absorbed from the middle sectors. The business elites are drawn largely from the true upper class or from ranks just on its fringes. Although the inner sanctum of the capitalist class seems to be opening up as younger enterpreneurs come on the scene, property is still easily transmitted in Brazil from one generation to the next. The same cannot be said of the transfer of political power. Finally, one elite corporation, the church, stands apart from these networks. Although supportive of the counterrevolution in its early days, the Brazilian bishops became increasingly critical of it, and some of them offered sanctuary from its excesses.

Thus, there are at least three institutional axes around which the Brazilian establishment is organized, and these cleavages go together only imperfectly. Even though power was extremely concentrated in Brazil during the early seventies, the parameters of latent conflict remained in place, making the power structure complex and difficult to consolidate.

The lines of ideological combat reflect the multiple dimensions of the power structure. The elites who favor a more socially oriented, distributive strategy of development are at odds with those committed, with an almost monomaniacal passion during the Médici years, to rapid economic growth. A related, but not identical, conflict pits the devotees of authoritarianism, those who have essentially given up on democracy as a process and as an end state, against the elites with some faith in political liberalization as either one or both.

Yet the moral issues—birth control, divorce, and abortion—escape these classifications, just as the bishops cannot be spotted unequivocally in the power structure. Such controversies are not harmless, nor are the bishops powerless. The moral issues, however, do not divide the elites in the same way as do the classic conflicts between left and right, and they add a measure of equivocation and ambivalence to the activities of the bishops, who are otherwise among the more progressive of the elites regarding political and economic change. The church in Brazil is compromised not only by traces of its earlier support for the 1964 coup but also by its doctrinal inhibitions with respect to moral and sexual issues.

Most generally, the separation of moral and religious controversies from other antagonisms prevents interelite conflict in Brazil from becoming more polarized than it already is. The lines of conflict are dispersed and confused, and furious crusades are the exception rather than the rule.

None of this means that the organization and the political thinking of the elites are in harmony. On the contrary, the Brazilian power structure is out of joint with elite ideology. The conflict-potential of this gap does not always carry over into overt combat because, among other things, political tension varies from issue to issue. It can be just as misleading to talk of an elite "ideology," in the singular, as to think in terms of a unified "elite."

The consequential point is that the explosiveness of issues varies systematically. By and large, the moral issues are the least controversial, the economic and distributive issues somewhat more tension-ridden, with questions that concern interelite governance and the autonomy of diverse elite organizations being the most sensitive of all. The inverse association between the structural seriousness of issues and their perception as conflictive on the part of the elites may be thought an exquisitely perverse demonstration of the invincible ignorance and irresponsibility of the Brazilian establishment. This I doubt, for two reasons.

First, implicit in the conflict hierarchy of the issues is a recognition that institutional deadlocks among the elites may forestall changes with far-reaching repercussions for those left out of an apparently superficial struggle. Second, the related facts that the issues are differentially explosive and that elite ideologies are multidimensional are not "all in the mind." They accord with the lineaments of Brazilian institutional and cultural history. It would take a very abstract brand of objectivity to characterize Brazilian elites as missing the point of what is truly at stake.

Not only are issues differentially polarized and cleavages multiple among Brazilian elites; the organizational mechanisms for expressing and resolving these conflicts are also weak. In part, it is precisely on account of this institutional miasma that the elites show such anxiety about the balance of collective power within the establishment. The sundering of policy preferences from the means for processing them makes Brazilian politics a limbo of ideologies and interests in which the more trivial as well as the most massive challenges are often dealt with by individual superheroes of the moment. This dissociation also helps account for the episodes, frequent in Brazilian history, in which elites make claims about the existence of conspiracies and secret associations (*dispositivos*) waiting to be given the signal for mobilization, only to have them vanish or turn out never to have existed.

The military on the one hand and the church on the other may be less prone to this empiricism and clientelism than the other elites because they are traditional organizations of national scope. The remaining elite sectors are "groups" only by generous standards, and their capacity for collective action, whatever their ideological compatibility, appears to be low. For the most part, what I have called the "institutional axes" of the Brazilian power structure are inchoate and fluid.[4]

Thus, the elites are exasperated with the organizational arbitrariness and precariousness of the regime, a misfortune that is ironic in light of the military's insistence on turning away from particularistic toward impersonal rule. The elites, even the conservatives, want the power of the mightiest among them—the military, the technocrats, and the multinationals—curtailed.

In one sense, this impulse is unexceptionable. The nadir of dictatorship had been reached by the early 1970s. It is not surprising that the elites who welcomed the suppression of mass politics in 1964 should, almost a decade later, become disillusioned with the perpetuation of restrictions on their own power.

Even if their protests at the time were mainly verbal, many of the elites were cognitively mobilized against a regime whose respect for the canons of limited pluralism, for interelite accommodation, gave way to its fascination with development on a gargantuan scale. The elites were not simply distressed at the inequities between their condition and the sorry state of the Brazilian people. The regime itself had turned sour; the rules of elite conduct had been persistently violated.

Time itself eroded the bases of support. The counterrevolution that was supposed to be self-liquidating, a reasoned drive to political house cleaning, economic recovery, and nothing more, took on airs of self-perpetuation. The Third Reich, which made no concessions whatsoever to democratic norms, lasted for only twelve years. At the end of the post-1964 decade, the Brazilian dictatorship appeared to be solidly entrenched. In the eyes of many of the elites, it had overstayed its welcome.

Still, the question remains of how the system lasted so long without provoking more resistance than it did. Part of the answer lies in the complicity of the social reformers, the elites whose primary concern is with a modicum of benefits for themselves and their constituents. If the economists, the headlong developmentalists without much in the way of scruples about due process, are antipolitical, many of the social reformers are

---

[4] It is possible that I have overestimated the underorganization of Brazilian elites, because of the dreamlike air that can afflict survey research with its emphasis on attitudes, et cetera. On the other hand, after four years spent in Brazil, no subterranean formal sociometry leaped out at me, except what I have summarized here. Most social anthropologists who have studied Brazil share these conclusions. See Anthony Leeds, "Brazil as a System," Amherst, Mass., Program in Latin American Studies Occasional Paper Series No. 5, University of Massachusetts, 1977.

apolitical. Some of them are given to a paternalistic sentimentalism. Usually, they fit without undue discomfort in the mainstream of the corporatist spirit in Brazil: respectful of the hierarchy of the moment and content with their own position in it. On most policy matters, these men went along with the regime's assumption about the need for discipline and trickle-down distribution. Against the zeal of the economists and the lethargy of the social reformers, the politicians were helpless.

Gradually, and then more brusquely, the social reformers defected. One reason was the failure of the regime on its own terms as a result of the post-1973 turmoil in the economy. Another was that by the early seventies, the slide into authoritarian intimidation had gone about as far as it could go, short of outright totalitarianism. For all their concern with material, tangible payoffs, the social reformers, like the other elites, care about their control over the distribution of these rewards. Without this control, or at least some semblance of it, their survival as elites is jeopardized. This is what the regime took from them.

Although many of the interviews resonate with skepticism about the economic accomplishments of the regime and with considerable dismay over its inattention to social needs, policy failures in these areas alone did not move the elites—in particular, the social reformers—to question the legitimacy of the regime. What did this, even for the social reformers, was a sense that the regime had plunged the country into a deepening reign of terror and arbitrary lawlessness from which the elites themselves were not safe.[5]

After the Médici presidency, the authoritarian system began to unwind. The incumbents were committed to progress with order, not to a thoroughgoing totalitarianism. Beyond the torture, the censorship, the harassment of the potential opposition, the downward pressure on wages and the ubiquitous restrictions on popular initiative, the major step that remained to be taken in the direction of total control was mass mobilization under the aegis of a single party. But the logic of Brazilian authoritarianism does not require such mobilization, and the regime settled for a public relations promotion of a stern yet populist image for its presidents.

Why should this be so? A principal reason is the ambiguous nature of cross-cutting cleavages among the elites. Conservatives and progressives

---

[5] The following excerpt, from "1974, A Mudança," *Isto É*, October 4, 1978: 38, captures the basic idea: "The torture of prisoners occurs, then, when the interrogator has a guarantee of impunity, something that generally happens in closed political systems (and not only in Brazil). If there is any possibility of punishment, the simplest way out is to free oneself of whoever saw or knows too much about the tortures. 'So the chain of transgressions grows,' comments Raymundo Faoro, president of the Brazilian Bar Association. 'One crime is committed to cover another'."

are not diametrically opposed on all issues. Moreover, the interviews reveal that the men who took power in 1964 were probably more concerned with those among their peers whom they considered as incompetents and demagogues than with a convulsion emanating spontaneously from the mass of the population, whom they tend to view as malleable and largely indifferent to politics. Repression was therefore selective rather than saturating. It was no less arbitrary and uncontrolled for being so; but it was less overwhelming than it might have been, had the precoup mobilization been massive and had the elites been ideologically predisposed to inaugurate a millennial reaction.

It need not be assumed that growing agitation among dissident elites drove the regime to modify the hard-line policies of the Médici era. If we accept the view that authoritarian governments in Brazil do not aim for absolute domination because they perceive such penetration as too costly or unnecessary, then the cautious relaxation of sanctions takes on a certain cadence, initiated deliberately by the government. After 1973, these controls were not working the way they used to anyway, for the economy had slumped. And there was enough ambivalence and embarrassment among supporters of the regime to call into question the utility of sustained despotism.

The earliest reforms were tentative: the halt to torture as an instrument of national security, the lifting of the more heavy-handed forms of press censorship, and the rethinking of a long-standing pronatalist policy. Toward the late seventies, with the transition from the Geisel to the Figueiredo presidencies, reforms came in a rush: the restoration of *habeas corpus*, partial amnesty, the elimination of most types of proscription and the ensuing return of political exiles, the upgrading of income redistribution as a national priority. The two-party system created in 1966 was abolished and a return to multipartism permitted, or rather, imposed from above.

There has been a loose progression to these changes, starting roughly with the most possible and leading toward the most difficult. This scale of feasibility was evident in the thinking of the elites as early as the Médici period. As issues go in Brazil, family planning and divorce are not acutely controversial, even though they fail to reach the status of virtual nonissues like some of the top-down welfare measures enacted since 1964. They do not trigger aggressive and defensive enmities at the heart of the authoritarian system, and they were among the first issues on which reformist settlements were reached. Changes in the authoritarian order itself—especially in the status of the military estate—have been the longest in coming, delayed even more than reforms in social and distributive policies.

The military, then, drew back from totalitarianism, and political life oscillated toward a kind of limited pluralism. But limited pluralism is not the rule of law; it is neither contractual nor constitutional. It is an ill-defined, or continuously redefined, set of prescriptions, like those involved in patron-client relations in a society where the traditional bases of such relations are breaking down. As such, the rules are subject to chronic breakage by ambitious elites or by elites who are not fully aware of the complexities of the game.

If anyone should know what is going on in the labyrinthine world of Brazilian politics, it is the elites themselves. But their perceptions of the political world can be drastically subjective. In some instances, when their vital interests are at stake, the ideological proclivities of the elites are given free rein.

Much of the confusion arises from the ambiguity of limited pluralism as both a normative and a descriptive set of guidelines—a statement about the way elites should behave toward one another as well as a sort of inside-dopesterism about what they actually do. Neither version is unequivocal, even to the elites themselves. The facts about elite behavior are inevitably filtered through rumor. And limited pluralism as an operational code is better understood as an assortment of standards about what outrages cannot be committed than as the codification of a positive political ideal.

Both the obscurity and uncertainty of limited pluralism and its negative quality as an ideology may encourage pragmatism in the behavior of the elites. It certainly gives the appearance that they are not finely tuned to ideological discourse. But the elites cannot live by piecemeal experimentation alone. They need to structure the reality of others in predictable ways: to "coordinate," at least in their own minds, the lopsided relations between a few powerful and many less powerful interests. And their own beliefs are quite patterned. This is especially true of their developmental priorities, about which they can be extremely adamant. The strategic vision implicit in these values functions as a surrogate for explicit ideology.

Limited pluralism is therefore unstable in Brazil. If the regime lacks ideology, contending elites try to supply their own. Ideology abhors chaos, just as power abhors a vacuum. Conflict between rival ideologies may add to the tribulations of the elites. In any event, the absence of a single, hegemonic ideology does not imply that the authoritarian situation is devoid of ideological currents, anymore than the habit of the elites of thinking about politics in multidimensional terms means that they are unideological.

The ideologies of the elites, their values, and their perceptions of one another provide a surreal clarity to a complex political environment. Of course, the world of Brazilian politics is far messier than we, or the elites, make it out to be. This is why case studies of Brazilian authoritarianism are appealing. They recognize the "garbage can" nature of elite politics from the inside: the inherently confused and overloaded jumble of cross-purposes, boilerplate, knee-jerk intrigue, shifting agenda, and imperfect perceptions that compose the day-to-day world of elites jockeying amid institutional lacunae. Yet a focus on what the elites actually do, and on the supposed outcomes of the policy process, inevitably requires some backtracking to the larger issues:

Garbage cans appear to be stimulated by a destabilization of the prevailing value structure, i.e., by a situation in which the dominant preference ordering begins to crumble and there is movement toward a new weighting of goals and values. Star billing seems to go to the kind of ambiguity featured in times of transition and reappraisal. . . . under these circumstances, the primary purpose of certain decision processes is not to produce a specific outcome, but rather, through the airing or "exercising" of problems, to maintain or change the organization as a social unit.[6]

Something like this realignment of priorities seems to have taken shape among Brazilian elites during the Médici regime, as it dawned on even the tamest of them, the social reformers, that the bargain they had struck with the military and the technocrats was yielding diminishing returns. As soon as the economic performance of the regime began to falter, starting late in 1973, there was little excuse for continued quiescence.

In sum, the analysis calls into question two standbys of interpretations of authoritarianism: the workability of limited pluralism and the notion that authoritarian elites are unideological. The framework suggested by limited pluralism comes out more intact than the imputation of ideological vacuity. It is a trifle uncertain, or so it would seem in the minds of Brazilian elites, and perhaps it makes more sense in a society such as Spain where the elites, during the Franco era, were probably more homogeneous and rigorously socialized than in the boisterous new world of Brazil.

The serious problem in understanding limited pluralism comes from the confusion between its normative and its descriptive variants. As a description of what goes on in elite circles, the construct is broad enough to include a variety of maneuvers, bargaining, and infighting. It is too general to be realistic and too imprecise for an ideology; it covers too large a multitude of sins. The latitude for internecine factionalism is so great that one wonders what might be peculiarly authoritarian about this sort of interelite squabbling.

As a normative statement—as a hypothesis about the legitimacy of certain kinds of elite behavior—it suggests that some of the elites may

[6] Lawrence B. Mohr, review of James G. March et al., *Ambiguity and Choice in Organizations* (Bergen: Universitetsforlaget, 1976), *American Political Science Review* 8 (1978): 217-220.

share assumptions about a line that the incumbents cannot cross without risking the loss of their authority. Yet in the absence of a hegemonic program, a dominant ideology, the normative version of limited pluralism offers only a negative consensus that is prone to chronic violation. The legitimate boundaries of authority and dissent are vague.

O sistema, the system, a term with suitably mocking as well as paranoid overtones, may lend a certain exhilaration and some charisma to those who maneuver in and around it, for their endurance in the midst of unpredictability. "I feel," a ministerial bureaucrat said in one of the interviews, "like a general going into battle." But the system is barely routinized, and it tires. Although authoritarian politics may constitute the modal type in Brazil, it cannot be thought of as especially legitimate or even workable over the long haul.[7]

The claim that elites in Brazil are unideological does not fare well. Rather, the problem is the multiplicity of ideologies that collide over the nature of the political system—over who has the right not only to the benefits of development but to compete for the command of developmental decision making—and that, at the same time, coincide only occasionally with organized collectivities. This is what gives Brazilian politics its unideological, experimental gloss. Rival ideologies among the elites take on critical significance, and some pathos, in the absence of accepted institutional mechanisms for settling conflicts and shaping alliances.

At the basis of the authoritarian compromise is a delicate, informal coalition between strong-minded and cooptable elites, between the economists and the social reformers. The coalition is tenable to the extent that the social reformers are given a modicum of control over their designated bailiwicks, at least a sense of access to the powerful. When they are persistently shut out, even when the economic programs of the government are successful, the acquiescence of the social reformers can no longer be taken for granted. Although they may not question fundamentally the economic and social policies of the regime, they begin to question their

---

[7] Many modern political systems may be only weakly institutionalized, in the sense that the formal organizations of government are largely a façade behind which the real work of a highly personalized politics goes on, and yet reasonably legitimate. Mexico comes immediately to mind. See Susan Kaufman Purcell and John F. H. Purcell, "State and Society in Mexico: Must a Stable Polity Be Institutionalized?" *World Politics* 32: 194-227, and Peter H. Smith, *Labyrinths of Power: Political Recruitment in Twentieth-Century Mexico* (Princeton: Princeton University Press, 1979). The key point is that the Mexican system has an organized, if not entirely routinized, way of dealing with the rotation of power at the peak of the polity and, therefore, with a central feature of the balance of power among elites. The Brazilian system has yet to devise a satisfactory mechanism for handling the succession problem.

future within it. They become politicized. The collapse of the government's economic program gives them the chance to express this dissatisfaction.

Why did the social reformers enter into such a coalition to begin with? Part of the reason must lie in the disaccreditation of the politicians not only because of their incidental corruption, which in retrospect does not seem any greater than that which was to afflict the beneficiaries of authoritarianism, but also because of the evident inability of most politicians to back up their ambitions with mass support. Unlike the anti-Allende movement in a highly mobilized Chile, the 1964 counterrevolution in Brazil did not provoke much popular resistance and bloodshed. For a time, the Brazilian military could rule by force alone, since it was the restoration of order that large sectors of the Brazilian populace, including the poorest, wanted. Under these conditions, the politicians were the clear losers. And it was under these conditions that the alliance between economists and social reformers took shape.

The coalition was also facilitated, from a longer-term perspective, by the corporatist strain in Brazilian politics, by the accustomed deference of labor leaders in Brazil to the bureaucratic state, and by the vision on the part of many of the rank-and-file of their own organizations as administrative appendages of the state. It is doubtful whether corporatism is the pre-eminent current in Brazilian political history. But it is a resilient one. It renders the politicians vulnerable to domination by elites who are impatient with pluralistic bargaining, and vulnerable as well to the indifference of the Brazilian public.[8]

The decline of authoritarianism in Brazil has therefore been halting. The break with the politics of accommodation has been only partial, and confrontation intermittent. The lines of conflict among Brazilian elites do not converge. In this sense, not only is it true that the state is—to use an overworked phrase—independent from society. It is also the case that the religious-moral dimension, which in simpler times might have given Bra-

---

[8] It is important to keep in mind that the social reformers, and indeed all of the elites, do not reflect closely the opinions of the general populace. Despite the gain in popularity of the opposition parties since 1974, and despite the crescendo of strikes in 1978 and afterwards, there is little evidence that the Brazilian public is dissatisfied with military government per se. An article published under the title "O João Mais Popular," *Veja*, October 3, 1979, shows that in August 1979, 57 percent of over 3,000 Brazilians interviewed in a Gallup poll approved strongly of the way General Figueiredo (João) was handling the government. Earlier, in October 1978, fully 64 percent gave the same rating to President Geisel. These figures are in line with the results of our 1972/1973 survey of the general population. Compare Fábio Wanderley Reis et al., *Os Partidos e o Regime: A Lógica do Processo Eleitoral Brasileiro* (São Paulo: Edições Simbolo, 1978), and "O Apoio à Livre Iniciativa e à Eficiência: A Sociedade Almejada," *Gazeta Mercantil*, April 29, 1980: 2-7.

zilian politics firmer ideological moorings and split it between absolutes, is divorced from the principal cleavages of elite thought and action.[9]

Nothing in the way of prophecy flows from a study that has been confined to fragments of the past; forecasts are as extraneous to most social science as are morals tacked on to works of art. The best that can be expected is some understanding of the structural, institutional, and ideological matrices within which the process of political change might unfold.[10]

Structurally, several major transformations have occurred since 1964. One is the continued absorption of Brazil into the capitalist international: its climb to the status as the leading borrower among late-developing nations and the increasing interpretation of domestic and international manufacturing in the country. This has been accompanied, since 1973, by an inflation induced not only from the outside but also by a swelling of the Brazilian state. The public sector erected to deal with the multinationals on equal terms has become the principal importer of loans. Another change is the rapid growth of a working class that the developmental policies of the regime have helped create.

The political implications of these changes are not transparent. It used to be thought that the chief reason for the military intervention of 1964 was to extirpate the menace of leftist revolution. This was how many observers, among them members of the elite, saw events at the time. Currently, it is common to argue that the severest pressures exerted on the Brazilian government come from the outside, from the dangers of a barely controllable foreign debt.

Popular mobilization in Brazil was not a phantasm during the early sixties, and the debt burden of Brazil during the eighties is staggering. Furthermore, foreign investment has not simply replaced domestic conflict

---

[9] It does not follow from any of this that, if only elite politics in Brazil were less multi-dimensional or if, in effect, the lines of conflict were sharpened and more polarized, the institutionalization of any Brazilian regime, authoritarian or democratic, would somehow be facilitated. What the argument does suggest, however, is that the apparently unideological nature of Brazilian politics—essentially the result of a severe disjunction between ideologies and organizations and not just of the complexity of ideologies per se—may not be especially "pragmatic." Brazilian politics is certainly personalistic, but this differs from accepted notions of efficient pragmatism. The tension between personalism and institutionalization is not necessarily anti-innovative or one-sidedly counterproductive. Yet it engenders an extreme imbalance between those in and out and power: vast discretion for the winners and bureaucratic strangulation for the losers. "For my friends," a Brazilian politician used to say, "everything; for my enemies, the law."

[10] See Francisco C. Weffort, "Menos Teoria, Mais Fatos," *Isto É*, November 5, 1980: 67.

as the big issue of the present decade. A more accurate diagnosis would be that the role of foreign capital has become more salient, while most of the social and political issues touching the majority of Brazilians remain unresolved.

The question, however, is: How politically explosive are these issues? Much of the literature on Brazil leaves the impression that the most acute conflicts stem from supposedly hard economic controversies. But there is an opacity to causal explanations that link macro-economic constraints to political crises in Brazil. The reasons offered for the onset of authoritarian rule—the exhaustion of economic creativity in the face of hyperbolic agitation, the failure to cope with the external economic environment, and the like—are sometimes the same as those given for its demise. Although there is nothing necessarily contradictory about this reasoning, it is difficult to see how economic frustration is translated into political action in either circumstance.[11]

In fact, the numerous, discrete debts owed by Brazilian firms and by agencies of the government continue to be negotiated in piecemeal fashion. Where the truly divisive potential of this complex of issues seems to lie is in the imported nature of part of the Brazilian inflationary spiral and in the temptation that this predicament offers for the imposition of drastic wage restraints. Given the difficulty of reversing the gains conceded to working-class syndicates following their zombielike condition under the Médici government, such measures would probably be unenforceable.

On the other hand, popular expectations and demands appear to be comparatively modest, and sustained demonstrations of working-class radicalism, while regionally serious, have not attained national scope.[12] Brazil is no longer the landlord-peasant society in which the spread of market relations has elsewhere precipitated successful revolutions in the twentieth century. In this regard, time may have run out not only for the more hidebound of Brazilian reactionaries but also for the traditionally more radical forces on the Brazilian left.[13]

---

[11] At times, this approach wanders into tautology, in effect identifying economic causes with political outcomes. See the otherwise insightful article by Ruth Berins Collier and David Collier, "Inducements versus Constraints: Disaggregating Corporatism," *American Political Science Review* 73 (1979): 967-986. Compare Michael T. Hannan and Glenn R. Carroll, "Dynamics of Formal Political Structure: An Event-History Analysis," *American Sociological Review* 46 (1981): 19-35.

[12] See the results of public opinion polls conducted in 1979 and 1980 reported in "Ficou o Desgaste," *Isto É*, May 21, 1980: 12-17.

[13] This is a possibility of which the Brazilian Communist Party, and the left generally, is well aware. See "A Queda do Cavaleiro: Contra o Radicalismo de Esquerda, o Comitê Central do Partido Comunista Demitiu Luís Carlos Prestes, o Mais Antigo Secretário Geral do Mundo," *Veja*, May 28, 1980: 20-23.

Institutionally, the future of Brazilian politics is muddled. This confusion stems from the regime's response not only to the threat from the outside but also to the threat from below. The state has expanded prodigiously. Controlled social programs have probably grown as rapidly as have the various mechanisms, such as joint ventures and the curbs on foreign capital, that the government uses as buffers against the international market.

In the absence of a corresponding political opening, such reform-from-above violates the sequence followed by earlier developers, in which political guarantees were extended before social rights. Nevertheless, it jibes with the growth-first, equity-second agenda of the Brazilian model. In one respect, the motivations behind the reforms are crystal clear: to deal with problems such as population growth, inadequate housing, limited health care, and so on that have become a drag on economic growth, and to alleviate them before they produce irremediable political damage.

In another sense, however, the burgeoning of social services and increased expenditures on compensatory measures may not yield the benefits that the advocates of rationalized authoritarianism desire. They involve remedial investments without commensurate political return; they do not necessarily or even typically stimulate gratitude among interests who do not take part in the formulation of policy. Because the channels of competition and consultation are so haphazard, whatever positive contribution the policies make is liable to go unnoticed in the midst of denunciations of their preemptive intent.

Thus the readjustment in priorities that has occurred since 1973, toward greater attention to social reform, seems to have been a largely defensive rather than institutionally creative step. This change has softened the impact of the developmental model, and has almost certainly bought the regime time. But it has not resolved the political deadlock among contending elites. It postpones the question of political representation, both formal and substantive, and raises issues that are more complex than the ones I have dealt with in the analysis, going beyond considerations of what political actions the elites will not tolerate toward the construction of political institutions that they and their followers are to live with.[14]

An obvious sign of the limits of guided reform has been the refusal of

[14] Inspired by the experience of the French Fifth Republic and the post-1974 institutional changes in Portugal, Maurice Duverger has argued for a semipresidential arrangement to overcome deadlocks between executive and legislative-representative interests. See "A New Political System Model: Semi-Presidential Government," *European Journal of Political Research* 8 (1980): 165-188. See also Giuseppe DiPalma, "Founding Coalitions in Southern Europe," *Government and Opposition* 15 (1980): 162-189.

some of the large labor syndicates, especially in São Paulo, to settle for wage concessions that leave their institutional subordination intact; Weffort is surely correct in pointing to the problem of the admission of the working class to full political rights as a major challenge to the authoritarian system.[15]

But this is not the only, and perhaps not even the most intractable, dilemma. What may be an even more remarkable symptom of the near-praetorianism of Brazilian political life is the degree to which two actors, the military and the church, who in the normal course of political combat in institutionalized politics stay at the margins of civilian affairs, square off against one another, sometimes without quarter.[16]

The antagonism between the church and the military is important, first, because it reflects the polarization of Brazilian elite politics, and, in particular, the loss of patience of the social reformers, many of whom are drawn from among the bishops, with the intolerance of the economists. Second, open enmity between the military and the bishops also means that the processing of economic and social conflicts has escaped conventional channels, evidently because the corporatist structure of compromise and conciliation does not work very well.

It is not just a matter of the clash of disembodied values and rival symbols; institutionalized bargaining among interests no longer contains or shapes strategic commitments. The streak of fundamentalist anarchism within the church, bent on social justice without regard to political formula, collides head-on with the military's commitment to order, in the last instance, of any kind.[17]

Third, while this combat between para-institutional estates entails a considerably greater dose of pluralism than ever existed during the grimmest period of authoritarianism in Brazil, it cannot be called a pluralist solution. In the classical pattern, either the military is subordinate to civilian authority, or it is not; in a pluralist system, the military is not allowed the

---

[15] In addition to the interview cited in footnote 1, see Francisco Weffort, "O Erro Constituído," *Isto É*, July 23, 1980: 46-48.

[16] Warren M. Hoge, "Brazil's Church-Military Feud Deepens," *New York Times*, December 28, 1980: 4.

[17] An intriguing question here involves the extent to which either the military or the church as organizations have control of their radical wings. Compare Warren Hoge, "Angry Brazilian Chief Vows to Halt Rightist 'Thugs'," *New York Times*, September 16, 1980: 2, and Charles A. Reilly, "Cultural Movements as Surrogates for Political Participation in Contemporary Latin America," paper presented at the annual meetings of the American Political Science Association, Washington, D.C., August 28-31, 1980. See also Tom J. Farer, "Reagan's Latin America," *New York Review of Books* 28 (March 19, 1981): 10-16.

freedoms enjoyed by other interests.[18] A similar restriction applies to the church in the secular versions of pluralism.

The expression of deeply rooted conflicts through the military and the church dramatizes the breakdown of conventional authoritarianism in Brazil; but it is an intermediate stage, and it does not signify the consolidation of a democratic order. Casual comparison might bring to mind the Spanish transition from fascism to parliamentary monarchy as a possible future for Brazil. The scenario is attractive not only because of certain similarities in the political pasts of the two countries but also because of a rough correspondence in their trajectories of economic growth.

However, a key factor in the relatively smooth changeover in Spain has been popular as well as elite identification with several traditional shibboleths, for example, with the monarchy and religious custom. The former is nonexistent in Brazil, and the church has never permeated Brazilian society very deeply. This does not rule out the possibility of a *pacto de los altos*—an accord among the mighty—for just this sort of resolution was devised by competing elites in Venezuela. But the absence of any strong traditional icons of traditional political community in Brazil makes such a denouement more difficult. It is this emptiness that the military has customarily filled in Brazil, to which has more recently been added an enormous state apparatus that the coming to power of a civilian government may affect very little.

A related obstacle blocking the development of representative democracy in Brazil is the corporatist and patrimonial heritage and the attendant difficulty that the elites have in dealing with open, inconclusive debate and conflict. Although I have not plumbed these materials extensively, the elite interviews are littered with references to the debilitating effects of particularistic, selfish interests and about the need to act in the interests of the nation as a whole.[19] To the pluralist (and Machiavellian) tradition, all this

---

[18] It is for this reason that the fate of the military in Brazil is not merely a technicality. As I argued in Chapter Five, it is not just the military's participation in politics that matters but also the exclusionary and irregular structure of decision making represented by the bureaucratic state. However, since the military monopolizes the means of coercion, under strict pluralism this elite corporation can never be *primus inter pares* without endangering the guarantees of free assembly, speech, et cetera.

[19] In tracing the roots of corporatist thought, Alfred Stepan captures the flavor of this perspective with the following citation from Aristotle: " . . . it is the cardinal issue of goodness or badness in the life of the polis which always engages the attention of any state that concerns itself to secure a system of good law well obeyed. . . . Otherwise, a political association sinks into mere alliance. . . . law becomes a mere covenant . . . 'a guarantor of men's rights against one another'—instead of being, as it should be, a rule of life such as will make the members of a polis good and just." *The State and Society: Peru in Comparative Perspective* (Princeton: Princeton University Press, 1978), p. 30.

sounds pious and tiresome. The assumption appears to be that a positive consensus must precede democratic practice, rather than vice versa.[20]

The yearning for holism beneath the widely advertised pragmatism of Brazilian elites is the product of cultural as well as institutional-historic forces. The struggle to reconcile the imperatives of accumulation and distribution and the demands for order and autonomy does not lead with any certainty to the formation of a political community, to a transcendental consensus. Taken literally, a political solution of this type can be thought utopian and archaic, hopelessly deviant from the practical and developmental mainstream of Brazilian public life. Yet the insistence by many of the elites that a constitutive agreement must precede the sorting-out of specific interests suggests that the idealist strain has deep roots in the political culture of Brazil.

One promising development is that authoritarianism of the coarsest variety, with troops in the streets and dissidents in prison, seems just about exhausted in Brazil, for the time being. A cycle of democratic experimentation is underway, if for no other reason than that blatant despotism is no longer seen as efficient, much less equitable, in most elite quarters. Although chronic deadlock is conceivable, the least likely outcome is one in which a unified social and ideological current gains political hegemony. The challenge comes in institutionalizing a nascent pluralism.[21] During the twentieth century in Brazil, previous attempts to reach this goal have drifted toward a disorganized populism and, then, onto a wintery but not unpopular authoritarianism.[22]

Ideologically, Brazilian elites present a mixed picture. The infirmity of their politics is the extreme difficulty they have in coming to a constitutive arrangement about the terms of conflict among themselves, even if they settle many other issues by way of pragmatic bargaining. Once the crisscrossing nature of the multiple cleavages in Brazilian politics is recognized, along with the great ambivalence—the simultaneous distrust of conciliation

[20] This point is elaborated by Fernando Henrique Cardoso, "Democracia, Simplesmente," *Isto É*, August 3, 1977: 33-37. The title of the interview is misleading, since Cardoso makes clear that the movement toward democracy in Brazil is anything but simple.

[21] The advantage that the military enjoys in a situation like this is that even if it cannot impose consensus, it can usually enforce unity within its own ranks. This discipline, compared to the clamoring of several voices from the opposition, has popular appeal. Furthermore, the breakdown in the more stringent authoritarian controls and the growing differentiation of Brazilian society do not automatically "converge" toward a stable and legitimate pluralism. Compare Stephen White, "Communist Systems and the 'Iron Law of Pluralism'," *British Journal of Political Science* 8 (1978): 101-117.

[22] See Francisco Weffort, *O Populismo na Política Brasileira* (Rio de Janeiro: Editora Paz e Terra, 1978).

and the fear of confrontation—that this fosters among the elites, it is fairly easy to understand the claim that while Brazilian politics is not generally polarized between extremes, neither does it possess a consensual center.[23]

This difficulty impedes a clean break with authoritarianism. Because most of the issues are not fused, such that abrupt political change might carry with it a clearly alternative social program, continued transition may involve an amalgam that is mostly nonviolent but virtually immobilist— a deadlock that is not a disaster yet is unsatisfactory to a majority of interests.

Another factor should also be mentioned. All of the values discussed in this book—economic growth, organizational autonomy, order, and social distribution—are clearly public goods. But, at least in the Brazilian context, one of these—the autonomy of competing interests—is perhaps the most truly collective, the least divisible. Revolutionary scenarios notwithstanding, the redistribution of material benefits in Brazil is a matter of degree, and it involves tangible, palpable rewards and compensations for specific groups. The problem of liberty for contending groups is less tangible and more general; it loses meaning as a collective good when tolerance is restricted and some groups excluded. This perspective on autonomy and liberty has fewer precedents in Brazilian political thought than does the corporatist tradition. Furthermore, because of its remoteness from the lives of many Brazilians, it is difficult to rally sustained support for this apparently empty, yet basic, tenet of the pluralistic ethic.

The manifest fallacy in drawing lessons about authoritarianism, about elites, and about the methods for studying them from the results presented here is that this has been a case study of a single country at a single slice in time. The observation is true enough; it is also overly earnest. Since much of what passes for epistemology in the social sciences is personal taste raised to the level of principle, I will limit my obiter dicta to one point only.

For some time, analysts of political development have been concerned with setting their interpretations in historical context, even at the risk of

[23] It bears stressing that it is probably less the multidimensional nature of Brazilian ideologies, alone, than their frustrated organizational expression that makes the elites so insecure about threats to their autonomy. This pair of factors also helps account for what looks like an ingrained tendency for the elites to categorize one another as in either a subordinate or superior position relative to themselves, and a trained incapacity to treat one another more or less as equals. Still, it is fairly clear that the multidimensionality of elite belief systems, by accustoming the elites to uncertainty, makes for a modicum of tolerance. It may also explain—although here I am in a realm of untested hypothesis—the comparative scarcity in Brazilian culture as well as politics of chiliastic and didactic treatises. Compare Heloisa Buarque de Hollanda, *Impressões de Viagem* (São Paulo: Brasiliense, 1980).

relying for their sources on second-hand history. But, despite an occasional nod in the direction of *mentalités*, there has been less concern about the danger of resorting to predigested psychology in order to understand the ideologies of political actors. More than enough bad analyses based on one psychological perspective or another have been written to make ignoring them a defensible position, and there is something to be said for the need to get structural and institutional forces straight before launching an investigation of cognitive and emotional variables whose causal relevance and explanatory significance seem less compelling.

But it is a tendentious step from these observations to the suggestion that ideologies are at most interior decoration, a matter perhaps of aesthetic, miniaturist interest but of no scientific concern within the grander architecture of structures and institutions. The validity of such judgments depends, in the first instance, on what it is that is to be explained. Even then, it is extremely difficult to come up with the conditions for a meaningful test of the importance of psychological, ideological, and cultural influences, relative to that of presumably less flimsy factors.

While it is no doubt useful to worry about this sort of thing, discussions of the problems associated with extrapolating back and forth from individual to aggregate levels rarely contain substantive ideas, and it may be that most of us manage to arrive at fresh conclusions despite, rather than with the aid of, our methodological inhibitions and paraphernalia. "Imagination and history," Thompson notes, "are separate and opposed only in the simple sociology that regards facts and values, social structure and ideology, as repetitive examples of objective truth and subjective falsehood."[24]

[24] William Irwin Thompson, *The Imagination of an Insurrection* (New York: Oxford University Press, 1967), p. 232. Compare Joyce Appleby, "Social Science and Human Nature," *democracy* 1 (1981): 116-126, and Clifford Geertz, "Blurred Genres: The Refiguration of Social Thought," *American Scholar* 9 (1980): 165-179. For my purposes, this literature is a matter of interest but not of great concern. It seems to me that the most pressing "levels of analysis" problem in the study of Brazilian politics is of a different sort, involving questions of elite-nonelite relations that the present volume touches hardly at all and that require book-length treatment in their own right. For a start, see Peter McDonough, "Repression and Representation in Brazil," paper presented at the Centennial Conference on Mosca's Theory of the Ruling Class, Northern Illinois University, DeKalb, Illinois, September 7-9, 1981.

Appendix

The Nature of the Evidence

The present volume is based on field work conducted in 1972 and 1973. It forms part of a research project involving interviews not only with various sectors of the Brazilian elite but also with a sample of the adult population in six states of the center-south of the country ($n = 1,314$) and with a sample of members of the largest labor syndicates in metropolitan Rio de Janeiro and São Paulo ($n = 352$).

The purpose of the study was to trace the variety and strength of political linkages between elites and nonelites as well as within the elite establishment itself. The study focused on two kinds of elite-mass connections: (1) those based on geographical units (the Brazilian states) through which the literate populace is supposed to be represented in the national congress, and (2) those based on functional units—that is, working-class syndicates organized around occupational categories. Comparison of the modes of representation is of special interest in the study of corporatist and conventional territorial politics. The larger study is therefore an offshoot not only of research traditions about Latin American authoritarianism but also of a program of investigation about political representation.

My focus is exclusively on the elite materials; the data on elite-mass relations are the subject of companion studies.[1]

The Elite Samples

At the most general level, there seem to be two rationales for the selection of elite groups for study. One stems from the tradition originating with Mosca and Pareto, the other from neo-Marxist explorations of the relative

---

[1] See Amaury G. de Souza, "The Nature of Corporatist Representation in Brazil," Ph.D. dissertation, Massachusetts Institute of Technology, 1978. Parts of the mass data are examined in doctoral dissertations by Fábio Wanderley Reis (Harvard), Carlos Hasenbalg (University of California, Berkeley), Marcus Figueiredo (University of Chicago), and Youssef Cohen (University of Michigan).

autonomy of the state.[2] Despite their theoretical differences, it is difficult to make out operative discrepancies between the approaches with respect to guidelines for sampling. The perspectives converge on the notion that business leaders (members of the capitalist class) and government executives (state managers) are key elements in the decision-making process. Beyond this agreement of common sense, the selection of elite actors is probably as much the result of resources and opportunity as of theoretical choice. In addition, neither approach has focused attention on explicitly authoritarian systems. For the most part, they have been concerned with advanced capitalist societies in the Western democratic tradition. Neither orientation determined our sampling strategy.[3]

Several years ago, the literature on elites was enlivened by a debate over the merits and drawbacks of various selection criteria: by institutional standards, by indicators of active weight in decision making, and by measures of reputational power. The interest of this discussion lay mostly in the possibility that, in nominally pluralist systems, the three dimensions of power might be partly independent of one another.[4]

But in Brazil, organizational and behavioral power overlap very closely. There are no gray eminences behind a façade of democratic pretensions; the system is avowedly elitist. Thus, the influence of this sampling debate on the present study was marginal.

We arrived, finally, at a sample composed of three types of actors: coercive, utilitarian, and normative elites. The labels are suggestive rather than definitive. They are not meant to indicate that the three categories are mutually exclusive. Furthermore, the typology was at best implicit when

[2] In addition to the literature cited in the Introduction, see the review article of Thomas R. Dye, *Who's Running America? Institutional Leadership* (Englewood Cliffs, N.J.: Prentice Hall, 1976), by Alan Stone, *American Political Science Review* 72 (1978): 673-674. See also Harold R. Kerbo and L. Richard Della Fave, "The Empirical Side of the Power Elite Debate: An Assessment and Critique of Recent Research," *Sociological Quarterly* 20 (1979): 5-22, and Michael Useem, "Studying the Corporation and Corporate Elite," *American Sociologist* 14 (1979): 97-107.

[3] There is considerably more literature on methods of elite interviewing than on elite sampling. See, for example, Joel D. Aberbach, James D. Chesney, and Bert A. Rockman, "Exploring Elite Political Attitudes: Some Methodological Lessons," *Political Methodology* 2 (1975): 1-28; Robert Leonardi, Raffaela Nanetti, and Robert D. Putnam, "Attitude Stability among Italian Elites," *American Journal of Political Science* 23 (1979): 463-494; and Harriet Zuckerman, "Interviewing an Ultra-Elite," *Public Opinion Quarterly* 36 (1972): 159-175.

[4] See, for example, Peter Bachrach, *The Theory of Democratic Elitism* (Boston: Little, Brown and Company, 1967); Seymour Martin Lipset and Aldo Solari, eds., *Elites in Latin America* (New York: Oxford University Press, 1967); Philip Stanworth and Anthony Giddens, eds., *Elites and Power in British Society* (London: Cambridge University Press, 1974); and Beth Mintz et al., "Problems of Proof in Elite Research," *Social Problems* 23 (1976): 314-324.

we began to design the sample. It evolved from a series of conceptual and practical considerations that had to be reconciled at the two main stages of sampling. The first stage entailed the selection of elite sectors, the second the selection of individual elites within sectors.[5]

The Selection of Elite Sectors

The fact that Brazil is a frankly authoritarian system makes the preliminary stage of sampling easy. There is hardly any doubt about the identity of the principal actors. In addition, with the exception of the bishops, the nationally powerful elites are centered in three areas: Brasília, Rio de Janeiro, and São Paulo. Unlike in the United States, most of the elites in Brazil are geographically accessible.

Three criteria entered into the selection process at the preliminary stage. First, an elite sector had to be considered powerful in national affairs by scholars acquainted with Brazil. By this standard, the top civil servants and the directors of the leading industrial and financial corporations entered the lists. The top civil servants include the executive officers of the large state-owned companies as well as high-level ministerial bureaucrats. The businessmen include directors of the large multinational and domestic enterprises.[6]

Second, an elite sector could be included, even if it did not meet the first criterion, if it exercised some formal representative function. This drew in the politicians from the opposition and government parties as well as the presidents of the national labor confederations, state federations, and the larger local syndicates in Rio and São Paulo. Leaders of the largest business interest groups in Rio and São Paulo were included by reason of both the first and second criteria. They form the counterpart, among the "productive classes," of the workers' organizations.

The second standard of selection derived from our interest in the modes of representation. It also stemmed from a recognition that there are various modes of power in Brazil. During the Médici era, neither the politicians nor the labor leaders exercised influence over strategic decisions at the national level. Yet even during the Médici era, they could not be dispensed with. They have a latent power that sets limits on the excesses of authoritarian politics. In their etiolated form, they also help prop up the author-

[5] Compare Helmut Palme, "Criteria for the Selection of Sectors and Positions in an Elite Study," paper presented at the meetings of the International Political Science Association, Montreal, August 19-25, 1973.

[6] It does not follow from the fact that these sectors are known to be powerful that all the businessmen and state managers are powerful, or equally so. This depends to some extent on their ranking within their respective hierarchies, a point to be clarified in the discussion of the sampling procedures used within each sector.

itarian state. The government regularly purged and otherwise intimidated dissident elements from the political and labor spheres, but it could not eliminate politicians and labor militants as such, and in some cases recalcitrant figures survived. In fact, the persecutory mania of the more repressive elements often turned their own appointees against the government from sheer outrage and out of sympathy with individuals who were not so much of the opposition as they were in the wrong place at the wrong time.

Third, a sector might be omitted from the study, even though it met one or both of the foregoing criteria, if problems of access were deemed insuperable. The most important group excluded by this test is the military. While some retired military personnel appear among the top civil servants, we have no proper sample of the active military command.

Another key group we did not interview is composed of the men assigned to the president's office: the heads of the civil and military "houses," the director of the National Information Service (the internal security apparatus), and so on. On the other hand, within the sectors chosen, the samples are properly representative. I shall have more to say later about the actual and putative effects of the third criterion.[7]

One group that does not fit under any of the sampling guidelines is the peak of the ecclesiastical hierarchy. The bishops are neither transparently powerful nor representative; moreover, access to them was made difficult by their dispersion throughout the country. In the end, a decision was taken to sample the bishops. They can be considered eminent on normative grounds. And in fact they enjoy a distinctive kind of power in Brazil. They cannot, as is sometimes believed, face down the military without fear of reprisal. But the bishops are exceptional in that they form an organized

[7] There are two other groups, besides the military and the inner circle of the presidency, that might have been included in an ideal sample but that were not approached for practical and prudential reasons. One is composed of large landowners, who presented two problems. First, they are difficult to reach because of their geographical dispersion. Second, there is no readily accessible and reliable listing of the population of Brazilian landowners, broken down by size of holding. The other group is composed of Brazilian high society-café society: the *alta roda*. This group intersects partially with some of the other estates—with the businessmen and the more prominent civil servants, for example; their names are given in standard blue-book type publications such as Marise de Ouro Prêto and Helena Gondim, *Sociedade Brasileira* (Rio de Janeiro: Muller, 1970). While the group constitutes a possibly fascinating addition to conventional elite samples (for one thing, it would have added some females to the elites), its status in the power hierarchy is nebulous. Moreover, the main avocation of persons in this group is gossip, a habit that could have jeopardized the completion of the study.

as well as normative center of power, and this gives them leverage for resistance.[8]

In summary, the selection of the elite sectors resulted from a mixture of theoretical interests and practical constraints, involving both inclusionary and exclusionary criteria. Certain groups are obvious candidates for elite sampling. The state managers and the businessmen are such elites by consensus. In more abstract terms, they are charged with the coercive and utilitarian functions of the system, sometimes in concert and sometimes against one another.

The other elite sectors—the labor leaders, the politicians, and the bishops—are important in different ways. While they are not powerful in the same sense or to the same degree as the civil servants, the industrialists, and the bankers, they have a certain kind of power—latent, symbolic, ideological, normative. The nomenclature matters less than the fact that, despite their virtual monopoly of the means of violence and production, the state managers and the businessmen cannot eliminate, and in some ways depend on, the labor leaders, the politicians, and the bishops for the legitimization of the system.[9]

The Selection of Elites within Sectors

Once the elite sectors had been chosen, the next stage of sampling involved the selection of respondents within each group. Since the internal structure of the estates differs, sampling procedures varied from sector to sector.

---

[8] See Thomas C. Bruneau, *The Political Transformation of the Brazilian Catholic Church* (London: Cambridge University Press, 1974).

[9] Mention should be made of one subsample that was interviewed but which is not analyzed in the present volume. The questionnaire was administered to eighteen leaders of the liberal professions (law, medicine, engineering) and prominent journalists and editorialists in Rio and São Paulo. These individuals are included in analyses presented in Peter McDonough and Amaury de Souza, *The Politics of Population in Brazil: Elite Ambivalence and Public Demand* (Austin: University of Texas Press, 1981).

The sample of "intellectuals" is not used here, for two reasons. First, it is uncertain in that it is extremely difficult to fix criteria for defining a population of such individuals. Their institutional affiliations are varied, quantitative measures of membership in the population are dubious, and reputational measures tend to be ideologically biased. While I believe the sample of intellectuals to be close to representative, it does not stand up to samples of the other sectors. At least, it is hard to document the representativeness of the sample. Second, and more important, the intellectuals turn out to be a very heterogeneous group on most attitudinal measures, and this suggests that the sample is a proper one. On the other hand, the heterogeneity of the intellectuals complicates analysis, especially when the number of interviews is small. The omission of this sample is particularly regrettable because intellectuals probably have greater influence in Latin America than in advanced industrial societies; they are, or are often thought to be, arbiters of the cultural community. For the sake of completeness, information about the sample of intellectuals is included in Table A.1.

For some groups, such as the industrial and the financial, hierarchies by size can be clearly discerned. Size was measured by liquid assets for the industrial firms and by deposits for the banks.[10] A similar process was adopted in sampling the syndical leaders, where "size" was defined by membership.[11]

Cutoff points for defining the universe to be sampled in the civil service are more problematic. They are obscured by the marked power differences between ministries (the ministry of finance, for example, being closer to the center of action than the ministry of health) and the occasional incomparability of similar-sounding job classifications, among other factors. We settled on the rank of "national institute director" as the minimal level in order to restrict the government sample to the higher reaches of the executive and the judiciary (ministers and secretaries-general of the ministries, supreme court judges, executive officers of public companies, and so on).[12]

[10] The populations are the top five hundred industrial corporations and the top two hundred banks. The sources are *Conjuntura Econômica*, published by the Fundação Getúlio Vargas, and *Quem é Quem na Economia Brasileira*, an annual special number of *Visão*. There are slight discrepancies between the figures released by these sources, but when considered as orders of magnitude the correlation between the rankings is very high. Other sources were used to check the sample of businessmen: for example, *As Grandes Companias*, an annual publication of Editora Banas in São Paulo. This is helpful because it gives the composition of the boards of directors for the major companies. A number of specialized publications were also consulted, most of them annual special numbers released by *Visão* in São Paulo. *Os Agentes do Desenvolvimento*, part of the *Perfil* series of *Visão*, contains a breakdown of the development-financing (public) and investment (private) banks in Brazil. Two other publications of the *Visão* group also proved useful. One is the monthly *Dirigente Industrial*, which often contains features on particular branches of Brazilian industry. The other is *Brazil Report*, an annual publication in English, directed at the foreign investment community, with a fairly detailed ranking of major industrial and commercial enterprises.

[11] Syndicates are nested within federations, and federations within confederations. For my purposes, the determining figure is the membership totals in the areas of metropolitan Rio and São Paulo. As of 1972, there were eighty-five labor syndicates in Rio and ninety in São Paulo. Variation in size is extreme. In Rio, the range was between 121 and over 36,000 members; in São Paulo, between 68 and nearly 160,000. The distribution of syndical members, like the size of industrial companies and banks, is skewed. In Rio, the mean and median membership figures were respectively 3,835 and 1,551; in São Paulo, 5,686 and 1,834. The cutoff for sampling was a membership of 5,000. Thus, the labor leaders are drawn from the larger organizations. See de Souza, "The Nature of Corporatist Representation in Brazil."

[12] The primary sources for the sample of civil servants (as well as of politicians) are (a) *Autoridades Brasileiras*, an annual mimeographed publication of the Agência Nacional, Serviço de Documentação, Rio de Janeiro, and (b) *Perfil da Administração Federal*, an annual special number published by *Visão* in São Paulo. The first publication is official; the *Agência Nacional* is attached to the president's office. However, the second publication is in some respects more useful. For example, it gives organization charts for the ministries and basic biographical information about major figures.

The result is to exclude a great many middle- and lower-rank *técnicos*. Some of these individuals are influential within their own spheres, especially if they are attached to powerful ministries. Furthermore, a few of them are rising stars of ministerial caliber. But their inclusion would have to be based on comparatively uncertain sampling methods, for example, by reputation. On the other hand, the top echelon of state managers is made up of an unequivocally powerful stratum of elites, all of whom command organizational resources.[13]

Results

All interviews were conducted by Brazilians. Most were done in the offices, but some were done in the homes of the respondents. Access was often facilitated by respondents who, once they were interviewed, provided introductions to their colleagues.

Table A.1 provides a detailed breakdown of the number and relative frequency of respondents in each sector. Table A.2 presents a simplified

TABLE A.1
The Elite Sample in Detail, in Descending Order of Response Rate

Elite Sector	Target N	Percent of Total	N Obtained	Percent of Sample	Response Rate
Labor Leaders	85	13.0	53	19.7	62.4
Business Associations	33	5.0	19	7.1	57.6
Public Companies	27	4.1	15	5.6	55.6
Liberal Professions[a]	33	5.0	18	6.7	54.8
ARENA Politicians	65	9.9	33	12.3	50.8
Multinationals	56	8.5	23	8.6	41.1
National Finance	43	6.6	16	5.9	37.2
MDB Politicians	39	5.9	14	5.2	36.9
National Industry	76	11.6	26	9.7	34.2
Civil Service	155	23.6	41	15.2	26.5
Bishops	44	6.7	11	4.1	25.0
Totals	656	100.0	269	100.0	41.0

[a] Included in sample but excluded from analysis. See footnote 9 for a description of the "liberal professionals" subsample.

[13] Certain details are left vague throughout this section to protect the anonymity of the respondents. I cannot cite the names of the labor syndicates, the states that the politicians represent, or break the sample of civil servants down by ministry. In fact, all such identifying information has been erased from the computer records of the interviews, and I can no longer match names to individual protocols.

TABLE A.2
Major Groups in the Elite Sample, as Aggregated for Data-Analysis

Elite Sector	N	Grouped N	Percent of Sample	Response Rate
Labor Leaders	53	53	21.1	62.4
ARENA Politicians	33	47	18.7	45.2
MDB Politicians	14			
National Industry	26			
Multinationals	24	84	33.5	35.6
National Finance	15			
Business Associations	19			
Civil Service	41	56	22.3	30.8
Public Companies	15			
Bishops	11	11	4.4	25.0
Totals	251	251	100.0	40.3

NOTE: ARENA and MDB are joined in the analysis of elite background but separated in the anlaysis of elite ideology.

version of the same information, with the elite groups aggregated in the format in which they are usually depicted during the analysis.

The target *n* is the number of elites selected within each sector as possible respondents. Sometimes, as with the labor leaders, the civil servants, the heads of the public companies, and the presidents of the business interest associations, this number comprises the entire population, defined by the within-sector cutoff criteria. For the remaining groups, such as the politicians, the bishops, and the directors of the industrial and financial enterprises, the target *n* is a fraction of the larger population. For example, from among the largest five hundred nonfinancial companies, every third company was selected by systematic random sampling.

At the outset of the study, we expected to obtain about a 50 percent response rate, and we also wanted to secure enough respondents in each sector to permit statistical analysis. So, in those sectors where the universe of elites is relatively small, as with the labor leaders and the civil servants, we kept the target *n* equivalent to the population. Where the elite population is larger, as in the case of the politicians and the businessmen, we sampled within the sector to arrive at the target *n*.

A second preliminary is in order. Table A.1 presents the relative size of the target *n* and the actual number of interviews, proportional to the total size of the target *n* and the sample. These figures are useful as documentation, but they are not very important for the analysis of the data.

First, with elites, numbers tend to be inversely related to power. The present case substantiates this tendency: the most numerous of the elites, the labor leaders, are probably the least powerful. Second, only under exceptional circumstances are the elites treated as a bloc, a procedure that would overrepresent the most numerous. Almost always, they are presented sector by sector, so that the variable number of cases across the groups does not affect the results.[14]

The overall response rate was 41 percent, ranging from a high of 62 percent among the labor leaders to a low of 25 percent among the bishops. The sample of labor leaders is the most complete. Unlike most of the other elites during the Médici era, the latter had time on their hands. They were not put off by the length of the interview schedule, which consumed on the average almost an hour and a half.[15]

The sample of opposition politicians is quite small because their congressional representation before the elections of 1974 was marginal. In fact, the MDB is overrepresented relative to the ARENA. We boosted the proportion of MDB politicians in order to reach a minimum number of cases for analysis.[16]

The number of bishops is reduced for a different reason. Very few of them are to be found in Rio, São Paulo, and Brasília, and the cost of travelling to their dioceses for interviews was prohibitive. However, the sample of bishops is not confined to individuals from these three areas. We interviewed bishops from the interior during their infrequent trips to Rio.[17]

[14] See Leslie Kish, "Sampling Organizations of Groups of Unequal Sizes," *American Sociological Review* 30 (1965): 564-572.

[15] It is difficult to establish a standard against which to judge the response rate for a study of this sort. The success rate is low in comparison to interview surveys of general populations and in line with the results of mailed questionnaire surveys. But neither of these provides a standard for the special population under study here. Sampling procedures and results for an elite study similar to ours are reported by Allen H. Barton and R. Wayne Parsons, "Consensus and Conflict among American Leaders," *Public Opinion Quarterly* 38 (1974-1975): 509-528.

[16] At the time the study was conducted, the Brazilian senate had 66 members, 3 for each unit of the federation. Of these, 59 senators belonged to the ARENA and 7 to the MDB. In the chamber of deputies, 221 were from the ARENA and 87 from the MDB out of a total of 308. All told, there were 374 directly elected national politicians. Over both houses, ARENA dominated MDB in the ratio of 2.98 to 1.0. In our sample, the ratio is 2.36 to 1.0.

[17] Still, there are disproportionately more bishops from the Rio-São Paulo region than there should be in a national sample. If there is any sector sample that may be biased, it is that of the bishops. This qualification should be kept in mind when reading the following paragraphs. It may be that the over-representation of bishops from Rio-São Paulo lends a progressive cast to the attitudes of individuals from this sector, but I have no side information against which to check this possibility. Indeed, some would argue that bishops located in the Amazon dioceses, or in the poverty-stricken northeast, are more progressive than the clergy

There is no indication that the differential response rates can be attributed to a variable propensity among the elite groups to refuse to be interviewed for political reasons. In other words, while some elites turned down requests for interviews out of caution and discretion, this tendency is not peculiar to certain sectors rather than others. Thus, none of the sector samples is biased in such a way as to prevent valid inferences about the elite populations. This is a strong claim, and it merits explanation.

First, a principal cause of nonresponse was the length of the questionnaire. Asking for more than fifteen minutes of a national figure's time for the purpose of conducting an academic interview reduces the response rate. But, with the partial exception of the labor leaders and in some instances the politicians, this refusal factor operates uniformly across the elite sectors.

Second, logistical and circumstantial factors operated to reduce response rates unevenly across the sectors. Simultaneously with the elite survey, we conducted two others: one of the general population and one of labor syndicate members. Resources were spread thin. We eliminated the northeast—an extremely interesting area for the study of agrarian politics—in order to complete the special sample in the labor syndicates. As for the elite sample, respondents in Rio and São Paulo were in closer reach than those in Brasília. The distance to Brasília and the costs of maintaining an interviewing staff there were the main reasons for the modest response rate among the politicians, who are actually quite approachable. Because of their schedules, the civil servants are less accessible, and their residence in Brasília compounds the problem.

In retrospect, we probably could have attained a greater than 50 percent response rate by devoting exclusive attention to the elite study. This hypothetical possibility does not change the results, but neither do the logistics of the study suggest that the fluctuating response rates are themselves indicative of bias.[18]

Another potential source of bias can be traced to the temptation to interview secondary figures for the sake of padding the sample. The temptation is particularly strong in the face of access problems and the need to obtain a statistically adequate number of interviews.

Our position on this difficulty was, first, not to attempt interviews at all

---

in other areas. In the absence of systematic data, however, most of this remains speculation. It should also be mentioned that no distinction among cardinals, archbishops, and bishops has been made, just as senators and deputies have been mixed together in the sample of politicians.

[18] One way to confirm this proposition is to compare the response rates given in Tables A.1 and A.2 with the left-right leanings of the elite sectors reported in Chapter Five (see especially Table 5.1). There is no correlation, at the level of elite groups, between response rates and ideological position.

in those sectors where problems of access were daunting (for example, the military); and second, to stick with the top figures in the sectors chosen. We could probably have managed to interview a handful of generals, but not more; the product would not have been worth the effort or the risk. Within the sectors chosen, however, sampling procedures were methodical. Again, this drags down the response rate, but it does not damage the quality of the sample in the sense of creating a bias within the sectors.

There are hierarchies within as well as between sectors. For example, the listing of industrialists includes the executive officers of the largest five hundred firms, and the bankers are drawn from among the executive officers of the top two hundred financial organizations. Both rankings are highly skewed, with a very small number of extremely large companies and a much larger incidence of relative pigmies. Yet for each of the companies selected, we interviewed the principal figures. We did not interview vice-presidents for public relations, corporate counsels, and other front men; we confined ourselves to members of the executive boards.[19]

Another reason for our decision not to interview middle- and lower-level elites stems from a judgment that they respond differently from the higher-ups. In the course of preparing for the survey, we examined interview protocols from an earlier study of middle managers and bureaucrats.[20] It became apparent that respondents in subordinate strata tend to qualify their answers for political reasons. They make a point of their agreement with the policies of the regime.

In our sample, we encountered greater self-confidence and a willingness

[19] The skew in assets among the leading corporations should be emphasized. Let us take as an example the top five hundred nonfinancial enterprises in Brazil by major type: state-owned, foreign-owned, and national-private, where "foreign-owned" means that a majority share of capital is controlled by non-Brazilian interests. All of the figures pertain to 1971, the last year for which complete data were available when our sample was designed. In thousands of *cruzeiros,* the mean and median liquid capital of the three types of companies are, in order: 447,800 and 134,780; 83,838 and 39,000; 45,889 and 29,494. This ranking is characteristic of the "tripod" dominated by the public companies in coalition with the multinationals, with Brazilian private enterprise taking up the rear. See Peter B. Evans, "Multinationals, State-Owned Corporations, and the Transformation of Imperialism: A Brazilian Case Study," *Economic Development and Cultural Change* 26 (1977): 43-64.

Our sample matches this hierarchy. When we pool the three types of enterprises and compare the proportions of public, foreign, and national-private capital between the target *n* and the respondents, the following ratios are obtained:

Ratio	Target N	Sample
Public/Private	4.57	4.51
Public/Foreign	3.46	3.29
Foreign/Private	1.32	1.37

[20] The study was conducted in 1968 and 1969 by Eli Diniz Ciqueira and Carlos Hasenbalg of the Instituto Universitário de Pesquisas do Rio de Janeiro.

to sound progressive. This pattern creates problems of its own, dealt with in the course of the analysis. But there is no reason to believe that we missed the true reactionaries by refraining from sampling the military and the president's staff. The middle and lower ranks of the elite hierarchy within an organization tend to follow the party line and to look over their shoulder while doing so. Those at the top tend to be less preoccupied with this sort of problem, probably because many of them are the originators of the party line.[21]

Thus, while our failure to obtain interviews at the supreme heights of the Brazilian state makes the elite sample incomplete, it is debatable whether the results are biased. Observers have noted the extreme concentration of power in Brazil and the manner in which key decisions are often taken, without consultation, by a small group of individuals or even by a single individual, the president himself.[22] But this affects the representativeness of the sample only if it can be assumed that the attitudes, values, and perceptions of the top military command and the men in the president's office differ markedly from those of the groups, especially conservative groups, from whom we obtained interviews. As Chapter Six demonstrates, the elites themselves do not perceive the military as being extraordinarily reactionary, compared to other generally conservative interests.[23]

In summary, the problem of bias—of systematic error in the elite sample—does not seem very troubling. But two other difficulties should be recognized. One is caused by the low response rates in some of the sectors; the other is due to the low absolute number of respondents, whatever the response rate.

---

[21] This does not mean that elites at the top are entirely fearless and frank but only that they tend to be more outspoken than those below them. The pattern also varies from sector to sector. The dissident elites generally have more reason to be cautious than the incumbents.

[22] See Jonathan Kandell, "Brazil's Chief Political Loner: Ernesto Geisel," *New York Times*, April 18, 1977: 5, and "A Eleição com um Voto Só," *Veja*, January 11, 1978: 20-55.

[23] There is another indication that we did not omit the genuine conservatives—that is, bias the sample toward the more progressive elites who, it might be thought, are more willing to be interviewed in the first place. (For what it is worth, this objection seems more common among the Brazilianists than the Brazilians with whom I have discussed the sample design and results.) Earlier I noted that the tendency to refuse interviews for political reasons does not vary across the elite sectors, even though the response rate varies markedly. Even if this is granted, however, it is still natural to argue that the entire sample of respondents leans toward the progressive side, irrespective of possible between-group variation. Although there is no hard-and-fast evidence to dismiss this charge, it should be set in the context of the reverse objection, also brought up in conversations about the sample, that we missed the true progressives, who might have been unwilling to let us past the door for fear of having their views publicized. Both concerns have been voiced with about equal frequency, and I suspect that in practice the potential biases have cancelled each other out.

When response rates go down, standard errors go up. Even though results might not be biased, they may be subject to random noise, which tends to deflate correlations, for example. This difficulty can be endured, since its worst effect is to encourage cautious rather than overstated inferences.[24]

Even if response rates were higher, however, it still might be the case that in certain sectors the number of interviews would have to remain small. The logic of sampling elites tends to be the reverse of that involved in sampling general populations. Large samples of elites are not necessarily more representative, since elites are by definition few in number. This restricts the applicability of conventional statistical techniques, which relies on a "reasonable" number of observations. This problem is handled by a mixture of common sense, qualitative analysis of the discursive responses of the elites, and an illustrative rather than rigorous use of tests of statistical significance.[25]

In summary, the elite sample seems satisfactory. Even a moderate amount of bias would probably not throw off by much estimates of the relative differences among elite estates or of the correlations between variables. It is also possible to fall back on the escape clause that, given the technical and political obstacles to conducting systematic research in Brazil, the wonder is not that the study was done well but that it was done at all and that any sample of Brazilian elites represents an advance. To claim more than this is to invite the skepticism of anyone who has tried to carry out field research in Latin America; anecdotes of disaster come to mind in plenty.

This being said, my assessment is that the sample is not only satisfactory but representative. The judgment is important for two reasons. First, although we could live with the defects of systematic error in parts of the analysis, the problem becomes unacceptable in at least two places: when differences in social background among the elite groups are examined and when the elites' own preferences are laid against their perceptions of the preferences of one another. In the first instance, sampling bias in one sector or another could jeopardize the validity of inferences about contrasts among the sectors. The second case is even more clear-cut: the elites are asked to make point-estimates of the opinions of others, and it is not the relative but the absolute difference between avowed and attributed opinion that makes for misperception. If the sample of any elite sector were unrepresentative, the "misperception" of that sector by the other elites might be a technically rather than a politically caused distortion.

[24] See Leslie Kish, *Survey Sampling* (New York: Wiley, 1965), pp. 509 ff.

[25] See Leslie Kish and Martin Richard Frankel, "Inference from Complex Samples," *Journal of the Royal Statistical Society*, Series B, 36 (1974): 1-36.

Finally, the purpose of a proper sample is to randomize the data, not the findings. The idea that such an approach is unduly mechanical, if not unworkable, has a surface attraction. But its realism is spurious. Conclusions about the unstable and aleatory nature of Latin American politics may be as much a function of the impromptu nature of the methodology employed as of the reality itself.[26]

The Interview Schedule

The questionnaire is long and structured; both properties run against the conventions of elite interviewing. The length of the questionnaire drove down the response rate. Brazilian elites, particularly the businessmen and state managers, budget their time.

Several considerations entered into the decision to employ a structured— that is, largely close-ended—format. One was that, even with the guarantee of confidentiality, the use of tape recorders did not seem advisable under the conditions prevailing in Brazil during the early seventies. Without this device, transcribing entire interviews becomes awkward. Another reason stemmed from the need to maintain some standardization and comparability across a variety of elite groups. This consideration dictated the collection of quantifiable data.

There are two dangers in presenting elites with structured questionnaires: they are likely to be put off by the format itself and, even when they do respond, doubts may arise about the quality of their answers. In order to reduce the first of these problems, we avoided using batteries that have come to be thought of as part of the standard machinery of opinion polls. The atmosphere of psychometric testing was brought to a minimum.

Furthermore, some kinds of measures that tend to baffle members of a general population with low rates of literacy can be used to good effect

---

[26] This statement probably sounds more rigid than it is meant to be. It definitely does not imply that questionnaires concocted according to predetermined schemata can be applied in virtually any setting, without much in the way of pretesting or contextual knowledge. I lived in Brazil continuously for two years before the research was launched. It does suggest, however, that claims regarding the arcane uniqueness of Brazil should be treated with suspicion. Carrying out the elite (and nonelite) surveys produced a number of *contratemps* and bizarre episodes, and the best that can be said for these incidents is that they are not unexpected in large-scale research. One that serves to dispel any notion of laboratorylike conditions involved an attempt by a member of the research staff to interview an elite figure who had already been interviewed by another. A minute or so through the second interview, the respondent asked, "Haven't I answered this before?" The interviewer said that this was impossible, that the study was being carried out according to the strictest scientific standards, that the principal investigators were "experts from the University of Michigan," and so forth. The interview proceeded to the end, the respondent hurrying through it.

with elites. An example is the series of 100-point scales on which the elites were asked to state their preferences pro or con on specific policy issues.[27] Such measures give considerably more latitude than a simple agree-disagree format, although it is doubtful that they yield more information than a 10-point scale. In any case, most of the elites found this approach challenging and interesting.

Still, some of the elites objected to the metric paraphernalia. One called the questionnaire "Kafkaesque"; another thought it was "subliminal." But most responded favorably, and even those who complained about the numbers took the time to respond to the open-ended probes interspersed among the scalar items. Information from these discursive responses provides a check on problems of validity.

The probes took the form of a brief follow-up to the metric scales: "Could you tell me more about that?" "Why do you think so?" et cetera. Responses were recorded verbatim in writing. This could not be done for all items; to do so would have expanded the questionnaire to unmanageable size. We concentrated on the basic priorities of the elites (the trade-offs among economic, social, and political goals) and on five key policy issues, from birth control to government-opposition relations.[28]

As it turned out, on narrowly technical grounds, we probably could have dispensed with many of the discursive probes. Only quite rarely do elites say one thing in responding to a close-ended item and something irrelevant or contradictory in explaining their response. The metric items are thus reasonably valid indicators of elite opinion, or at least of their private opinions. The fact that the scales discriminate well between conservative and progressive groups gives them a prima facie credibility.

The quantitative measures are not "wrong," but they can be rather cryptic, and it is for this reason that the open-ended probes are useful. They reveal that the elites give different, although not mutually exclusive, reasons, for apparently identical responses. They also help us understand

[27] A typical question in this format is the following: "In comparison with the situation nowadays in Brazil concerning the limits of opposition to the government, where would you place yourself on this scale?" The respondent was handed a card, on which was printed the scale, thus:

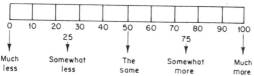

[28] See Robert M. Groves, "On the Mode of Administering a Questionnaire and Responses to Open-Ended Probes," *Social Science Research* 7 (1978): 213-256.

the variations in shading behind a score of "25" and one of "45" on the 100-point scale. Some of them are presented in the following pages.

A final note: matters of form and style, of the presentation and flow of the questionnaire, are crucial to eliciting meaningful responses that can be organized in an intelligible way. For all this, the primary element remains the content of the questionnaire. It is overtly political, directed at what we believe to be some of the touchiest and most vital issues in Brazil. Once we had decided to attempt to interview the leading figures in Brazilian public life, it made little sense to us to tone down the survey instrument. The elites, of course, were well aware of the political content of the survey. As one of them said, "Once in a while, it is good to lay down on the couch and think things over."[29]

Categorization of Elite Groups

Since the objective is to understand the structure and the ideology of multiple elite sectors, no one group is singled out for special analysis. I do not disaggregate certain elite sectors that might, for other purposes, be examined in greater detail. For example, the labor leaders are treated as a unit, even though this group contains three distinct tiers (confederation, federation, and syndicate levels). Similarly, the businessmen could be divided between the industrialists and the bankers, and the industrialists themselves might be split between the directors of nationally owned and the directors of multinational corporations. Analogous divisions can be

---

[29] One factor not mentioned directly in this how-to discussion concerns the quotidian politics of the study. Around the turn of the century, a Portuguese politician was quoted as saying "If these people [figures in public life] knew what they had to gain by being honest, they would be honest for the wrong reasons [*por maldade*]." There is a certain wisdom to this stance; "strategy" is probably not the right word. The arbitrary nature of repression under the Médici regime may not have been particularly efficient, but then it probably was not meant to be. In any event, it became clear very early on that any attempt to pull the study off by resorting to deception could prove very dangerous, although almost certainly not to me as a foreigner. Playing by being devious was not a game that could be won, even supposing a talent or a liking for it. Such considerations prompted us to be sure that the identity of the organizations collaborating in the study as well as the sources of funding were made known to the respondents, that copies of the questionnaire were sent to scholars not participating, and so on. In retrospect, I suppose this approach can be said to have paid off, although at the time it was not so much purposeful as obligatory. One defense available in carrying out research of this sort is *idoneidade*, a disinterested and perhaps disarmingly naive professionalism. See the article, by Jon Elster that concludes with the sentence, "we need to question the assumption of most political science—that the successful politician is one who is better at politics than his rivals" ("Irrational Politics," *London Review of Books*, August 21-September 3, 1980: 11-13). John Huston's *Beat the Devil* carries the same dumb luck message. Compare Mário de Andrade, *Macunaíma: O Herói sem Nenhum Carater*, 6th ed. (São Paulo: Martins, 1971).

imagined for the top civil servants—for example, between the ministerial bureaucrats and the managers of the public companies.

Results are usually presented for less than the maximum possible number of elite sectors for reasons of simplicity. In practice, depicting an analysis for more than half a dozen groups produces confusing arrays of data. Besides, it is often unnecessary. Thus, for example, in the analysis of the social background of the elites, the businessmen are treated as a bloc because the social origins of the executive officers of the national private manufacturing concerns, of the banks, of the multinational corporations, and of the presidents of the business associations do not differ significantly. A similar pattern holds for members of the ARENA and the MDB, and they are treated simply as "politicians" in the analysis of elite origins and mobility.

In the analysis of elite ideology, however, politicians of the government and opposition parties are kept separate. Whatever the similarity in their social origins, the ARENA and the MDB are at odds on most issues. At the same time, on most issues, the businessmen can be treated as a unit, and I do not generally distinguish among the various subsectors of the business community.

It is important to understand the consequences of this aggregation of elite groups. Some loss of information is inevitable. When the industrialists and the financiers are joined together, the implication is not that they are all alike but only that, on a given dimension of social status or opinion, they resemble one another. In statistical terms, there is a significant difference between the businessmen as a whole and the rest of the elites, even though there remains a good deal of variation within the business community.

This within-group heterogeneity constitutes residual, unexplained variance that, were the number of cases sufficient, I could try to reduce by standard multivariate techniques. But I seldom follow this route because the respondents in certain sectors are so few. This is one instance where the logic of elite sampling collides with the logic of quantitative analysis. Qualitative analysis—the exploration of open-ended responses—alleviates this problem to some extent, but there does not seem to be a neat solution to it; nor am I convinced that it requires one.

In summary, the sectoral division of the elites depends to a great extent on the particular dependent variable under consideration. Sometimes the fact that no significant difference between certain elite sectors is uncovered can be an important finding in itself. Such is the case with the general ideological similarity between the national and multinational branches of the business elite. Again, this does not mean that the groups live in perfect harmony; it does mean that vis-à-vis other sectors of the elite they are rather similar. In any event, the presentation of results showing "the business community," or the "state managers," or "the politicians" as simplified categories derives from a group-by-group analysis that enabled me to conclude that a given elite sector could be treated as a single actor without grievous distortion of the facts.

The Substance of Elite Ideology

My purpose here is twofold. I want to transmit a sense of what the elites mean when they declare themselves in favor or opposed to "foreign investment," "income redistribution," and similarly broad issues. Second, I want to specify the notion of the variable polarization of these issues.

Usually, there is no difficulty in making out the relative positions of the elites. The state managers are predictably conservative and the MDB politicians progressive. But the fit between the sectoral location of the elites and their opinions is loose, and it is reasonable to suspect that part of this slack can be traced to the vague phrasing of some of the items.

One way to reduce the problem is to formulate unambiguous questions. The trouble with this solution is that a query that is comprehensible to elites specializing in one area—for example, the regulation of foreign exchange rates—may be perplexing to another—to the bishops, for instance. An alternative way to assess the validity of the responses of the elites is to probe the discursive explanations they give for their positions. This is the approach used here.

Inspection of the open-ended responses of the elites yields detail, not necessarily meaning. On the other hand, it may be arbitrary to reduce the responses to a small number of categories. There seemed to be enough richness to the responses to justify, for any given question, about a dozen categories. The differences between some of the types of answers are occasionally very slight; nevertheless, in such cases, I decided to err on the side of detail. The purpose is not to verify whether the elites know what they are talking about—that is, to check whether they understand the questions at all. Instead, it is to show how the elites define the issues and how several somewhat different rationales and interpretations may underlie identical positions on the closed preference scales.

The discursive responses also convey a feel for the polarization of the issues; elites at either extreme of the debate over government-opposition relations, a strongly politicized issue, defend their views quite forcefully. However, the variable polarization of issues also lends itself to more precise assessment.

Some conventional measures of issue-polarization are, of course, useful. The standard deviations of the policy preferences reported in Chapter Five, and the etas-squared measuring the extent of intersectoral disagreement, provide estimates of issue-polarization.[30] But such measures are not entirely satisfactory. Issues may generate identical coefficients of polarization, and yet there may be some element of conflict or of the potential for conflict that escapes the statistics.

My argument is that, between any two issues with an apparently equivalent potential for generating interelite antagonism, it is the one that directly and unequivocally engages the group rivalries of the elites that stands to produce the greater conflict. The question of government-opposition relations is one such issue. An issue like income redistribution, while highly charged in left-right terms, is not.

Thus, the analytical purpose is to assess the polarizing potential of selected issues. I do this, in part, by scrutinizing the open-ended responses of the elites. This is done not only in connection with the scalar preferences of the elites but also with reference to the importance that the elites assign the issues. The procedure is complicated by the fact that "importance" is notoriously polysemous. But the general idea is fairly simple, and it can be summarized as follows: most of the time, elites who take a positive position on an issue—favoring a more rapid redistribution of income, for example—also attribute high importance to the issue. Conversely, those who opt for a go-slow approach to income redistribution tend to assign the matter less importance. In both cases, importance is a surrogate for priority.

But there are some issues for which importance connotes intensity. It may be that on the question of government-labor relations, for example, the elites who assume a conservative stance give the issue just as much importance as the progressives. By this criterion, government-labor relations have more potential for interelite conflict than the question of income redistribution.

In schematic terms: relatively conflictive issues are those for which the adherents of opposing positions attach about the same importance to their preferences. Persons on one side of the issue give it as much priority as those on the other side. By contrast, on less conflict-ridden issues, the proponents of one alternative give the issue more importance than the advocates of the opposing position. Opinion in the sense of pro-con preferences may be about equally divided. What matters is that one side

[30] That is, the greater the variation of opinion, as measured by the standard deviation on an issue, the greater the conflict-potential of the issue, all things being equal. For example, the controversy over the restoration of *habeas corpus* is pretty much a noncontroversy, since the elites are nearly unanimous in their support for such a measure. The etas-squared are a better measure of issue-polarization, for they indicate the degree of dissension among the elite sectors.

upgrades the issue while the other ranks it lower in priority with the result that logrolling and other forms of compromise are facilitated.[31]

A possible flaw in this reasoning derives from the ambiguity of the meager importance that conservative elites attribute to an issue like income redistribution. It is not at all evident that the low priority they give the issue means that they feel less strongly about the matter than the advocates of rapid redistribution. This is where the discursive responses of the elites come in handy, as a qualitative check on inferences about issue-polarization that are difficult to make on the basis of statistical methods alone.[32]

The Agenda of Issues

A primary function of elites is agenda setting: deciding which issues reach the discussion stage before decisions in favor or against alternative courses are taken.[33] Although I do not reconstruct the processes by which certain issues find a place in the elite forum, while others are tabled, it is possible to make a first approximation of the salience of various issues.

The elites were asked how important they felt each of fifteen different issue-areas were. The issues themselves are a sampling of the topics of elite discourse during the Médici era. With the exception of the question of the legalization of divorce, all of them remain objects of contention in Brazil. Table A.3 gives the average importance attributed to each of the fifteen issues, in descending order, by each of the major sectors.

Very roughly, the ordering of issues from top to bottom corresponds to the climate of the Médici administration, with developmental issues enjoying greater salience than explicitly political controversies. The ordering suffers from the same partial indeterminancy that afflicts the group attention and support/opposition measures analyzed in Chapter Three. It does not represent a precise ranking, since the elites did not establish comparative priorities down the line of issues. In a moment, this inflation will be corrected. However, despite the methodological distortion, the outline of issue-priorities is visible. The human capital issue of educational reform is accorded almost universal priority, and population planning is relegated to the status of a nonproblem.

[31] Compare David Butler and Donald E. Stokes, *Political Change in Britain* (New York: St. Martin's Press, 1971), and Robert A. Dahl, *A Preface to Democratic Theory* (Chicago: University of Chicago Press, 1956).

[32] For a coverage of the problems involved in measuring the polarization of issues, see Douglas W. Rae and Michael Taylor, *The Analysis of Political Cleavages* (New Haven: Yale University Press, 1970). See also Shlomit Levy, "Involvement as a Component of Attitude: Theory and Political Examples," in *Theory Construction and Data Analysis in the Behavioral Sciences*, ed. Samuel Shye (San Francisco: Jossey-Bass, 1978).

[33] See Richard W. Cobb and Charles D. Elder, "The Politics of Agenda-Building: An Alternative Perspective for Modern Democratic Theory," *Journal of Politics* 33 (1971): 898-915.

TABLE A.3
Average Importance Attributed to Fifteen Issues, by Elite Sector

			Elite Sector					
Issue	*MDB*	*Labor*	*Civil Service*	*Business*	*Bishops*	*Arena*	*Mean*	ETA^2
Educational Reform	95	91	86	83	80	84	86	.05
Income Redistribution	85	90	79	77	92	79	82	.07
Occupation of Amazon	83	92	74	74	71	78	79	.10
Government-Student Relations	88	83	72	66	78	72	74	.09
Agrarian Reform	86	86	69	62	87	74	73	.13
Government-Labor Relations	80	82	66	63	75	64	69	.09
Foreign Investment	65	58	73	75	55	67	68	.12
Leadership of Brazil	57	75	68	57	45	74	65	.08
Censorship	65	55	64	58	58	47	58	.04
Participation of Military	60	49	64	62	38	51	57	.07
Government-Opposition Relations	64	55	56	57	59	48	56	.01
Legalization of Divorce	49	70	53	59	36	35	55	.11
Participation of Church	67	59	48	45	72	45	50	.09
Subversion	46	31	52	59	46	55	50	.09
Birth Control	35	50	51	55	42	33	48	.06
Mean	68	68	65	63	62	61	65	.05

NOTES: "What degree of importance [*importância*] do you attribute to each of the following issues [*questões*]?" A score of 0 = no importance, and 100 = extremely important.
ETA^2 of .07 or greater significant at p ≤ .01.

Still, the hierarchy of issues, while discernible, is not particularly well-defined. One wonders whether "subversion," for example, is as unimportant to the elites as they claim. Similar doubts can be raised about the question of the political participation of the military, to which the elites appear to attach only modest importance.

Table A.3 contains another jarring pattern. If we are to judge from the overall differences in the importance ascribed by the various sectors to the issues, indexed by the mean values in the bottom row, it would appear that the elites are not far from consensus in their priorities.[34]

[34] One other, minor difficulty with the results reported in Table A.3 should be noted. I correlated the importance attributed to each of the issues with the interviewer-assessed hes-

But it is evident that the importance that the elites ascribe to some issues is closely tied to their preferences on these issues. The bishops assert that the question of the legalization of divorce has little importance not because they feel the issue is trivial but because they oppose a prodivorce policy. The businessmen give less priority to income redistribution than do the other elites because they are not very enthusiastic about positive policies in the area. The MDB politicians, the labor leaders, and the bishops declare that agrarian reform has greater importance because they favor agrarian reform. And so on.

Not all of the importance ratings are confounded in this way by the preferences of the elites. Yet for many issues, priorities and pro-con opinions cannot be considered independent dimensions. Conservative elites downgrade certain issues, progressive elites upgrade them, and vice versa on other issues. The result is that the importance ratings tend to cancel one another out, so that on the average there does not seem to be serious disagreement among the elite sectors. Yet this composite bottom line is misleading, precisely because the elites disagree substantially on the importance of particular issues.[35]

In brief, we are confronted with two difficulties in interpreting the importance ratings of the elites. One is the familiar problem brought on by the propensity of the elites systematically to inflate or deflate the significance of issues in general. This makes it difficult to retrieve a precise rank-ordering of controversies on the policy agenda.[36]

Second, the priorities that the elites assign some issues are virtually inseparable from their positions on the issues. This correlation is diagnostic of the tendency of the elites to treat certain controversies as nonissues—that is, to prevent them from reaching the agenda in the first place. At the

itancy of the respondents. None of the correlations is significant, except for that associated with the political participation of the military ($r = .21$). Apparently, there is a slight tendency for the "nervous" elites to up their estimates of the weight of the military, because they favor, more than the progressives, the participation of the military in politics.

[35] It may be objected that the problem is traceable to the supposedly different meanings of the Portuguese *importância* and the English "importance." But the confusion between importance as priority and importance as preference is common to both languages; it is not a semantic artifact peculiar to either.

[36] To the extent that the importance ratings and the opinions of the elites are correlated, the propensity of the elites to inflate or deflate their attributions of importance to the issues across the board is minimized. The conservatives inflate the importance of the "conservative" issues (for example, foreign investment); the progressives inflate the importance of the "progressive" issues (for example, income redistribution). While there is some tendency to inflate and deflate issues despite ideological leanings, the more serious problem is created by the fact that the elites were not asked to rank the issues in precise order. That is, they did not make pairwise comparisons between the fifteen issues—an exercise that would have required 105 comparisons. The result is that the precise agenda of elite concerns remains somewhat indeterminate. The pattern is not unrealistic.

same time, the association also contributes to a distortion in the ranking of issues. It would be naive to take the average ratings toward the right side of Table A.3 as an exact portrayal of the elite agenda.

Let us consider each of these difficulties in turn. Table A.4 presents the pairwise correlations between fifteen issues. The matrix is calculated from the importance ratings assigned to each of the issues by the elites, without any adjustment for the failure of the elites to establish precise rankings among the issues.

The result is a set of largely positive correlations, with a few negative (and insignificant) coefficients. In many instances, the patterns are comprehensible as, for example, with the correlation of .61 between the importance assigned to government-student relations and the importance assigned to government-labor relations, and with the correlation of .34 between income redistribution and agrarian reform. The elites who give high priority to one such issue also give high priority to others of a similar progressive-conservative cast.

But in other cases the results are disturbing. We would expect a negative correlation between agrarian reform and subversion, if the importance ratings of the elites reflect their policy preferences. As it is, the correlation is .03—not entirely meaningless but lacking in the contrast associated with genuinely conflictive positions.

The relationship between priorities on the issues comes into sharper focus when the importance scores of individual elites are adjusted for their tendency to under- and overrate issues generally. The operation involves subtracting the average importance attributed by each elite, calculated across the fifteen issues, from the importance he assigns each issue. These standardized values are then correlated with the results shown in Table A.5.[37]

The prevalence of negative correlations reflects, imperfectly but more sharply than before, the rank-ordering implicit in the agenda setting of the elites. Some positive associations remain between issues that tap similar concerns. The correlation between the importance attributed to educational reform, for example, and government-student relations is .16; between foreign investment and the participation of the military, the correlation is .19.

Still, most of the linkages are negative, indicating that issues compete for a place on the elite agenda. The negative correlations are strongest between issues on which the elites take characteristically progressive and conservative stands. For example, the association between agrarian reform and foreign investment is −.32. The elites who promote one tend not to

---

[37] The algorithm is the same as that used in Chapter Three, where the elites' perceptions of the attention paid to various groups by the government were standardized.

TABLE A.4
Correlations between Importance Ratings, Fifteen Issues

	(1)	(2)	(3)	(4)	(5)	(6)	(7)	(8)	(9)	(10)	(11)	(12)	(13)	(14)	(15)
(1) Education Reform	—														
(2) Income Redistribution	.27	—													
(3) Occupation of Amazon	.26	.27	—												
(4) Government-Student Relations	.39	.26	.39	—											
(5) Agrarian Reform	.36	.34	.42	.41	—										
(6) Government-Labor Relations	.32	.35	.38	.61	.44	—									
(7) Foreign Investment	.15	.08	.06	.15	-.06	.09	—								
(8) Leadership of Brazil	.22	.07	.43	.29	.34	.32	.07	—							
(9) Censorship	.09	.16	-.02	.18	.07	.20	.20	.03	—						
(10) Participation of Military	.08	.02	-.03	.02	-.06	.10	.28	.04	.32	—					
(11) Government-Opposition Relations	.06	.14	.02	.09	.04	.09	.15	.00	.44	.14	—				
(12) Legalization of Divorce	.11	.08	.18	.11	.05	.13	.11	.05	.09	.02	.11	—			
(13) Participation of Church	.12	.20	.09	.25	.19	.18	-.05	.04	.26	.13	.29	-.05	—		
(14) Subversion	.05	.00	.00	-.02	.03	.01	.21	.00	.24	.08	.21	-.05	.09	—	
(15) Birth Control	.02	-.05	.00	-.04	.03	.04	.13	-.02	.09	.08	.15	.26	-.05	.17	—
	(1)	(2)	(3)	(4)	(5)	(6)	(7)	(8)	(9)	(10)	(11)	(12)	(13)	(14)	(15)

TABLE A.5

Correlations between Importance Ratings (Ipsatized), Fifteen Issues

	(1)	(2)	(3)	(4)	(5)	(6)	(7)	(8)	(9)	(10)	(11)	(12)	(13)	(14)	(15)
(1) Education Reform	—														
(2) Income Redistribution	.10	—													
(3) Occupation of Amazon	.03	.07	—												
(4) Government-Student Relations	.16	.01	.15	—											
(5) Agrarian Reform	.12	.12	.21	.16	—										
(6) Government-Labor Relations	-.01	.09	.10	.41	.19	—									
(7) Foreign Investment	.02	-.07	-.15	-.09	-.32	-.21	—								
(8) Leadership of Brazil	-.01	-.17	.27	.06	.15	.08	-.13	—							
(9) Censorship	-.21	-.09	-.36	-.15	-.26	-.13	.00	-.25	—						
(10) Participation of Military	-.05	-.13	-.23	-.24	-.30	-.14	.19	-.13	.17	—					
(11) Government-Opposition Relations	-.22	-.09	-.28	-.24	-.25	-.26	-.04	-.24	.27	-.02	—				
(12) Legalization of Divorce	-.08	-.08	.00	-.13	-.17	-.13	-.01	-.12	-.14	-.13	-.08	—			
(13) Participation of Church	-.06	.05	-.13	.01	-.03	-.09	-.19	-.17	.06	-.01	.13	-.24	—		
(14) Subversion	-.14	-.18	-.20	-.29	-.19	-.26	.08	-.17	.07	-.05	.06	-.20	-.06	—	
(15) Birth Control	-.15	-.21	-.19	-.29	-.17	-.21	.03	-.19	-.10	-.03	.00	.16	-.21	.06	—

promote the other. Likewise, the correlation between income redistribution and subversion is − .18.

One of the more intriguing patterns emerges in the links among foreign investment, the occupation of the Amazon region, and the leadership of Brazil in Latin America. In the previous matrix, all correlations between these items are positive. Given the crosscurrents of dependence and development associated with foreign investment in Brazil, such a configuration is not implausible. But it fails to capture the sense of the elites that the trade-offs between international and national factors are not all part of an expanding-sum game.

When this expansiveness is removed, the correlation between occupation of the Amazon regions and the role of Brazil in Latin America remains significantly positive. However, the associations of both these items with the importance attributed to foreign investment become negative. There is a tacit recognition that receptivity to foreign investment may not be the optimal path toward the rise of Brazil as a regional and world power.

Table A.5 does not uncover a rank-order of "pure" importance among the issues, from one through fifteen. It would be difficult to interpret such a ranking, since it is natural for the elites to confound the priority of the issues with their preferences on them and since the agendas of the elites are probably not neatly ordered in reality. Nevertheless, the matrix does give an impression of the perceived trade-offs between priorities.

I have argued that elites tend to raise and lower the importance of many issues according to their opinions about the issues. Empirically, this means a strong correlation between their importance ratings and their preference scores on an issue. For example, the more the elites favor agrarian reform, the greater the priorities they give the issue.

I have also suggested that there may be some issues for which the fit between importance and priority is less perfect. Elites on either side of an issue give it about equal priority, so that there is at most a weak correlation between importance and opinion. This type of issue is polarized, because the intensity with which opinions are held is spread more or less evenly across preferences on the issue. It may be that other issues that do not display this pattern are also conflictive. This is likely to be true of issues that are clearly aligned on a left-right continuum. Yet if an issue is both intelligible in left-right terms and structured such that elites with discrepant opinions admit to feeling equally strongly about it, then this issue is likely to be extremely polarized.[38]

---

[38] It is instructive to interpret the connection between preference and intensity graphically. Preferences on either side of an issue can be distributed laterally, on a horizontal axis. The intensity of opinion can then be plotted vertically, against each preference. A flat or U-shaped, bimodal distribution of intensity by preference would represent a polarized issue.

Table A.6 presents the correlations between the importance ratings and the preference scores for thirteen issues. The correlations have been computed for the elite sample as a whole, as well as for each of the sectors. The mean correlations in the panel to the right are simply the averages calculated across the six sectors; they are very similar to the results for the elites considered as a whole.

The issues are arrayed from top to bottom in descending order of the magnitude of the correlation between importance and preference or, by the working definition, in ascending order of polarization. It is the explicitly political issues, like censorship, subversion, government-opposition relations, and government-labor relations, that tend to have the greatest conflict-potential.[39]

TABLE A.6

Correlations between Importance Ratings and Preference Scores on Thirteen Issues, by Elite Sector

| Issue | All | Elite Sector | | | | | | Mean |
		MDB	Labor	Civil Service	Business	Bishops	Arena	
Legalization of Divorce	.69	.53	.82	.68	.71	.11	.68	.59
Agrarian Reform	.65	.80	.27	.67	.65	.26	.65	.55
Leadership of Brazil	.59	.51	.75	.47	.60	.21	.33	.48
Birth Control	.52	.79	.43	.50	.54	.21	.69	.53
Income Redistribution	.51	.21	.58	.42	.45	.35	.57	.43
Participation of Church	.47	.31	.65	.20	.42	.48	.36	.40
Participation of Military	.46	.03	.65	.10	.53	.41	.52	.37
Foreign Investment	.41	.39	.43	.32	.36	.47	.36	.39
Government-Student Relations	.36	.66	.06	.19	.41	.45	.42	.37
Subversion	.16	− .29	− .01	.39	.36	− .07	.12	.05
Government-Opposition Relations	.12	.25	.12	.11	.20	.02	− .12	.14
Government-Labor Relations	.11	.46	− .22	− .03	.14	− .35	.05	.01
Censorship	.03	− .07	− .20	.18	.05	− .38	− .31	− .12

NOTES: Since the pro-con opinions of the elites were not elicited for two issues—educational reform and the occupation of the Amazon region—thirteen rather than fifteen issues appear in Table A.6.

The correlations computed across the entire sample are usually greater than the average correlations computed from each sector, because the variance across the entire sample is larger than the variance within sectors.

A unimodal or skewed distribution of intensity would suggest a less conflict-ridden issue.

[39] The signs of the correlations in Table A.6 are arbitrary. They depend on which end of

Let us take as an example the question of government-opposition relations. In none of the elite sectors is the association between importance
and preference on the issue significant. Elites in opposing camps give the
issue about the same importance.

The question of the "fight against subversion" furnishes another striking
example of polarization. Within the progressive sectors—the MDB, the
labor leadership, and the church—the connection between pushing the fight
against subversion and the priority given to the issue tends to be reversed.
The elites who are themselves most likely to be victimized by witch hunting
consider the issue fairly important. Yet, for obvious reasons, they do not
push for an increase in witch hunting.

The general pattern is clear. As we move toward the issues that evoke
the group interests of the elites, and in particular of the elites who are not
dominant in the power structure, we begin to pick up signs of intensity
and polarization. Group rivalries come to the fore; gains and losses are
clear-cut; friends and enemies are plainly visible.

By contrast, on broader issues like agrarian reform and income redistribution, and on issues like population planning and the legalization of
divorce that elude categorization in left-right terms, polarization falls off.
This does not mean that elite preferences are consensual. Rather, the
progressive elites, and the progressives within the conservative sectors,
attach great importance to the issues, while the conservatives downplay
them.

The progressives give great priority to the group-rivalry issues. What
changes is that the conservatives take these issues seriously, too. The issues
engage the interests of the elites in the struggle for power and autonomy,
and the stakes are manifest. The conservatives can deal with a basic issue
like income redistribution, or agrarian reform, by mouthing moderately
liberal-sounding views, while putting the issue itself on the back burner.
They are less disposed to ignore issues that place their own positions on
the line.

In summary, two tendencies dominate the expression of elite opinion
on matters of policy. One is the inclination to adopt rather progressive
views on the issues, with the disclaimer that these issues are not very

---

the preference scale for each issue was coded low (0) and high (100). As a rule, a positive
correlation signifies agreement with the alternative posed (for example, legalization of divorce,
agrarian reform, and so on) and high importance attributed to the issue (or, conversely,
disagreement and low importance). A negative correlation means that preferences go in one
direction and intensity in another. For example, the correlation of −.22 within the labor
leadership on the government-labor relations issue indicates that the labor leaders who oppose
government domination tend to give the issue more importance than those who support a
strong role for the government.

important. In principle, income redistribution may be a good thing; so is agrarian reform. But they will have to wait.

The second tendency runs counter to the first. When the group interests of the elite come into play, the conservatives take a less condescending view of the issues. In such instances, the importance attributed to the issues, relative to the elites' preferences, tends to be uniformly high.

The difference between more and less polarizing issues forms a continuum, not a dichotomy. Toward the foggier end are issues like birth control. Preferences on issues such as these are difficult to pin down in the conventional vocabulary of left versus right. They are not uncontroversial, but they are probably less conflictive and threatening than is usually assumed. After all, divorce has been legalized in Brazil, at the prompting of an authoritarian and moralizing government.

Issues that can be understood in left-right terms probably have greater conflict-potential. It is easy to identify typically conservative and progressive opinions on issues like income redistribution and agrarian reform. If there is one "ideological" issue that evades precise classification in left-right terms, it is the question of foreign investment. There is a progressive—that is, antiforeign—position on this issue. But the position is not a matter of black versus white; it is as fraught with ambivalence as the conservative stance on the issue.[40]

Finally, there are issues that are charged not only with left-right tensions but also with extra conflict-potential because they evoke the specific group interests of the elites. Government-labor relations and government-opposition relations are the most graphic examples.

The evidence presented so far has been entirely statistical. It is useful now to turn to an examination of how the elites themselves interpret the issues.

Elite Rationales

It was not possible to elicit open-ended responses for all the issues. Here I concentrate on four: foreign investment, income redistribution, government-labor relations, and government-opposition relations.[41]

[40] When the relations between the four issues that are the main subject of this analysis are examined (foreign investment, income redistribution, government-labor relations, and government-opposition relations), it turns out that opinions regarding foreign investment are imperfectly related to the left-right cleavage; see Chapter Five. They cannot be located at the extremes, as can preferences about income redistribution, for example. As noted in the text, the issue of foreign investment is seldom treated in either-or terms in Brazil; the question involves the amount rather than the wholesale acceptance or rejection of foreign capital and technology.

[41] The open-ended responses to a fifth question, birth control, are examined in McDonough and de Souza, *The Politics of Population in Brazil*.

The issues are submitted to the same analytic procedure. The discursive responses are first categorized, then compared with the preference scores and importance ratings given by the elites. The purpose of the first comparison is to get an idea of the intentions of the elites in choosing progressive and conservative alternatives. The second comparison is a bit more subtle. The objective is to understand the rationales offered by elites who assign varying degrees of importance to an issue. In this way, it is possible to gain a more precise understanding of the difference between importance as priority and as intensity.

Commentary on the discursive responses of the elites is kept to a minimum. The idea is to let the elites speak for themselves. For the most part, the reasons they offer for their opinions are self-explanatory.

Foreign Investment

Immediately after stating their location on the 100-point scale designed to measure preferences with regard to foreign investment, the elites were asked to give the reasons for their position. The follow-up probe (''Could you tell me more about that?'') produced a variety of rationales. They are grouped under ten headings, from the least to the most favorable toward foreign investment.

1. *Exploitation, Underdevelopment.* ''Foreign investment leads to a development that is not development. Incentives for foreign capital based on the availability of cheap labor should not continue. But withdrawing this capital is not justified either, since it is already part of the national plan.'' (Rio de Janeiro labor leader)

''Foreign investment never promoted development in any country. Capitalism acts the same way in every area it penetrates, as Rosa Luxembourg saw.'' (ARENA politician)

''Foreign investment comes to collect selfish economic benefits, like Greeks bearing gifts. I would be all for it, if only the benefits went into social programs.'' (São Paulo labor leader)

2. *Political Dependence.* ''The multinationals are practically absorbing the decision-making power of governments themselves.'' (Bishop)

''The next stage of economic development has to be characterized by the localization in the country of the critical decisions regarding the sectors of strategic importance for national development. We cannot eliminate foreign capital completely. That would not be viable.'' (Ministerial bureaucrat)

''National capital should have a greater share. The amount of foreign investment is already substantial. The decision-center should be reversed for Brazilians. We must maintain decision-making autonomy.'' (Rio de Janeiro industrialist)

3. *Threat to National Bourgeoisie.* "Foreign investment is not adequately controlled under the law. Instead of being a help, it has gained a privileged position in the competition with national companies and has become a nuisance in the economy of the country." (MDB politician)

"Foreign investment goes into areas where it does not bring new jobs and where there is no need for foreign technology. These are the areas where national business can contribute most. For example: in medium-light industry, in housing, in finance, agriculture, and services. There should be less foreign investment in order to avoid the denationalization of the country." (São Paulo banker)

4. *No Longer Necessary.* "Brazil does not need foreign capital. Internal sources of income do not have to be supplemented by foreign inputs. What we need is reforms: agrarian reform, tax reform, increased exports, a larger domestic market, less sending of profits overseas, and more people working in production, more consumption." (São Paulo labor leader)

"Brazil is already in a position to develop her industry with her own capital. The Revolution of 1964 has made this possible. It has expanded the market and given confidence to Brazilians." (Rio de Janeiro labor leader)

5. *Balance between National and Foreign Capital.* "To be a nationalist is to invite foreign capital. We can nationalize the companies and not let the profits get out." (São Paulo industrialist)

"Foreign investment is necessary, and nowadays it enters in a dosage that is compatible with our stage of development." (MDB politician)

"Foreign investment is indispensable for economic development. There is no problem since there are laws to control this investment. The foreigners obey the laws better than the Brazilians." (São Paulo business association leader)

6. *More, but with Control.* "Brazil does not have enough resources to grow on its own. Foreign investment is necessary for the country to develop, with the necessary restrictions, of course. The profits of the foreign companies should not be exorbitant but relative." (Rio de Janeiro labor leader)

"I have nothing against foreign investment. It can even help, so long as we keep control over the return of profits overseas." (ARENA politician)

7. *Lack of Capital and Resources.* "We are a poor country and we need investment to develop. We are on the road to development, and the maximum that domestic capital can give does not amount to enough to reach development. What matters is not the investment itself but the control of foreign capital. We need to have this control." (Director of public company)

"Foreign investment subsidizes national resources that, in the present moment of development, are insufficient for all the needs of national development. However, such investments should be controlled so that they carry out a supplementary role, never as a suction pump on the national wealth.'' (ARENA politician)

8. *Lack of Know-How and Technology.* ''It should only complement economic activities essential for development and that require great resources and up-to-date technology—in infrastructure, health, electrical energy, et cetera. It should not compete with already existing Brazilian enterprises.'' (Rio de Janeiro banker)

''The efficiency of foreign investment is greater. Technology is transfered faster and at less cost, and foreign savings stay here.'' (Rio de Janeiro industrialist)

9. *Accelerates Development.* ''We are at the take-off stage in the process of economic development. We need a large sum of capital to reach this objective.'' (ARENA politician)

''It speeds up development with the least sacrifice for the population. The national private sector should be capitalized to maintain whatever control is possible. But if it loses, it's lost. In this matter, the position of the festive left, still tied to Stalinism, is identical with the position of the obsolete private capitalists who are against foreign investment because they want to keep their monopolies in the internal market. The left has lots of objections, but nowadays nationalism is irrelevant. Capital itself is no longer American or anything else. It is international capital.'' (Rio de Janeiro director of public company)

10. *Creates Jobs.* ''Foreign investment works to create new industries and a larger labor market. We should make sure the policy works to this end.'' (Rio de Janeiro labor leader)

''Foreign investment helps national development, and it increases the number of jobs necessary in a country like ours.'' (São Paulo labor leader)

Table A.7 presents the average preferences of the elites giving different rationales.[42] Once again, distinctions between some of the rationales are minute. Almost all of the elites want some control over foreign investment. The ''more-but-with-control'' category serves as a residual placement for those who say little else besides this.

[42] The eta-squared at the bottom of Table A.7 is extraordinarily high. The reason is that the scalar measures of preference and the follow-up probes are not independent; thus, the statistic is used only for reference. It should also be noted that ''rationale'' is in no sense a predictor of the preferences of the elites. In fact, since the rationales are coded from the probes that follow the 100-point scale, the arrangement of Table A.7 might well be the other way around, with the scalar scores grouped as the independent variable. I maintain the present format throughout the chapter, mainly for aesthetic reasons. It would be clumsy, although possibly more correct, to reverse the variables. So long as it is understood that there is variance about the mean preference scores for each of the rationales, little harm is done.

TABLE A.7
Average Preference, Foreign Investment,
by Rationale of Preference

Rationale	Average	N
Exploitation, Underdevelopment	75	13
Political Dependence	72	18
Threat to National Bourgeoisie	61	15
No Longer Necessary	59	18
Balance Between National and Foreign Capital	43	46
More, but with Control	25	28
Lack of Capital, Resources	24	31
Lack of Know-How, Technology	24	26
Accelerates National Development	22	37
Creates Jobs	14	15
Totals	38	247

NOTES: High score = against foreign investment
$ETA^2 = .55$

Toward one side are the elites who believe that foreign investment brings nothing but economic ruin and the loss of national autonomy. Toward the opposite end are those who argue that foreign capital supplies the added investment to keep economic growth going faster and to expand the job market. Most of the elites in between follow a "necessary evil" line. Foreign investment is supposed to compensate for what is lacking domestically—capital and/or know-how; the proviso that it should be regulated is standard.

Foreign investment is a strategic developmental controversy, and the elites react to options on the issue in light of their assumptions about what will impede and accelerate national development. The strongest positions against foreign investment focus on the threat to national power.

Table A.8 maps the importance attributed to the issue of foreign investments against the pro and con rationales.[43] With one major exception, the elites who favor foreign investment give the issue more importance than those who oppose it.

The exception is formed by the elites who are worried about foreign capital as a menace to Brazilian industry. These men assign about as much

[43] The eta-squared association with "importance" is much lower than the corresponding statistic for "preference." To some degree, this is because the importance ratings were elicited at a separate point in the interview from the preference scores. But this is not the crucial point. What matters is the difference in the etas-squared for importance across the four issues discussed in this chapter. The smaller the eta-squared, the more evenly spread is the importance attributed to an issue across the various priorities.

TABLE A.8
Average Importance, Foreign Investment,
by Rationale of Preference

Rationale	Average	N
More, but with Control	74	28
Creates Jobs	74	15
Threat to National Bourgeoisie	73	16
Accelerates National Development	72	37
Lack of Know-How, Technology	72	26
Lack of Capital	69	31
Balance Foreign and Domestic Capital	68	45
Exploitation, Underdevelopment	61	13
No Longer Necessary	59	17
Political Dependence	52	18
Totals	68	246

NOTES: High score = great importance
ETA^2 = .08

importance to the issue as any of the other elites. The intensity of their concern about the threat to the national bourgeoisie matches the expectation that an issue takes on conflict-potential to the extent that the elites perceive their group interests to be at stake in vivid, direct terms.

But the recognition that foreign capital tends to dominate and undercut domestic interests, concretely, remains an exceptional view. For the most part, the elites who object to foreign investment place the issue low on their agenda. The majoritarian assumption is that Brazil is poor but enormous and that it can turn a profit, even after some short-term losses, from foreign investment.[44]

Income Redistribution

The question of income redistribution—or rather, of the increasing maldistribution of income—was one of the few sources of heated polemics during the Médici years. It has continued to be a prime topic of controversy through subsequent governments. The reason for the explosiveness of the

[44] The generally optimistic tone of responses to the foreign investment question is at least in part a reflection of the "era of good feeling" represented by the 1968 to 1973 boom. Were the survey conducted now, more responses directed at the foreign debt burden would no doubt appear. Nevertheless, it is worth noting that even in 1972 and 1973, the incidence of responses referring to the necessity of "control over foreign capital" is quite high. While the impression of alarm is mild, the insistence on the need for control is present, and it is this sense of control over external forces that the soaring debt has shaken.

issue is evident. The maldistribution of income represents the dark side of the Brazilian miracle.

Ten rationales behind the opinions of the elites on the question of income redistribution emerged:

1. *Increasing Maldistribution, Inequities.* "What has happened in Brazil is redistribution in the wrong way, and this should be neutralized in the right way, which is to benefit the great masses of the Brazilian population. In Brazil in recent years, there has been an accentuated concentration of income in the financial sectors. This has meant economic sacrifice for the middle classes and for the great masses of workers. It is necessary to give back what was unduly taken away from those who already had little. Just look at the figures in the last census!" (Rio de Janeiro business association leader)

"Brazil is a country with one of the lowest per capita incomes in the world. Income is concentrated in the hands of a small group. The much celebrated [*festejado*] Brazilian miracle has been carried out at the expense of most of the population." (ARENA politician)

"The majority of the population has been tightening its belt for the benefit of a minority, and this has been going on for a long time. The pie has to be cut up in equal pieces as soon as possible." (Rio de Janeiro labor leader)

2. *Now Possible, Time has Come.* "We have a situation nowadays, regarding the creation of wealth, that justifies the implementation of policies aimed at a better distribution of income." (ARENA politician)

"Brazil has reached a point of development where the workers should receive more for the collaboration they have shown with the revolutionary powers." (Rio de Janeiro labor leader)

3. *Social Peace, Political Stability.* "The government is trying, but there is a natural tendency towards concentration when a country enters the take-off stage. Income should be redistributed more rapidly to alleviate the burden which the worker suffers and to avoid the creation of a discontented people, a subversive people." (São Paulo industrialist)

"It is the number one problem in Brazil today, these islands of development that exist within the country. There are developed regions, and within the underdeveloped regions there are islands of development, showing up the maldistribution of income. This creates social imbalances, with all the attendant problems." (Ministerial bureaucrat)

"Economic development should be accompanied by social welfare. Political stability depends on social stability." (Leader of São Paulo businessmen's association)

4. *Speeds Development.* "The abysmal income of the greater part of the population is one of the major problems now. The sooner redistribution

occurs, the sooner the country will live better from the social point of view, as well as in terms of productivity. Satisfied people produce more.'' (São Paulo banker)

"Economic growth is presently benefiting only a minority. We must increase the number of people who receive benefits, since development is a collective process in which everybody should take part. The greater the participation, the greater the motivation for development. This creates conditions to maintain growth, since consumption increases. I don't think the creation of economic conglomerates promotes development, since this implies income concentration.'' (Rio de Janeiro banker)

5. *Expands Domestic Market.* "We have to look to the development of the domestic market, which in the long run is one of the great potential forces in a country with 100 million inhabitants.'' (Rio de Janeiro industrialist)

"The great problem is to balance savings and distribution and to expand the domestic market. Possibly, a bit more generous and immediate distribution would improve the level of individual liquidity in savings, and that would certainly expand the domestic market.'' (ARENA politician)

6. *Gradual Distribution, Without Jeopardizing Development.* "First the country has to develop so that afterwards redistribution can be encouraged. But redistribution should proceed a little faster, because many people are dying of hunger.'' (Rio de Janeiro industrialist)

"In Brazil, as in almost every developing country, there are a few rich and many poor. It is a question of social justice, but it cannot be resolved from one moment to the next. It should be done in accord with a long-run plan. Redistribution should be carried out according to realistic conditions, so as not to upset development. Premature redistribution would slow down the rate of development.'' (São Paulo industrialist)

7. *Improvement of Current Policy.* "Today we are already redistributing quite a bit. But this has to be done more rapidly, because Brazil is growing very quickly, without being able to think of long-run projects. The problems are being resolved with development, without social disturbance. The present government has redistributed more in ten years than any other government has in fifty, because economic development has made this possible.'' (Rio de Janeiro leader of business association)

"There still exists in a poor country like ours a concentration of income in a small percentage of the population, despite the government's attempts to change the situation. The redistributive mechanisms should be intensified, so that the people feel closer to the process of economic development.'' (São Paulo labor leader)

8. *Indirect Distribution, Education, Welfare.* "Concentration of income is a necessity. For some time we will have to favor a certain formation of

savings in areas that facilitate investment. On the other hand, support for education and the creation of new job opportunities will effectively contribute to the growth of family income. This you can see in practice. Look at the progress made by poor families and the educational opportunities opening up for their children.'' (São Paulo industrialist)

''As the country develops, income tends to accumulate among those with a knack for saving. Since the country needs internal savings, only afterwards can people take part in the deconcentration of income, through programs such as PIS, FGTS, and so on [pension funds].'' (Ministerial bureaucrat)

9. *Balance between Accumulation and Distribution.* ''Given the present situation, the rate of redistribution is reasonable. Since the economy is still not absolutely solid, we first need to consolidate the economy so that afterwards we can think of reformulating policy. Therefore, in present terms, redistribution is being carried out as it has to be to meet the rate of economic growth that is required.'' (São Paulo industrialist)

''The idea would be to redistribute income much more rapidly. But at the present time this ideal collides with the interests of national development. I support the present policy. It permits a satisfactory degree of accumulation and investment.'' (Ministerial bureaucrat)

10. *Capital Accumulation.* ''We have to create wealth so that later we can think of redistributing it. It is impossible to distribute something that doesn't exist. It is impossible to redistribute poverty.'' (Rio de Janeiro industrialist)

''Income redistribution is utopian. The deconcentration of capital would impede economic growth.'' (Manager of public company)

''High-income Brazilians are already taxed too much. These taxes go for education, public services, and so on. Even higher taxes would be counterproductive for economic development.'' (Rio de Janeiro banker)

Although very few of these men admit to being against income redistribution in principle, their views of the sheer feasibility of such a policy are discrepant. They also differ sharply about the timing of redistribution. Many of those who advocate some sort of redistribution do so with the understanding that it will take place very gradually and in the long run. Table A.9 summarizes the preferences of the elites with more and less distributive rationales.

Three major groupings emerge. Beginning with the elites who desire an expansion of the domestic market and culminating with those who want to reverse the growing maldistribution, the preference is for a much more rapid redistribution of income. Next come the gradualists and those who believe that current policy only needs fine tuning. Finally, the least enthusiastic about income redistribution are the elites preoccupied with the

TABLE A.9
Average Preference, Income Redistribution,
by Rationale of Preference

Rationale	Average	N
Increasing Maldistribution, Inequity	88	53
Now Possible, Time has Come	84	27
Social Peace, Political Stability	83	19
Speeds Development	82	25
Expands Domestic Market	82	12
Gradual, without Jeopardizing Development	72	31
Improvement of Current Policy	69	19
Indirect Distribution, Education, Welfare	58	20
Balance Consumption and Savings	53	19
Capital Accumulation	47	21
Totals	74	246

NOTES: High score = favors redistribution
$ETA^2 = .51$

TABLE A.10
Average Importance, Income Redistribution,
by Rationale of Preference

Rationale	Average	N
Speeds Development	91	25
Expands Domestic Market	89	12
Now Possible, Time has Come	88	27
Increasing Maldistribution, Inequity	87	53
Indirect Distribution	81	20
Gradual Redistribution	78	31
Improvement of Current Policy	77	19
Social Peace, Political Stability	75	19
Balance Consumption and Savings	74	19
Capital Accumulation	63	21
Totals	81	246

NOTES: High score = great importance
$ETA^2 = .13$

continued need to accumulate capital for further investment. The most they are liable to grant is a package of indirectly distributive programs of the sort that delay redistribution.

Table A.10 reveals a similar pattern. The elites who stress capital accumulation give income redistribution low priority. The only significant departure from the earlier configuration is the tendency for the elites who stress the pre-emptive and politically stabilizing effects of redistribution to give the issue less than top priority. They are not so much concerned with the injustice of the present situation or with the possible economic benefits to be reaped from enlarging the internal market as they are with averting the disruption generated by unbridled greed.

Two further points should be noted. Generally, the level of importance ascribed to the issue of income redistribution is high. Even the gradualists assign the problem great priority. The verbal ambience is so favorable to redistribution that only the elites who insist on the brute primacy of capital accumulation place themselves to the right of ''the situation nowadays in Brazil.'' In the main, the conservativism of the elites comes out not in their general approval of the idea of redistribution but in their caution about its timing.

Second, the extreme conservatives tend to be defensive rather than on the attack. Their strategy is to deny that income redistribution has importance for the present and to postpone it to an unset date. The objective is to keep the issue low on the elite agenda.

Government-Labor Relations

Just as income redistribution is the macro-issue of authoritarian Brazil, the autonomy-versus-subjugation of the labor syndicates is the great class issue. The wage policy of the government is enforced through its containment of the labor organizations.

However, there is one clear difference between the issues. The question of income redistribution is susceptible to various sorts of high-toned waffling. The question of government-labor relations is more immediate and less disembodied. It involves the physical repression and material cooptation of a visible, growing class. The sense of threat and intergroup confrontation is undeniably present, even for the elites who might wish in the abstract for a more humane distribution of the benefits of economic growth.

Ten rationales are prominent in elite discussions of the issue.

1. *Political Opening.* ''The syndicate should be free. It is like a dove. If you squeeze it in your hand, it will die. Its essence is liberty and since liberty requires responsibility, it is naturally controlled. The freedom of the syndicate is one of the conditions of representative democracy.'' (Rio de Janeiro labor leader)

2. *Class and Interest Representation.* ''A controlled syndicate does not exist, in the sense that it cannot act effectively. The demands of the working class should be ventilated with the fullest liberty. For this purpose, the syndicate is the representative organ. The syndicate is important for the

workers because economic conditions themselves, as such, limit their power of making demands." (São Paulo banker)

"Greater liberty would give the syndicates a chance to negotiate with the employing class. The workers want to bargain with their labor power for a just price without the interference of the government. What the worker has is the instrument of work, his labor power. It is his property, and it is inadmissible that there should be prohibitions against negotiating what belongs to him." (Rio de Janeiro labor leader)

"Instead of representing the workers, the syndicates are forced to represent the government to the workers. This is ridiculous." (Rio de Janeiro labor leader)

3. *Bureaucratic Distortion, Interference.* "Everything that we do is subject to the control of the government. In every activity of the workers' syndicates, from buying furniture to wage policy, there are bureaucratic obstacles that get in the way of any attempt at reform on the part of the syndicates." (Rio de Janeiro labor leader)

"The syndicates have stopped being syndicates. They have become government agencies, recreational and welfare agencies." (MDB politician)

"The present level of control practically nullifies syndical action. The workers can't say anything. The government and the bosses rule. This contradicts the encyclical 'Mater et Magistra.' Not to give the workers a voice in planning is a failure. This would not affect the political situation of the country. It would give much more incentive to the workers to produce." (Rio de Janeiro labor leader)

4. *No Longer Necessary.* "In the present climate in which subversion is controlled, every measure aimed at liberalizing the syndicates as representative organs should be taken." (MDB politician)

"The syndicate is the supreme expression of class defense but without political involvement beyond its legal activities. The government only intervenes to maintain order when these extraordinary political actions occur, as it already has. Now this is no longer necessary. The syndicates confine themselves to defending their interests." (São Paulo industrialist)

5. *Mild Control Only, Regulation.* "The syndicates should be free. The role of the government is to regulate, to check the expenditures of money collected from the syndical members. By international obligation, the syndicates should be free. This is what the International Labor Organization says. But with this liberty comes government regulation, instead of control. To leave the syndicates completely free is like leaving a loaded gun in the hands of a child. This means I favor liberty with responsibility." (Rio de Janeiro labor leader)

6. *Economic Growth, Anti-Inflationary Restrictions.* "The present policy

has produced good results. It has eliminated class conflicts and favored economic development.'' (Rio de Janeiro industrialist)

''The present level of control allows for a certain amount of demands without entering into questions about exorbitant wages. We must control inflation and promote savings.'' (São Paulo industrialist)

7. *Harmony, Equilibrium, Compromise.* ''The current degree of control is adequate. No labor problems have arisen, and there has been no deterioration of the harmonious situation between capital and labor. They work in unison, especially in comparison with the situation in other countries of Latin America.'' (Rio de Janeiro industrialist)

''The syndicates are free in the present situation. They have freedom of action as long as they act in accord with the policy of the government.'' (Rio de Janeiro labor leader)

8. *Paternalism, Best for Workers.* ''There is an understanding between the syndical leaders and the authorities, so as to benefit the working classes and, at the same time, not to create problems for production.'' (ARENA politician)

''The control is well-balanced. The present situation does not create dissatisfaction among the workers. They feel that the syndicates have passed from a merely political phase to one of protection for the workers.'' (Bishop)

''The government does not control, it regulates. The government provides incentives, for example, through scholarships [for the children of workers]. This is not a restriction on freedom. It is an incentive for future leaders.'' (Ministerial bureaucrat)

9. *Anti-Communism, Subversion.* ''The present level of control is high. The country is convalescing from an extremely grave pathological state that preceded the revolution of 1964. The patient is not ready to act normally. To shorten the period of convalescence would mean a return to the pathological state. The syndicates were used as a means of political action and not in the interests of the workers.'' (São Paulo leader of business association)

''Control of the syndicates is necessary, so that they don't become as they were in the past, with communist agents waiting to take over.'' (Rio de Janeiro syndical leader)

10. *Leaders Corrupt, Workers Gullible.* ''Control is still necessary because the syndicates are not ready to carry out their role. The leaders are practically illiterate, they don't have the capacity to lead. It's not like in Germany or the United States, where the syndicates help the government.'' (Ministerial bureaucrat)

''The syndicate is nothing more than a collectivity, and our people are still not prepared for this. Government control prepares them so that, later, there can be less control.'' (ARENA politician)

For all the diversity of response, a certain tone typifies many of the explanations of the elites on either side of the question of government-labor relations. Except for those who argue that capital and labor are in harmony or that the government policy actually benefits the workers, the elites exhibit real anger and fear. Conservatives describe the syndical leadership as illiterate, corrupt, and possibly infiltrated by communists. Progressives are exasperated with the heavy-handedness of the government. Income redistribution is an important issue, but it is also somewhat distant; the question of government-labor relations is more concrete, and discussions of it take on a harsher tone.

Table A.11 breaks down the average preferences of the elites on the government-labor issue according to their rationales. The modal rationale, used by nearly a quarter of the elites, invokes the necessity of restoring a representative function to the syndicates. Another popular progressive rationale is, in effect, the obverse: bureaucratic interference by the government vitiates what is supposed to be the true role of the syndicates, that is, class defense.

The moderates argue that state control is either no longer necessary or required only in mild doses. It is among the elites who believe that the government knows best, or that the labor leadership is incompetent, or that the syndical membership is befuddled, or in some combination of all these

TABLE A.11
Average Preference, Government-Labor Relations,
by Rationale of Preference

Rationale		Average	N
Political Opening		93	10
Class, Interest Representation		87	53
Bureaucratic Distortion, Interference		87	21
No Longer Necessary		75	7
Mild Control Only, Regulation		70	14
Economic Growth, Anti-Inflation		52	14
Harmony, Equilibrium, Compromise		50	29
Paternalism, Best for Workers		50	21
Anti-Communism, Subversion		47	38
Leaders Corrupt, Workers Gullible		46	32
	Totals	64	239

NOTES: High score = progressive
$ETA^2 = .48$

things, that we encounter the true conservatives. The clearest division is between those who argue for bottom-up representation or for some autonomy from the state, and those who insist that the state must remain dominant over a dangerous and ignorant working class.

Table A.12 gives the importance ratings associated with each of the rationales. The striking property of these data is that they show little variation. The differences among the elites giving various rationales in the importance they ascribe to the issue are not statistically significant.

On this issue, the usual pattern of progressive opinion-high importance and conservative opinion-low importance does not hold. Even disregarding the criterion of statistical significance, it can be seen that the elites who view the syndical leadership as corrupt and the membership as unprepared to seek its own best interests attach about the same importance to the issue as the progressives. By this standard, the issue of government-labor relations is polarized.

Government-Opposition Relations

The issue of government-opposition relations is confrontational. Conservatives are inclined to think in terms of a direct threat to the incumbent powers. Progressives define it less as a question of the right to take power than as a matter of the right to political autonomy vis-à-vis the state. In either case, the question is controversial, for it involves the fate of specific actors. The elites reveal eleven rationales for their positions on the issue.

TABLE A.12
Average Importance, Government-Labor Relations,
by Rationale of Preference

Rationale	Average	N
Bureaucratic Distortion, Interference	75	22
Mild Control Only, Regulation	74	14
No Longer Necessary	74	7
Leaders Corrupt, Workers Gullible	73	34
Paternalism, Best for Workers	72	22
Class, Interest Representation	71	54
Economic Growth, Anti-Inflation	68	13
Anti-Communism, Subversion	64	38
Harmony, Equilibrium, Compromise	64	30
Political Opening	62	10
Totals	69	244

NOTES: High score = great importance
$ETA^2 = .03$

1. *Democratic Imperative*. "There should be no limits on the opposition as such, because it is part of the very structure of democracy. Let there be opposition, and let it be of iron." (Bishop)

"Limited opposition cannot fulfill its duty. It is simply not opposition. In order to be an opposition and exercise its role, it has to have complete freedom." (ARENA politician)

"There should be no limits on the opposition. The government should not fear the opposition. There should be a living-together [*convivência*] of opposites in order to have a true democracy." (São Paulo business association leader)

2. *Balance of Power*. "The big decisions about social objectives are essentially political questions. They depend on a functioning of the three branches of government." (Ministerial bureaucrat)

"Today there is no opposition. A bit of opposition is necessary to clear up possible errors of the government and to avoid an excess of flattery and servility, which normally grows when the opposition can't exercise its functions." (São Paulo industrialist)

3. *Political Development, Enlightened Opinion*. "What gives authenticity to the powers-that-be [*a situação*] is the greatest freedom of opposition. When the opposition is very restricted and cannot express itself, the authorities overextend themselves and cease to represent the collective will, which can only be formed through freedom of opposition. This requires ample debate and criticism." (São Paulo banker)

"We need more opposition so that national opinion, using its common sense, can get the true facts about the national condition." (Rio de Janeiro banker)

4. *Corrects Errors of Executive*. "Even when the government means well, it needs opposition. Today the opposition is surrounded. Without opposition, the executive makes mistakes, endangering the majority that is prevented from expressing itself." (São Paulo business association leader)

"Economic development is going well within the present political limits. But there should be fewer limits, so as to gather more opinions about things that may not be going well." (Ministerial bureaucrat)

"The danger with this government is that it doesn't listen. It talks to itself and answers to no one. It is so centralized that sooner or later, without opposition, it is going to make mistakes." (Rio de Janeiro industrialist)

5. *Constructive Criticism*. "It's the same as with the syndicates. The opposition needs to grow to exercise its rights, but it needs to educate itself in order to carry out its true obligations. Opposition for the sake of opposition is worthless." (ARENA politician)

"Opposition is needed in every democracy. A government without opposition can turn down paths that at times even the government itself is not aware of. The opposition regulates constructively the action of the government. And the opposition we have now behaves exactly in this sense, without acting contrary to the interests of the nation.'' (Ministerial bureaucrat)

6. *Opposition of Quality*. ''Opposition is always healthy and should not be limited, as long as it is an opposition of ideas. With people who don't think in general terms, but only in terms of immediate benefits, there can be no opposition. It should operate through people who by reason of their education can criticize the government responsibly.'' (ARENA politician)

''I think that there should be a more intelligent opposition. The problem is quality, not quantity. The lack of intelligence is especially noticeable in the political class, among the majority of politicians.'' (Director of public company)

7. *Avoid Confrontation*. ''The purpose of the present government is not to limit opposition but to do away with confrontation. This will disappear as the democratic regime consolidates itself, to the point where confrontation is no longer a problem.'' (ARENA politician)

''What we have now is a balance between criticism and confrontation. This enables us to reach our national goals, without disturbance.'' (Ministerial bureaucrat)

8. *Status Quo Satisfactory*. ''The current opposition expresses itself respectfully and within the boundaries that a democracy permits.'' (Rio de Janeiro labor leader)

''The opposition checks on [*fiscaliza*] the government. The Congress approves the budget. We don't need more. The rest is 'tea'.'' (São Paulo industrialist)

9. *Anti-Communism, Populism, Subversion*. ''The government is following the right course. When you come out of a storm, as we did, the government has to have freedom to act and consolidate the situation, or the storm will return. Afterwards, opposition can and should develop. But at the moment this would be counterproductive.'' (Rio de Janeiro labor leader)

''The tendency of the opposition is to return to the situation before the revolution, to fight for power, and so on. What Brazil really needs is political peace, so we can get down to work. Our success over the past ten years is due to this political peace.'' (Ministerial bureaucrat)

''If there were no limits on the opposition, the politicians would get up and slander the President or fool with the budget for their own sake, as they did before 1964.'' (São Paulo industrialist)

10. *Strong Government*. ''The political process was interrupted ten years ago. We were being led toward the unknown, without objectives or ideol-

ogies. It was anarchy and demagogy. It will take time to form a new political consciousness, and only a strong government can do this." (Director of public company)

"We are in a phase of political reconstruction. The political class needs time to renovate itself. Our institutions are so fragile that we need more time to consolidate them. With economic development, these institutions will grow strong and they won't depend on persons or groups. Right now, we can't afford another tumult, everybody has to work hard." (ARENA politician)

"As long as there are not enough jobs and social benefits for everyone, we need a strong government that can give us a unified direction, that can plan and carry out its plans. Then the people will become conservative. That is, they will want to hold on to what they have gained: schools, housing, groceries, etc. For the time being, opposition would only create instability, because the people follow those who promise the most." (São Paulo labor leader)

11. *Politicians Incompetent, Irrelevant.* "There is no real opposition in the country. The role of the opposition is above all to promote the welfare of the population. This the government has done, not the opposition. Flying off on political tangents [*partindo para tèses políticas*], the opposition fails to carry out its true function." (Ministerial bureaucrat)

"The little opposition that there is might as well not exist because it is unnecessary. The government is meeting the needs of the country; it is making progress. The opposition only criticizes the government, and it is not consistent. There is no real opposition because the reasons for it don't exist." (São Paulo industrialist)

The lines of conflict on the issue of government-opposition relations are clearly drawn. On one side are the elites who believe that freedom of opposition is a fundamental political right that cannot be denied. On the other are the elites who argue that political opposition is insidious or outmoded.

There is, however, something of a middle ground. As Table A.13 shows, this is occupied by the elites who contend that without opposition, the government is liable to fall in upon itself.

What is remarkable about these figures is the tendency of the elites who give entirely respectable reasons for opposition ("constructive criticism") to place themselves far in advance of the "situation" nowadays in Brazil. Their progressivism can be read in two ways: as hypocrisy, or as a demonstration of the illegitimacy of political repression and of their likelihood of defection from the impositions of the military. Both factors are no doubt at work. The consequential point is the skewing of preferences toward a

TABLE A.13
Mean Preference, Government-Opposition Relations,
by Rationale of Preference

Rationale	Average	N
Democratic Imperative	92	33
Balance of Power	88	27
Political Development, Enlightened Opinion	86	24
Correct Errors of Executive	71	26
Constructive Criticism	69	18
Opposition of Quality	65	10
Avoid Confrontation	63	17
Status Quo Satisfactory	52	35
Anti-Communism, Subversion, Populism	52	21
Strong Government	51	21
Politicians Incompetent, Irrelevant	47	8
Totals	69	240

NOTES: High score = progressive
ETA^2 = .48

less stifling political condition. It is extremely difficult for the elites to sanction outright repression.

When the importance that elites with different rationales give to the issue is considered in Table A.14, the results are similar to those encountered

TABLE A.14
Mean Importance, Government-Opposition Relations,
by Rationale of Preference

Rationale	Average	N
Opposition of Quality	72	9
Democratic Imperative	63	33
Balance of Power	57	27
Anti-Communism, Subversion, Populism	57	22
Political Development, Enlightened Opinion	56	22
Constructive Criticism	54	18
Correct Errors of Government	53	26
Strong Government	52	20
Avoid Confrontation	52	115
Status Quo Satisfactory	50	34
Politicians Incompetent, Irrelevant	41	8
Totals	55	234

NOTES: High score = great importance
ETA^2 = .04

with the government-labor question. Although the progressive elites seem to give the issue slightly greater priority, the difference in intensity between them and the conservatives is insignificant.

The elites who claim that the politicians are obsolete also claim that the issue of political opposition is relatively unimportant. But they are not typical. Evidently, the anticommunists have strong feelings about the matter. Even those who downgrade the issue cast their opinions harshly: the politicians, as a class, are inadequate and must be passed by.

Bibliography

Aberbach, Joel D.; Chesney, James D.; and Rockman, Bert A. 1975. "Exploring Elite Political Attitudes: Some Methodological Lessons." *Political Methodology* 2: 1-28.

Abercrombie, Nicholas, and Hill, Stephen. 1976. "Paternalism and Patronage." *British Journal of Sociology* 27: 413-429.

Achen, Christopher H. 1977. "Measuring Representation: Perils of the Correlation Coefficient." *American Journal of Political Science* 21: 805-815.

Adelman, Irma, and Morris, Cynthia Taft. 1974. *Economic Growth and Social Equity in Developing Countries*. Stanford: Stanford University Press.

"A Eleição com um Voto Só." 1978. *Veja*, January 11: 20-55.

"A Estrutura do Poder no Basil: Quem Decide?" 1974. *Visão*, June 24: 16-22.

"A Face Cruel do Brasil." 1980. *Veja*, July 16: 84-92.

"A Fera Ganhou os 100%." 1980. *Veja*, June 18: 80-87.

"Alívio com a Dívida." 1980. *Veja*, July 9: 90-91.

Allardyce, Gilbert. 1980. "What Fascism is Not: Thoughts on the Deflation of a Concept." *American Historical Review* 85: 367-388.

Almond, Gabriel A.; Flanagan, Scott C.; and Mundt, Robert D., eds. 1973. *Crisis, Choice, and Change: Historical Studies of Political Development*. Boston: Little, Brown and Company.

Anderson, Charles W. 1967. *Politics and Economic Change in Latin America*. Princeton: D. Van Nostrand.

Andrews, Frank M. et al. 1973. *Multiple Classification Analysis*. Ann Arbor: Institute for Social Research.

Appleby, Joyce. 1981. "Social Science and Human Nature." *democracy* 1: 116-126.

"A Queda do Cavaleiro: Contra o Radicalismo de Esquerda, o Comitê Central do Partido Comunista Demitiu Luís Carlos Prestes, o Mais Antigo Secretário Geral do Mundo." 1980. *Veja*, May 28: 20-23.

Armstrong, John A. 1973. *The European Administrative Elite*. Princeton: Princeton University Press.

Arns, Dom Paulo Evaristo. 1980. "Deus o Acompanhará." *Veja*, November 5: 146.

Asheshove, Nicholas, and Reich, Cary. 1980. "Has Delfim Worked his Last Miracle?" *Institutional Investor*, August: 174-193.

"As Palavras de João Paulo II." 1980. *Isto É*, July 9: 27-29.

Bacha, Edmar L. 1976. *Os Mitos de uma Década: Ensaios de Economia Brasileira*. Rio de Janeiro: Editora Paz e Terra.

———. 1977. "Issues and Evidence on Recent Brazilian Economic Growth." *World Development* 5: 47-67.

———, and Taylor, Lance. 1978. "Brazilian Income Distribution in the 1960s: 'Facts,' Model Results, and the Controversy." *Journal of Development Studies* 14: 271-297.

Bachrach, Peter. 1967. *The Theory of Democratic Elitism*. Boston: Little, Brown and Company.

Baer, Werner. 1973. "The Brazilian Boom, 1968-1972: An Explanation and Interpretation." *World Development* 1: 1-15.

———. 1978. "The Impact of Industrialization on Brazil's External Development." Paper presented at the meetings of the Midwest Political Science Association, Chicago, Illinois, April 20-22.

———; Kerstenetsky, Isaac; and Villela, Annibal V. 1973. "The Changing Role of the State in the Brazilian Economy." *World Development* 1: 23-34.

———, and Villela, Annibal V. 1979. "The Changing Nature of Development Banking in Brazil." Paper presented at the meetings of the Latin America Studies Association, Pittsburgh, Pennsylvania, April 5-7.

Bailes, Kendall E. 1978. *Technology and Society Under Lenin and Stalin: Origins of the Soviet Technical Intelligentsia, 1917-1941*. Princeton: Princeton University Press.

Bailey, Kenneth B. 1974. "Interpreting Smallest Space Analysis." *Sociological Methods and Research* 3: 3-29.

Bakota, Carlos Steven. 1979. "Getúlio Vargas and the Estado Novo: An Inquiry into Ideology and Opportunism." *Latin American Research Review* 14: 205-210.

Barnett, Steve, and Silverman, Martin G. 1979. *Ideology and Everyday Life: Anthropology, Neomarxist Thought, and the Problem of Ideology and the Social Whole*. Ann Arbor: University of Michigan Press.

Barton, Allen H. 1980. "Fault Lines in American Elite Consensus." *Daedalus* 109: 1-24.

———, and Parsons, R. Wayne. 1974-1975. "Consensus and Conflict among American Leaders." *Public Opinion Quarterly* 38: 509-528.

Bastide, Roger. 1978. *The African Religions of Brazil: Toward a Sociology of the Interpenetration of Civilizations*. Baltimore: The Johns Hopkins University Press.

Bell, Daniel. 1978. *The Cultural Contradictions of Capitalism*. New York: Basic Books.

———. 1980. *The Winding Passage: Essays and Sociological Journeys 1960-1980*. Cambridge, Mass.: ABT Books.

Bell, Wendell, and Stevenson, David L. 1979. "Attitudes toward Social Equality in Independent Jamaica." *Comparative Political Studies* 11: 499-532.

Bem, Daryl J., and Allen, A. 1974. "On Predicting Some of the People Some of the Time: The Search for Cross-Situational Consistencies in Behavior." *Psychological Review* 81: 506-520.

Bennett, Douglas C. 1977. "Defining Ideology: The Danger of Methodological Distortion." In *Terms of Conflict: Ideology in Latin American Politics*, edited by Morris J. Blachman and Ronald G. Hellman. Philadelphia: Institute for the Study of Human Affairs.

Bennet, W. Lance. 1980. "Culture, Communication, and Political Control." Paper presented at the annual meetings of the American Political Science Association, Washington, D.C., August 28-31.

Berger, Peter L., and Luckman, Thomas. 1966. *The Social Construction of Reality.* New York: Doubleday & Company, Inc.

Berlin, Isaiah. 1980. *Against the Current: Essays in the History of Ideas.* New York: Viking Press.

Berman, Marshall. 1970. *The Politics of Authenticity: Radical Individualism and the Emergence of Modern Society.* New York: Atheneum.

Berner, Joel B. 1976. "Educational Backgrounds of Latin American Legislators." *Comparative Politics* 6: 617-634.

Bernstein, Richard J. 1978. *The Restructuring of Social and Political Theory.* New York: Harcourt, Brace, Jovanovich/University of Pennsylvania Press.

Bettman, James R. 1977. "Measuring Individuals' Priorities for National Goals: A Methodology and Empirical Example." *Policy Sciences* 2: 373-390.

Billington, James H. 1966. *The Icon and the Axe: An Interpretative History of Russian Culture.* New York: Alfred A. Knopf, Inc.

Biondi, Aloysio. 1978. "País dos Coitadinhos. Ou dos Espertinhos?" *Isto É*, February 15: 7-10.

Blackwell, Robert E., Jr. 1972. "Elite Recruitment and Functional Change: An Analysis of the Soviet Obkom Elite, 1950-1968." *Journal of Politics* 34: 124-152.

Blau, Peter M. 1962. "Inferring Mobility Trends from a Single Study." *Population Studies* 16: 79-85.

Block, Fred. 1977. "The Ruling Class Does Not Rule: Notes on the Marxist Theory of the State." *Socialist Revolution* 7: 6-28.

———. 1978. "Class Consciousness and Capitalist Rationalization: A Reply to Critics." *Socialist Review* 40-41: 212-220.

Bonacich, Phillip. 1972. "Factoring and Weighting Approaches to Status Scores and Clique Identification." *Journal of Mathematical Sociology* 2: 113-117.

Bonilla, Frank, and Silva Michelena, José A. 1967. *The Politics of Change in Venezuela: A Strategy for Research on Social Policy.* Vol. 1. Cambridge, Mass.: M.I.T. Press.

Booth, John. 1979. "Political Participation in Latin America: Levels, Structure, Context, Concentration and Rationality." *Latin American Research Review* 14: 29-60.

———, and Seligson, Mitchell A., eds. 1978. *Political Participation in Latin America.* New York: Holmes & Meier.

Brading, D. A., ed. 1980. *Caudillo and Peasant in the Mexican Revolution.* London: Cambridge University Press.

"The Brazilian Gamble: Why Bankers Bet on Brazil's Technocrats." 1977. *Business Week*, December 5: 72-81.

Bresser Pereira, Luís Carlos. 1978. *O Colapso de uma Aliança de Classes.* São Paulo: Editora Brasiliense.

Broder, David S. 1980. *Changing of the Guard: Power and Leadership in America.* New York: Simon & Schuster.

Bruneau, Thomas C. 1974. *The Political Transformation of the Brazilian Catholic Church*. London: Cambridge University Press.

————. 1980. "The Catholic Church and Development in Latin America: The Role of Basic Christian Communities." *World Development* 8: 535-544.

Buarque de Gusmão, Sérgio. 1980. "Um João Paulo II para Cada Gosto." *Isto É*, July 9: 30-35.

Buarque de Hollanda, Heloisa. 1980. *Impressões de Viagem*. São Paulo: Brasiliense.

Bullard, Monte Ray. 1979. "People's Republic of China Elite Studies: A Review of the Literature." *Asian Survey* 19: 789-800.

Bunce, Valerie. 1979. "Leadership Succession and Policy Innovation in the Soviet Republics." *Comparative Politics* 11: 379-401.

————, and Hicks, Alexander. 1980. "Capitalism, Socialisms, and Democracy: Beyond Present Political Economic Tradeoffs." Paper presented at the annual meetings of the American Political Science Association, Washington, D.C., August 28-30.

Buroway, Michael. 1978. "Contemporary Currents in Marxist Theory." *American Sociologist* 13: 55-56.

Burt, Ronald S. 1975. "Corporate Society: A Time Series Analysis of Network Structure." *Social Science Research* 4: 271-328.

————. 1976. "Positions in Networks." *Social Forces* 55: 93-122.

————. 1977. "Positions in Multiple Network Systems, Parts One and Two." *Social Forces* 56: 106-131, 551-575.

Butler, David, and Stokes, Donald E. 1971. *Political Change in Britain*. New York: St. Martin's Press.

Camargo, José Márcio. 1980. "A Nova Política Salarial, Distribuição de Renda, e Inflação." Mimeographed. Rio de Janeiro: Pontifícia Universidade Católica.

Campbell, Donald T. 1958. "Common Fate, Similarity, and Other Indices of the Status of Aggregates of Persons as Social Entities." *Behavioral Science* 3: 14-25.

Caporaso, James A. 1980. "Dependency Theory: Continuities and Discontinuities in Development Studies." *International Organization* 34: 605-628.

Cardoso, Fernando Henrique. 1974. *O Modêlo Político Brasileiro*. São Paulo: Difusão Européia do Livro.

————. 1977. "Democracia, Simplesmente." *Isto É*, August 3: 33-37.

————. 1978. Interview. *Isto É*, September 13: 35-38.

————. 1980. "A Coragem de um Gesto." *Veja*, August 27: 130.

————, and Faletto, Enzo. 1973. *Dependência e Desenvolvimento na América Latina: Ensaio de Interpretação Sociológica*. Rio de Janeiro: Zahar Editores.

Chalmers, Douglas A., and Robinson, Craig H. 1980. "Why Power Contenders Choose Liberalization: Perspectives From Latin America." Paper presented at the annual meetings of the American Political Science Association, Washington, D.C., August 28-31.

Chamberlain, Neil W. 1972. *Beyond Malthus: Population and Power*. Englewood Cliffs, N.J.: Prentice-Hall.

Chandler, Alfred D., Jr. 1977. *The Visible Hand: The Managerial Revolution in American Business*. Cambridge Mass.: The Belknap Press of Harvard University Press.

Chapman, William. 1980. "New Leaders in Seoul Exploit General Yearning for Stability." *Washington Post*, September 4: A33.

Chelliah, Raja J.; Baas, Hessel J.; and Kelly, Margaret R. 1975. "Tax Ratios and Tax Effort in Developing Countries, 1969-71." *International Monetary Fund Staff Papers* 12: 187-205.

Chenery, Hollis et al. 1974. *Redistribution with Growth*. London: Oxford University Press.

Chirot, Daniel. 1977. *Social Change in the Twentieth Century*. New York: Harcourt, Brace, Jovanovich.

Clausen, Aage R. 1977. "The Accuracy of Leader Perceptions of Constituent Views." Paper presented at the annual meetings of the American Political Science Association, Washington, D.C., September 1-4.

Cobb, Richard W., and Elder, Charles D. 1971. "The Politics of Agenda-Building: An Alternative Perspective for Modern Democratic Theory." *Journal of Politics* 33: 898-915.

Coelho, Edmundo Campos. 1976. *Em Busca da Identidade: O Exército e a Política na Sociedade*. Rio de Janeiro: Forense Universitária.

Cohen, Abner. 1981. *The Politics of Elite Culture*. Berkeley: University of California Press.

Cohen, Youssef. 1979. "Popular Support for Authoritarian Governments: Brazil Under Medici." Ph.D. dissertation, University of Michigan.

Collier, David. 1978. "Industrialization and Authoritarianism in Latin America." *Items of the Social Science Research Council* 31/32: 5-13.

————, ed. 1979. *The New Authoritarianism in Latin America*. Princeton: Princeton University Press.

Collier, Ruth Berins, and Collier, David. 1979. "Inducements versus Constraints: Disaggregating Corporatism." *American Political Science Review* 73: 967-986.

Converse, Philip E. 1964. "The Nature of Belief Systems in Mass Publics." In *Ideology and Discontent*, edited by David E. Apter. New York: The Free Press.

————. 1975. "Some Mass-Elite Contrasts in the Perception of Political Spaces." *Social Science Information* 14: 49-83.

Coveyou, Michael R., and Pierson, James. 1977. "Ideological Perceptions and Political Judgment: Some Problems of Concept and Measurement." *Political Methodology* 4: 77-102.

Cox, Robert W. 1979. "Ideologies and the New International Economic Order: Reflections on Some Recent Literature." *International Organization* 33: 257-302.

Crittenden, Ann. 1979. "Brazil Sets Historic Plans to Redistribute Income." *New York Times*, September 4: D1, D4.

Cunningham, William H.; Cunningham, Isabella C. M.; and Green, Robert T.

1977. "The Ipsative Process to Reduce Response Set Bias." *Public Opinion Quarterly* 41: 379-384.

Cupertino, Fausto. 1976. *As Muitas Religiões do Brasileiro*. Rio de Janeiro: Editora Civilização Brasileira.

Dahl, Robert A. 1956. *A Preface to Democratic Theory*. Chicago: University of Chicago Press.

Das Gupta, Jyotirindra. 1978. "A Season of Caesars: Emergency Regimes and Development Politics in Asia." *Asian Survey* 28: 315-349.

Davis, James. 1980. "Contingency Table Analysis." *Quality and Quantity* 80: 117-154.

————, and Leinhardt, Samuel. 1972. "The Structure of Positive Interpersonal Relations in Small Groups." In *Sociological Theories in Progress*, edited by Joseph Berger. Boston: Houghton-Mifflin Company.

Dealy, Glen Caudill. 1977. *The Public Man: An Interpretation of Latin American and Other Catholic Countries*. Amherst, Mass.: University of Massachusetts Press.

Dean, Warren. 1969. *The Industrialization of São Paulo, 1880-1945*. Austin: University of Texas Press.

de Barros, José Roberto Mendonça, and Graham, Douglas H. 1978. "The Brazilian Economic Miracle Revisited: Private and Public Sector Initiative in a Market Economy." *Latin American Research Review* 13: 5-38.

de Camargo, Apásia Alcântara. 1979. "Authoritarianism and Populism: Bipolarity in the Brazilian Political System." In *The Structure of Brazilian Development*, edited by Neuma Aguiar. New Brunswick, N.J.: Transaction Books.

de Castro Andrade, Regis. 1980. "Política Salarial e Normalização Institucional no Brasil." Mimeographed. São Paulo: CEDEC.

de Lima Figueiredo, Euríco. 1979. "Abertura Política: Processo de Conservar o Ontem." *Jornal do Brasil*, September 30: 7.

Della Cava, Ralph. 1976. "Catholicism and Society in Twentieth Century Brazil." *Latin American Research Review* 11: 7-50.

————. 1980. "Church Leads the Cause of Human Rights in Brazil." *International Development Review* 22: 40-43.

Demerath, Nicholas J. 1976. *Birth Control and Foreign Policy: The Alternatives to Family Planning*. New York: Harper & Row, Publishers.

de Oliveira, Maria Lúcia. 1977. "A Tendência à Centralização e o Fenômeno do Autoritarismo no Brasil." *Dados* 15: 83-99.

de Ouro Prêto, Marise, and Gondim, Helena, 1970. *Sociedade Brasileira*. Rio de Janeiro: Muller.

de Souza, Amaury. 1978. "The Nature of Corporatist Representation in Brazil." Ph.D. dissertation, Massachusetts Institute of Technology.

————, and Lamounier, Bolivar. 1980. "Escaping the Black Hole: Government-Labor Relations in Brazil in the 1980s." Paper presented at the Symposium on "Brazil 1980-2000," sponsored by the Research Institute on International Change, Columbia University, Rio de Janeiro, August 20-22.

de Souza, Maria do Carmo C. Campbello. 1976. *Estado e Partidos Políticos no Brasil (1930 a 1964)*. São Paulo: Editora Alfa-Omega.

Dias, Marcelo. 1979. " 'Miracles' en Chaine au Bresil." *Le Monde Diplomatique*, January: 1, 14-15.

Dias, Maurício. 1979. "Os Anos Faoro, Tempo de Bom Combate." *Isto É*, April 4: 28-30.

Diggins, John P. 1978. "Barbarism and Capitalism: The Strange Perspectives of Thorstein Veblen." *Marxist Perspectives* 1: 138-156.

―――. 1978. *The Bard of Savagery: Thorstein Veblen and Modern Social Theory*. New York: Seabury Press.

Dillman, C. Daniel. 1978. "Absentee Landlords and Farm Management in Brazil during the 1960s." *American Journal of Economics and Sociology* 37: 1-8.

Diniz Cerqueira, Eli. 1978. "Os Limites Políticos do Empresariado." *Isto É*, June 7: 70-71.

―――. 1979. "Industrial and Agro-Export Sectors in Brazil: Interest Differentiation and Institutional Changes (1930-1945)." Paper presented at the annual meetings of the Latin American Studies Association, Pittsburgh, Pennsylvania, April 5-7.

DiPalma, Giuseppe. 1980. "Founding Coalitions in Southern Europe." *Government and Opposition* 15: 162-189.

Dodson, Michael. 1980. "Prophetic Politics and Political Theory in Latin America." *Polity* 12: 388-408.

Dogan, Mattei, ed. 1975. *The Mandarins of Western Europe*. Beverly Hills: Sage Publications.

"Dom Antônio Exercita seu Poder." 1980. *Isto É*, December 31: 68.

dos Santos, Wanderley Guilherme, 1977. "Liberalism in Brazil: Ideology and Praxis." In *Terms of Conflict: Ideology in Latin American Politics*, edited by Morris J. Blachman and Ronald G. Hellman. Philadelphia: Institute for the Study of Human Issues.

―――. 1978. *Ordem Burguesa e Liberalismo Político*. São Paulo: Livraria Duas Cidades.

―――. 1979. *Cidadania e Justiça: A Política Social na Ordem Brasileira*. Rio de Janeiro: Editora Campus.

"Dossiê da Repressão: 1974: A Mudança." 1978. *Isto É*, October 4: 38-48.

Dunham, Vera S. 1976. *In Stalin's Time: Middleclass Values in Soviet Fiction*. London: Cambridge University Press.

du Plessix Gray, Francine. 1970. *Divine Disobedience: Profiles in Catholic Radicalism*. New York: Alfred A. Knopf.

Duverger, Maurice. 1980. "A New Political System Model: Semi-Presidential Government." *European Journal of Political Research* 8: 165-188.

Eagleton, Terry. 1976. *Criticism and Ideology*. London: New Left Books.

Easton, David. 1975. "A Re-Assessment of the Concept of Political Support." *British Journal of Political Science* 5: 435-457.

Echols, John M., III. 1981. "Does Socialism Mean Greater Equality? A Comparison of East and West Along Several Major Dimensions." *American Journal of Political Science* 25: 1-31.

Eckstein, Susan. 1977. "Politicos and Priests, the Iron Law of Oligarchy and Interorganizational Relations." *Comparative Politics* 9: 463-481.

Edelman, Murray. 1977. *Political Language: Words That Succeed and Policies That Fail*. New York: Academic Press.

Eldersveld, Samuel J. 1978. Critique of Eulau and Czudnowski's *Elite Recruitment in Democratic Polities: Comparative Studies Across Nations. American Political Science Review* 72: 727-728.

Elkins, David J., and Simeon, Richard E. B. 1979. "A Cause in Search of Its Effect, or What Does Political Culture Explain?" *Comparative Politics* 11: 127-145.

Elster, Jon. 1980. "Irrational Politics." *London Review of Books*, August 21-September 3: 11-13.

Ensor, Richard. 1980. "The Great Brazilian Tightrope." *Euromoney*, January: 50-68.

Erickson, Kenneth P. 1977. *The Corporative State and Working-Class Politics in Brazil*. Berkeley: University of California Press.

Estevam Martins, Carlos. 1977. *Capitalismo de Estado e Modelo Político no Brasil*. Rio de Janeiro: Editora Graal.

———. 1977. "Reflexões de um Cidadão Mal Informado." *Escrita* 2: 6-14.

Etheredge, Lloyd. 1979. "Hardball Politics: A Model." *Political Psychology* 1: 3-26.

Eulau, Heinz, and Czudnowski, Moshe M., eds. 1976. *Elite Recruitment in Democratic Polities: Comparative Studies Across Nations*. New York: John Wiley and Sons.

Evans, Peter B. 1977. "Multinationals, State-Owned Corporations, and the Transformation of Imperialism: A Brazilian Case Study." *Economic Development and Cultural Change* 26: 43-64.

———. 1979. *Dependent Development: The Alliance of Multinational, State, and Local Capital in Brazil*. Princeton: Princeton University Press.

Faase, Thomas P. 1980. "Bulwark-Catholics and Conciliar-Humanists in the Society of Jesus." *Sociological Quarterly* 21: 511-527.

Fagan, Richard R., ed. 1979. *Capitalism and the State in U.S.-Latin American Relations*. Stanford, Calif.: Stanford University Press.

Faoro, Raymundo. 1968. *Os Donos do Poder: A Formação do Patronato Político Brasileiro*. Porto Alegre: Editora Globo.

Farer, Tom J. 1981. "Reagan's Latin America." *New York Review of Books* 28 (March 19): 10-16.

Farnsworth, Clyde H. 1980. "Strikes in Poland: The Risk for Western Banks." *New York Times*, August 31: F1, 4.

Fausto, Boris. 1970. *A Revolução de 1930*. São Paulo: Editora Brasiliense.

Fernandes, Florestan. 1972. *Sociedade de Classes e Subdesenvolvimento*. Rio de Janeiro: Zahar Editores.

Feuer, Lewis S. 1975. *Ideology and the Ideologists*. New York: Harper & Row, Publishers.

"Ficou o Desgaste." 1980. *Isto É*, May 21: 12-17.

Fiechter, Georges-André. 1975. *Brazil Since 1964: Modernization Under a Military Regime*. New York: John Wiley.

Fields, Gary S. 1977. "Who Benefits from Economic Development?—A Reexamination of Brazilian Growth in the 1960s." *American Economic Review* 67: 570-582.

Fields, James M., and Schuman, Howard. 1976-1977. "Public Beliefs about the Beliefs of the Public." *Public Opinion Quarterly* 40: 427-448.

Figueiredo, Argelina Cheibub. 1975. "Política Governamental e Funções Sindicais." Master's thesis, Universidade de São Paulo.

Figueiredo, Marcus Faria. 1977. "Política de Coerção no Sistema Político Brasileiro." Master's thesis, Instituto Universitário de Pesquisas do Rio de Janeiro.

Filho, Paulo Nogeuira. 1965-1967. *Idéais e Lutas de um Burguês Progressista*. 3 vols. Rio de Janeiro: José Olympio.

Fishlow, Albert. 1980. "Brazilian Development in Long-Term Perspective." *American Economic Review* 70: 102-108.

Fitzpatrick, Sheila. 1979. *Education and Social Mobility in the Soviet Union, 1921-1934*. London: Cambridge University Press.

Fleischer, David. 1976. "Thirty Years of Legislative Recruitment in Brazil: An Analysis of the Social Background and Career Advancement Patterns of 1548 Federal Deputies, 1945-1975." Paper presented at the Tenth World Congress of the International Political Science Association, Edinburgh, Scotland, August 16-20.

Flynn, Peter. 1974. "Class, Clientelism, and Coercion: Some Mechanisms of Internal Dependency and Control." *Journal of Commonwealth and Comparative Politics* 12: 133-156.

————. 1978. *Brazil: A Political Analysis*. Boulder, Colo.: Westview Press.

Fona, Paulo, and Kuntz, Rolf. 1980. "A Cruz e a Caldeirinha." *Isto É*, April 30: 84-86.

Forman, Shepard. 1975. *The Brazilian Peasantry*. New York: Columbia University Press.

Frank, André Gunder. 1967. *Capitalism and Underdevelopment in Latin America*. New York: Monthly Review Press.

Frieden, Jeff. 1980. "Third World Debt Industrialization: International Finance and State Capitalism in Mexico, Brazil, Algeria and South Korea." Paper presented at the annual meetings of the American Political Science Association, Washington, D.C., August 28-31.

Galbraith, John Kenneth. 1978. "A Hard Case." *New York Review of Books* 25 (April 20): 6-7.

Gall, Norman. 1977. "The Rise of Brazil." *Commentary* 63: 45-55.

Gamson, William. 1975. *The Strategy of Social Protest*. Homewood, Ill.: Dorsey.

Garg, Ramesh C. 1978. "Brazilian External Debt: A Study in Capital Flows and

Transfer of Resources.'' *Journal of Interamerican Studies and World Affairs* 20: 341-351.

Gay, Peter. 1968. *Weimar Culture: The Outsider as Insider*. New York: Harper & Row, Publishers.

Geertz, Clifford. 1973. *The Interpretation of Cultures*. New York: Basic Books.

———. 1975. ''Common Sense as a Cultural System.'' *Antioch Review* 33: 5-26.

———. 1980. ''Blurred Genres: The Refiguration of Social Thought.'' *American Scholar* 9: 165-179.

Germani, Gino. 1978. *Authoritarianism, Fascism, and National Populism*. New Brunswick, N.J.: Transaction Books.

Gerwitz, Carl. 1980. ''Varied Terms Sought for Brazil.'' *International Herald Tribune*, July 21: 9.

''Golbery na ESG: Abertura pelo Centro.'' 1980. *Isto É*, July 9: 36.

Goode, William J. 1970. ''Family Systems and Social Mobility.'' In *Families in East and West*, edited by Reuben Hill and Rene Konig. The Hague: Mouton.

Goodman, D. E. 1976. ''The Brazilian Economic 'Miracle' and Regional Policy: Some Evidence from the Urban Northeast,'' *Journal of Latin American Studies* 8: 1-27.

Goodheart, Eugene. 1978. *The Failure of Criticism*. Cambridge, Mass.: Harvard University Press.

Goodwyn, Lawrence. 1978. *The Populist Moment: A Short History of the Agrarian Revolt in America*. London: Oxford University Press.

Gouldner, Alvin W. 1975-1976. ''Prologue to a Theory of Revolutionary Intellectuals.'' *Telos* 26: 3-36.

———. 1976. *The Dialectic of Ideology and Technology*. New York: Seabury Press.

Gourevitch, Peter. 1978. ''The International System and Regime Formation.'' *Comparative Politics* 10: 419-438.

———. 1978. ''The Second Image Reversed: The International Sources of Domestic Politics.'' *International Organization* 32: 881-911.

Graham, Lawrence S. 1968. *Civil Service Reform in Brazil*. Austin: University of Texas Press.

Granberg, Donald, and Jenks, Richard. 1977. ''Assimilation and Contrast Effects in the 1972 Election.'' *Human Relations* 30: 623-640.

Granovetter, Mark S. 1973. ''The Strength of Weak Ties.'' *American Journal of Sociology* 78: 1360-1380.

———. 1978. Critique of Edward O. Laumann and Franz U. Pappi's *Networks of Collective Action*. *American Journal of Sociology* 83: 1538-1542.

———. 1979. ''The Idea of 'Advancement' in Theories of Social Evolution and Development.'' *American Journal of Sociology* 85: 489-515.

Greenberg, George D. et al. 1977. ''Developing Public Policy Theory: Perspectives from Empirical Research.'' *American Political Science Review* 71: 1532-1543.

Greenwald, Howard P. 1979. ''Scientists and Technocratic Ideology.'' *Social Forces* 58: 630-650.

Gregor, A. James. 1969. *The Ideology of Fascism*. New York: The Free Press.

————. 1979. *Italian Fascism and Developmental Dictatorship*. Princeton: Princeton University Press.

Grey, Jack. 1973. "The Two Roads: Alternative Strategies of Social Change and Economic Growth in China." In *Authoritary, Participation, and Cultural Change in China*, edited by Stuart R. Schram. London: Cambridge University Press.

Grindle, Merilee. 1977. "Power, Expertise and the 'Tecnico': Suggestions from a Mexican Case Study." *Journal of Politics* 39: 399-426.

Groth, Alexander J. 1979. "USSR: Pluralist Monolith?" *British Journal of Political Science* 9: 445-464.

Groves, Robert M. 1978. "On the Mode of Administering a Questionnaire and Responses to Open-Ended Probes." *Social Science Research* 7: 213-256.

Gunther, Richard. 1980. *Public Policy in a No-Party State: Spanish Planning and Budgeting in the Twilight of the Franquist Era*. Berkeley: University of California Press.

Gurevitch, Michael, and Weingrod, Alex. 1978. "Who Knows Whom? Acquaintanceship and Contacts in the Israeli National Elite." *Human Relations* 31: 195-214.

Gurr, Ted Robert. 1974. "Persistence and Change in Political Systems, 1800-1971." *American Political Science Review* 68: 1482-1504.

Haller, Archibald O.; Holsinger, Donald B.; and Saraiva, Hélcio U. 1972. "Variations in Occupational Prestige Hierarchies: Brazilian Data." *American Journal of Sociology* 77: 941-945.

Hamilton, Nora. 1979. "Possibilities and Limits of State Autonomy in Latin American Countries." Paper presented at the meetings of the Latin American Studies Association, Pittsburgh, Pennsylvania, April 5-7.

Hammergren, Linn A. 1977. "Corporatism in Latin American Politics: A Reexamination of the 'Unique' Tradition." *Comparative Politics* 9: 443-461.

Hannan, Michael T., and Carroll, Glenn R. 1981. "Dynamics of Formal Political Structure: An Event-History Analysis." *American Sociological Review* 46: 19-35.

Hansen, Susan B. 1975. "Participation, Political Structure, and Concurrence." *American Political Science Review* 69: 1181-1199.

Harman, Harry H. 1967. *Modern Factor Analysis*. 3d ed. Chicago: University of Chicago Press.

Harris, Paul, and Heelas, Paul. 1979. "Cognitive Processes and Collective Representations." *Archives Européennes de Sociologie* 20: 211-241.

Harvey, John H.; Ickes, William John; and Kidd, Robert F., eds. 1976. *New Directions in Attributions Research*. Vol. 1. Hillsdale, N.J.: Lawrence Erlbaum Associates.

Hazelrigg, Lawrence E., and Garnier, Maurice A. 1976. "Occupational Mobility in Industrial Societies: A Comparative Analysis of Differential Access to Occupational Ranks in Seventeen Countries." *American Sociological Review* 41: 498-511.

Hechter, J. H. 1979. *Reappraisals in History*. 2d ed. Chicago: University of Chicago Press.

Heckathorn, Douglas. 1979. "The Anatomy of Social Network Linkages." *Social Science Research* 8: 222-252.

Heclo, Hugh. 1977. *A Government of Strangers: Executive Politics in Washington*. Washington, D.C.: Brookings Institution.

Herzon, Frederick D. 1980. "Ideology, Constraint, and Public Opinion: The Case of Lawyers." *American Journal of Political Science* 24: 233-258.

Hicks, Norman L. 1979. "Growth vs. Basic Needs: Is There a Trade-Off?" *World Development* 7: 985-994.

———, and Streeten, Paul. 1979. "Indicators of Development: The Search for a Basic Needs Yardstick." *World Development* 7: 567-580.

Higham, John, and Conkin, Paul K., eds. 1979. *New Directions in American Intellectual History*. Baltimore: The Johns Hopkins University Press.

Higley, John; Field, C. Lowell; and Groholt, Knut. 1976. *Elite Structure and Ideology*. New York: Columbia University Press.

Hirschman, Albert O. 1979. "The Turn to Authoritarianism in Latin America and the Search for its Economic Determinants." In *The New Authoritarianism in Latin America*, edited by David Collier. Princeton: Princeton University Press.

Hoberman, Louisa S. 1980. "Hispanic American Political Theory as a Distinct Tradition." *Journal of the History of Ideas* 41: 199-218.

Hoge, Warren M. 1979. "It's Back on the Firing Line for Brazil's 'Miracle' Worker." *New York Times*, October 7: E3.

———. 1980. "Angry Brazilian Chief Vows to Halt Rightist 'Thugs'." *New York Times*, September 16: 2.

———. 1980. "Brazilians Battle Over Land, with Church Backing Poor." *New York Times*, March 4: A2.

———. 1980. "Brazil's Army Regime Under Attack from All Sides." *New York Times*, April 30: A3.

———. 1980. "Brazil's Church-Military Feud Deepens." *New York Times*, December 28: 4.

———. 1980. "Land Dispute in Brazil Pits Church against Regime." *New York Times*, June 18: A2.

Holsti, Ole R. 1965. "The 1914 Case." *American Political Science Review* 59: 365-378.

Horowitz, Irving Louis. 1972. "The Norm of Illegitimacy: Toward A General Theory of Latin American Political Development." In *Latin America: The Dynamics of Social Change*, edited by Stefan A. Halper and John R. Sterling. New York: St. Martin's Press.

———, and Trimberger, Ellen Kay. 1976. "State Power and Military Nationalism in Latin America." *Comparative Politics* 8: 223-244.

Hough, Jerry F. 1977. *The Soviet Union and Social Science Theory*. Cambridge, Mass.: Harvard University Press.

———. 1980. *Soviet Leadership in Transition*. Washington, D.C.: Brookings Institution.

Humphrey, John. 1980. *As Raízes e os Desafios do 'Novo' Sindicalismo da Indústria Automobilística*. São Paulo: Estudos CEBRAP.

Huntington, Samuel P. 1968. *Political Order in Changing Societies*. New Haven: Yale University Press.

————, and Nelson, Joan M. 1976. *No Easy Choice: Political Participation in Developing Countries*. Cambridge, Mass.: Harvard University Press.

Hyman, Richard. 1978. "Pluralism, Procedural Consensus, and Collective Bargaining." *British Journal of Industrial Relations* 16: 16-40.

Inglehart, Ronald, and Klingeman, Hans D. 1976. "Party Identification, Ideological Preference and the Left-Right Dimension among Western Mass Publics." In *Party Identification and Beyond*, edited by Ian Budge, Ivor Crewe, and Dennis Farlie. New York: John Wiley.

Insko, Chester A. 1967. *Theories of Attitude Change*. New York: Appleton-Century-Crofts.

Iutaka, Sugiyama, and Bock, E. Wilbur. 1973. "Determinants of Occupational Status in Brazil." In *Social Stratification and Career Mobility*, edited by Walter Muller and Karl Mayer. The Hague: Mounton.

Jackman, Robert W. 1976. "Politicians in Uniform: Military Governments and Social Change in the Third World." *American Political Science Review* 70: 1078-1097.

Jaguaribe, Helio. 1958. *O Nacionalismo na Atualidade Brasileira*. Rio de Janeiro: Instituto Superior de Estudos Brasileiros.

————. 1968. *Economic and Political Development: A Theoretical Approach and a Brazilian Case Study*. Cambridge, Mass.: Harvard University Press.

————. 1974. *Brasil: Crise e Alternativas*. Rio de Janeiro: Zahar.

Jannen, William, Jr. 1976. "National Socialists and Social Mobility." *Journal of Social History* 9: 339-366.

Jones, F. Lancaster, and McDonnell, Patrick. 1977. "Measurement of Occupational Status in Comparative Analysis." *Sociological Methods and Research* 5: 437-459.

Juruna, Julia. 1980. "Les Limites de la Libéralisation au Brésil." *Le Monde Diplomatique*, July: 19-20.

Kaeble, Hartmut. 1980. "Long-Term Changes in the Recruitment of the Business Elite: Germany Compared to the U.S., Great Britain and France since the Industrial Revolution." *Journal of Social History* 13: 404-423.

Kalleberg, Arne L., and Griffin, Larry J. 1980. "Class, Occupation, and Inequality in Job Rewards." *American Journal of Sociology* 85: 731-768.

Kandell, Jonathan. 1976. "The Bonus Babies of Brazil." *New York Times*, July 11: F3.

————. 1977. "Brazil's Chief Political Loner: Ernesto Geisel." *New York Times*, April 18: 5.

Kaufman, Robert R. 1974. "The Patron-Client Concept and Macro-Politics: Prospects and Problems." *Comparative Studies in Society and History* 16: 284-308.

————. 1979. "Industrial Change and Authoritarian Rule in Latin America." In

The New Authoritarianism in Latin America, edited by David Collier. Princeton: Princeton University Press.

Kautsky, John H. 1969. "Patterns of Elite Succession in the Process of Development." *Journal of Politics* 31: 359-396.

Kedward, H. R. 1978. *Resistance in Vichy France: A Study of Ideas and Motivation in the Southern Zone 1940-1942*. London: Oxford University Press.

Kelley, Robert. 1977. "Ideology and Political Culture from Jefferson to Nixon." *American Historical Review* 82: 531-562.

Kemper, Theodore D. 1976. "Marxist and Functionalist Theories in the Study of Stratification: Common Elements that Lead to a Test." *Social Forces* 54: 559-578.

Kenworthy, Eldon. 1973. "The Function of the Little-Known Case in Theory-Building, or What Peronism Wasn't." *Comparative Politics* 6: 17-45.

———. 1976. "Nonparticipation in Latin America: How We Explain the End of Democracy There." Paper presented at the meetings of the American Political Science Association, Chicago, Illinois, September 2-5.

Kerbo, Harold R., and Della Fave, L. Richard. 1979. "The Empirical Side of the Power Elite Debate: An Assessment and Critique of Recent Research." *Sociological Quarterly* 20: 5-22.

Kessler, Allan. 1967. "The Internal Structure of Elites." In *A Strategy for Research on Social Policy*, vol. 1 of *The Politics of Change in Venezuela*, edited by Frank Bonilla and José A. Silva Michelena. Cambridge, Mass.: M.I.T. Press.

Keyfitz, Nathan. 1976. "World Resources and the World Middle Class." *Scientific American* 235: 28.

Kinder, Donald R. 1978. "Political Person Perception: The Asymmetrical Influence of Sentiment and Choice on Perceptions of Presidential Candidates." *Journal of Personality and Social Psychology* 36: 859-871.

King, Michael. 1977-1978. "Assimilation and Contrast of Presidential Candidates' Issue Positions, 1972." *Public Opinion Quarterly* 41: 515-522.

Kish, Leslie. 1965. "Sampling Organizations and Groups of Unequal Sizes." *American Sociological Review* 30: 564-572.

———. 1965. *Survey Sampling*. New York: Wiley.

———, and Frankel, Martin Richard. 1974. "Inference from Complex Samples." *Journal of the Royal Statistical Society*, Series B, 36: 1-36.

Korte, Charles. 1977. "Pluralistic Ignorance about Student Radicalism." *Sociometry* 35: 576-587.

Krane, Dale. 1980. "Opposition Strategy and Survival in Praetorian Brazil." Paper presented at the annual meetings of the Southern Political Science Association, Atlanta, Georgia, November 6-8.

Kritzer, Herbert M. 1978. "Ideology and American Political Elites." *Public Opinion Quarterly* 42: 484-502.

Kruskal, Joseph B., and Wish, Myron. 1977. *Multidimensional Scaling*. Beverly Hills: Sage Productions.

Kupfer, José Paulo. 1980. "Nas Asas da Inflação." *Isto É*, June 4: 66-71.

Kurth, James R. 1979. "Leading Sectors, Timing of Industrialization, and Political

Change: A European Perspective." In *The New Authoritarianism in Latin America*, edited by David Collier. Princeton: Princeton University Press.

Labovitz, Sanford. 1971. "In Defense of Assigning Numbers to Ranks." *American Sociological Review* 36: 521-522.

Lafer, Celso. 1975. *O Sistema Político Brasileiro*. São Paulo: Perspectiva.

Lamounier, Bolivar. 1968. "Ideologia Conservadora e Mundanças Estruturais." *Dados* 5: 1-26.

———. 1977. "O Mito da Tecnocracia." *Isto É*, May 25: 72-73.

———. 1979. "O Discurso e o Processo: Da Distensão às Opções do Regime Brasileiro." In *Brasil 1990*, edited by Henrique Rattner. São Paulo: Editora Brasiliense.

———. 1980. "Notes on the Study of Re-Democratization." Washington, D.C.: Working Paper No. 58, The Wilson Center, Smithsonian Institution.

Lancaster, Thomas D. "Toward an Assessment of the Spanish Social Security System." *Economic Development and Cultural Change*. Forthcoming.

Landsberger, Henry A., and Saavedra, Antonio. 1967. "Response Set in Developing Countries." *Public Opinion Quarterly* 31: 214-229.

Larkin, Emmet. 1975. "Church, State, and Nation in Modern Ireland." *American Historical Review* 80: 1244-1276.

Larson, Magali Sarfatti. 1977. *The Rise of Professionalism*. Berkeley: University of California Press.

Laslett, Barbara. 1980. "The Place of Theory in Quantitative Historical Research." *American Sociological Review* 45: 214-228.

Laumann, Edward O. 1969. "Friends of Urban Men: An Assessment of Accuracy in Reporting Their Sociometric Attributes, Mutual Choice, and Attitude Agreement." *Sociometry* 32: 54-69.

———, and Pappi, Franz U. 1976. *Networks of Collective Action*. New York: Academic Press.

Lawrence, David G. 1976. "Procedural Norms and Tolerance: A Reassessment." *American Political Science Review* 70: 80-100.

Leeds, Anthony. 1964. "Brazilian Careers and Social Structure." *American Anthropologist* 66: 1321-1347.

———. 1977. "Brazil as a System." Amherst, Mass. Program in Latin American Studies Occasional Paper Series No. 5, University of Massachusetts.

Leff, Nathaniel H. *Economic Retardation and Development in Brazil, 1822-1947*. Forthcoming.

Legg, Keith R. 1975. *Patrons, Clients, and Politicians: New Perspectives on Political Clientelism*. Berkeley: Institute of International Studies.

———. 1980. "Political Participation, Ideologies of Participation, and Regime Stability: A Comparison of Pluralist and Clientelist Systems." Paper presented at the annual meetings of the Mid-West Political Science Association, Chicago, Illinois, April 24-26.

Leinhardt, Samuel, ed. 1977. *Social Networks: A Developing Paradigm*. New York: Academic Press.

Lemgruber, Antonio C. 1977. "Inflation in Brazil." In *Worldwide Inflation: Theory and Recent Experience*, edited by Lawrence B. Krause and Walter S. Salant. New York: Academic Press.

Leonard, H. Jeffrey. 1980. "Multinational Corporations and Politics in Developing Countries." *World Politics* 32: 454-483.

Leonardi, Robert; Nanetti, Raffaela; and Putnam, Robert D. 1979. "Attitude Stability among Italian Elites." *American Journal of Political Science* 23: 463-494.

Lernoux, Penny. 1980. *Cry of the People*. New York: Doubleday & Company, Inc.

———. 1980. "Brazil Spends Its Way to the Guardhouse." *The Nation*, June 28: 780-782.

———. 1980. "The Latin American Church." *Latin American Research Review* 15: 201-211.

———. 1980. "Latin America: The Revolutionary Bishops." *The Atlantic* 246 (July): 6-14.

Levin, Linda. 1979. "Some Historical Implications of Kinship Organization for Family-Based Politics in the Brazilian Northeast." *Comparative Studies in Society and History* 21: 262-292.

Levy, Shlomit. 1978. "Involvement as a Component of Attitude: Theory and Political Examples." In *Theory Construction and Data Analysis in the Behavioral Sciences*, edited by Samuel Shye. San Francisco: Jossey-Bass.

Lewis-Beck, Michael S. 1979. "Some Economic Effects of Revolution: Models, Measurement, and the Cuban Evidence." *American Journal of Sociology* 84: 1127-1149.

Lijphart, Arend. 1978. *Democracy in Plural Societies*. New Haven: Yale University Press.

Lincoln, James R., and Miller, Jon. 1979. "Work and Friendship Ties in Organizations: A Comparative Analysis of Relational Networks." *Administrative Science Quarterly* 24: 181-199.

Linz, Juan J. 1964. "An Authoritarian Regime: Spain." In *Cleavages, Ideologies, and Party Systems*, edited by Erik Allardt and Yrjo Littunen. Helsinki: Academic Bookstore.

———. 1973. "The Future of an Authoritarian Situation or the Institutionalization of an Authoritarian Regime: The Case of Brazil." In *Authoritarian Brazil: Origins, Policies and Future*, edited by Alfred Stepan. New Haven: Yale University Press.

———. 1973. "Opposition in and Under an Authoritarian Regime: The Case of Spain." In *Regimes and Oppositions*, edited by Robert A. Dahl. New Haven: Yale University Press.

———. 1975. "Totalitarian and Authoritarian Regimes." In *Handbook of Political Science*, vol. 3, edited by Fred I. Greenstein and Nelson W. Polsby. Reading, Mass.: Addison-Wesley.

———. 1978. *The Breakdown of Democratic Regimes: Crisis, Breakdown, and Reequilibration*. Baltimore: The Johns Hopkins University Press.

————. 1979. "Europe's Southern Frontier: Evolving Trends Toward What?" *Daedalus* 108: 175-209.

Lipset, Seymour Martin. 1969. *Political Man*. New York: Doubleday & Company, Inc.

————, and Solari, Aldo, eds. 1967. *Elites in Latin America*. New York: Oxford University Press.

Lowi, Theodore. 1964. "American Business, Public Policy, Case-Studies and Political Theory." *World Politics* 16: 677-715.

Luckmann, Thomas, ed. 1978. *Phenomenology and Sociology: Selected Readings*. London: Penguin Books.

Lustick, Ian. 1979. "Stability in Deeply Divided Societies: Consociationalism versus Control." *World Politics* 31: 325-344.

McCauley, Clark, and Stitt, Christopher L. 1978. "An Individual and Quantitative Measure of Stereotypes." *Journal of Personality and Social Psychology* 36: 929-940.

McDonald, Ronald H. 1979. "Patterns of Patrimonial Leadership in Latin America." Paper presented at the annual meetings of the American Political Science Association, Washington, D.C., August 31-September 3.

McDonough, Peter. 1981. "Repression and Representation in Brazil." Paper presented at the Centennial Conference on Mosca's Theory of the Ruling Class, Northern Illinois University, DeKalb, Illinois, September 7-9.

————, and de Souza, Amaury. 1981. *The Politics of Population in Brazil: Elite Ambivalence and Public Demand*. Austin: University of Texas Press.

————; López Pina, Antonio; and Barnes, Samuel H. 1981. "The Spanish Public in Political Transition." *British Journal of Political Science* 11: 49-79.

Macedo, Roberto B. M. 1977. "A Critical Review of the Relation between the Post-1964 Wage Policy and the Worsening of Brazil's Size Income Distribution in the Sixties." *Explorations in Economic Research* 4: 117-140.

McFarland, David, and Brown, Daniel. 1973. "Social Distance as a Metric: A Systematic Introduction to Smallest-Space Analysis." In *Bonds of Pluralism*, edited by Edward O. Laumann. New York: John Wiley.

MacRae, Duncan, Jr. 1960. "Direct Factor Analysis of Sociometric Data." *Sociometry* 23: 360-371.

Maguire, John M. 1978. *Marx's Theory of Politics*. London: Cambridge University Press.

Maier, Charles S. 1975. *Recasting Bourgeois Europe: Stabilization in France, Germany, and Italy in the Decade after World War I*. Princeton: Princeton University Press.

————. 1979. "The Politics of Productivity: Foundations of American International Economic Policy After World War II." *International Organization* 31: 607-633.

Malan, Pedro S., and Bonelli, Regis. 1977. "The Brazilian Economy in the Seventies: Old and New Developments." *World Development* 5: 19-45.

Malloy, James M. 1979. *The Politics of Social Security in Brazil*. Pittsburgh: University of Pittsburgh Press.

Malloy, James M., ed. 1977. *Authoritarianism and Corporatism in Latin America.* Pittsburgh: University of Pittsburgh Press.

Mandle, Jay R. 1980. "Marxist Analyses and Capitalist Development in the Third World." *Theory and Society* 9: 865-876.

Marsh, James G. 1980. "Footnotes to Organizational Change." Unpublished paper, Stanford University.

Marshall, T. H. 1964. *Class, Citizenship and Social Development.* New York: Doubleday & Company, Inc.

Martin, Andrew. 1977. "Political Constraints on Economic Strategies in Advanced Industrial Societies." *Comparative Political Studies* 10: 323-354.

Martin, David. 1978. *A General Theory of Secularization.* New York: Harper & Row, Publishers.

Martin, Everett G. 1980. "Big Borrower: Brazil Counts on Banks to Lend More Billions as Tough Year Looms." *Wall Street Journal,* February 4: 1, 17.

Martin, Heloísa Helena T. S. 1979. *O Estado e a Burocratização do Sindicato no Brasil.* São Paulo: Editora Hucitec.

Martins, Luciano. 1977. "A Expansão Recente do Estado no Brasil: Seus Problemas e Seus Atores." Unpublished manuscript, São Paulo.

Mass, Bonnie. 1976. *Population Target: The Political Economy of Population Control in Latin America.* Brampton, Ontario: Charters Publishing Company.

Mauer, Harry. 1978. "Is Brazil on the Brink of Democracy?" *New York Review of Books* 25 (September 28): 43-48.

Mayer, Arno J. 1975. "The Lower Middle Class as Historical Problem." *Journal of Modern History* 47: 409-436.

Meek, Ronald L., ed. 1971. *Marx and Engels on the Population Bomb.* Berkeley: Ramparts Press.

Meirelles Passos, José. 1980. "A Tortura Ainda é uma Rotina nas Delegacias." *Isto É,* November 5: 26-27.

Mendelson, Sara Heller, and Slater, Miriam. 1979. "The Weightiest Business: Marriage in an Upper-Gentry Family in Seventeenth-Century England." *Past and Present* 85: 126-140.

Mendes, Cândido. 1980. "The Post-1964 Brazilian Regime: Outward Redemocratization and Inner Institutionalization." *Government and Opposition* 15: 48-74.

Mercadante, Paulo. 1965. *A Consciência Conservadora no Brasil.* Rio de Janeiro: Editôra Saga.

————. 1978. *Militares e Civis: A Ética e o Compromisso.* Rio de Janeiro: Zahar Editores.

Mericle, Kenneth S. 1977. "Corporatist Controls of the Working-Class: The Case of Post-1964 Brazil." In *Authoritarianism and Corporatism in Latin America,* edited by James Malloy. Pittsburgh: University of Pittsburgh Press.

Merton, Robert K. 1957. *Social Theory and Social Structure.* Rev. ed. Glencoe: The Free Press.

Mesa-Lago, Carmelo. 1979. *Social Security in Latin America: Pressure Groups, Stratification, and Inequality.* Pittsburgh: University of Pittsburgh Press.

Mintz, Beth et al. 1976. "Problems of Proof in Elite Research." *Social Problems* 23: 314-324.

Modigliani, Andre, and Gamson, William A. 1979. "Thinking About Politics." *Political Behavior* 1: 5-30.

Mohr, Lawrence B. 1978. Review of James G. March et al., *Ambiguity and Choice in Organizations*. Bergen: Universitetsforlaget, 1976. *American Political Science Review* 8: 217-220.

Mokken, Robert J., and Stokman, Frans N. 1978-1979. "Corporate-Governmental Networks in the Netherlands." *Social Networks* 1: 333-358.

Moon, J. Donald. 1975. "The Logic of Political Inquiry: A Synthesis of Opposed Perspectives." In *Political Science: Scope and Theory*, edited by Fred I. Greenstein and Nelson W. Polsby, vol. 1 of *Handbook of Political Science*. Reading, Mass.: Addison-Wesley.

Moore, Barrington Jr. 1966. *Social Origins of Dictatorship and Democracy*. Boston: Beacon Press.

Moore, Clement Henry. 1980. *Images of Development: Egyptian Engineers in Search of Industry*. Cambridge, Mass.: M.I.T. Press.

Moore, Gwen. 1979. "The Structure of a National Elite Network." *American Sociological Review* 44: 673-692.

Moreno, J. L. 1953. *Who Shall Survive? Foundations of Sociometry, Group Psychotherapy and Sociodrama*. New York: Beacon House.

Morrison, Donald F. 1976. *Multivariate Statistical Methods*. 2d ed. New York: McGraw-Hill.

Morse, Richard M. 1970. *Formação Histórica de São Paulo*. São Paulo: Difusão Européia do Livro.

Mota, Carlos Guilherme. 1974. *Ideologia da Cultura Brasileira, 1933-1974*. São Paulo: Editora Atica.

Mulaik, S. A. 1972. *The Foundations of Factor Analysis*. New York: McGraw-Hill.

Nagle, John D. 1977. *System and Succession: The Social Bases of Political Elite Recruitment*. Austin: University of Texas Press.

"Negociar É Possível." 1980. *Veja*, June 11: 20-22.

Netto, Delfim. 1972. Address to the Conference on Indicators of Nation Building, Rio de Janeiro, April.

Neubauer, Deane E., and Kastner, Lawrence D. 1969. "The Study of Compliance Maintenance as a Strategy for Comparative Research." *World Politics* 21: 629-640.

Nicholls, William H. 1978. "Professor Forman on the Brazilian Peasantry." *Economic Development and Cultural Change* 26: 359-383.

"1974, A Mudança." 1978. *Isto É*, October 4: 38.

Nisbet, Richard, and Ross, Lee D. 1980. *Human Inference: Strategies and Shortcomings of Social Judgment*. Englewood Cliffs, N.J.: Prentice-Hall.

Noble, David F. 1977. *America by Design: Science, Technology, and the Rise of Corporate Capitalism*. New York: Alfred A. Knopf, Inc. "O Apoio à Livre

Iniciativa e à Eficiência: A Sociedade Almejada.'' 1980. *Gazeta Mercantil*, April 29: 2-7.

Oberschall, Anthony. 1979. ''Protracted Conflict.'' In *The Dynamics of Social Movements*, edited by Mayer N. Zald and John D. McCarthy. Cambridge, Mass.: Winthrop Publishers.

O'Donnell, Guillermo A. 1973. *Modernization and Bureaucratic-Authoritarianism*. Berkeley: Institute of International Studies.

————. 1978. ''Reflections on the Patterns of Change in the Bureaucratic-Authoritarian State.'' *Latin American Research Review* 8: 3-38.

————. 1978. ''State and Alliances in Argentina, 1956-1976.'' *Journal of Development Studies* 15: 3-33.

O'Gorman, Hubert J., with Garry, Stephen L. 1976-1977. ''Pluralistic Ignorance— A Replication and Extention.'' *Public Opinion Quarterly* 40: 449-458.

''Oh, Brazil.'' 1979. *The Economist*, August 4-10: 1-22.

''O João Mais Popular.'' 1979. *Veja*, October 3: 9-16.

Oksenberg, Michael. 1970. ''Getting Ahead and Getting Along in Communist China: The Ladder of Success on the Eve of the Cultural Revolution.'' In *Party Leadership and Revolutionary Power in China*, edited by J. W. Lewis. London: Cambridge University Press.

————. 1976. ''The Exit Pattern from Chinese Politics and Its Implications.'' *China Quarterly*: 501-518.

Okun, Arthur M. 1975. *Equality and Efficiency: The Big Tradeoff*. Washington, D.C.: The Brookings Institution.

Olson, Richard Stuart. 1979. ''Expropriation and Economic Coercion in World Politics: A Retrospective Look at Brazil in the 1960s.'' *Journal of the Developing Areas* 13: 247-262.

''O Poder e os Novos Poderes da Presidência.'' 1974. *Visão*, June 24: 16-19.

Organski, A.F.K. 1965. *Stages of Political Development*. New York: Alfred A. Knopf, Inc.

Packenham, Robert A. 1974. *Liberal America and the Third World: Political Development Ideas in Foreign Aid and Social Science*. Princeton: Princeton University Press.

Palme, Helmut. 1973. ''Criteria for the Selection of Sectors and Positions in an Elite Study.'' Paper presented at the meetings of the International Political Science Association, Montreal, August 19-25.

Perkin, Harold. 1978. ''The Recruitment of Elites in British Society since 1800.'' *Journal of Social History* 12: 222-234.

Perlman, Janice. 1976. *The Myth of Marginality: Urban Poverty and Politics in Rio de Janeiro*. Berkeley: University of California Press.

Pike, Frederick B., and Stritch, Thomas, eds. 1974. *The New Corporatism*. South Bend: University of Notre Dame Press.

Pipes, Richard. 1974. *Russia Under the Old Regime*. New York: Charles Scribner's Sons.

''Planalto Não Desmentirá Boatos.'' 1980. *Veja*, June 4: 31.

Pocock, J.G.A. 1975. *The Machiavellian Moment: Florentine Political Thought and the Atlantic Republican Tradition*. Princeton: Princeton University Press.

Portes, Alejandro. 1979. "Housing Policy, Urban Poverty, and the State: The *Favelas* of Rio de Janeiro, 1972-76." *Latin American Research Review* 14: 3-24.

———, and Ferguson, D. Frances. 1977. "Comparative Ideologies of Poverty and Equity: Latin America and the United States." In *Equity, Income, and Policy: Comparative Studies in Three Worlds of Development*, edited by Irving Louis Horowitz. New York: Praeger.

Poulantzas, Nicos. 1979. "La Crise des Partis." *Le Monde Diplomatique*: 28.

Purcell, Susan Kaufman, and Purcell, John F. H. 1980. "State and Society in Mexico: Must a Stable Polity Be Institutionalized?" *World Politics* 32: 194-227.

Putnam, Robert D. 1973. *The Beliefs of Politicians*. New Haven: Yale University Press.

———. 1976. *The Comparative Study of Political Elites*. Englewood Cliffs, N.J.: Prentice-Hall.

———. 1977. "Elite Transformation in Advanced Industrial Societies: An Empirical Assessment of the Theory of Technocracy." *Comparative Political Studies* 10: 383-412.

Rabinow, Paul, and Sullivan, William M., eds. 1979. *Interpretative Social Science*. Berkeley: University of California Press.

Rae, Douglas W. 1979. "The Egalitarian State: Notes on a System of Contradictory Ideals." *Daedalus* 408: 37-54.

———, and Taylor, Michael. 1970. *The Analysis of Political Cleavages*. New Haven: Yale University Press.

Ray, J. J. 1976. "Do Authoritarians Hold Authoritarian Attitudes?" *Human Relations* 29: 307-325.

Reed, Theodore L. 1978. "Organizational Change in the American Foreign Service, 1925-1965: The Utility of Cohort Analysis." *American Sociological Review* 43: 404-421.

Reilly, Charles A. 1980. "Cultural Movements as Surrogates for Political Participation in Contemporary Latin America." Paper presented at the annual meetings of the American Political Science Association, Washington, D.C., August 28-31.

Reis, Fábio Wanderley et al. 1978. *Os Partidos e o Regime: A Lógica do Processo Eleitoral Brasileiro*. São Paulo: Edições Símbolo.

Rejai, Mostafa, with Philips, Kay. 1979. *Leaders of Revolution*. Beverly Hills: Sage Publications.

Remmer, Karen L. 1979. "Military Rule and Political Demobilization in Latin America." Paper presented at the annual meetings of the American Political Science Association, Washington, D.C., August 31-September 3.

———. 1979. "Public Policy and Regime Consolidation: The First Five Years of the Chilean Junta." *Journal of Developing Areas* 13: 441-461.

Rigby, Ken, and Rump, Eric E. 1979. "The Generality of Attitudes to Authority." *Human Relations* 32: 469-487.

Rimlinger, Gaston V. 1971. *Welfare Policy and Industrialization in Europe, America, and Russia.* New York: John Wiley & Sons.

Rochon, Thomas R. 1980. "Local Elites and the Structure of Political Conflict: Parties, Unions, and Action Groups in the Netherlands." Ph.D. dissertation, University of Michigan.

Rockman, Bert A. 1976. "Studying Elite Political Culture: Problems in Design and Interpretation." *Papers of University Center for International Studies,* University of Pittsburgh.

Rodrigues, José Honório. 1965. *Conciliação e Reforma no Brasil.* Rio de Janeiro: Editora Civilização Brasileira.

Roett, Riordan, ed. 1976. *Brazil in the Seventies.* Washington, D.C.: American Enterprise Institute.

————. 1978. *Brazil: Politics in a Patrimonial Society.* Rev. ed. New York: Praeger.

Rose, Richard. 1969. "Dynamic Tendencies in the Authority of Regimes." *World Politics* 21: 602-628.

Rosenbaum, H. Jon, and Tyler, William G., eds. 1973. *Contemporary Brazil: Issues in Economic and Political Development.* New York: Praeger.

Rosenthal, Robert, and Rubin, Donald B. 1979. "A Note on Percent Variance Explained as a Measure of the Importance of Effects." *Journal of Applied Social Psychology* 9: 395-396.

Ross, Lee D. 1977. "The Intuitive Psychologist and his Shortcomings: Distortions in the Attribution Process." In *Advances in Experimental Social Psychology,* edited by Leonard Berkowitz. New York: Academic Press.

————. 1977. "Problems in the Interpretation of Self-Serving Asymmetries in Causal Attribution." *Sociometry* 40: 112-114.

————; Amabile, Teresa M.; and Steinmetz, Julia L. 1977. "Social Roles, Social Control, and Biases in Social-Perception Process." *Journal of Personality and Social Psychology* 35: 485-494.

————; Greene, David; and House, Pamela. 1977. "The 'False Consensus Effect': An Egocentric Bias in Social Perception and Attribution Processes." *Journal of Experimental Social Psychology* 13: 279-301.

Roy, William G. 1974. "Inter-Industry Membership in a National Polity Over Time." Unpublished manuscript, Ann Arbor, University of Michigan.

Rubenstein, W. D. 1977. "Wealth, Elites, and the Class Structure of Modern Britain." *Past and Present* 26: 99-126.

Rummel, R. J. 1970. *Applied Factor Analysis.* Evanston: Northwestern University Press.

Sanders, Thomas G. 1980. "Human Rights and Political Process in Brazil." American Universities Field Staff Reports, No. 11, Washington, D.C.

São Paulo Justice and Peace Commission. 1978. *São Paulo: Growth and Poverty.* London: Bowerdean Press.

Sardenberg, Carlos Alberto. 1980. "O Mundo das Fichas." *Isto É*, June 25: 12-17.

Sarfatti, Magali. 1966. *Spanish Bureaucratic-Partimonialism in America*. Berkeley: Institute of International Studies.

Sartori, Giovanni, 1969. "Politics, Ideology, and Belief Systems." *American Political Science Review* 53: 398-411.

———. 1979. "Liberty and Law." In *The Politicization of Society*, edited by Kenneth S. Templeton, Jr. Indianapolis, Ind.: Liberty Press.

Schaffer, Bernard. 1977. "Organization is not Equity: Theories of Political Integration." *Development and Change* 8: 19-43.

Schmidt, Steffen W. et al. 1977. *Friends, Followers, and Factions: A Reader in Political Clientelism*. Berkeley: University of California Press.

Schmitter, Philippe C. 1971. *Interest Conflict and Political Change in Brazil*. Stanford: Stanford University Press.

———. 1972. "Paths to Political Development in Latin America." In *Changing Latin America*, vol. 3, edited by Douglas A. Chalmers, Proceedings of the Academy of Political Science, Columbia University.

———. 1974. "Still the Century of Corporatism?" *Review of Politics* 36: 85-131.

Schneider, Ronald M. 1971. *The Political System of Brazil: Emergence of a "Modernizing" Authoritarian Regime*. New York: Columbia University Press.

Schneider, William. 1978. "Democrats and Republicans, Liberals and Conservatives." In *Emerging Coalitions in American Politics*, edited by Seymour Martin Lipset. San Francisco: Institute for Contemporary Studies.

Schoultz, Lars. 1977. "The Socio-Economic Determinants of Popular-Authoritarian Electoral Behavior: The Case of Peronism." *American Political Science Review* 71: 1423-1446.

Schuman, Howard, and Presser, Stanley. 1977. "Question Wording as an Independent Variable in Survey Analysis." *Sociological Methods and Research* 6: 27-46.

Schwartzman, Simon. 1970. "Representação e Cooptação Política no Brasil." *Dados* 7: 9-41.

———. 1973. "Twenty Years of Representative Democracy in Brazil." In *Mathematical Approaches to Politics*, edited by Hayward Alker, Jr., Karl Deutsch, and Antoine H. Stoetzel. San Francisco: Jossey-Bass.

———. 1975. *São Paulo e o Estado Nacional*. São Paulo: Difusão Européia do Livro.

Scott, James C. 1976. *The Moral Economy of the Peasant*. New Haven: Yale University Press.

Searing, Donald D. 1978. "Measuring Politicians' Values." *American Political Science Review* 72: 65-79.

Seliger, Martin. 1976. *Ideology and Politics*. New York: The Free Press.

Serra, José. 1979. "Three Mistaken Theses Regarding the Connection between Industrialization and Authoritarian Regimes." In *The New Authoritarianism in Latin America,* edited by David Collier. Princeton: Princeton University Press.

Shapiro, David. 1965. *Neurotic Styles.* New York: Basic Books.

Sheahan, John. 1980. "Market-oriented Economic Policies and Political Repression in Latin America." *Economic Development and Cultural Change* 28: 267-291.

Sherif, Muzafer, and Hovland, Carl. 1961. *Social Judgment: Assimilation and Contrast Effects in Communications and Attitude Change.* New Haven: Yale University Press.

Shiner, L. E. 1975. "Tradition/Modernity: An Ideal Type Gone Astray." *Comparative Studies in Society and History* 17: 245-252.

Sigmund, Paul. 1973. "Latin American Catholicism's Opening to the Left." *Review of Politics* 35: 61-76.

Skidmore, Thomas E. 1967. *Politics in Brazil, 1932-1964: An Experiment in Democracy.* New York: Oxford University Press.

―――. 1975. "The Historiography of Brazil, 1889-1964: Part I." *Hispanic-American Historical Review* 55: 716-748.

Skocpol, Theda. 1979. *States and Social Revolutions.* London: Cambridge University Press.

Smith, Kent W. 1974. "Forming Composite Scales and Estimating Their Validity Through Factor Analysis." *Social Forces* 53: 158-180.

Smith, Peter H. 1979. *Labyrinths of Power: Political Recruitment in Twentieth-Century Mexico.* Princeton: Princeton University Press.

Snyder, Mark, and Swann, William B., Jr. 1978. "Behavioral Confirmation in Social Interaction: From Social Perception to Social Reality." *Journal of Experimental Social Psychology* 14: 148-162.

―――; Tanke, Elizabeth Decker; and Berscheid, Ellen. 1977. "Social Perception and Interpersonal Behavior: On the Self-Fulfilling Nature of Social Stereotypes." *Journal of Personality and Social Psychology* 35: 656-666.

Soares, Glaucio Ary Dillon. 1973. *Sociedade e Política no Brasil: Desenvolvimento, Classe e Política durante a Segunda República.* São Paulo: Difusão Europeía do Livro.

Spalding, Rose J. 1980. "Welfare Policymaking: Theoretical Implications of a Mexican Case Study." *Comparative Politics* 12: 419-438.

Srinivas, M. N. 1967. *Social Change in Modern India.* Berkeley: University of California Press.

Stanworth, Philip, and Giddens, Anthony, eds. 1974. *Elites and Power in British Society.* London: Cambridge University Press.

Stauffer, Robert B. 1974. "The Political Economy of a Coup: Transnational Linkages and Philippine Political Response." *Journal of Peace Research* 11: 161-177.

Stepan, Alfred. 1971. *The Military in Politics.* Princeton: Princeton University Press.

―――. 1978. *The State and Society: Peru in Comparative Perspective.* Princeton: Princeton University Press.

————, ed. 1973. *Authoritarian Brazil: Origins, Policies, and Future.* New Haven: Yale University Press.

Sternheimer, Stephen. 1980. "Administration for Development: The Emerging Bureaucratic Elite." In *Russian Officialdom: The Bureaucratization of Russian Society from the Seventeenth to the Twentieth Century*, edited by Walter McKenzie Pinter and Don Karl Rowney. Chapel Hill: University of North Carolina Press.

Stinchcombe, Arthur L. 1965. "Social Structure and Organizations." In *Handbook of Organizations*, edited by James G. March. Chicago: Rand McNally.

————. 1968. "Political Socialization in the Latin American Middle Class." *Harvard Educational Review* 38: 506-527.

Stone, Alan. 1978. Review of Thomas R. Dye's *Who's Running America? Institutional Leadership*, in *American Political Science Review* 72: 673-674.

Strauss, David J. 1977. "Measuring Endogamy." *Social Science Research* 6: 225-245.

Strickland, D. A., and Johnston, R. E. 1970. "Issue Elasticity in Political Systems." *Journal of Political Economy* 78: 1069-1092.

Stycos, J. Mayone. 1971. *Ideology, Faith, and Family Planning in Latin America.* New York: McGraw-Hill.

Suleiman, Ezra N. 1978. *Elites in French Society: The Politics of Survival.* Princeton: Princeton University Press.

Sullivan, William M. 1979. "Shifting Loyalties: Critical Theory and the Problem of Legitimacy." *Polity* 12: 253-272.

Synder, Mark; Tanke, Elizabeth Decker; and Berscheid, Ellen. 1977. "Social Perception and Interpersonal Behavior: On the Self-Fulfilling Nature of Social Stereotypes." *Journal of Personality and Social Psychology* 35: 656-666.

Szuchman, March D., and Sofrer, Eugene F. 1976. "The State of Occupational Stratification Research in Argentina." *Latin American Research Review* 11: 159-171.

Tait, Alan A.; Gratz, Wilfrid I. M.; and Eichengreen, Barry J. 1979. "International Comparisons of Taxation for Selected Developing Countries, 1972-76." *International Monetary Fund Staff Papers* 16: 123-153.

Taussig, Michael T. 1980. *The Devil and Commodity Fetishism in South America.* Chapel Hill: University of North Carolina Press.

Taylor, Lance, and Bacha, Edmar L. 1976. "The Unequalizing Spiral: A First Growth Model for Belinda." *Quarterly Journal of Economics* 90: 197-218.

Therborn, Göran. 1978. *What Does the Ruling Class Do When It Rules?* London: New Left Books.

————. 1979. "The Travail of Latin American Democracy." *New Left Review* 113-114: 71-109.

Thompson, Richard A. 1973. "A Theory of Instrumental Social Networks." *Journal of Anthropological Research* 29: 244-265.

Thompson, William Irwin, 1967. *The Imagination of an Insurrection.* New York: Oxford University Press.

Ting, William Pang-Yu. 1979. "Coalitional Behavior among the Chinese Military Elite." *American Political Science Review* 73: 478-493.

Todaro, Michael P. 1976. "Rural-Urban Migration, Unemployment, and Job Probabilities: Recent Theoretical and Empirical Research." In *Economic Factors in Population Growth*, edited by Ansley J. Coale. New York: Halsted.

Treiman, Donald J. 1970. "Industrialization and Social Stratification." In *Social Stratification: Research and Theory for the 1970s*, edited by Edward O. Laumann. Indianapolis: Bobbs-Merrill.

Trimberger, Ellen Kay. 1978. *Revolution from Above: Military Bureaucrats and Development in Japan, Turkey, Egypt, and Peru*. New Brunswick, N.J.: Transaction Books.

Tucker, Robert C. 1977. "Stalinism as Revolution from Above." In *Stalinism: Essays in Historical Interpretation*, edited by R. C. Tucker. New York: W.W. Norton & Company, Inc.

Uricoechea, Fernando. 1980. *The Patrimonial Foundations of the Brazilian Bureaucratic State*. Berkeley: University of California Press.

Useem, Bert and Michael. 1979. "Government Legitimacy and Political Stability." *Social Forces* 57: 840-852.

Useem, Michael. 1978. "The Inner Group of the American Capitalist Class." *Social Problems* 25: 225-240.

———. 1979. "Studying the Corporation and the Corporate Elite." *American Sociologist* 14: 97-107.

Vaillant, George E. 1977. *Adaptation to Life: How the Best and the Brightest Came of Age*. Boston: Little, Brown and Company.

Van Der Plight, Joop, and Van Dijk, Jos A. 1979. "Polarization of Judgment and Preference for Judgmental Labels." *European Journal of Social Psychology* 9: 233-241.

Vanneman, Reeve. 1977. "The Occupational Composition of American Classes." *American Journal of Sociology* 82: 783-807.

Velho, Otávio Guilherme. 1976. *Capitalismo Autoritário e Campesinato*. São Paulo: Difel.

Veliz, Claudio. 1979. *The Centralist Tradition in Latin America*. Princeton: Princeton University Press.

Vera, Hernan, and Francis, Michael J. 1977. "A Totalitarianism in Latin America: Chile's New Military Messiahs." *Third World Review* 3: 21-30.

Verbrugge, Lois M. 1979. "Multiplexity in Adult Friendships." *Social Forces* 57: 1286-1308.

Vianna, Luis Werneck. 1976. *Liberalismo e Sindicato no Brasil*. Rio de Janeiro: Paz e Terra.

Vincente-Wiley, Leticia. 1979. "Achievement Values of Filipino Entrepreneurs and Politicians." *Economic Development and Cultural Change* 27: 467-483.

Vogel, David. 1977. "Why Businessmen Distrust Their State." *British Journal of Political Science* 8: 45-78.

Volgyes, Ivan. 1978. "Modernization, Stratification, and Elite Development in Hungary." *Social Forces* 57: 500-521.

Wachtel, Howard M. 1980. "A Decade of International Debt." *Theory and Society* 9: 504-518.

Wallerstein, Immanuel. 1976. "Class Conflict in the Capitalist World-Economy." Working Paper Series, Fernand Braudel Center for the Study of New Economies, Historical Systems, and Civilizations, State University of New York, Binghamton.

———. 1976. "From Feudalism to Capitalism: Transition or Transitions?" *Social Forces* 55: 273-283.

Wallerstein, Michael. 1980. "The Collapse of Democracy in Brazil." *Latin American Research Review* 15: 3-40.

Waring, Joan M. 1975. "Social Replenishment and Social Change: The Problem of Disordered Cohort Flow." *American Behavioral Scientist* 19: 237-256.

Wasserman, Stanley. 1980. "Analyzing Social Networks as Stochastic Processes." *Journal of the American Statistical Association* 75: 280-294.

Weffort, Francisco. 1977. "Por um Novo Pacto Social." *Veja*, June 29: 3-6.

———. 1978. *O Populismo na Política Brasileira*. Rio de Janeiro: Editora Paz e Terra.

———. 1980. "Menos Teoria, Mais Fatos." *Isto É*, November 5: 67.

———. 1980. "O Erro Constituído." *Isto É*, July 23: 46-48.

Weisskoff, Richard. 1979. "Trade, Protection and Import Elasticities for Brazil." *Review of Economics and Statistics* 61: 58-66.

Welsh, William A. 1970. "Methodological Problems in the Study of Political Leadership in Latin America." *Latin American Research Review* 5: 3-34.

White, Stephen. 1978. "Communist Systems and the 'Iron Law of Pluralism'." *British Journal of Political Science* 8: 101-117.

Whitmore, Don. "Brazilian Positivism and the Military Republic." In *Religion in Latin American Life and Literature*, edited by Lyle C. Brown and William F. Cooper. Waco, Tex: Baylor University Press. Forthcoming.

Wiarda, Howard. 1978. "Corporatism in Iberian and Latin American Political Analysis: Criticisms, Qualifications, and the Context of 'Whys'." *Comparative Politics* 10: 307-312.

———. 1978. "Corporatism Rediscovered: Right, Center, and Left Variants in the New Literature." *Polity* 10: 416-428.

———, ed. 1974. *Politics and Social Change in Latin America: The Distinct Tradition*. Amherst, Mass.: University of Massachusetts Press.

———, ed. 1980. *The Continuing Struggle for Democarcy in Latin America*. Boulder: Westview, 1980.

Wilder, David A. 1978. "Perceiving Persons as a Group: Effects of Attributions of Causality and Beliefs." *Social Psychology* 41: 13-23.

———. 1978. "Reduction of Intergroup Discrimination through Individuation of the Out-Group." *Journal of Personality and Social Psychology* 36: 1361-1374.

Williamson, Jeffrey G. 1979. "Inequality, Accumulation and Technological Imbalance: A Growth-Equity Conflict in American History?" *Economic Development and Cultural Change* 27: 231.

"Will Foreign Bankers Blow the Whistle on Brazil?" 1979. *Business Week*, November 19: 56-63.

Wilson, Bryan. 1979. "The Return of the Sacred." *Journal for the Scientific Study of Religion* 18: 268-280.

Wolf, Eric R. 1969. *Peasant Wars of the Twentieth Century*. New York: Harper & Row, Publishers.

Wolfe, Alan. 1978. "Has Social Democracy a Future?" *Comparative Politics* 11: 100-125.

Wright, James D. 1976. *Dissent of the Governed*. New York: Academic Press.

Yahuda, Michael. 1979. "Political Generations in China." *China Quarterly* 80: 793-805.

Yap, Lorene Y. L. 1976. "Internal Migration and Economic Development in Brazil." *Quarterly Journal of Economics* 90: 119-137.

———. 1976. "Rural-Urban Migration and Urban Underdevelopment in Brazil." *Journal of Development Economics* 3: 227-243.

Zaluar, Guimarães, Alba. 1980. "On the Logic of Popular Catholicism." In *Brazilian Social Studies Annual*, edited by Simon Schwartzman. New Brunswick, N.J.: Transaction Books.

Zartman, I. William. 1974. "The Study of Elite Circulation." *Comparative Politics* 6: 465-488.

Zeitlin, Maurice. 1974. "Corporate Ownership and Control: The Large Corporation and the Capitalist Class in Chile." *American Journal of Sociology* 79: 1073-1119.

———; Ewen, Lynda; and Ratcliff, Richard. 1974. "New Princes for Old? The Large Corporation and the Capitalist Class in Chile." *American Journal of Sociology* 80: 87-123.

———, and Ratcliff, Richard Earl. 1975. "Research Methods for the Analysis of the Internal Class Structure of Dominant Classes: The Case of Landlords and Capitalists in Chile." *Latin American Research Review* 10: 5-61.

Zeller, Richard, and Carmines, Edward. 1976. "Factor Scaling, External Consistency, and the Measurement of Theoretical Constructs." *Political Methodology* 3: 215-252.

Zuckerman, Alan. 1977. "The Concept of 'Political Elite': Lessons from Mosca and Pareto." *Journal of Politics* 39: 324-344.

Zuckerman, Harriet. 1972. "Interviewing an Ultra-Elite." *Public Opinion Quarterly* 36: 159-175.

Zuckerman, Michael. 1978. "Dreams that Men Dare to Dream: The Role of Ideas in Western Modernization." *Social Science History* 2: 332-345.

Index

abortion, legalization of, xxiv, 26, 175-177, 184-187, 229. *See also* moral issues

agrarian reform, 29, 175-178, 184, 188, 267-275

Amazon, 178-179n, 267-272

amnesty, political, 175-182, 184-188

Anderson, Charles W., 46-47, 111n, 200

ARENA, 32, 59n, 102, 113-117, 120, 122-124, 126-127, 141; perceptions of, 207-222, 225-227; policy preferences of, 175-189

authoritarianism, xx, xxvii; cultural explanation of, xx, 15-16; "generation of," 4; literature on, 5-11; structural explanation of, xx, 5-6, 15. *See also* corporatism, despotism, dictatorship

"authoritarians," xxix

Bacha, Edmar, 4n, 29n, 132n

Baer, Werner, 4n, 8n, 19n

bankers, 22, 120, 123, 224n; perceptions of, 207-221, 226; recruitment of, 17

belief system, *see* ideology

bipartism, 32n-33n

birth control, 20, 26, 34, 172, 175-178, 184-188, 225, 229, 233, 266-275; perceptions of, 209, 213-217, 225-226. *See also* moral issues

bishops, 10, 90-91; perceptions of, 207-221, 226; policy preferences of, 175-189; and social justice, 20. *See also* church

Block, Fred, 170n

Bruneau, Thomas C., 20n, 21n, 251n

bureaucratic-authoritarianism, 6, 47, 189-203. *See also* authoritarianism

Burt, Ronald, 85n, 88n, 204

businessmen, 22; mobility of, 55-56, 59; policy preferences of, 176-189; recruitment of, 18, 99-102, 141-143, 229. *See also* bankers, industrialists

Campos Coelho, Edmundo, xxv

capital accumulation, 131-132, 203, 276-289

capitalism, 50n, 201

Cardoso, Fernando Henrique, 6n, 28n, 44n, 89n, 133-134n, 243n

Catholicism, xxvn, 20-21, 30n, 48, 102n. *See also* bishops, church

censorship, xvii, 176-180, 184-186, 233, 267-275

Chalmers, Douglas A., 46n

Chile, 237

church, xxiv, xxvi, xxxi, xxxiiin, 48, 114-115, 120, 123, 126-127, 141-142, 229-231; and grass-roots communities, 21n; political participation of, 176-181, 184-189, 267-275; relations with state, 20, 241

civil servants, 114-116, 141-143; mobility of, 60-61; perceptions of, 207-221, 226; policy preferences of, 175, 189; recruitment of, 18. *See also* state managers

class: as basis of mobility, 18, 70-74; counterrevolution, 10; fractions, 9-10, 11; marriage between, 19, 75-82

cleavages: accumulation-versus-distribution (class), xxi-xxii, xxx; cross-cutting, 232-233, 243; generational, 23-24; moral (religious), xxiii-xiv, xxx-xxxi, 27; order-autonomy (political), xxii-xxiii, xxx

coalitions, xxxi, 48, 125-129, 133, 171, 200-201, 236-237

Cohen, Youssef, 117n

cohorts, 68-69, 80-81n

Collier, David, 13n, 205n, 239n

Collier, Ruth Berins, 239n

communism, 4, 239n, 287-289

community, cultural, xxxi, 242

consensus, 25, 46, 133, 171, 185, 203, 243

consociational politics, 47

Converse, Philip E., 16n, 209n

corporatism, xxxiii, 6, 30n, 34n, 35n, 40n, 110, 232, 237, 239n, 242, 247

Dean, Warren, 76n
death penalty, 176-182, 184-189
democracy, xxxiii, 44, 155. *See also* political liberalization
denationalization, xxxii, 189, 277
dependent development, 6, 8n, 276-280
de Souza, Amaury, 117n, 170n, 247n,
251n, 252n, 275n
despotism, xxvi, xxxiii, 233, 243
dictatorship, xxi, 20, 231
divorce, legalization of, 26, 34, 172, 176-
179, 229, 233, 266-275. *See also* moral
issues
dos Santos, Wanderley Guilherme, 30n,
132n, 148n, 166n

economic growth, xxviii, xxix, xxx, 3, 40,
43-44, 131, 156-163, 224
economic policy, xxviii, 201
"economists," xxix, 42-45, 50, 136-147,
153-168, 193-199, 231-232, 236-237
education, 55, 62-68; as investment, 158,
266-267; reform of, 267-271; regional
variations in, 63-68; relation to class,
70-74
elites: mobility of, 17-19, 55-84, 229;
sample of, 247-260, 262-264
engineers, 64-66
Erickson, Kenneth, P., 30n
Evans, Peter, 8, 28n

family planning, *see* birth control
Faoro, Raymundo, 7n, 232n
fascism, 16n, 37, 242
Fausto, Boris, 23n
Fernandes, Florestan, 28n
Figueiredo, Gen. João, 175, 233, 237n
foreign debt, 3, 28, 224, 238-239
foreign investment (capital), 28-29, 238-
240; ambiguity of, xxxii, 189; importance of, 267-280; opinions about, 175-
180, 184-189; perceptions of, 208-217,
221, 225-227
friendship ties, 22, 92-98, 208n, 229

Geertz, Clifford, 14n, 245n
Geisel, Gen. Ernesto, 3, 130, 146, 175,
233, 237n, 258n
generations, 57, 229
Germani, Gino, 5n
Goodwyn, Lawrence, xxxiiin

Goulart, João, 191n
governors, 120, 176-179
Gregor, A. James, 16n

habeas corpus, 175-177, 199n
hegemony, 46, 48, 200, 203, 236, 243
Hirschman, Albert O., 38-39
human rights, 20n, 40, 170. *See also* political rights
Huntington, Samuel P., 131n, 148n

ideology, xxi, xxiiin, xxvii, 11, 25-46,
264-294; dimensionality of, xxi, xxv,
14, 172-173, 200, 229-230, 234, 244; as
systemic, 15
income redistribution, 29-30, 34, 132n,
156-160, 174-189, 202n, 224, 233; importance of, 267, 270-271, 273, 280-
285; perceptions of, 208-217, 221, 225-
227
industrialists, 22, 114-116, 120-123; perceptions of, 207-221; recruitment of, 18
industrialization, xx, 6, 133, 200
inflation, xixn, 3-4, 132, 156-158, 202n,
224n, 239
intellectuals, 251n
interest groups, 44, 230
interest representation, 47, 50, 189-203,
240

Jaguaribe, Helio, 29n, 89n

Keyfitz, Nathan, 18n
kinship ties, 22, 92-98, 208n, 229
Kubitschek, Juscelino, 41
Kurth, James R., 16n

labor leaders: ostracism of, 207-208; perceptions of, 207-221, 226; policy preferences of, 175-199; recruitment of, 18,
60-61, 73, 229
labor syndicates: autonomy of, 31, 114-
117, 120, 176-189; importance of issue,
266-275, 285-289; perceptions of issue,
209-217, 221-227
Lafer, Celso, 4n, 90n
Lamounier, Bolivar, 34n, 119n, 129n
landowners, 22, 114-116, 120, 123-126,
239
lawyers, 64-66, 68, 127n
Leeds, Anthony, 22n, 85n, 231n

Leff, Nathaniel H., 8n
left-right continuum, 26-27, 29, 171-173, 183-189
legitimacy, xxvii, xxx-xxxi, 13, 25, 43, 46, 48, 50, 137, 169-203, 235-237
Linz, Juan J., xixn, xxivn, 6n, 7n, 11, 13n, 43

Malloy, James M., 15n
marriage ties, 57-58; as mechanism of mobility, 75-82
Martin, David, xxivn
MDB, 32, 59n, 102, 113-117, 120, 122-124, 126-127, 140-143, 174; perceptions of, 207-221, 226; policy preferences of, 176-185
Médici, Gen. Emílio Garrastazú, 98-101, 132n, 136, 147, 162, 166, 168, 175, 181n-182n, 191, 198, 208, 229, 232-233, 235, 239, 249, 255, 262n, 266
Mendes, Cândido, 104n
mentalities, 13-17, 200, 245
Mercadante, Paulo, xxiiin
Mericle, Kenneth S., 30n
Mexico, xxviin, 13n, 24n, 47n, 83n, 98n, 236n
middle class, 55, 57-59, 71-72, 83, 94-98, 114-116, 229
military, xxvn, 3, 43, 114-116, 120, 122-129, 224, 231, 241; perceptions of, 210-211, 226; political participation of, 32, 174, 177-183, 195-203, 242n, 267-275
mobilization, mass, 57, 132-133, 232, 238. *See also* participation, mass
Mohr, Lawrence B., 235
moral issues, 34, 172, 176-189, 199, 229-230
Mosca, Gaetano, 247-248
multinationals, 114-115, 120, 122-129, 201, 231, 238, 257, 276-280
multipartism, 32-33, 175-189, 195-199

Netto, Delfim, 49n, 98n-99, 186n, 224
networks, 85-106

occupation, 58-59n, 70-82
O'Donnell, Guillermo A., 6n, 7n, 8n

Packenham, Robert A., 135n
Pareto, Vilfredo, 247-248

participation, mass, 3, 13, 33, 45, 110, 204, 231. *See also* mobilization, mass
party system, 32, 195-199, 233
peasants, 5, 30, 114-117, 120, 123, 125-126, 239; political participation of, 176-184, 188
perceptions, 35-38, 109, 111-118, 204-227, 234
pluralism, limited, xxviii, 11-13, 16, 38, 45, 47n, 51, 200, 231, 233-236
pluralistic ignorance, 36, 205n
polarization of issues, 37, 40, 195-199, 211-227, 229-230, 244, 264-294
policy preferences, 171-172, 175-183; dimensionality of, 183-189
political culture, xxv-xxvi, 40n, 243
political liberalization, 131, 201, 229, 240-241
political opposition, 37, 176-189, 196-203; importance of, 266-275, 289-294; perceptions of, 208-217, 221-227
political parties, freedom of, 31, 176-189, 195-199
political rights, 33, 175. *See also* human rights
politicians, recruitment of, 18, 58-74
"politicians," xxix-xxx, 42, 49, 136-143, 147-149, 153-168, 193-199, 232-233, 237
population planning, ambiguity of, xxxii. *See also* birth control
populism, 43, 131-132, 204, 243
power: concentration of, xxviii, 258; crisis of, xxx, 128-129; dimensions of, 19-21, 229-230; structure of, 17-21, 86-91
priorities, 25, 130-168, 190-199, 240
projection, 36, 212-225
Purcell, John F. H., xxviin, 13n, 236
Purcell, Susan Kaufman, xxviin, 13n, 236
Putnam, Robert D., 9n, 56n, 217

Quadros, Jânio, 191n
questionnaire, design of, 260-262

regional differences, 56, 63-68, 156-159
Reis Veloso, João Paulo, 66
religion, xxiii-xxiv, 229-230, 237-238; popular, xxvii, 21n, 48n. *See also* moral issues
repression, xvii-xix, xxviii, xxx, 44, 99, 201, 233, 262n. *See also* torture

Rio de Janeiro, 56, 63n, 64-65, 247, 249, 252n
Rio Grande do Sul, 63n
rules of the game, 25, 32-35, 45-46, 173-175, 195-203, 234

São Paulo, 56, 63n, 64-65, 241, 247, 249, 252n
Sartori, Giovanni, xxiiin, 40n
Schmitter, Philippe C., 6n, 40n
Schwartzman, Simon, 7n, 21n, 63n
Scott, James C., 47
Skidmore, Thomas E., 14n
Smith, Peter H., 47n, 83n, 236n
Soares, Glaucio Ary Dillon, 23n
socialism, 40n
social issues, 29-31, 153-168
social justice, 33n, 137n, 240, 281, 284-285
"social reformers," xxix-xxx, 42-46, 50, 136-143, 150-167, 193-199, 231-232, 235-237
social security, 30n, 156-162
Spain, xxiv, xxvii, 30-31n, 33n, 172, 235, 242
Spalding, Rose J., xxxiiin
state, Brazilian, xviii; organization of, xxxiii; size of, 19, 203, 238, 240
state managers, 22-23, 55, 117n. *See also* civil servants

Stepan, Alfred, 7n, 60n, 68n, 242n
stereotyping, 36, 212-227
strikes, 4, 31n, 237n
students, 114-115, 120, 176-178, 184, 188, 267-271
subversion, 157-160, 176-181, 184-185, 266-275
Superior War College, 67

taxation, xviin
technocrats, 23, 32, 42, 57, 60, 99-103, 114-116, 120, 122-128, 163, 201, 229, 231, 235. *See also* civil servants
Therborn, Göran, xix, xxin
torture, xvii-xviii, 4, 232-233
totalitarianism, 5, 7, 24, 233
Trimberger, Ellen Kay, 18n, 28n

Vargas, Getúlio, 17n, 23, 30, 41
Venezuela, 7, 242
Vianna, Luis Werneck, 161n

Weffort, Francisco, 228, 238n, 241, 243n
welfare, xxix, 188, 233, 240. *See also* social security
Wiarda, Howard J., 10n, 15n

Zeitlin, Maurice, 19n